Well-being and Beyond

NEW HORIZONS IN MANAGEMENT

Series Editor: Cary L. Cooper, CBE, *Distinguished Professor of Organizational Psychology and Health, Lancaster University, UK and Chair of the Academy of Social Sciences*

This important series makes a significant contribution to the development of management thought. This field has expanded dramatically in recent years and the series provides an invaluable forum for the publication of high quality work in management science, human resource management, organizational behaviour, marketing, management information systems, operations management, business ethics, strategic management and international management.

The main emphasis of the series is on the development and application of new original ideas. International in its approach, it will include some of the best theoretical and empirical work from both well-established researchers and the new generation of scholars.

Titles in the series include:

Psychological Ownership and the Organizational Context
Theory, Research Evidence, and Application
Jon L. Pierce and Iiro Jussila

Handbook of Stress in the Occupations
Edited by Janice Langan-Fox and Cary L. Cooper

The New Knowledge Workers
Dariusz Jemielniak

Narcissism in the Workplace
Research, Opinion and Practice
Andrew J. DuBrin

Gender and the Dysfunctional Workplace
Edited by Suzy Fox and Terri R. Lituchy

The Innovation Imperative in Health Care Organisations
Critical Role of Human Resource Management in the Cost, Quality and Productivity
Equation
Edited by Peter Spurgeon, Cary L. Cooper and Ronald J. Burke

Human Resource Management in the Nonprofit Sector
Passion, Purpose and Professionalism
Edited by Ronald J. Burke and Cary L. Cooper

Human Resource Management in the Public Sector
Edited by Ronald J. Burke, Andrew Noblet and Cary L. Cooper

The Psychology of the Recession on the Workplace
Edited by Cary L. Cooper and Alexander-Stamatios G. Antoniou

How Can HR Drive Growth?
Edited by George Saridakis and Cary L. Cooper

Voice and Whistleblowing in Organisations
Overcoming Fear, Fostering Courage and Unleashing Candour
Edited by Ronald J. Burke and Cary L. Cooper

Proactive Personality and Behavior for Individual and Organizational Productivity
Andrew J. Dubrin

Well-being and Beyond
Broadening the Public and Policy Discourse
Edited by Timo J. Hämäläinen and Juliet Michaelson

Well-being and Beyond

Broadening the Public and Policy Discourse

Edited by

Timo J. Hämäläinen

Sitra Fellow, The Finnish Innovation Fund, Finland

Juliet Michaelson

Senior Researcher and Programme Co-ordinator, Centre for Well-being, new economics foundation, UK

NEW HORIZONS IN MANAGEMENT

Edward Elgar
Cheltenham, UK • Northampton, MA, USA

Published by
Edward Elgar Publishing Limited
The Lypiatts
15 Lansdown Road
Cheltenham
Glos GL50 2JA
UK

Edward Elgar Publishing, Inc.
William Pratt House
9 Dewey Court
Northampton
Massachusetts 01060
USA

A catalogue record for this book
is available from the British Library

Library of Congress Control Number: 2013949885

This book is available electronically in the ElgarOnline.com Business
Subject Collection, E-ISBN 978 1 78347 290 1

Published in the Sitra Publication series (Sitra 306)
ISSN 1457-5736 (printed book)
ISSN 0785-8388 (electronic version)

ISBN 978 1 78347 289 5

Typeset by Servis Filmsetting Ltd, Stockport, Cheshire
Printed and bound in Great Britain by T.J. International Ltd, Padstow

Contents

List of figures   vii
List of tables   ix
List of contributors   x

1   New theories and policies for well-being: introduction   1
Juliet Michaelson and Timo J. Hämäläinen

PART I   THE NEED FOR COHERENCE

2   In search of coherence: sketching a theory of sustainable
well-being   17
Timo J. Hämäläinen

3   The salutogenic framework for well-being: implications for
public policy   68
Monica Eriksson and Bengt Lindström

4   Well-being and well-becoming: reauthorizing the subject in
incoherent times   98
Maureen O'Hara and Andrew Lyon

PART II   RESTORING THE CENTRALITY OF THE
SOCIAL

5   Understanding and improving the social context of well-being   125
John F. Helliwell

6   Buying alone: how the decreasing American happiness turned
into the current economic crisis   144
Stefano Bartolini

7   Creating supportive environments to foster reasonableness
and achieve sustainable well-being   182
Avik Basu, Rachel Kaplan and Stephen Kaplan

PART III   REVISING ECONOMIC PRINCIPLES

8   What implications does well-being science have for economic
     policy?   221
     Charles Seaford

9   Well-being in organizations   244
     Jill Flint-Taylor and Cary L. Cooper

PART IV   POLICY RESPONSES

10   The politics of consciousness   271
     Mihaly Csikszentmihalyi

11   Well-being, capitalism and public policy: from generalization
     to granularity   283
     Geoff Mulgan

12   Well-being for growth and democracy in the EU   296
     Agnès Hubert

13   Policies for well-being and health   311
     Pekka Puska

14   Practical models for well-being-oriented policy   321
     Juliet Michaelson

Index   345

Figures

2.1 Key determinants of well-being in everyday life   24
2.2 Hurried life in affluent society   30
2.3 Socio-economic transformation weakens the sense of
    coherence   32
2.4 Dimensions of individual coherence and consequences of
    incoherence   40
3.1 The health ease–dis-ease continuum   70
3.2 The salutogenic umbrella   73
3.3 Mental health as flourishing   76
3.4 Well-being in the context of health research   85
3.5 The river of life   86
3.6 The impact of the SOC in a lifetime perspective   89
4.1 Transformation   109
5.1 Happiness by age, on weekdays and weekends   128
6.1 Private consumption, wages and excess consumption   147
6.2 Personal saving rate as a percentage of disposable personal
    income   147
6.3 Private consumption-to-GDP ratio across countries   148
6.4 Total consumption-to-GDP ratio across countries   148
6.5 Ratio between US household debt (mortgage debt and total
    debt) and wages   149
6.6 Change in US household total debt, mortgage debt and
    current account balance   150
6.7 Home price indexes   151
6.8 Ratio between the value of US residential mortgages and
    residential home values (primary residence only)   152
6.9 Trend of self-reported happiness in the US   164
6.10 Trends in total working time across countries   166
6.11 Differences in the use of time between Germany and the US   167
6.12 Trends in European well-being   168
6.13 Outstanding mortgage-backed securities by issuer   173
7.1 Three interrelated domains of the Reasonable Person
    Model   187
9.1 The ASSET model of employee well-being   250

14.1 The dynamic model of well-being 324
14.2 The links between good functioning, represented by the components of self-determination theory, and the key features of co-production 334
14.3 The Five Ways to Well-being messaging 338

Tables

3.1 A theoretical comparison between salutogenesis and resilience 74

3.2 A theoretical comparison between salutogenesis and empowerment 79

6.1 Trends of US social capital 1975–2004, General Social Survey data 163

6.2 Growth rates of GDP 1980–2005 in the US and in some big European economies 165

6.3 Work supervisors as a percentage of the total labour force: 18 advanced economies in 2002 169

8.1 Estimated typical pay range (per annum) for non-graduates in sample sectors 237

9.1 Estimated annual number of working days lost through presenteeism attributable to mental ill health in an organization with 1000 employees (United Kingdom) 252

9.2 The prevalence of presenteeism 252

9.3 Health risk indicator improvement at Johnson & Johnson over time 262

Contributors

Stefano Bartolini
Department of Political Economy and Statistics, University of Siena
Siena (Italy)
Email: stefano.bartolini@unisi.it

Avik Basu
School of Natural Resources and Environment, University of Michigan
Ann Arbor, Michigan (USA)
Email: abasu@umich.edu

Cary L. Cooper
Lancaster University Management School
Lancaster (UK); and
Academy of Social Sciences
Email: c.cooper1@lancaster.ac.uk

Mihaly Csikszentmihalyi
Claremont Graduate University
Claremont, California (USA)
Email: mihaly.csikszentmihalyi@cgu.edu

Monica Eriksson
Department of Nursing, Health and Culture, University West
Trollhättan (Sweden)
Email: monica.eriksson@hv.se

Jill Flint-Taylor
Rusando Ltd and Ashridge Business School
Berkhamsted (UK)
Email: jill@rusando.com

Timo J. Hämäläinen
Strategy Unit, Finnish Innovation Fund, Sitra
Helsinki (Finland)
Email: timo.hamalainen@sitra.fi

John F. Helliwell
Canadian Institute for Advanced Research, Vancouver School of
Economics, University of British Columbia
Vancouver (Canada)
Email: john.helliwell@ubc.ca

Agnès Hubert
Bureau of European Policy Advisers, European Commission
Brussels (Belgium)
Email: agnes.hubert@ec.europa.eu

Rachel Kaplan
School of Natural Resources and Environment, University of
Michigan
Ann Arbor, Michigan (USA)
Email: rkaplan@umich.edu

Stephen Kaplan
Department of Psychology, University of Michigan
Ann Arbor, Michigan (USA)
Email: skap@umich.edu

Bengt Lindström
Department of Social Work and Health Science, NTNU
Trondheim (Norway)
Email: bengt.lindstrom@svt.ntnu.no

Andrew Lyon
International Futures Forum
Aberdour (UK)
Email: andrew@internationalfuturesforum.com

Juliet Michaelson
Centre for Well-being, new economics foundation
London (UK)
Email: juliet.michaelson@neweconomics.org

Geoff Mulgan
NESTA
London (UK)
Email: geoff.mulgan@nesta.org.uk

Maureen O'Hara
Department of Psychology, National University
La Jolla, California (USA)
Email: mohara@nu.edu

Pekka Puska
National Institute for Health and Welfare
Helsinki (Finland)
Email: pekka.puska@thl.fi

Charles Seaford
Centre for Well-being, new economics foundation
London (UK)
Email: charles.seaford@neweconomics.org

1. New theories and policies for well-being: introduction

Juliet Michaelson and Timo J. Hämäläinen

What are the essential attributes of a person? What is it to be human? These eternal questions are of course the domain of philosophy, literature and religion, but implicit answers to these questions also drive the real-world business of policy making.

The urge to provide new answers to these questions underpins the ever more prominent discussions about the concept of well-being. Such discussions seek to provide an answer from the point of view of what makes human lives *go well*.

The motivation for suggestions that improving human well-being should become the primary focus of modern societies is the view that policy making currently takes too narrow an approach to answering these fundamental questions and, in particular, that policy making ought to widen its scope beyond an overarching focus on economic success. The economics discipline has had great success in getting its own models, notably that famous abstraction of rational self-interest, *homo economicus*, to be those which policy makers use by default. Turning the discussion to well-being opens the door to the understanding gained by a much broader tranche of those researching human lives across the social and health sciences.

The sense that our lives and societies are more complex now than at any other time in the past is a key reason why many are seeking new means of explaining them. And, with ongoing global economic and environmental crises – and signs of growing social distress – posing seemingly insurmountable challenges to existing policy frameworks, there is considerable urgency for the task of constructing a broader, more holistic framework.

The contributions in this volume represent a multidisciplinary attempt to work towards a new set of models for policy, which represent what is required to achieve good lives.

WHY WE NEED NEW MODELS

The success of economic models in policy making rests to a large extent on the appealing simplicity of being able to value potential costs and benefits of any course of action in a common unit, those of a currency. Economic theory acknowledges that monetary wealth is ultimately a means to the end of human welfare: the economic concept of *utility* acknowledges that the monetary value of a gain to an individual merely proxies for her ability to use the money to satisfy her preferences, with satisfaction of one's preferences treated as equivalent to well-being (Dolan et al. 2006).

However, a wealth of evidence now suggests that this approach represents an over-simplification – that reducing policy focus to monetary gains risks excluding a wealth of both costs and benefits that cannot be adequately represented in economic utility models.

Diener and Seligman, who between them have pioneered much of the field of well-being research, argue that a concern with economic issues was 'understandably primary' when '[m]eeting simple human needs for food, shelter and clothing was not assured, and satisfying these needs moved in lockstep with better economics' but that, while 'economic progress can enhance the quality of life even in industrialized nations, it no longer serves as a strong barometer of well-being because there are substantial discrepancies between economic indices and other measures' (Diener and Seligman 2004).

Such discrepancies are highlighted by now considerable evidence within well-being research. Most commonly, this uses large-scale survey data that includes subjective measures of well-being – which directly capture people's experiences of their lives – to identify the factors which result in lives going well. The evidence shows, for example, that there are diminishing returns to well-being from increased income and that the strength of the relationship between national income and well-being is 'substantially reduced once quality of government, democracy and social capital is controlled for' (Stoll et al. 2012). Hence these factors explain much of the variation in well-being which income does not. Even factors usually regarded as firmly in the economic sphere have impacts on well-being that go beyond money – for example, research on unemployment shows that the loss of well-being from being unemployed far exceeds the reduction that would be expected from the loss of income (Carroll 2007), and that negative effects on well-being remain even after re-employment (Louis and Zhao 2002). There are also discrepancies which arise from the focus on aggregate national income, which masks differences in the distribution of income, consumption and wealth (Stiglitz et al. 2009). Furthermore, research from psychology and other fields provides reasons to doubt a number of the assumptions of standard economic models, for example that more choice is always good for well-being (Schwartz 2004).

BEYOND 'BEYOND GDP'

The recognition of these flaws in old models has instigated a turn towards well-being within policy circles. Much of the policy attention to date has focused on the issue of measurement. There is now a broad consensus that producing new headline political measures is a necessary first step in going beyond economic models of human welfare in policy making. The body of evidence which establishes that subjective measures of well-being, which capture directly people's experiences of their lives, are robust, valid and useful to policy (see for example Helliwell and Wang 2012) has been crucial in establishing that there are viable means of creating such new measures.

Hence the emergence of the 'Beyond GDP' agenda to establish new measures of national progress, which, since 2007, has been given serious attention by international bodies including the OECD and the European Commission, and by national governments, including France's 'Stiglitz Commission' in 2009, the UK's Measuring National Well-being Programme launched in 2010, and Finland, which is one of the other European countries collecting subjective well-being measures in official surveys (Abdallah and Mahony 2012). The United Nations has demonstrated that it too places importance on this issue, with a High-level Meeting on 'Happiness and Well-being' in April 2012 followed closely by the Rio Conference on Sustainable Development, whose outcome document recognized 'the need for broader measures of progress to complement GDP in order to better inform policy decisions' (UNCSD 2012, p. 6). These initiatives encompass new measures of progress based on adjusted versions of standard economic indicators, subjective measures of well-being, objective measures of well-being within a variety of life and policy domains, and measures relating to the natural environment, resource use and sustainability.

Providing new headline measures by which the success of governments is judged has the power to reframe ideas of national success and to provide new incentives for political action (Michaelson et al., forthcoming). But measurement in fact sits between two other key areas. First, knowing what and how to measure relies on the existence of strong theoretical *models of what it is that one intends to measure.* For example, in their influential review of approaches to well-being measurement, Dolan et al. make clear that their starting point is 'concepts of well-being' (2006, p. 14). The first aim of this volume is therefore to explore different conceptual approaches to well-being. In doing this, it takes a deliberately multidisciplinary perspective, including contributors whose work has not previously been seen as part of the 'well-being discourse'. The concepts discussed here therefore go beyond the approaches which Dolan and colleagues set out, which are tied closely to established well-being measurement approaches. One implication from the breadth of conceptual approaches included here, therefore, is that current well-being measurement initiatives may need to be revised to take account of them.

Ultimately, of course, measurement exists to produce evidence about what is being measured. In the case of well-being measurement, the salient evidence relates to the aspects of people's lives and broader conditions which promote or detract from their well-being. The *implications of this evidence for decision-makers* are therefore the second key area to which this volume relates. It is certainly not the first effort to draw out such conclusions from well-being research. Notable publications which have made useful contributions in this area include Diener et al. (2009) and Bok (2010), with others forthcoming (e.g. Huppert and Cooper, forthcoming) as the research in the field continues to grow. The current volume adds to these through its multidisciplinary approach which draws on a wider range of both sources and forms of evidence than these others. It also includes shorter contributions from commentators working in policy-facing settings who reflect deliberately on the extent to which the evidence can and should change policy processes and decisions. But there is no hard-and-fast distinction between the different types of contribution included here, with those writing from the research perspective also delineating clear policy implications.

A RANGE OF STARTING POINTS

Our claim that this book takes a multidisciplinary approach may seem strange given that well-being research is itself a relatively new, and far from homogeneous, discipline. What has come to be regarded as 'mainstream' well-being science – as practised, for example, by contributors to the *Journal of Happiness Studies* – has a number of roots.

One strand comes from the economics discipline, specifically 'the rediscovery within economics of [subjective well-being] accounts, by Easterlin (whose 1974 paper is often cited as a beginning of this process)' (MacKerron 2011). This rediscovery and Easterlin's paper, titled 'Does economic growth improve the human lot? Some empirical evidence' (Easterlin 1974), sparked an interest among economists and social scientists in exploring the range of factors which do contribute to the human lot, leading to the 'extraordinary growth' in journal articles on the topic, particularly from the mid-1990s onwards (MacKerron 2011).

The other key root of modern well-being science is work within the psychology discipline, particularly the advent of the positive psychology movement, which sought to move beyond an understanding of 'how people survive and endure under conditions of adversity' and focus on 'how normal people flourish under more benign conditions' (Seligman and Csikszentmihalyi 2000). Psychologists who are more or less closely associated with the movement have worked on issues including: the extent to which mental illness and health form a separate dimension from positive and negative well-being (Keyes 2002); how epidemiological models can be applied to the promotion of positive well-being across a population and result in a reduction of the incidence of mental disorders (Huppert 2009); how experiencing positive emotions expands horizons for action and over time builds personal resources (Frederickson 2001); and the identification of basic psychological needs (Deci and Ryan 2000). Many of these psychologists have been associated with a 'eudaimonic' approach to well-being, in which well-being is viewed as the life well lived, with an emphasis on how well people function in, or interact with, the world around them, in addition to the positive feelings and judgements about life that are emphasized by other approaches.

This volume contains research contributions from authors working within both the economic (Helliwell, Bartolini, Seaford) and the psychological (Csikszentmihalyi, Cooper and Flint-Taylor) strands of well-being research. But its aim has been deliberately to extend more broadly than this to bring a range of other disciplinary perspectives, although many explicitly draw on and complement the 'mainstream well-being approach' while bringing in other strands of thought. The interest which some economists have taken in subjective well-being sits in parallel with other economists' exploration of more objective aspects of human welfare and capacities, particularly in the capabilities approach of Sen and Nussbaum, which is the starting point for Hämäläinen's chapter (Chapter 2). Other complementary perspectives included in the volume are Antonovsky's medical sociology (Chapter 3 by Eriksson and Lindström and elsewhere) and the field of environmental psychology (Chapter 7 by Basu, Kaplan and Kaplan). And the contribution by O'Hara and Lyon (Chapter 4), written from the perspective of holistic complexity, aims to challenge some elements of well-being research.

In setting out to produce this book we have deliberately aimed to establish a dialogue between these perspectives. During the writing process we convened two workshops, in London and Helsinki, to bring together the authors of the different chapters and allow them to probe each other's ideas and uncover themes and tensions.

The key theme that emerged as common to all the research contributions has already been mentioned – the need to overturn old models of what makes human lives go well. A number of these 'new takes' directly challenge elements of the dominant models from economics. Bartolini (Chapter 6) and Seaford (Chapter 8) both challenge the notion of economic growth as an unproblematic primary policy aim. Helliwell (Chapter 5) contests the assumption of economic models that humans are inherently selfish and individualistic. Hämäläinen (Chapter 2) challenges the economic tenet that choice is always good for people. And Flint-Taylor and Cooper (Chapter 9) call into question the idea that having a concern with employee well-being is an expensive luxury for employers.

Other contributions address models within other policy spheres. Eriksson and Lindström (Chapter 3) challenge the notion that health policy is a matter of combating disease. O'Hara and Lyon (Chapter 4) go as far as questioning basic Enlightenment models of human beings as individual autonomous agents and of our ability to discover regular, reliably predictable causal relationships within the social sciences.

Of course, while such challenges are of theoretical interest, viewed on their own they do nothing to help policy makers in their role of taking practical decisions about the generation and allocation of public resources. Such help comes in providing new, workable models which can be genuinely useful in policy making. The contributions in this volume do just this – providing a range of alternative models (which complement each other to different degrees). We now describe the key themes around which these new models cluster.

THE NEED FOR COHERENCE

The first strong theme is that people – and societies – have a need to make sense of the world around them. A sense of rapid change and the multiple pressures of modern life contribute a sense of urgency to the need to produce societal conditions which address this fundamental need.

This analysis of what is wrong is very much the starting point of Timo J. Hämäläinen's contribution (Chapter 2). He focuses on the problems of market-oriented industrialized societies, which, he argues, often provide 'too much choice' for people's decision-making capacity. Critiquing the capabilities approach, he argues that an individual's well-being arises from the physical, institutional and cultural environment together with material and mental resources, which impact on everyday activities and roles (as worker, consumer, family member, etc.), which in turn determine the extent to which a range of physical and psychological needs are met. All this, he concludes, suggests a required reduction in the complexity of modern life through a new cultural paradigm which can restore balance and what Antonovsky called 'coherence' to daily activities.

Antonovsky's sense of coherence theory forms the basis of the chapter by Monica Eriksson and Bengt Lindström (Chapter 3). They describe evidence which suggests that coherence – viewing the world as comprehensible, manageable and meaningful – is a crucial element in what promotes physical and mental health, and ultimately well-being. In their view, health policy, and public policy more generally, should adopt a 'salutogenic orientation', which asks how health and well-being can be promoted, rather than how disease and risk can be avoided. This involves promoting the resources – material, cognitive, emotional, social, cultural – which protect from countless stressors encountered through life. With applications in educational settings and workplaces as well as health services, this approach involves creating the conditions which allow people to understand, cope with and see meaning in their everyday situations.

Maureen O'Hara and Andrew Lyon (Chapter 4) go even further in describing both the extent of current incoherence and the degree of transformation required to escape it. They raise doubts about the adequacy of the standard science model in the social sciences to describe the current 'change of eras'. In particular, they question the ability of subjective measures of well-being to genuinely represent internal states rather than reflect the biases of the researchers (arguments which readers should consider during presentations of such results in later chapters). O'Hara and Lyon urge a move beyond a focus on the aggregated well-being of individuals, towards a holistic view where well-being is seen as a 'function of whole systems'. They argue that interlocking problems such as growing rates of mental distress, increasing inequalities, climate change and economic crises require moving beyond the defensive strategies, such as denial and distortion, which are commonly used to restore coherence and reduce complexity. Instead, they describe the need for a 'learning culture' that enables learning to be disruptive of the status quo to allow new forms of action.

RESTORING THE CENTRALITY OF THE SOCIAL

Each of the contributions which focuses on the need to promote coherence as a crucial element of well-being highlights social relationships and collective solutions as a key means of achieving this. Thus it is no surprise that the volume's second major theme is the need to restore our social nature to the centre of the picture of human well-being.

Redressing the bias within the theory and practice on well-being which treats people as individuals is the explicit starting point of the chapter by John F. Helliwell (Chapter 5). He describes the evidence which establishes, first, that humans are fundamentally social beings – with our big brains arising from the complexities of social groups, and, second, that the enjoyment of social relationships leads to an evolutionary advantage so that people benefit from their practical outcomes such as physical health and alertness to threats. Furthermore, Helliwell argues, humans are inherently *pro-social* and altruistic, receiving a bigger boost to well-being from giving than receiving. Helliwell outlines a number of practical policy implications, particularly the 'how' of policy delivery and the way that institutions are managed. For example, he argues that considerably greater importance for well-being of the social context within workplaces than salary and bonuses has real-life consequences for what employers prioritize. He also argues that the findings have applications at the macroeconomic level, for example in the priority which national governments give to avoiding unemployment.

This idea, that macroeconomic conditions can influence social relationships, with resulting impacts on well-being, is core to the chapter by Stefano Bartolini (Chapter 6). He describes how a decline in common goods – crucially including networks of relationships – can cause the defensive response of additional consumption of private goods, while economic growth that is based on high levels of consumerism can itself be a cause of the decline in relationships, particularly through the isolating nature of modern cities and emphasis on materialistic values. He produces evidence to argue that the US economy has many of these characteristics, with high expenditure on home entertainment and means of social control, deteriorating experienced well-being and social capital, and increasing inequality and working hours. Hence he argues that a primary cause of the economic crisis of recent years, which began as a debt crisis in the USA and was exported to the rest of the world, was the USA's relationship-damaging form of economic growth.

Another take on the centrality of the social – and its link to surrounding environments – is provided in the chapter by Avik Basu, Rachel Kaplan and Stephen Kaplan (Chapter 7). They describe the concept of 'reasonableness', which 'addresses the issues that help (or hinder) us in being civil and sociable, developing trust, and cooperating with one another in the face of shared challenges'. In their conception, reasonableness rests on the ability to build mental models to make sense of the world, function effectively with a sense of competence, and take meaningful action – a framework with strong parallels with both the sense of coherence model (discussed by Hämäläinen in Chapter 2 and Eriksson and Lindström in Chapter 3) and Deci and Ryan's (2000) self-determination theory. Basu, Kaplan and Kaplan describe the environments – physical, but also rule and custom based – which, they argue, support these types of elements of reasonableness: those which can restore depleted mental capacity, particularly natural settings; environments that promote social connectivity, such as the walkability of cities; and social contexts designed to enable community participation and involvement, from community gardens to microcredit schemes.

REVISING ECONOMIC PRINCIPLES

The chapters by Helliwell (Chapter 5) and Bartolini (Chapter 6) demonstrate that well-being evidence produces implications both for economic policy making and for businesses. This theme is examined further in the following two chapters.

In Chapter 8, Charles Seaford questions the traditional policy distinction between supposedly neutral 'economic' objectives, such as maximizing GDP, and more 'political' objectives, such as reducing inequality. He argues that, in fact, all major objectives for governments can and should be justified with reference to the evidence about what promotes well-being. Reviewing findings from well-being research such as the diminishing well-being returns of income, and beyond-economic damage from unemployment, Seaford derives a set of economic policy principles. Focusing on the first of these – that there should be a target band of income for all – and using the UK as an example case, he identifies the need for strategies to improve pay in non-graduate sectors: paying more than current market rates where the government is the key employer, putting in place a strong minimum wage and encouraging unionization. A coherent programme for well-being across government departments, he argues, will require a set of simple, evidence-based principles which can replace those such as 'Find a market solution', 'Increase choice' or 'Cut spending' which have been so effective in guiding policy under conventional economic theory.

Businesses as well as governments should revise conventional thinking about key economic principles: instead of a focus on employee well-being being seen as desirable but costly, it should be recognized as contributing to a range of positive business outcomes, including improved productivity, customer satisfaction and staff retention. This is the case made by Jill Flint-Taylor and Cary L. Cooper (Chapter 9), who describe why businesses should seek to actively manage employee well-being. This is not, they say, a matter simply of schemes promoting physical health or eliminating sources of stress. Instead, businesses should recognize that employees experience different sources of workplace pressure – both negative and positive – and of support, and therefore seek to create an appropriate balance between them. Practical means towards this include: auditing exercises; considering well-being in employee assessment and selection; paying close attention to the impact of leaders and managers on workgroup well-being; and national guidance and policy action on employee well-being.

POLICY RESPONSES

The first nine chapters clearly do not present a single conceptual view of well-being, despite their many overlaps, nor do they examine the same sorts of evidence or draw a unified set of conclusions. Hence the job of policy makers required to make sense of and respond to this sort of research may well seem daunting. The key themes which we have identified here provide a starting point: the need for coherence, the centrality of the social, and the importance of reviewing economic principles. As well as these broad thematic strands, the volume contains five contributions that explore policy responses to the evidence and arguments of the preceding chapters. All of these contributions are shaped by the different perspectives of their authors.

Mihaly Csikszentmihalyi (Chapter 10) discusses what is required to bring about social and political change, asking how so many communist governments of the twentieth century, despite almost total control of their populations, fell in the face of popular uprisings. His answer is human 'consciousness' – the ability to organize one's own previous experience in order to imagine existing alternatives to reality – which is the basis of autonomous action. He argues that governments that do not do enough to help people achieve what (they think) will make them happy risk falling in similar ways. Good governance, he says, consists of promoting the conditions which allow consciousness to flourish: freedom to hear and express the truth; hope – societal goals to which citizens can aspire; and enjoyable activities – not just pleasant distractions, but experiences which allow challenge and mastery of skills, and ultimately the experience of 'flow' – the concept of losing oneself in an appropriately challenging task, which Csikszentmihalyi famously introduced into the psychological discourse.

Geoff Mulgan (Chapter 11) has been a key figure in introducing the concept of a focus on the good life and well-being into the policy discourse in the UK and beyond. Despite this, his perspective is one of relative caution about the extent to which well-being evidence can inform policy making. He points to the lack of ability to confidently predict a direct link between the implementation of any specific policy to a measurable improvement in well-being, and to the trade-offs which remain to be made once well-being has been adopted as a goal, for example between well-being now and in the future. But he notes that there are some *overall* features of social systems we do know are related to well-being, such as peace, the rule of law and democracy. And he is more optimistic about using disaggregated and granular-level information to explore the effects of particular programmes and services, as well as issues covered in this volume such as the effects of environments, the salutogenic approach, the nature of workplaces, and consumption. His conclusion is that governments should adopt a 'partial planning' approach to well-being – arguing that, while well-being should not override everything else as a goal, there is currently too little rather than too much serious attention on the issue.

The contribution by Agnès Hubert (Chapter 12) is written from the perspective of a genuine Brussels insider examining the European Union's response to the well-being agenda. She notes that, while the EU stated an explicit aim of 'promoting well-being' in the 2007 Treaty of Lisbon, the economic crisis has since brought an intensive focus to the question of how to restore growth. But, she argues, it has also demonstrated that business as usual is not an option – further questions which remain to be answered are 'What type of growth?' and 'How can we enter the virtuous circle of happiness that produces growth?' Hubert notes a range of existing European initiatives likely to contribute to promoting well-being, but cites reasons why well-being should be given even greater emphasis. Better frameworks guiding the use of scarce financial resources are required, and the need to strengthen Europe-level democracy points to a role for well-being in building a narrative which resonates with citizens. Hence, she argues, EU action is most needed to develop political take-up of the agenda to 'allow well-being to "count" in policy making'.

Pekka Puska (Chapter 13) discusses the well-being agenda from the viewpoint of his considerable contributions to the field of public health, asking what lessons it holds for health policy. He suggests that the salutogenic approach, where the question is not about determinants of risk factors but what creates health (as described in Chapter 3 by Eriksson and Lindström), is a consequence of applying a well-being perspective to health policy. However, he describes this as sitting on a spectrum of focal points for health policy, all with potentially useful applications: disease prevention and treatment; risk factors for diseases, particularly behaviours and lifestyles; the socio-economic determinants linked to those risk factors; and (relatedly) welfare policies. But, Puska argues, developing policies for well-being also has implications for economic policy. Echoing Hubert, he emphasizes the need to encourage the *kind* of economic growth that improves rather than damages health and well-being. This, he says, will require grassroots action and legislation to restrict intensive commercialism, marketing and consumerism, support social interaction, increase the flexibility and control of employees and deepen the democratic process.

In the final chapter (Chapter 14), Juliet Michaelson reflects on the book's contributions through the lens of the well-being policy frameworks devised by the new economics foundation think tank. Its dynamic model of well-being describes an individual's well-being arising from a dynamic interaction between her external conditions, both material and social, and her inner resources, such as optimism and self-esteem; together these enable her to experience eudaimonic good functioning as well as good feelings. Michaelson makes the case that this model can help guide thinking about different levers to influence well-being, particularly when linked to approaches such as co-production, which provides means to improve meaning, autonomy and relationships through the design and delivery of public services. But, she warns, policy makers should be wary of substitutes for some of the model's core concepts, for example choice rather than control. Instead, she argues, they should turn to deliberately designed heuristics, such as the Five Ways to Well-being messages, which bring together many of the book's themes around social connection, paying attention to environments, and acting for and with other people.

SUMMING UP THE THEMES

At the end of the second workshop held with the book's contributors, we asked the authors to sum up in a few words the key themes they felt were emerging from the discussions of the different chapters. The key common themes which emerged from this exercise provide a summary that might be helpful in further guiding readers through the contributions in this volume. They were: the importance of empowering people and enabling them to create good lives; the significance of participation, cooperation and belonging; and the need to comprehend complex environments to create coherence and meaning in everyday life.

REFERENCES

Abdallah, S. and S. Mahony (2012), *Stocktaking of Subjective Well-being*, report for e-Frame, European Framework for Measuring Progress research project, available at: www.eframeproject.eu.

Bok, D. (2010), *The Politics of Happiness: What Government Can Learn from the New Research on Well-being*, Princeton, NJ: Princeton University Press.

Carroll, N. (2007), 'Unemployment and psychological well-being', *Economic Record*, **83**, 287–302.

Deci, E.L. and R.M. Ryan (2000), 'The "what" and "why" of goal pursuits: human needs and the self-determination of behaviour', *Psychological Inquiry*, **11**, 227–68.

Diener, E. and M.E.P. Seligman (2004), 'Beyond money: toward an economy of well-being', *Psychological Science in the Public Interest*, **5**, 1–31.

Diener, E., R. Lucas, U. Schimmack and J. Helliwell (2009), *Well-being for Public Policy*, New York: Oxford University Press.

Dolan, P., T. Peasgood and M. White (2006), *Review of Research on the Influence of Personal Well-being and Application to Policy Making*, London: Defra.

Easterlin, R.A. (1974), 'Does economic growth improve the human lot? Some empirical evidence', in P.A. David and M.W. Reder (eds), *Nations and Households in Economic Growth: Essays in Honor of Moses Abramowitz*, New York: Academic Press.

Frederickson, B.L. (2001), 'The role of positive emotions in positive psychology: the broaden-and-build theory of positive emotions', *American Psychologist*, **56**, 218–26.

Helliwell, J.F. and S. Wang (2012), 'The state of world happiness', in J.F. Helliwell, R. Layard and J.D. Sachs (eds), *World Happiness Report*, New York: Earth Institute, Columbia University.

Huppert, F.A. (2009), 'Psychological well-being: evidence regarding its causes and consequences', *Applied Psychology: Health and Well-being*, **1** (2), 137–64.

Huppert, F.A. and C. Cooper (forthcoming), *Interventions and Policies to Enhance Well-being*, Oxford: Wiley-Blackwell.

Keyes, C. (2002), 'The mental health continuum: from languishing to flourishing in life', *Journal of Health and Behaviour Research*, **43**, 207–22.

Louis, V.V. and S. Zhao (2002), 'Effects of family structure, family SES, and adulthood experiences on life satisfaction', *Journal of Family Issues*, **23**, 986–1005.

MacKerron, G. (2011), 'Happiness economics from 35000 feet', *Journal of Economic Surveys*, doi: 10.1111/j.1467-6419.2010.00672.x.

Michaelson, J., C. Seaford, S. Abdallah and N. Marks (forthcoming), 'Measuring what matters', in F.A. Huppert and C. Cooper (eds), *Interventions and Policies to Enhance Well-being*, Oxford: Wiley-Blackwell.

Schwartz, B. (2004), *The Paradox of Choice: Why More Is Less*, New York: HarperCollins.

Seligman, M.E.P. and M. Csikszentmihalyi (eds) (2000), Positive psychology [Special issue], *American Psychologist*, **55** (1).

Stiglitz, J.E., A. Sen and J.-P. Fitoussi (2009), *Report by the Commission on the Measurement of Economic Performance and Social Progress*, available at: http://www.stiglitzsen-fitoussi.fr/documents/rapport_anglais.pdf.

Stoll, L., J. Michaelson and C. Seaford (2012), *Well-being Evidence for Policy: A Review*, London: new economics foundation.

UNCSD (United Nations Conference on Sustainable Development) (2012) 'The future we want', outcomes document from the Rio Conference on Sustainable Development, available at: http://www.uncsd2012.org/content/documents/727The%20Future%20We%20Want%2019%20June%201230pm.pdf (accessed 17 July 2012).

PART I

The need for coherence

2. In search of coherence: sketching a theory of sustainable well-being

Timo J. Hämäläinen

INTRODUCTION

A new, more holistic framework of human well-being is urgently needed. The growing affluence, freedoms and market orientation of industrialized societies has fundamentally changed the nature of their citizens' everyday well-being. Today, only a small minority of them suffer from absolute material deprivation problems, while the majority's basic needs are fairly well met. The post-war welfare state policies have more or less reached their original Beveridgian goals of eradicating 'Want, Disease, Ignorance, Squalor and Idleness' (Giddens 2007). However, this does not mean that the vast majority of people are happy and feeling well. Social inequalities are rising again, and a growing number of people suffer from mental health problems. In the United States, for example, only one-fifth of the people are truly flourishing, having their higher social and psychological needs well satisfied (Keyes 2005).

Changes in individual opportunities, everyday life and living environments have created new challenges to well-being which are still poorly understood by policy makers, media and citizens. The public well-being discourse tends to be framed in the old deprivation framework, which has little to say about these new challenges. In the field of health care, for instance, a few nations have recently gone through an 'epidemiological transition', a historical change in the cause of death and illness from acute and infectious to chronic and modifiable lifestyle causes (Keyes 2007, p. 96). However, as Corey Keyes points out, their health care strategies and systems are still based on the pathogenic paradigm that focuses on acute illnesses and the prevention of premature death. As a result, these countries have not been very effective in promoting positive health, subjective well-being and human flourishing (Keyes 2007, p. 96). Keyes's argument can be generalized to the post-war success of industrialized societies in meeting Beveridge's five goals, and the subsequent stagnation of their public policies and institutions with the old welfare problems. The current socio-economic transformation calls for new, more holistic theories that can incorporate both the traditional and the new dimensions of well-being.

A widespread dissatisfaction with the old material perspective to well-being and its key national indicator, GDP, has led to an international drive to develop new well-being measures.[1] National statistical offices, international organizations (e.g. the European Union, the OECD and the United Nations) and various research institutions around the world are actively engaged in this activity. However, none of the new well-being indices has, yet, gained wide-enough acceptance to really challenge the dominance of GDP in policy making. The development of appropriate well-being measures lags behind the structural and cultural change in advanced societies. The established statistics tend to reflect the dominant human needs and societal structures of the post-Second World War decades.

The current rush to develop new well-being indicators is not entirely unproblematic. It is not matched with an equally strong effort in new theory building. Many of the new well-being indices seem to reflect more the availability of suitable data than a well-grounded theoretical framework. Different well-being indices tend to emphasize different sources of well-being, and none of them is sufficiently comprehensive to include all key dimensions of well-being identified in the relevant disciplines, such as biology, psychology, sociology, economics, medicine, cognitive science, organizational theory, political science, cultural studies and philosophy. O'Hara and Lyon (this volume, Chapter 4) discuss the problems of well-being indicators in more depth.

Without a more holistic and up-to-date theoretical framework of well-being, individuals, organizations and policy makers may begin to follow and act on inappropriate or outdated well-being indicators, since usually 'you tend to get what you measure' (Hirsch 1977). Ideally, a more holistic theory should include both 'objective' and 'subjective' as well as 'physical' and 'psychological' dimensions of well-being. It should also pay attention to the short-term feelings and long-term sustainability of well-being.

This chapter sketches such a theory. Despite individual differences in preferences and circumstances, we believe that an intermediate-level theory of well-being can be developed that captures the key drivers of individual well-being in industrialized societies. These determinants of well-being are manifested in different ways in each individual's life. For example, the physiological needs for food and shelter are shared by all individuals, though they are met by very different foodstuffs and buildings in different cultures and living environments. A more holistic theory may help individuals, researchers and policy makers to pay more attention to the new challenges and opportunities for well-being that were not well incorporated in the post-war welfare paradigm.

The next section of the chapter assesses the strengths and weaknesses of the capability approach (CA), which is currently the dominant and most comprehensive framework of well-being. The CA is found insufficient for advanced societies, where people face new well-being challenges that stem from the complexity and uncertainty of their everyday lives. A more holistic framework is then introduced. Besides individual capabilities and freedoms, it incorporates a more detailed analysis of human needs, everyday life and living environments. The chapter continues by analysing the impacts of the current socio-economic transformation and increasing individual choice on subjective well-being. It turns out that these forces put increasing pressure on individuals' sense of coherence (SOC), which is an important determinant of health and subjective well-being. The chapter then focuses on the sustainability of well-being. It analyses the three pervasive decision-making problems in affluent societies – short-termism, selfishness and path-dependence – which create major unintended consequences for individual and social well-being. The small unintended consequences of individual micro-level decisions tend to accumulate into major sustainability problems (such as substance abuse, obesity, broken marriages and environmental problems). This section then underlines the importance of systemically coherent decision making for sustainable development, and concludes by discussing the 'general governance crisis' in industrialized societies that stems from the growing mismatch between the complexity and uncertainty of socio-economic systems and the control capacities of individuals, organizations and governments. The chapter then draws the policy implications by emphasizing the limitations of human mental capacity and discussing the various ways in which the control capacity of individuals could be improved and the complexity of choice situations reduced. This section provides new insights into the social exclusion processes of youth. The chapter concludes by calling for a cultural paradigm shift that could lead to a more sustainable socio-economic model.

WHY IS THE CAPABILITY APPROACH NOT SUFFICIENT?

The capability approach of Amartya Sen, Martha Nussbaum and their collaborators is probably the most comprehensive and influential of the existing well-being theories. It has inspired the development of the United Nations' Human Development Index, influenced the practical development work of the World Bank and shaped the new 'societal progress framework' of the OECD (Hall et al. 2010) as well as the report of the

Stiglitz Commission on new well-being indicators (Stiglitz et al. 2009). The CA has several advantages over the more traditional economic theories of well-being which have focused on collective utilities, economic resources and individual 'happiness' (Sen 2001, 2009; Nussbaum 2003, 2011):

a. It focuses on the ultimate goals – human capabilities and well-being – rather than instruments such as GDP growth or welfare services.
b. It is a broad, multidimensional framework that includes many non-economic variables that are important to individual well-being (e.g. food and shelter, health, physical security, knowledge, social needs, rights and freedoms, rule of law, natural environment).
c. It takes a human-centric perspective to well-being by focusing on individual capabilities and differences in personal ability to convert income and other resources to well-being. This is quite different from the traditional 'universalist' approach to well-being in welfare states.
d. It is aimed at empowering people in their everyday life, which fits well with the increasingly individualized and complex world where the traditional top-down, standardized approaches to enhancing citizens' welfare are more likely to fail.
e. It focuses on agency in real living environments. It sees individuals as active agents operating within local institutional constraints and opportunities rather than passive recipients of income transfers and public services. Besides rights and freedoms, it calls for personal responsibility for one's own actions.
f. It underlines the value of having choice and options even if they are not used.
g. Finally, it acknowledges the fact that expressed utility, or subjective happiness, is not always a sufficient indicator of well-being, since people tend to adapt their expectations in adverse conditions.

The CA is strongly associated with the economic development community (Nussbaum 2011). Sen's (2001) classic book *Development as Freedom*, UNDP's Human Development Index and the practical applications of the capability framework by the World Bank are good examples of this link. The theory resonates particularly well in developing countries, where basic human capabilities and rights cannot be taken for granted and social inequalities are pervasive. The CA has also been usefully applied to the analysis of deprivation problems in industrialized societies (Wolff and de-Shalit 2010). In these contexts, offering more opportunities, freedoms and choice can safely be assumed to improve people's lives. However, the changing nature of everyday life in highly developed societies has created new types of well-being problems that are not adequately incorporated in the CA.

The growing affluence, freedoms and market orientation of industrialized societies have created new types of life management and mental health problems (O'Hara 2007). Quite surprisingly, the origins of these problems are opposite to those emphasized by the CA. People in affluent societies do not suffer from having too little choice and freedom; they often have too much of them (Schwartz 2005; Hämäläinen 2009)!

The 'problem of choice' highlights an important weakness of the CA. It does not analyse the implications of the human being's limited mental capacities on well-being (Baumeister and Tierney 2011; Basu et al., this volume, Chapter 7). As a consequence, the CA cannot explain the widespread mental malaise in affluent societies (Pugno 2005). Despite having more capabilities, choice and freedoms than ever before, 'large parts of the population in high-income countries experience extended feelings of stress and fatigue, and depression and related mental health problems have become common and widespread' (Weehuizen 2005, p. 3).[2]

These mental problems are also likely to explain why the subjective well-being of people in affluent societies tends to adapt in the opposite way to that of the deprived people in poor countries (Pugno 2005): 'In the case of rich countries adaptation seems to work in the reverse direction, i.e. well-being is self-rated less than what material indices would have predicted. In this case, policy action clearly cannot ignore subjective indices of well-being.' At least part of the famous 'Easterlin paradox' may be caused by the negative impacts of increasing wealth and choice on psychological well-being.

In general, the CA pays very little attention to the highly interdependent and complex nature of everyday life in industrialized societies. Various capabilities and functionings tend to be analysed separately, and there is very little analysis of how these functionings are chosen, what specific human needs they satisfy, how they interact in shaping individual well-being, or how an individual's whole 'portfolio' of functionings is managed.[3] We will address these 'demand-side' questions of well-being in this chapter.

The CA acknowledges the importance of living environments for well-being. For example, Nussbaum argues that social, political, familial and economic conditions may sometimes prevent individuals from using their 'internal' capabilities. However, neither Nussbaum nor Sen analyse the well-being consequences of different aspects of living environments in any depth (Sen 2009, pp. 245–6; Nussbaum 2011, p. 31). As a consequence, the CA has sometimes been accused of 'methodological individualism'.

The exclusion of a more careful analysis of living environments was a prudent choice to limit the scope of the original research into manageable proportions. However, numerous decision makers whose decisions shape real living environments need to know what kinds of environments support everyday well-being. And, indeed, there is interesting research on the role and impact of nature, noise, infrastructure, organizations, housing, media, marketing, technologies, security, culture and arts on individual well-being (see e.g. Basu et al., this volume, Chapter 7; Flint-Taylor and Cooper, this volume, Chapter 9). This research needs to be integrated into a more holistic theory of well-being.

Wolff and de-Shalit (2010) point out that the CA does not pay sufficient attention to the fact that uncertainty and the risk of losing one's capabilities are important determinants of well-being. Those who feel uncertain and vulnerable find it more difficult to plan their lives. They call this situation 'planning blight'. At the extreme, '[s]ome people faced with pervasive uncertainty no longer know what to do, losing their confidence to make decisions and take action' (Wolff 2006). This is an important argument, because the current socio-economic transformation is causing great uncertainty in people's minds.

Wolff and de-Shalit (2010) also argue that individual capabilities (and functionings) are interdependent. This may lead individuals to virtuous circles of improving capabilities or vicious circles of deteriorating ones (Rönkä 1999). Some capabilities and functionings are more likely than others to produce such circles. Wolff and de-Shalit (2010) call them 'fertile functionings' and 'corrosive capabilities'. These capabilities can be targeted by policy makers to initiate virtuous circles or to prevent vicious ones.

Wolff and de-Shalit's (2010) analysis brings uncertainty and decision-making capacity to the capability analysis. Wolff believes that the 'planning blight . . . is a central, pervasive, and, to date, under-theorized, aspect of disadvantage' (Wolff 2006, p. 6). We agree with him and argue below that the capability to make prudent decisions in a highly uncertain and complex world is the key fertile functioning (or corrosive capability) in advanced societies. The rapid transformation of industrialized societies and living environments has fundamentally challenged the decision-making capacity of individuals. Besides direct negative impacts on psychological well-being, an individual's poor choices may 'spill over' to his or her other capabilities and create a vicious circle that leads to more tangible deprivation problems such as unemployment, low income, poor health and insecurity (Rönkä 1999; Lämsä 2009). We will discuss the relationship between life management problems and these deprivation problems later in the policy implications of this chapter.

The key terms of the capability approach – 'capabilities' and 'functionings' – are rather vaguely defined. In the CA literature, they are exemplified by various determinants of well-being, many of which are incommensurable (Sen 2009, p. 239; Wolff and de-Shalit 2010). For example, an individual's key functionings are said to include resources, such as 'being healthy' and 'having a job', and needs, such as 'having self-respect' and 'being safe', as well as feelings such as 'being happy'. Since the sources of well-being are plural it would be important to know how the various capabilities and functionings are interrelated beyond just being related to an individual's well-being.

The incommensurability of various capabilities and functionings explains why Sen, unlike Nussbaum, has not been willing to provide a specific list of core capabilities (Sen 2009, p. 242). He rightly points out that the required capabilities are context and culture dependent. However, Nussbaum also has a point in her attempt to develop a list of core capabilities that are generally important to well-being. Without any practical guide, decision makers would find it very difficult to implement the CA.

During major societal transformations, societies must revisit and re-evaluate their ultimate goals and values (von Wright 1981). Besides well-being and the good life, the current transformation emphasizes another fundamental goal of humankind, namely sustainable development. Individuals and societies are complex systems that must maintain their internal and external coherence in order to survive (Maturana and Varela 1998; Laszlo 2008, 2011).[4] The currently dominant lifestyles and behavioural patterns in industrialized societies are not sustainable. They create contradictions and incoherence at all levels of the society (individual, organizational, national and international). These contradictions are exemplified by, for example, the growth of lifestyle-related chronic diseases, widespread mental health problems, severe environmental problems and the malfunctioning international monetary and economic institutions (see also O'Hara and Lyon, this volume, Chapter 4). The CA approach needs to be augmented also in this respect. It focuses mainly on individual capabilities and prerequisites for social sustainability. A more comprehensive theory of sustainable well-being must integrate everyday life and well-being into a broader framework of sustainable development which includes the social, economic and ecological dimensions. Otherwise the well-intended efforts to improve individual well-being will not be sustainable in the long term (see also Basu et al., this volume, Chapter 7).

A MORE HOLISTIC FRAMEWORK

An improved theory of well-being should move beyond simple listings of incommensurable factors. It should explore the interdependencies and dynamic processes between various determinants of well-being. And

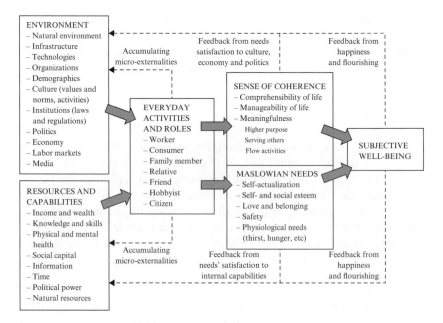

Figure 2.1   Key determinants of well-being in everyday life

it should provide a framework that makes sense of these relationships and processes as a whole. The traditional CA is a good basis for developing such a framework, but it must be augmented with an analysis of the human decision-making problems, higher social and psychological needs, and changing nature of living environments in affluent societies. Figure 2.1 proposes a more holistic theoretical framework that includes the key elements of the CA as well as the 'new dimensions' of well-being that will be discussed in this chapter.[5] It also incorporates the important feedback loops from the individual's behaviour to his or her own and collective well-being.

The subjective well-being of individuals stems from the satisfaction of their needs in various everyday activities (functionings) and communities. The principal human needs include the traditional Maslowian needs – physiological (thirst, hunger, etc.), safety, love and belonging, self- and social esteem and self-actualization – as well as Antonovsky's sense of coherence, i.e. the 'comprehensibility', 'manageability' and 'meaningfulness' of life (Maslow 1970; Antonovsky 1987). At the highest levels of well-being, or 'flourishing', a person is filled with social, psychological and emotional well-being; he or she is 'feeling good and functioning effectively' (Keyes 2006; Huppert 2009). Besides meeting the basic human needs, flourishing requires the satisfaction of higher Maslowian needs (love and belonging, self- and social esteem and self-actualization) as well as the three determinants of Antonovsky's sense of coherence, and is reflected in perceived and expressed happiness and satisfaction with life (see Keyes 2005, Table 1).

Individuals satisfy their needs in various everyday activities, roles and communities as workers, consumers, family members, relatives, friends, hobbyists, citizens and so on. In these activities, they seek to achieve their personal goals by using their internal resources and capabilities as well as those available in their living environment. These include: income and wealth, knowledge and skills, physical and mental health, social relationships and social capital, information, time, political power and natural resources. The subjective well-being and happiness of everyday life depend on the progress that individuals can make toward their personal goals as a whole. Thus, well-being is not a goal that can be pursued and reached directly; it emerges from successful goal pursuits in everyday life (Nesse 2004).

The behaviour and choices of individuals are influenced by the environmental constraints and supports within which the everyday life takes place: natural environment, prevailing technologies, organizational arrangements, demographics, cultural values, norms and activities, laws and regulations, public policies, economic situation, labour market practices and the media. These important aspects of living environments may either empower individuals and facilitate their needs' satisfaction, or constrain them and the satisfaction of their needs.[6]

The individual choices in everyday life involve small unintended consequences or 'micro-externalities' which can accumulate over time or in large groups to influence the individual's resources and capabilities and his or her living environment (Hirsch 1977).[7] These accumulating impacts can be negative, such as obesity, deteriorating social relationships, traffic jams or environmental pollution, or they can be positive, such as improving physical and mental health, increasing social support and more pleasant living environments.[8] The negative consequences follow from internally or externally incoherent behaviour which creates contradictions within the individual's mind and body, or in his or her relationship with the social and natural environment. The positive effects, in turn, stem from internally and externally coherent behaviour, which improves the dynamic balance and consistency of human and natural systems.

The satisfaction of an individual's needs has a direct feedback link to the level and quality of his or her resources and capabilities. Unsatisfied needs tend to weaken the individual's resources and capabilities, while satisfied needs do the opposite. For example, an individual's sense of coherence and social relationships have an important influence on his or her physical and mental health (Keyes 2005; Lindström and Eriksson 2005). At the societal level, the degree of needs satisfaction and subjective well-being can have a major impact on health-related costs and the collective mood, which in turn shapes the economy and politics (Keyes 2005; Casti 2010). For example, long-term economic success may lead to a pleasant collective sense of coherence and unwarranted complacency while the socio-economic environment is changing rapidly. On the other hand, major socio-economic transformations and crises create a collective cognitive dissonance and sense of incoherence which are a fertile ground for new political entrepreneurs (Hämäläinen 2003). Thus, there is a feedback loop also from needs satisfaction and subjective well-being to changes in living environments.

TRANSFORMATION, THE PROBLEM OF CHOICE AND PSYCHOLOGICAL WELL-BEING

Most industrialized societies focused on improving the material well-being of their citizens after the Second World War. This was a rational policy goal in the immediate post-war situation of pervasive material scarcity and unsatisfied basic needs. During the next few decades, their governments prioritized the development of two instrumental subsystems of the society: the economy and the welfare state (Inglehart 1997). Both of these systems developed their own strong proponents, experts and policy makers who still dominate the policy discourse in industrialized societies. Economists and economic policy makers argue for economic growth, productivity and competitiveness, while welfare state scholars and social policy makers are concerned with socio-economic inequalities, income transfers and public welfare services. However, neither of these two groups pays much attention to the changing nature of everyday life and well-being – the ultimate goal that these instrumental systems should serve. They seem to assume that the determinants of well-being are so well understood that they do not need to be discussed.

Unfortunately, this assumption is no longer valid. The nature of several key determinants of well-being has changed considerably during the past few decades in industrial societies as they have become wealthier, basic material needs have been met, physical health has improved, information has become more abundant, environmental problems have escalated, technologies have advanced, cultures have become more individualistic, deregulation has opened markets for competition, work and consumption have taken more important roles in everyday life, and women have increased their participation in the labour force. This 'silent revolution' in well-being has gone largely unnoticed in public policy discourse, which still tends to frame well-being mainly in terms of material consumption and deprivation.

The younger generations in many industrialized countries are no longer content with the material goals. They take material security for granted and are worried about the ecological sustainability of the post-war growth model. As a result, their values have shifted towards quality of life and subjective well-being (Inglehart 1997). In terms of human needs, the emerging cultural shift means that social and psychological needs have become more prominent relative to basic physiological and safety needs. These 'higher needs' include love and belonging, self- and social esteem, self-actualization and the sense of coherence, i.e. the comprehensibility, manageability and meaningfulness of life (Maslow 1970; Antonovsky 1987). Unfortunately, both social relations and the mental capacity of individuals are under severe pressure in today's affluent societies (see Bartolini, this volume, Chapter 6; Basu et al., this volume, Chapter 7).

The citizens of advanced societies are now living in a fundamentally changed world. In particular, their rights, freedoms and behavioural options have multiplied as a result of growing wealth and incomes, advance of the welfare states, liberalization of cultural norms, deregulation of the economy and society, growth of markets and differentiation of product offerings, increasingly powerful marketing and advertising, and the World Wide Web. Combined with the limited mental capacity and rationality of human beings, the new freedoms and behavioural options have created a 'problem of choice' for individuals, who need to make numerous decisions each day which have important well-being consequences (Schwartz 2005; Offer 2006; Beinhocker 2007). This problem is not made any easier by the current socio-economic transformation, information overload and high degree of specialization in modern societies, which magnify the uncertainty and complexity of decision-making situations.

The problem of choice is aggravated by emotions that shape human decision making. Different emotions motivate individuals in their various daily roles and activities. For example, hunger drives individuals to search for food and fear to look for shelter. Both emotions and cognition affect the allocation of effort between the various pursuits of life. The problem is that emotions have been shaped by evolution and may not always give useful behavioural guidance in today's fundamentally changed living environments (Nesse 2004). For instance, the lust for high-energy food may have been useful in prehistoric times when food was scarce and starvation was a real threat, but it creates problems in today's well-fed societies. Moreover, Nesse points out that our brains have not been designed for the highly specialized tasks and long-term efforts of modern societies.

The problem of choice is not only limited to the affluent or the middle-class. Thaler and Sunstein (2008, p. 134) argue that, '[w]hen markets get more complicated, unsophisticated and uneducated shoppers will be especially disadvantaged by the complexity'. For example, in a normal supermarket, the daily choice of food includes thousands of alternatives. People also face numerous options in other life domains: in social relationships, leisure-time activities, alternative commuting options, different technology and clothing alternatives, and so forth – not to mention the different brands and suppliers.[9] People have not, yet, learned to live with these plentiful options. The societal transformation and problem of choice put growing pressure on the satisfaction of social and psychological needs in advanced societies.

The relationship between the current socio-economic transformation and psychological well-being can be analysed with the salutogenesis theory of Aaron Antonovsky (1987). This theory was originally developed to explain health.[10] Antonovsky criticized modern medicine for focusing too much on individual diseases and forgetting that human beings and their health form a whole of many interdependent and interacting factors. He did not see health and disease as mutually exclusive categories – you are either sick or healthy – but rather argued that people are always located on some part of the health–disease continuum. Sometimes we are closer to the health end of it, and at other times nearer the disease end. According to Antonovsky, the key question is: why do the majority of people remain healthy despite being continuously surrounded by various bacteria, viruses, accidents and the natural laws of entropy? To answer this question he focused his research on the 'generalized resistance resources' which allow individuals to resist different diseases.

Antonovsky synthesized the various resistance resources in the concept of 'sense of coherence'. According to Antonovsky (1987), SOC is:

> a global orientation that expresses the extent to which one has a pervasive, enduring though dynamic feeling of confidence that 1) the stimuli, deriving from one's internal and external environment in the course of living are structured, predictable and explicable; 2) the resources are available for one to meet the demands posed by these stimuli; 3) these demands are challenges, worthy of investment and engagement.

As indicated before, these dimensions are: *comprehensibility, manageability* and *meaningfulness*.[11] Briefly put, a person's SOC is determined by the balance between the challenges posed by everyday life and the living environment and the resources and capabilities available to the person. If the challenges continuously exceed the person's resources and capabilities the person will be stressed and his or her health and well-being will suffer.

Towards the end of his career Antonovsky (1991) wrote a paper that emphasized the importance of socio-cultural and historical living environments in shaping individuals' SOC. In that paper, Antonovsky suggested that today's uncertain and complex living environments with plentiful information, freedoms and choice are particularly problematic for the development and maintenance of SOC:

> Different sources bombard us with conflicting information. Rules are often vague or inconsistent. Facing this perpetual danger of chaos, the human being finds it difficult to make sense of her or his world, to know how to feel, think, or behave . . . [W]ithout rules, guidelines, criteria for setting priorities; without some significant thread of continuity between past, present, and the future; without some degree of harmony, we are lost . . . A terrorizing environment, a suprasystem which sets inherently insoluble, simultaneously conflicting, or random, disconnected problems before one makes it impossible to know what to do. It is most important to know that these no-win situations . . . include those which impose an overload of freedom and choice. (Antonovsky 1991)

Antonovsky built an important theoretical link between the individual's well-being and the individual's living environment. However, he did not attempt to dynamize his model by asking how socio-economic changes would affect people's health and well-being.

The current transformation of industrialized societies puts considerable pressure on all three dimensions of SOC. First, the rapid transformation of society has increased the subjective uncertainty of individuals and decision makers. The higher uncertainty stems from the unpredictability of economic and social development, the splintering of social norms, information overload, growing specialization, the interdependence and complexity of everyday life and social processes, the increasing intensity of communication and the insufficiency of individuals' interpretative frames (Michael 2000; Hämäläinen 2003, O'Hara 2007). For an individual, the increased uncertainty reduces the comprehensibility of life and creates cognitive dissonance and stress (Festinger 1957; O'Hara and Lyon, this volume, Chapter 4).

Second, the growing uncertainty and decision-making problems also make life management more difficult. This problem is aggravated by the problem of choice described above. The affluent, free and market-oriented societies offer a huge number of options for building one's identity and life. In the increasingly individualized culture, these new opportunities encourage people to engage in all sorts of interesting activities and communities, both at work and in their leisure time, which they believe to enhance their well-being. However, in their new freedom to choose, people tend to forget that there are two limiting factors in their capacity to handle the whole portfolio of their activities, namely mental capacity and time. The various

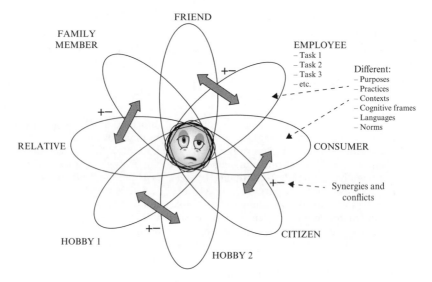

Figure 2.2   Hurried life in affluent society

activities of a person draw on the same fixed mental capacity and available time (24/7) (Baumeister and Tierney 2011; Basu et al., this volume,
Chapter 7). Moreover, the different activities and communities have their
own specific goals, practices, rhythms, contexts, shared frames, languages
and behavioural norms, which are not always easy to fit together in everyday life, particularly if the number of activities is large (Figure 2.2).[12]

Finally, the life management challenges are not made any easier by
the fact that the declining size of households has made cooperative and
shared solutions to everyday tasks increasingly rare. Unlike in the past,
when individual households could include many generations, relatives and
servants, and communal support was more common, today individuals,
parents and families must often deal with their complex everyday lives
alone without much external social support.

The problems with work–life balance have attracted a lot of public and
scholarly attention in recent years. However, the challenge of maintaining
a manageable balance and coherence among the various daily activities
is a more general one. Moreover, the mental burden of life management
is not only related to one's current activities. Individuals use their brains
also to reflect on and evaluate their past activities and to plan for future
ones. They may also have a responsibility for arranging the activities and
matters of their close dependants, such as children or parents. Bianchi
suggests that one reason for the increased time that American parents

spend engaged with their children's activities is that they are 'concerned with giving [them] a wide range of opportunities': 'A number of studies suggest that American parents, at least middle-class parents, are engaged in an ever more intensive form of child-rearing. Middle-class children participate in a large number of extracurricular activities that often require parental involvement and require parents to transport children to and from these activities' (Bianchi 2011).

Many people try to cope with these problems by performing many activities at the same time, by engaging in 'multitasking'. However, empirical research has shown that people are not very good at multitasking (Wallis 2006; Rosen 2008), particularly when the tasks involve active thinking (Kahneman 2011). They achieve worse results, make more mistakes, learn less and take longer to complete tasks than people who complete one task before taking up the next. In practice, the multitasking people do not parallel-process; they oscillate between various tasks and perform them in a sequential manner. Between each task the brain is compelled to restart and refocus. This takes time and mental capacity, and results in growing stress.

The hurried and overcrowded lifestyles of modern societies take a toll on well-being also indirectly through their negative impact on social relationships (Bianchi 2011; Bartolini, this volume, Chapter 6). As people engage in more and more activities, they have less time and mental energy for each of them (Hirsch 1977; Baumeister and Tierney 2011). As a result, their social relationships tend to become more numerous but also weaker. Moreover, human relationships, organizational affiliations, living places and other social commitments are changed more easily as a result of the increased choice and ease of switching.[13] The more rapid changes in personal commitments can be motivated by positive or negative reasons. On the one hand, one may want to try something new because 'the grass is greener on the other side of the fence'. According to Baumeister and Tierney (2011), people are not very good at making strong commitments to a single life option when they have many of them available. On the other hand, as Hirschman's (1970) theory of 'exit, voice and loyalty' suggests, dissatisfied people are likely to choose the exit option more often than staying loyal and voicing their complaints when the number of attractive alternatives grows.

As a result, the increasing choice in affluent societies leads to more short-term behaviour (Offer 2006; Steel 2011). In addition, it makes the development and maintenance of deep social relationships more difficult.[14] Such relationships are the most important ones for subjective well-being (Pulkkinen et al. 2011). The negative well-being effects of hurried life seem to peak when people have young children. Helliwell shows in his chapter that individual happiness tends to follow a U-shaped curve over the life course. The bottom is reached at around the age of 45 (Helliwell, this volume, Chapter 5).

The third dimension of Antonovsky's theory, meaningfulness, is also under pressure in advanced societies as they have become more individualistic and selfish. Already in the late 1970s, Viktor Frankl observed that Western civilization was suffering from a massive lack of meaning, an 'existential vacuum' (Frankl 1978). In his definition, a meaningful life meant exceeding one's own interests by serving others. Although highly important for well-being (see Helliwell, this volume, Chapter 5), this kind of altruistic behaviour is increasingly rare in today's self-centred and market-driven society (Gerhardt 2011). The currently dominant market ideology is based on Adam Smith's theory of the 'invisible hand', which allows individuals to focus on their own selfish endeavours instead of worrying about the common good. Powerful marketing and advertising surround the citizens of affluent societies and transform the market ideology into very practical pressures to make selfish choices in everyday life. The sense of meaninglessness is further reinforced by the weakening of strong social relationships which encourage pro-social behaviour, and the disintegration of traditional communal and religious norms which emphasize the common good (Fromm 1976; Csikszentmihalyi 2006).

In conclusion, the rapid transformation of society and everyday life has weakened the social relationships and sense of coherence of individuals, which has put new pressure on their mental health and subjective well-being (Figure 2.3).[15] These pressures can have serious consequences in the increasingly knowledge-intensive working life, since the productivity of a knowledge worker drops drastically with even slight mental health

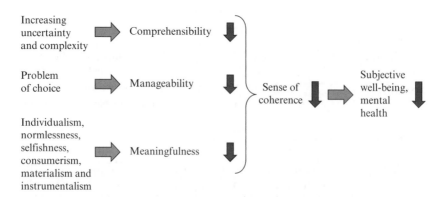

Figure 2.3   Socio-economic transformation weakens the sense of coherence

problems (Weehuizen 2005). The combination of weaker individual SOC and greater mental demands of knowledge work may explain why depression and other mental illnesses have become a major reason for disability leave and early retirement in industrialized countries.

DECISION MAKING, COHERENCE AND SUSTAINABLE WELL-BEING

So far, our analysis of well-being has focused on the individual level. However, individuals do not live solitary and independent lives maximizing their own well-being without any external ties or effects. They are an integral part of larger natural and social systems whose various interdependencies ultimately determine the sustainability of their well-being. Ultimately, it is the decisions that individuals make in their private lives, organizations and political institutions that collectively determine the sustainability of their well-being – and that of humankind. It is the nature of these individual decisions and the ways in which they influence the world that we must study if we want to promote sustainable well-being.

In the previous section, we argued that decision making has become more problematic as a result of the increased specialization and complexity of industrialized societies and the higher uncertainty stemming from the current societal transformation. Traditional mental frames and established social theories are becoming outdated in the rapidly changing world. At the same time, information overload and the problem of choice burden decision makers more than ever. Widely shared cultural norms have disintegrated and no longer give proper behavioural guidance.

The current decision-making environment generates three types of decision-making problems that create most well-being and sustainability problems in advanced societies. These are *short-termism*, *selfishness* and *path-dependence*. Individual short-term, selfish and path-dependent decisions create small unintended consequences that we call *micro-externalities*. These micro-externalities may produce either coherence and stability or incoherence and chaos in the biological, social, physical and natural systems that they influence. Financial markets and national economies provide good examples of both alternatives. Sometimes individual and seemingly independent decisions of economic agents create coherence and stability (e.g. Adam Smith's 'invisible hand'); at other times, they produce crisis and chaos. Individual decision makers do not usually even notice the micro-externalities they create in individual decisions. However, these small unintended consequences can accumulate *over time* or in *large crowds* into major well-being or sustainability problems.[16] We will next analyse the causes and well-being consequences of each of the three kinds of decision-making problems.

Short-termism

The widespread short-termism in today's society can be explained with a few mutually reinforcing causes. As we saw above, the growing wealth, freedoms and market pressures in affluent societies decrease the loyalty of individuals and increase their mobility between various life options. Combined with the fixed time available (24/7), engaging in more activities and commitments leads to more short-term behaviour.

Moreover, psychological research has shown that the willpower of individuals is a limited resource and its depletion will lead to myopic choices and unsocial behaviour. Three factors are particularly taxing to willpower: difficult problem solving and decision making, resisting temptations (to instant gratification) and multiple simultaneous projects (tasks) (Baumeister and Tierney 2011; Steel 2011). It is easy to see how the problem of choice, increased uncertainty and hurried life reinforce short-term behaviour by depleting the limited mental energy and willpower of individuals. Indeed, researchers suggest that the willpower and self-control of people are under more strain than ever: 'Self-regulation failure is the major social pathology of our time' (Baumeister and Tierney 2011; Baumeister et al. 1994).

People are very poor decision makers when it comes to their own well-being, especially if the effects of their decisions materialize only in the long term and if their living environment is changing considerably (Kahneman and Thaler 2006) – as it is doing in the current transformation.

A particularly difficult decision-making situation involves choices which have positive short-term but negative long-term effects on the individual's well-being. Research shows that most people tend to put more emphasis on the immediate impacts of their decisions than on the more distant ones (Ainslie 2001). Such 'hyperbolic discounting' is particularly common in situations where the expected longer-term impact of an individual decision is considered to be small relative to the immediate pleasures. Some examples of such short-term behaviour include: substance abuse, unhealthy meals, skipping physical exercise, infidelity, over-consumption with credit cards, and choosing individual hobbies over some extra time with family.

People tend to consider each individual decision independently. However, the well-being impacts of individual decisions are not really independent. The evaluation of the true well-being consequences of individual decisions is difficult, because the micro-externalities of similar decisions can accumulate over time: unhealthy meals and lack of exercise can lead to obesity and chronic diseases, infidelity to broken marriages, overspending to personal bankruptcies, and so forth. Taking these potential cumulative impacts into account with each decision requires considerable foresight and willpower. Then 'every episode must be treated as a reflection of the general need to resist temptations' (Baumeister and Tierney 2011, p. 16).

Selfishness

There are also many reasons behind the widespread selfishness of advanced societies (Gerhardt 2011). As we noted above, moral values and norms have become more individualistic and differentiated, which allows more self-centred behaviour to flourish (Inglehart 1997; Offer 2006). Traditionally, more widely shared values and behavioural norms promoted socially harmonious and unselfish behaviour. The growing specialization of economic and social processes and the urbanization of industrialized societies have also brought individuals and organizations into more intensive communication and interdependence with each other. Selfish behaviour has more negative external impacts in a tightly interconnected system. Moreover, the higher uncertainty and complexity in decision making have also made it more difficult to understand the full effects of one's decisions, even if one wanted to take them into account. A simple product choice in the local supermarket may have repercussions far away in the production network, often on the other side of the globe. In addition, the prevailing market ideology has made selfish behaviour increasingly legitimate, or even socially desirable. A well-functioning market economy is supposed to need self-centred consumers (Friedman and Friedman 1990). Finally, as we have already suggested above, the problem of choice and hurried lifestyles tend to deplete the willpower and civility of individuals, which has a negative impact on their social behaviour and relations (Baumeister and Tierney 2011; Basu et al., this volume, Chapter 7).[17]

Experimental research suggests that only a minority of people always behave in a selfish way and, in similar way, only a minority of people always behave in an altruistic way. Most people are 'strongly reciprocal', inclined to behave in unselfish and socially beneficial ways if other people also do so. They are also willing to punish rule breakers and free riders even at their own cost. This kind of conditionally cooperative behaviour is argued to be the result of long gene-culture co-evolution (Gintis et al. 2005; Ostrom 2005). However, if the strongly reciprocal people see many free riders who pursue their own interests they will also turn selfish. Thus, a gradual increase in selfish behaviour may start to snowball after some critical threshold. As a result, most people will end up acting in a selfish way (Fehr and Fischbacher 2005; Kahan 2005).

This kind of escalating process may explain the pervasiveness of selfish behaviour in many fields of life. Witness for example the miserable state of some urban neighbourhoods and unguarded public spaces. Littered streets, broken windows, vandalized playgrounds and empty houses as well as graffiti-covered walls signal that traditional social norms and rules are not being obeyed.[18] However, examples of accumulating selfishness are not limited to poor neighbourhoods. Widespread speeding in traffic, tax evasion and social security abuses suggest that many people have lost their trust in responsible behaviour. Moreover, the current consumption culture legitimizes many behaviours which are not consistent with environmental sustainability. Since the majority of people in affluent societies do not behave in environmentally unsustainable ways, not at least in terms of their countries' carbon footprint, many people think that trying to reduce one's own footprint does not make much sense, since it would have an insignificant impact on the overall situation. In these kinds of situations, people may ask themselves: why should I care about the common good if others do not? Strongly reciprocal people want fairness in altruism.

The growth of selfish behaviour decreases the overall well-being in the society both in the short and in the long term. Sometimes selfish choices accumulate immediately into major macro-level problems, such as traffic jams or littered parks at outdoor concerts; in other cases, the negative consequences take a longer time to accumulate, such as with the neglect of family responsibilities or unsustainable use of natural resources.[19] The increased wealth, interdependence and complexity of advanced societies have magnified this problem, because selfish choices have bigger impacts and diffuse more widely than ever before.

Path-dependence

The third common decision-making problem is path-dependence. At the most general level, path-dependence means that decisions in a particular situation depend on past decisions and their outcomes even if the past circumstances are no longer relevant. Path-dependence is particularly important in the current transformation in which the physical, natural and socio-economic environments of individuals, organizations and policy makers change rapidly and often in unexpected ways. Decision makers can be 'locked in' in less-than-optimal paths which are difficult to reverse. Eventually, the increasing mismatch, or incoherence, between the decision maker's system and the evolutionary path of its environment may lead to an adjustment crisis.

Path-dependence has mainly been analysed in economic history, economics and organizational management literature (see e.g. David 1985;

Krugman 1991; Arthur 1994; Garud and Karnøe 2001). However, it is interesting to think how path-dependence affects individual decision making and well-being. Path-dependence can be related to various determinants of well-being: the individual's resources and capabilities, living environments and everyday activities and roles. First, individual limitations in health, income, knowledge and skills are the most basic sources of path-dependent behaviour. Individuals cannot do more than what their personal resources and capabilities allow. Established cognitive frames and behavioural routines may also tie thinking and behaviour to traditional paths. Such unconscious mental rigidities are often the most important roadblocks to change (Hämäläinen 2007).

Second, individuals may have economic interests or large investments associated with the traditional ways of doing things which may slow down their adaptation to changing circumstances. For example, many citizens strongly support the established model of the welfare state because they are afraid of personally losing some benefits if it is fundamentally reformed. A difficult-to-sell house in a declining factory town provides an example of a major investment that may cause path-dependence by tying its owner down to a particular location.

A third source of path-dependent behaviour is strong social relationships. An individual may think twice before changing his or her behaviour if that will cause negative externalities to close partners. 'Rocking the boat' in social networks can easily result in ostracism, with immediate consequences to well-being. Thus strong social capital may sometimes also be detrimental to long-term well-being if changes in the living environment demand new types of behaviour.

Tight environmental constraints are the fourth possible source of path-dependence (Nussbaum 2011). For example, local climate and natural conditions as well as prevailing technologies, organizational arrangements and cultures, institutional norms and rules, economic conditions and the available information put numerous constraints on behavioural choices.

Finally, the interdependencies among an individual's various activities and roles constrain his or her behavioural changes. Changing a lifestyle may involve a whole cluster of interdependent activities with their own stakeholders and dynamics. Some of these interdependencies may produce undesirable negative side effects. For example, selling one's car and shifting to mass transportation would require more daily commuting time, but also provide more time for reading. In addition, it would make some hobbies and social contacts less accessible, but also increase the money available for other activities. As another example, improving one's sense of coherence and well-being could require 'downshifting', which would require a fundamental rearrangement of one's life. Despite the many benefits of downshifting, very few are still willing to do such a fundamental reshuffle in their everyday activities.

Why is path-dependent decision making a problem for individual well-being? An individual's resources, capabilities and behavioural patterns determine how well he or she can function in the ever-changing living environment. If path-dependent decision making prevents the adaptation of these resources, capabilities and behaviours to the changing environmental demands it may cause various well-being problems: unemployment, illnesses, lack of important social relationships, outdated mental frames, and so on. The widespread sense of incoherence in industrialized societies is a good example of what the combination of rapid environmental change and path-dependent cognitive frames and behaviour can do to subjective well-being (see also O'Hara and Lyon, this volume, Chapter 4).

Short-term, selfish and path-dependent decision making is not limited to the individual level. Various organizations and national governments regularly make such decisions too (Hämäläinen 2008). The short-termism, selfishness and path-dependence in corporate decision making can largely explain the current financial, economic and environmental crises. Similar problems in political decision making have contributed to the current structural adjustment and debt crises in industrialized countries. Thus, short-term, selfish and path-dependent decision making is pervasive in advanced societies and a fundamental challenge to sustainable well-being. Sustainable well-being requires behaviour which takes into account the accumulating micro-externalities of individual decisions. Sustainable choices maintain or improve the coherence of natural and social systems.

Coherence and Sustainability

Evolutionary processes create coherence in the cosmos, nature and society (Maturana and Varela 1998; Laszlo 2008, 2011). Ervin Laszlo argues that all 'viable systems are coherent both in themselves and with the world around them. A breakdown of coherence within them, and between them and their surroundings, is a sign of maladjustment – at worst, a life-threatening malady' (Laszlo 2011). This suggests that the key to sustainable well-being is coherent decision making at all levels of the society. Humberto Maturana (2011), in turn, notes that 'we can do anything if we respect the operational coherence of the domain'. He emphasizes the dynamic nature of coherence: 'The history of living systems is the history of coherent transformation of the organism and its niche.' Laszlo even suggests that coherence should be a key moral norm in our highly interdependent and complex world:

A healthy system is internally as well externally coherent. Its internal coherence defines its own health and viability, and its external coherence defines it contribution to the health of its environment. These principles apply to your life, and to mine. It is objectively good, and hence moral, to maintain your coherence, and to promote your coherence with your environment. Conversely it is objectively bad, and thus immoral, to damage your integrity and have destructive relations with other people and with nature. (Laszlo 2011)

Laszlo further notes that human beings are the only species that lives significantly below the level of coherence required for its own existence. Natural selection has already weeded out other species that had evolved incoherence to a comparable degree.

The sustainability of our civilization and well-being requires behaviour that is more coherent internally with our own mental and physical requirements as well as externally with those of our social, material and natural environments. Most likely, such behaviour was more common earlier in history when communities were much smaller, less specialized, more local and less well resourced than today. In such communities, short-sighted, selfish and non-adaptive behaviours would produce immediate and severe feedback that would quickly restore systemic coherence. On the other hand, in today's highly specialized, affluent and globalized societies, internally and externally coherent decision making requires human capacities – such as reflexivity, foresight and systemic intelligence, willpower, self-regulation and emotion control, and intra- and interpersonal attunement, as well as compassion and empathy (Nesse 2004; Cole and Deater-Deckard 2009; Siegel 2009; Saarinen and Hämäläinen 2010) – that very few individuals have. We need to develop new institutional norms, technologies and other decision support mechanisms that will help individuals to make more coherent and sustainable decisions. Ken Wilber may be right when he suggests that humanity cannot be saved unless it can rise to a higher level of 'conscious evolution' where it becomes aware of its impact on the evolutionary processes in human beings, nature and society, and individuals are empowered to take more responsibility for the full consequences of their behaviour (Wilber 2011).[20]

Figure 2.4 tries to capture the different dimensions of coherence at the individual level. In this framework, the accumulation of short-sighted decisions and the related micro-externalities creates internal incoherence in the mind and body of the individual. This may result in both mental and physical problems (depression, obesity, etc.). Laszlo sums up the relationship between internal coherence and health in a way that is entirely consistent with Antonovsky's sense of coherence theory:

	IMMATERIAL	PHYSICAL
INTERNAL	**Psychological** **(mind, will, heart)** e.g. stress, dissonance, and depression	**Physiological** **(health)** e.g. obesity and lifestyle diseases
EXTERNAL	**Social** e.g. broken marriages, loneliness, xenophobia, segregation	**Environmental** e.g. littering, vandalism, tragedy of the commons

Figure 2.4   Dimensions of individual coherence and consequences of incoherence

> In a biological organism the level of internal coherence decides the level of organic health. When the organism is internally coherent, its bodily functions are coordinated and effective: it is healthy. When the overall level of coherence is low, the organism's immune system is weak and the organism is subject to malfunction and disease. (Laszlo 2008, p. 119)

In a similar way, the accumulating micro-externalities of selfish decisions produce incoherence in the individual's relationship with the social and natural environment. This may lead for example to poor social relations, broken marriages and environmental problems. Finally, in times of transformation, the accumulation of path-dependent decisions will decrease the dynamic coherence of the individual with his or her rapidly changing environment. The individual's resources, capabilities and behavioural patterns may lose their previous relevance and cause adjustment and well-being problems at both individual and societal levels.[21]

Cybernetic Governance Crisis

As we noted above, short-term, selfish and path-dependent behaviour is also prevalent in organizations, governments and international institutions. Narrow, short-term interests and traditional solutions produce incoherence and unsustainable development at all levels of the society. These problems reflect a more general governance crisis in advanced societies (Beer 1973; Michael 1973; Zuboff and Maxmin 2002; Hämäläinen 2007; Hamel 2007; Heckscher and Adler 2007; Laszlo 2008). The uncertainty, interdependence and complexity of the governance challenge exceed the capacity of traditional governance arrangements at each systemic level, be it an individual, organization, national government, or intergovernmental institution such the European Commission or the International Monetary Fund. We do not, yet, seem to have the required 'systems intelligence' to successfully deal with our new governance challenges (Sterman 1994; Saarinen and Hämäläinen 2010).

John Casti (2012) calls this problem the 'complexity gap' based on Ashby's (1958) Law of Requisite Variety. Ashby's Law states that the variety (complexity) of the controller has to be at least equal to the variety (complexity) of the system for it to remain stable. Ashby was one of the founding fathers of cybernetics, the general theory of control systems. Stafford Beer, another pioneer of cybernetics, had recognized the emerging governance crisis already in the early 1970s. Resonating well with our previous analysis, he attributed the crisis to the increasing freedoms and opportunities afforded by 'education, technology, prosperity and the way those possibilities interact to generate yet more variety' (Beer 1973, pp. 10, 12):

> In the real world we find that increasing freedom (including new opportunities) proliferates variety to a point where our respected institutions cannot anymore cope with it . . . In order to regulate a system, we have to absorb its variety. If we fail in this, the system becomes unstable . . . [and] at worst, there is a catastrophic collapse.

Beer's analysis is extremely relevant for today's industrialized societies. Consider, for example, the chaotic responses of the European Union leaders to the recent financial, economic and debt crises. New turns in these crises have taken them by surprise even before the policy responses to the previous ones have been implemented. None of the EU leaders claim that these crises are in their control. In a similar vein, global business leaders admit that complexity is their number one challenge today (IBM 2010; *HBR* 2011). They are developing new organizational arrangements, such as 'collaborative communities', 'experimentalist governance' and various types of networks, to manage the increased variety of their business systems (Adler and Heckscher 2007; Galbraith 2007; Sabel and Zeitlin 2012). According to Casti (2012), the complexity gap can even explain the big 'x-events', or 'Black Swans' (Taleb 2007), in which major social systems are unexpectedly transformed or collapse. The implosion of the Soviet Union and the Arab Spring are two recent examples of x-events (Casti 2012).

Major governance crises are not an entirely new phenomenon in human history. Joseph Tainter discusses several historical governance crises in his book *The Collapse of Complex Societies* (Tainter 1988). Laszlo argues that governance crises are typical in major evolutionary bifurcations, and they may result in evolutionary breakdown or breakthrough (Laszlo 2008). The industrialized societies have been able to overcome the previous governance crises of capitalism by creating more complex governance arrangements (Freeman and Louca 2002; Adler and Heckscher 2007). However, there is no guarantee that they will be equally successful in the current crisis.

In the present context, a breakdown could result from a situation in which the governance challenges of the increasingly complex and uncertain world overwhelmed the decision makers. Particularly, solutions that are based on old frames and simplistic causal logic are likely to fail in the new environment (Michael 1973; O'Hara and Lyon, this volume, Chapter 4). A breakthrough, in turn, would require the development of a new cultural paradigm (shared frames, values and norms) that supported more sustainable behaviour and the development of new governance solutions with the requisite variety (Beer 1973; Laszlo 2008).

As we noted earlier, Antonovsky (1991) had important insights about the impact of uncertain and complex living environments on well-being. At the end of his seminal paper, he argued that systems theory could provide a valuable framework for analysing the well-being challenges of current living environments and how the external determinants of individual SOC could be improved. Antonovsky seemed to be well aware of Ashby's Law of Requisite Variety.[22]

At the individual level, sustainable behaviour and well-being require a strong personal sense of coherence, both internally and externally. The individual should:

- be aware of the 'bounded rationality' of human beings and systematic biases in their decision making (Thaler and Sunstein 2008; Kahneman 2011);
- understand the individual-level (internal) and collective (external) well-being consequences of his or her behaviour in the complex and dynamic systems that he or she operates in (comprehensibility);
- have the capability to act successfully in such systems despite the challenges they pose to intelligent behaviour (manageability);[23] and
- have the willpower, self-control and ethical norms to take into account the long-term well-being consequences of his or her choices as well as their impact on other human beings and the natural environment (meaningfulness).

As we can see, sustainable behaviour and well-being are not easy to achieve in today's complex and uncertain world characterized by the 'problem of choice'. Individuals need all the help they can get in making prudent choices in their everyday lives. Adapting a term from health promotion (Koelen and Lindström 2005), they need to develop a new 'well-being literacy' to achieve more sustainable lifestyles (see also O'Hara 2007). Researchers and education systems can play an important role in the development and diffusion of such literacy. However, the whole reductionist scientific approach may have to change towards a more holistic, relational and systemic approach before it can properly support a more sustainable culture (Hollingsworth and Muller 2008; Brown and Garver 2009). Besides education for sustainable well-being, policy makers can support individual decision making in various ways that reduce the complexity gap. We will discuss these policy options in the next section.

TOWARDS MORE SUSTAINABLE LIFESTYLES

The general governance crisis is at the heart of the new well-being problems of individuals. The growing uncertainty, complexity and choice in everyday life have created increasing problems in decision making, life management and psychological well-being for the citizens of affluent societies. In their daily life, people often have difficulties in making prudent decisions that will lead to sustainable well-being for themselves and their fellow citizens. Many feel their everyday life is not sufficiently under their control any more.[24] The hurried and chaotic life, in turn, reduces the time and mental energy that people have for maintaining the social relationships that are so important to their well-being. The mental burden of the complexity gap may also explain the frequent examples of unreasonable behaviour in modern life, such as irritability, impatience, intolerance, lack of respect, incivility and a sense of hopelessness (Basu et al., this volume, Chapter 7).

People have particular problems with choices that they make rarely and/or that involve high uncertainty and complexity, delayed and ambiguous well-being effects, and poor feedback information (Thaler and Sunstein 2008). In terms of Figure 2.4, the uncertainty and complexity of decision making tend to create mental incoherence, while the delayed and ambiguous well-being effects produce physical health problems, and the poor feedback and understanding of the consequences of one's choices can lead to social and environmental problems. Hence, achieving internal and external coherence and, hence, sustainable behaviour is, to a large extent, a decision-making challenge. As a result, we will focus in this section on how human decision making could be supported to make lifestyles more sustainable.[25]

Limited Mental Capacity

Both Ashby and Beer emphasized the limited capacity of the human brain in the development of the complexity gap (Ashby 1958; Beer 1973).[26] The fact that 'brains are finite' in comparison to the ever-increasing variety of life creates the problems with comprehensibility and manageability discussed earlier in this chapter. Beer was probably one of the first to notice this problem: 'Perhaps we cannot actually understand our lives, our environment, any longer . . . Can it be, perhaps, that we all suffer from a variety overload that we cannot map onto our [mental] models, and from an ungovernable oscillation in our search for mental equilibrium?' (Beer 1973, p. 30).[27]

More recently, the 'heuristics and biases' approach to decision making has also underlined the limited mental capacities of human beings (see Thaler and Sunstein 2008; Kahneman 2011). In this stream of research, psychologists and behavioural economists focus on human frailties in everyday choice situations. 'Heuristics' refers to the rules of thumb that people use to simplify their decision making, while systematic 'biases' result from the mistakes they make in their choices. The empirical results of the heuristics and biases research have fundamentally challenged the assumption of fully rational *homo economicus* in mainstream economics.

Many heuristics and biases – such as 'anchoring', 'availability' and 'representativeness' heuristics, 'status quo bias', 'planning fallacy', 'framing', 'priming' and 'post-completion error' – help individuals to reduce the uncertainty and complexity of decision-making situations (Thaler and Sunstein 2008, p. 95): 'The picture that emerges is one of busy people trying to cope in a complex world in which they cannot afford to think deeply about every choice they make. People adopt sensible rules of thumb that sometimes lead them astray.'

People are not always using their limited mental capacity very effectively. The empirical research on *conscious* and *unconscious* thought shows that these two thinking modes have different strengths and weaknesses that make them appropriate to different decision-making situations (Dijksterhuis and Nordgren 2006).[28] The effortful and deductive conscious thought has rather limited information-processing capacity and is good at solving relatively simple problems. It leads people to focus on a limited number of attributes and is guided by established schemas and stereotypes. It tends to have problems in weighting the various attributes of the decision-making situation. However, conscious thought is good when strict decision rules need to be followed. To a certain extent, it can also control the short-term temptations and emotions that drive the unconscious mind (Thaler and Sunstein 2008).

The effortless unconscious thought, in turn, is generally superior at making complex decisions. It can use a much bigger mental capacity and it tends to weight the relative importance of various attributes very well. The unconscious thought can also organize and improve the individual's mental representations. It is very good at detecting recurring patterns and associations, even highly complicated ones. In addition, the unconscious thought works 'aschematically', or 'bottom up', which is important for creativity and helps in avoiding premature conclusions. However, it tends to rely on heuristics instead of strict decision rules, and produces the systematic biases discussed above (Dijksterhuis and Nordgren 2006; Thaler and Sunstein 2008).

The differing capacities of conscious and unconscious thought have clear implications for the decision-making strategies of individuals. In general, the more complex and uncertain decision-making environments of today's society suggest that people should try to rely not only on reflective conscious thinking. Particularly the more complex problems which involve multiple and incommensurable attributes, and for which there are no established schemas or frameworks available, can often be better solved by intuitions from the unconscious mind. However, the unconscious mind does not work well without a prior stage of conscious and comprehensive information gathering. Moreover, it takes time for the unconscious to integrate all the relevant data to form an objective summary judgement. The old advice to 'sleep on it' with important decisions has a strong scientific foundation (Dijksterhuis and Nordgren 2006).

The attempts to develop sustainable lifestyles must take these evolutionary characteristics and limitations of human beings into account. In the remainder of this section, we will focus on how individuals could be helped in satisfying their higher social and psychological needs. In particular, we will discuss various ways in which the complexity gap could be bridged and the manageability of everyday life improved. The Law of Requisite Variety has two very simple policy implications that will guide our analysis. It suggests that an individual's sense of coherence and well-being can be improved by measures that either (1) increase the capacity (variety) of the controller or (2) reduce the complexity (variety) of the system. We will discuss each of them in turn.

Improving Control Capacity

Several authors have argued that the more dynamic, uncertain and complex living environments demand new types of knowledge and skills (Rogers 1995; Gardner 2006; O'Hara 2007; Saarinen and Hämäläinen 2010). In particular, the need for a broad individual knowledge base, cross-disciplinary cognitive frames and 'combinative capabilities' is growing (Kogut and Zander 1992).[29] Thus, Laszlo (1987) has pointed out that there is an increasing demand for 'generalists', and Gardner (2006) has stressed the growing importance of 'synthesizing minds'. The increasingly differentiated knowledge in advanced societies requires 'meta-cognitive skills' that enable individuals to identify, combine and synthesize relevant knowledge from different sources, and cooperate with others in doing so (Hakkarainen et al. 2004; Adler and Heckscher 2007). Saarinen and Hämäläinen (2010) argue that people need more holistic, relational and contextual 'systems intelligence' to successfully cope with today's complex and ever-changing world. However, developing such intelligence is not easy, owing to the many problems of learning processes in complex systems (Sterman 1994).

Lombardo (2012) emphasizes the benefits of 'future consciousness' in building integrative understandings, improving personal adaptability, developing self-control and self-coherence, giving meaning and purpose to life and fostering mental health.[30] He argues that future consciousness can be developed by, for example, brainstorming about alternative visions of the future, learning about history (especially long-term trends) and challenging the existing beliefs about the future and one's possibilities in it. Lombardo equates heightened future consciousness with wisdom, which, in the light of our analysis, is an appropriate goal for all learning that aims for the good life and well-being: 'Wisdom is the continually evolving understanding of and fascination with the big picture of life and what is important, ethical and meaningful; it includes the desire and ability to apply this understanding to enhance the well-being of life, both for oneself and for others' (Lombardo 2010, p. 34).

A broad knowledge base improves the comprehensibility of the world and manageability of everyday life. However, it is not sufficient alone in today's highly specialized knowledge society. The complexity and uncertainty of everyday life create new problems that require specialized knowledge and skills. Unfortunately, such 'life management skills' are not usually taught in education systems. Thus, individuals feel increasingly helpless with the variety and specificity of everyday problems.[31] It is often easier to find technical and other support in work organizations than in leisure time, particularly if the local service markets are not very well developed. Specialized knowledge and expertise are also highly valued in the increasingly networked working life. For example, the knowledge-intensive interpersonal networks ('collaborative communities') in and among high-tech firms require contributions that reflect deep disciplinary expertise (Adler and Heckscher 2007). In conclusion, an ideal individual knowledge base is likely to be 'T-shaped' – broad but also deep in some specific area.

The media is another factor that affects the mental capacity of individuals. As Beer suggested, the media can either increase or decrease the variety overload of individuals (Beer 1973). The programmes and stories can build new understandings and reduce cognitive dissonance, but they can also add to individuals' confusion and sense of incoherence. Unfortunately, much of today's commercial media tends to be highly differentiated, fast paced, superficial and entertainment oriented. Individual news is treated separately, and their interdependencies and causal relationships with other events are not explained. This does not help people in their sense making and life management (Csikszentmihalyi 2006). However, some public broadcasting companies (e.g. the BBC) and quality newspapers still play an important role in the collective learning processes through which individuals develop their understanding of the rapidly changing world.

Technology can also have both positive and negative effects on individuals' variety overload. At best, the internet, search engines, computers, smartphones and other 'knowledge devices' support an individual's information gathering, problem solving and memory. However, their non-intuitive user interfaces, unexpected perturbations and information overload can also create more stress and dissonance than the mental burden they alleviate.

Human capabilities need to be continuously maintained and renewed. The harried and knowledge-intensive life requires countervailing periods of tranquillity, rest and sleep during which the brain can recover from the strains of modern life. Mental capacities can also be improved by physical exercise and healthy nutrition (Muller 2007; Baumeister and Tierney 2011; Basu et al., this volume, Chapter 7).

Meditation can improve the mental coherence and capacity of its practitioners. For example, mindfulness training, a Western derivative of Buddhist meditation, focuses the mind on present activities and thoughts and prevents it from ruminating on the past or the future (Kabat-Zinn 2004). This releases mental capacity and allows the powerful unconscious part of the brain to create new understandings (Dijksterhuis and Nordgren 2006). Mindfulness training also supports the internal and external coherence of individuals by improving their emotional balance, response flexibility (reflection between impulse and response), body regulation, social attunement, empathy and morality (Siegel 2009). In addition to these benefits of mindfulness, meditation can reduce stress, increase willpower and help with seeing the bigger picture.[32]

Good social relationships can also augment the mental capacity of individuals (Oldroyd and Morris 2012). People can learn life management capabilities from their parents, relatives, friends or acquaintances. They can ask for others' help in trying to understand difficult issues or solving complex problems. In addition, peer groups can play an important role in strengthening the willpower of individuals when commitments to important decisions are at risk (e.g. Weight Watchers, Alcoholics Anonymous). The social media plays an important role in facilitating this kind of peer support.

Reducing Variety and Choice

There are many trends in contemporary societies which suggest that people are already reacting to the variety overload problem. For example, *downshifting, outsourcing, slow life, gated communities, cocooning, retro fashion*, the popularity of *strong brands*, and *fundamentalism* can be seen to reflect people's wishes to simplify their lives and living environments in ways that make those lives and environments more bearable. They reduce the number of daily activities, slow down life rhythms, make living environments more homogeneous and familiar, simplify consumer choice, and provide a clear worldview and strict rules that give structure to life.

Policy makers have two primary options when they are trying to support individual decision making by shaping their living environments (John et al. 2011). They can either study the heuristics and biases of human decision making and then seek to influence the living environment to get the behaviour that is more beneficial to the individual and the society, or they can shape the living environment in ways that reduce its complexity and uncertainty and thus help people to make better decisions. The former is the influential 'Nudge' strategy promoted by Thaler and Sunstein (2008). The latter strategy, which John et al. (2011) call 'Think', looks at how the bounded rationality and complexity gap could be overcome, or at least reduced. While John et al. focus on the potential of *open citizen deliberation* in changing individual behaviour, we will extend their approach to various aspects of living environments whose complexity and uncertainty can be reduced.

Sustainable well-being is supported by social and institutional environments that help individuals to strengthen their SOC and social relationships. According to Antonovsky, such environments provide individuals with *consistent experiences*, a *good load balance* and *participation opportunities*: 'Consistent experiences provide the basis for the comprehensibility component; a good load balance for the manageability component; and ... participation in shaping the outcome, for the meaningfulness component' (Antonovsky 1991).

In a study of child development, Sagy and Antonovsky (2000) added 'emotional closeness' to the above three factors. They argued that it was important for the development of meaningfulness. These four factors should be taken into account in the development of social and institutional arrangements such as organizations, public services and regulations.

Following Antonovsky (1991), the complexity of everyday life can be attenuated by building *coherent living environments* (see Basu et al., this volume, Chapter 7). Living nature provides the ultimate benchmark in coherence. Evolutionary processes guarantee that different species coexist in coherent patterns which minimize disturbing contradictions and cognitive dissonance. There is plenty of evidence about the mentally restoring and healing effects of access to nature. This knowledge can be utilized in the planning of living environments and the design of buildings and infrastructure. For example, community planners, architects and real estate developers can create communities in which easy access to nature is equally distributed among citizens.

Physical stimuli such as aesthetics, lights and sounds also play an important role in the coherence of living environments and well-being. Dissonant structures, disturbing lights and noise burden the brain with unnecessary incoherence.

Traffic and commuting can create a lot of pressure on the mental capacity and well-being of individuals. Driving a car in busy traffic is one of the least pleasant daily activities for most people (Layard 2005). The possibility of getting lost in an unfamiliar place may further intensify the unpleasant experience. Basu et al. (this volume, Chapter 7) suggest that these negative feelings can be alleviated by reducing the reliance on automobiles by supporting other types of travelling – such as walking, biking, going by train, sharing rides and going by bus – which circumvent many of the annoyances of driving. Moreover, they emphasize the coherence-enhancing effects of good signage, landmarks, grid-based street systems, unique city districts with clear boundaries, and smaller mixed communities where different travel destinations (work, shopping, hobbies, etc.) are closer to each other.

Organizational arrangements can either strengthen or weaken the employees' SOC. The best companies take a holistic perspective to their employees' lives and create working environments in which their higher social and psychological needs are adequately met. Flint-Taylor and Cooper (this volume, Chapter 9) suggest that, besides adequate resources and information, workplace well-being is determined by five factors that are closely associated with employees' sense of coherence and social needs: control over one's work, balance between work and home life, job security and well-managed change, collaborative relationships, and meaningful and rewarding work. At the same time, these factors reduce the uncertainty and complexity of working life.

Information overload is one of the principal causes of mental incoherence and stress for today's knowledge workers. Oldroyd and Morris (2012) suggest that organizations can reduce the information overload of their highly networked employees by various measures that improve their information-processing capacity (e.g. broadening cognitive frames through job rotation) and reduce their information burden by developing organizational processes and systems, using human and technological 'gatekeepers' to guard their time, and focusing their work-related networks to ease employees' responsibilities.

Cultural norms, shared visions and ideologies, and social regulations can improve the coherence of living environments by aligning people's expectations, synchronizing interdependent social activities (e.g. transportation schedules, school days, working times, store opening hours, holiday periods, etc.) and, hence, making their rhythms more compatible. At worst, incoherent frames, norms and rules can puzzle individual decision makers by providing ambiguous or contradictory signals and making life management very difficult. The needs, situations and contexts of individuals are increasingly differentiated. The private sector has increasingly moved towards tailored services to meet these differentiated needs, but the hierarchical welfare state lags behind with its 'universal' services. Citizens are often frustrated with the sequential and incoherent treatment of their multidimensional needs by the rigid silos of public hierarchies. A more human-centric and tailor-made approach is clearly needed. There are already some signs that such an approach is emerging in the public sector (Noonan et al. 2009; Sabel et al. 2011; Sabel and Zeitlin 2012).

The human-centric approach can also reduce the complexity of technological environments in everyday life. For example, the recent success of Apple's products was largely based on Steve Jobs's vision of making the everyday use of technologies as simple as possible (Isaacson 2011). Another example of the importance of the human-centric approach is a small Finnish fund management company that became hugely successful by applying human-centric design thinking in reducing the cognitive complexity, dissonance and uncertainty that their clients associated with traditional fund management services (Ruckenstein et al. 2011). There is a lot of hidden value in improving the comprehensibility and manageability of people's lives.

As we saw before, the increasing variety in product markets is a major contributor to the problem of choice. The cognitive pressures of product choice are multiplied by powerful marketing activities whose intrusive messages create a lot of cognitive dissonance and mental incoherence in everyday life. Marketing restrictions are not very popular in free market economies but, from the complexity perspective, the well-being effects of 'marketing overload' warrant further research (see also Bartolini, this volume, Chapter 6; Seaford, this volume, Chapter 8). Would people be happier with less exposure to powerful marketing despite the loss of some relevant product information?

The complexity of everyday life can also be attenuated with *better life management*. The complexity and stress of life can be attenuated by focusing on the most important activities for well-being. The choice of these activities can be based on individual purpose, needs, values and key capabilities, as well as the utility and compatibility of different activities. For example, 'flow activities' combine the clarity of objectives, concentration on one task at a time, sufficient balance between the challenge and personal capabilities, and an intensive focus on the task (Csikszentmihalyi 2006). Flow activities are a good example of a situation where the variety of the governance task is nicely balanced with the variety of the controller.

Moreover, activities that are not so important to an individual's well-being can be outsourced to external partners to release time and mental capacity for the more important activities and commitments (Lair and Ritzer 2009). Outsourcing reduces the complexity of everyday life by reducing the number of daily activities and the need to manage the different interdependencies of outsourced activities. Thus, individuals can take advantage of the 'near decomposability' (Simon 1962) and modularization (Baldwin and Clark 2003) of activities.

Zuboff and Maxmin (2002) have argued that the whole economy should be reorganized in such a way as to support individuals in their everyday life. This 'support economy' would empower people for activities in which they could reach their best potential and well-being. The government can play an important role in facilitating the growth of needed personal and household services with its tax and regulatory policies.

The size of the household is also important for the division of labour in everyday life. Traditionally, everyday tasks were divided and shared within households. Over time, the declining size of households has reduced opportunities for this kind of cooperation. As the number of household members has declined, the complexity of potential social relationships among them has declined even faster.[33] Hence, individuals and households have been forced to meet the increasing complexity of everyday life with a decreasing complexity of households. According to Ashby's Law, it is no surprise that life management problems have become the new well-being challenge of advanced societies!

Lampinen has proposed experimentation with new types of communities that could solve the complexity gap in everyday life.[34] These communities do not need to be based on a shared living place, though some shared space would be good. In order to build trust, these communities should be able to select their members and have a rather limited membership (e.g. 20–60 persons). A heterogeneous membership of people with different ages and backgrounds would be preferable, since it includes more complementary capabilities and allows a better division of labour. Besides reducing the complexity gap, such communities offer many other benefits (Lampinen 2012). They:

- improve well-being by reducing loneliness (especially of children and the elderly), building social relationships and improving the meaningfulness of life;
- save resources by sharing durable goods ('collaborative consumption');
- benefit from economies of scale and save nature by pooling similar tasks (grocery shopping, care of children, transportation, etc.); and
- reduce the society's service responsibilities and costs.

Many daily activities and roles are not decomposable and dividable, however. They form interdependent systems, or 'practice or role complexes' (Latour 2007; Pantzar and Shove 2009). From the perspective of Simon (1962) and Baldwin and Clark (2003), the manageability and coherence of life can be increased by treating such complexes as individual 'modules of life'. There needs to be tight coordination among the activities within such complexes, but also complementarity and compatibility between them and life's other activities. For example, the various housekeeping and work activities should be coordinated among themselves, but there should also be a good match and balance between them.

Individuals can learn from organizational theory in coordinating their everyday activities. The coordination of interdependent activities requires different *coordination mechanisms* depending on the nature of the interdependence (Thompson 1967).[35] The key decision of what activities to engage in should be based on the consideration of the limited amount of time and mental capacity available. These shared resources set the limit that should not be exceeded by the portfolio of activities chosen. Besides such 'pooled interdependence', individuals must organize consecutive activities that involve 'sequential interdependence'. This calls for *planning* and *scheduling*. The more intensive 'reciprocal interdependence' requires *mutual adjustment* as, for example, the overlapping and conflicting demands of an individual's different roles need to be co-adjusted to fit together. Finally, the 'systemic interdependence' among life's various interdependent activities can be best coordinated with *personal values* and the *purpose of life*. Strong purpose and values form a sound basis for a coherent lifestyle.

Preventing Social Exclusion

The prevention of social exclusion is one of the core functions of the welfare state. Welfare states have traditionally emphasized various deprivation problems (poverty, housing, education, etc.) in their fight against social exclusion processes. More resources and better rights for individuals have been the key solutions to these problems. However, in today's increasingly complex and uncertain society, many of the traditional deprivation and well-being problems are also associated with growing life management problems. Hence, Lämsä (2009) has framed the social exclusion process as movement in a continuum from 'life management' through 'helplessness' to 'social exclusion'. In her study of social exclusion in Finland, the path from life management to social exclusion involved the accumulation of various disadvantages and an increased control by the social welfare authorities, which further decreased the individual's own life management capacity.

Also in Finland, Anna Rönkä (1999) made a comprehensive empirical study of the accumulation of 'social functioning problems' (disadvantages) in the transition from childhood through adolescence to adulthood. She described three paths through which risks for personal disadvantages accumulated over time. These were *poor living environments* (e.g. problems of parenting, a deviant peer group, low education, and career instability), *self-related cognitions* (low self-esteem and self-efficacy, low sense of control, lack of supportive adult relationships, and increased likelihood of failure), and *individual dispositions* (difficult temperament, weak emotion regulation, aggressiveness, or shyness and anxiety). The three types of vulnerabilities identified by Rönkä make individuals' life management exceedingly difficult by (1) increasing the environmental uncertainty and complexity that they must deal with, (2) weakening their capacity to deal with everyday challenges, and (3) leading to problems in social situations. The life management problems, in turn, can cause the accumulation of the more traditional disadvantages and deprivation problems (unemployment, poverty, poor health, etc.) (Lämsä 2009).

A study of 15- to 24-year-old European NEETs ('not in employment, education or training') is consistent with the view that life management problems can cause the accumulation of disadvantages and eventually social exclusion (Eurofound 2012). According to the study, the probability of becoming a NEET is positively associated with personal characteristics that weaken the individual's life management capabilities (e.g. 'some disability' or 'immigration background') or make his or her living environments more challenging (e.g. 'living in remote areas', 'low household income' or 'unemployed, poorly educated or divorced parents'). Those families are particularly challenging growth environments for those young people whose parents also suffer from life management problems. Finally, young people must meet all these challenges with a relatively low 'sense of coherence' (comprehensibility, manageability and meaningfulness of life), because it only develops gradually with growing life experience (Antonovsky 1987; Eriksson and Lindström, this volume, Chapter 3).

In their best-selling book *The Spirit Level*, Wilkinson and Pickett (2010) suggest that income inequality leads to various social ills such as *drug use*, *obesity*, *teenage births* and *criminal activity*. Our analysis suggests an alternative interpretation for their multiple bivariate correlations between inequality and the above social problems. The causality may also run in the opposite direction. Drug use, obesity, teenage births and criminal activities signal serious *life management problems*, which are also likely to cause the accumulation of other types of disadvantages, such as low income and poor health. As a result, the life management problems may be the underlying cause for both the above social ills and income inequality.

Since life management problems play an important role in the early accumulation of personal disadvantages, the traditional reactive policy responses – such as employment policies, transfer payments, and career counselling for the NEETs – are not likely to be sufficient in fighting social exclusion. For example, the Finnish social policy authorities intervene rather late in the social exclusion process when the person often already has multiple serious and prolonged well-being problems. Moreover, the person's situation tends to be discussed in the traditional deprivation frame, which focuses on monetary issues and treats the person as an object of standard policy measures (Lämsä 2009; Palola et al. 2012). Such a policy approach hides the underlying life management problems, which often started to accumulate some time before.

Our analysis suggests that policy makers should pay more attention to proactive measures that could identify and solve the life management problems early, and thus prevent the accumulation of various well-being problems. Such measures would empower individuals for everyday life instead of focusing on the already accumulated problems. The research of James Heckman, a Nobel laureate in economics, supports our argument:

> [I]mprovements early in the life cycle of disadvantaged children have much higher economic and social returns than later-life remediation targeted towards disadvantaged adolescents, such as reduced pupil–teacher ratios, public job training, convict rehabilitation programs, adult literacy programs, tuition subsidies, or expenditures on police . . . The longer society waits to intervene in the life cycle of a disadvantaged child, the more costly it is to remediate disadvantage. (Heckman 2011)[36]

Unfortunately, there is still relatively little research about the processes by which the personal disadvantages of young people accumulate (Palola et al. 2012). However, the prevention of such processes is likely to require an early, tailored and well-coordinated intervention by parents, service professionals and those significant others who can support the young person in his or her everyday tasks (Sabel et al. 2011). Individuals with life management problems are not very good at navigating complex service systems. Poor access to support services may allow the initial life management problems to accumulate into major well-being problems before traditional service providers will react to them.

At the same time, individual service professionals are not alone able to provide sufficient help with complex well-being problems. A more horizontal and cross-functional approach is needed in service provision. The service personnel need to engage in deep and intimate dialogue with the individuals at risk, because people are often not willing to reveal their life management problems (Lämsä 2009). Palola et al. (2012) suggest that youngsters at risk of social exclusion should be provided with a 'trusted person' whom they could contact once the service system feels too difficult to approach.

The Scottish Government provides an interesting example of how these ideas can be implemented in policy making (Scottish Government 2010; GCPH 2011; Burns 2012). It has practical policy experiments that build on Antonovsky's sense of coherence framework. The Scottish policy makers fight the deprivation problems of children with three key principles: (1) focusing on early intervention and prevention, (2) taking an asset-based approach (leveraging individuals' and the community's existing assets and improving their sense of coherence) and (3) ensuring that the child is at the centre of policy making and service provision. The Scottish strategy acknowledges the complexity of an individual's accumulated well-being problems. Hence, it emphasizes that 'the early years provide the first and best opportunity to set children off on the right trajectory and reduce the need for later interventions that are more costly in both financial and social terms'. The strategy puts particular weight on coherent parenting and living environments:

> Parental attachment in the early years in particular, and good, consistent parenting more generally, are the key factors in building a sense of coherence and, in turn, increasing a person's chances of experiencing a range of positive social outcomes. On the other hand, chaotic surroundings and lack of coherence can produce consistently higher stress levels as children grow up. This impacts directly on cognitive and emotional development, and can lead to a higher likelihood of experiencing problems in later life, such as poor health, low educational attainment, substance misuse and offending. (Scottish Government 2010, 3.2.1).

Rather than focusing on problems and disadvantages, the asset-based approach attempts to empower individuals, families and communities by highlighting their assets and potential. These assets can be of any kind: psychological, social, financial, physical, environmental, or human resources. The child-centred approach, in turn, aims to improve outcomes for all children and young people through a shared and tailored approach to service provision. This requires a new mindset from service providers. They no longer produce services for the users; instead, services are co-created with them (GCPH 2011; Burns 2012).

CONCLUSIONS

In the past few decades, industrialized societies have focused on two instrumental subsystems of the society – the economy and the welfare state. This will no longer be sufficient in the future. The structural problems of advanced economies and welfare states cannot be solved without an improved understanding of the ultimate goals of all policy making, that is, sustainable development and well-being. Hence, this chapter has sketched an outline of a new theory of sustainable well-being.

Such a theory is urgently needed in the current transformation. Policy makers have recognized the unsustainability of the current socio-economic model but have no vision of a more sustainable model that could replace it. As a consequence, there is a lot of loose talk about the 'need for structural change'. An improved understanding of sustainable well-being can form a sound basis for a new socio-economic model. A deeper and more holistic understanding of well-being would make the necessary structural changes much easier to identify and carry out. The goal of intended structural changes would be clear, and the uncertainty around them would dissolve. Governments, firms and civic actors would know more specifically what kinds of products and services, organizational arrangements, institutions and policies best served the everyday life and well-being of their stakeholders.

This chapter has analysed the new well-being problems in advanced societies. The problem of choice, sense of incoherence and unintended consequences of individual decisions pose new challenges to individual and social well-being which are not adequately incorporated in the current well-being theories and policies. Some of these challenges can be met within the established cultural and institutional framework. Hence, we identified some potential areas for policy action. However, since the new well-being problems have emerged from the post-war materialistic mass-consumption paradigm, sustainable improvements in well-being will also require a cultural paradigm shift (Michael 1973; Rogers 1995; Laszlo 2008; Bartolini, this volume, Chapter 6). The development of a new cultural paradigm is not going to be easy, since the current paradigm is deeply embedded in the society's institutions. The cultural paradigm can only emerge from a collective learning (and unlearning) process (Hämäläinen 2007; O'Hara and Lyon, this volume, Chapter 4).

In the new cultural paradigm, sustainable well-being and development must be the ultimate goals of all human activities. Technology, the economy, the welfare state and other instrumental systems must be subordinated to these ultimate goals. This means, for example, that technology development and economic growth are pursued only when and where they are likely to improve the sustainable well-being of human beings.

At the same time, the model of a human being must be broadened from *homo economicus* – the self-regarding, atomistic maximizer of neoclassical economics – to a more holistic view of human beings as, *inter alia*, biological, psychological, social, political and economic creatures. Besides self-interest and rational economic calculus, human behaviour is shaped by for example biological urges, cognitive biases, limited willpower, social norms and political ambitions. Human beings are motivated not only by the extrinsic motivations, such as money and material goods, but also by their intrinsic motivations, such as empathy, responsibility and values. A sustainable culture and socio-economic model must be based on a holistic model of human beings and their needs. Developing such a multidisciplinary model is an urgent priority for academia.

The mechanistic worldview of the industrial era is becoming outdated in the increasingly complex and uncertain environment. The human being, the economy and society are complex adaptive systems with highly interdependent and interactive subsystems and environments.[37] These complex systems have a recursive structure, and they operate at multiple interlinked levels. They produce emergent phenomena where individual micro-level choices can lead to major macro-level impacts. This holistic and systemic conceptualization of the world differs radically from the traditional reductionist and mechanistic view that dominated the industrial era. A more advanced and sustainable cultural paradigm will have to embrace the increased complexity in everyday life, organizations, governments and science. As has happened so many times throughout history, humankind must learn to live with higher levels of interdependence and complexity (Michael 1973; Laszlo 2008).

Finally, the more uncertain and complex world requires more decentralized governance mechanisms. The crucial information and understanding about individual needs and local circumstances cannot otherwise be integrated in decision making. As Stafford Beer (1973) argued, the governance of complex systems demands the contribution of all brains. The decentralized governance system must also give individuals more responsibility about the consequences of their choices. Increased decision-making powers and responsibilities should go hand in hand. However, owing to the decision-making problems described in this chapter, people must not be left alone with their increased responsibilities. New mechanisms need to be developed to support the decision making of individuals and to empower them to make more coherent and sustainable decisions. Only this will enable humankind to live sustainably at a higher level of complexity.

NOTES

1. A recent international review found 15 different indices that covered various aspects of well-being (Hoffren et al. 2010).
2. For example, in the United States, almost 20 per cent of the people are 'mentally unhealthy' or 'languishing', which exposes them to a risk of developing a real mental illness (Keyes 2005).
3. Sen does acknowledge such interdependencies but chooses not to analyse them in detail: 'Even though it is often convenient to talk about individual capabilities . . . it is important to bear in mind that the capability approach is ultimately concerned with the ability to achieve combinations of valued functionings . . . [We] have to see the person's overall capacity in terms of combined achievements that are open to her. And yet it is often convenient to talk about individual capabilities' (Sen 2009, p. 233).
4. In this chapter, coherence refers to the consistency, harmony and integration of systems with diverse elements and relationships.
5. The CA of Amartya Sen (2001, 2009) focuses mainly on the available resources and capabilities and some parts of the living environments which have a direct impact on an individual's freedoms and rights. Martha Nussbaum's (2011) list of 'ten central capabilities' covers many elements in Figure 2.1 at a very general level, but her analysis has very little to say about the new well-being problems in affluent societies.
6. See Antonovsky (1991) for an early discussion of the impact of socio-cultural and institutional contexts on individuals' choices and sense of coherence. Basu et al. (this volume, Chapter 7) provide a comprehensive review of 'supportive environments'.
7. We will analyse micro-externalities more carefully later in this chapter.
8. For example, social activities enhance physical and probably also mental capabilities besides their direct well-being benefits. On the other hand, long working hours gradually accumulate problems in maintaining social relationships (see Helliwell, this volume, Chapter 5; Bartolini, this volume, Chapter 6).
9. The tighter budget constraints of low-income people could either increase or decrease their problem of choice. On the one hand, the trade-offs between different consumption alternatives tend to become more difficult to solve with fewer resources; on the other hand, lower incomes also close some options as too expensive and thus decrease choice. The fact that serious lifestyle-related health problems tend to be more common in lower-income deciles suggests that the problem of choice is very real also at these income levels.
10. Eriksson and Lindström (this volume, Chapter 3) discuss the implications of the salutogenesis theory from the health perspective. We will use it to examine the impacts of the current transformation in living environments on well-being.
11. The 'Reasonable Person Model' of Basu et al. (this volume, Chapter 7) is very similar

to Antonovsky's theory. Its key dimensions are: 'model building', 'being effective' and 'meaningful action'. In the future, both fields of research would benefit from cross-fertilization.

12. Nesse (2004) argues that, historically, the evolutionary success of human beings has depended on their ability to manage these trade-offs successfully. For most of human history, misallocated attention and effort have often led to premature death. Nesse also highlights the stress that arises from the conflicting demands of different pursuits. According to him, it is the overall coherence of life – 'the degree to which all major goals can be pursued successfully without unduly compromising others' – that determines its viability.

13. For example, 10 per cent of US women have had three or more partners (either husbands or cohabiting partners) by the time they reach age 35 (Bianchi 2011).

14. In the United States, the share of people who have nobody to talk to about matters of importance to them has risen from 10 to 25 per cent in two decades (Mulgan 2009). At the same time, many American parents feel that they have too little time for each other and their children (Bianchi 2011).

15. Empirical research has shown that an individual's mental health and quality of life correlate strongly with his or her sense of coherence (Lindström and Eriksson 2005).

16. The economic examples suggest that a dynamically sustainable systemic balance (or coherence) requires that the accumulation of individual decisions with similar micro-externalities should not go too far to cause a system breakdown. As an example, Engelen et al. (2011) argue that the current economic crisis 'resulted from an accumulation of small, and in themselves relatively harmless, decisions made by many individual traders or bankers and banks'. A generally depressed mood among consumers and investors can produce individual choices whose external impacts tend to reinforce each other and create a serious imbalance between supply and demand, and ultimately an economic crisis. Similarly, an overly positive mood can lead to an unsustainable spending spree and a financial bubble.

17. The research results presented by Baumeister and Tierney (2011, p. 12) show that strong willpower and self-control promote other-regarding behaviour and good social relations: 'In workplaces, managers scoring high in self-control were rated more favourably by their subordinates as well as their peers. People with good self-control seemed exceptionally good at forming and maintaining secure, satisfying attachments to other people. They were shown to be better at empathizing with others and considering things from other people's perspectives.'

18. The 'broken windows' theory suggests an antidote to the problem of accumulating selfishness (Kelling and Coles 1996). Quickly fixing the signs of selfish and irresponsible behaviour will diminish the signalling effect of broken windows, litter, vandalism and so on which people use to judge the responsibility of others' behaviour. Not seeing these signs suggests that most people are obeying the shared norms and, hence, the large group of strongly reciprocal individuals is willing to do it too. Another remedy is to target the committed free riders and rule breakers with effective policy measures. Such targeted interventions do not ruin the general trust in cooperative behaviour which more general policies and incentives could do (Kahan 2005).

19. Long working hours and heavy investments in one's career may cause unintended consequences in marriage. According to Bianchi (2011), increases in work hours are associated with declines in marital quality and, for middle-class professionals, with higher levels of marital tension. In such cases, people are not likely to pay enough attention to the possible long-term, accumulating consequences of their individual decisions.

20. Siegel suggests that the prefrontal cortex in the human brain plays an important role in shaping the degree of coherence ('attunement', 'integration') in human decision making. Early childhood development, particularly the relationship between the baby and his or her parents, is crucial in the development of the prefrontal cortex. During the first 24 months of the baby's life, emotionally attuned parents can foster the development of mental capacities that support the internal and external attunement and

coherence of their children throughout their lives. These same capacities can also be shaped by training and meditation practices (Siegel 2009).

21. See O'Hara and Lyon (this volume, Chapter 4) for a discussion of the psychological consequences of maladapted mental frames in the rapidly changing environment.

22. The following quotation is from his discussion of 'socializing agencies': '[T]he self has been shaped by socializing agencies . . . What must be stressed in the present context is that the greater the internal integrated complexity which has been developed, the greater the capacity to handle complex input' (Antonovsky 1991).

23. Saarinen and Hämäläinen (2010) call this capability 'systems intelligence'. See Sterman (1994) for a good analysis of the difficulties that complex adaptive systems pose to intelligent behaviour and learning processes.

24. The research on children's school fatigue and stress suggests that problems with the complexity gap and life management are not limited to adults. The restlessness and negative atmosphere in schools as well as the lack of support from teachers and school health care workers are positively associated with feelings of insufficiency and cynicism among students (Salmela-Aro 2010). In a similar vein, a study by Bowen et al. (1998) found that the 'sense of school coherence' has an important impact on students' school performance.

25. We understand that our focus leaves out many important policy areas in which social and environmental sustainability could be promoted. See for example Bartolini's discussion (this volume, Chapter 6) of modern cities and consumer culture, and Basu et al.'s discussion (this volume, Chapter 7) of community gardens and participatory decision making.

26. Beer was very explicit about the limitations of the brain: 'The brain is a slightly alkaline three-pound electromechanical computer, running on glucose at 25 watts. It contains 10^{10} (that is ten thousand million) nerve cells or neurons, which are its computing elements operating on a scanning rhythm of ten cycles per second' (Beer 1973, p. 33).

27. Beer's observations resonate well with our earlier discussion of multitasking individuals and the EU decision makers. Basu et al. (this volume, Chapter 7) also echo Beer: 'The demands on attention in modern environments are rapidly increasing, but the evolution of our brains has not kept pace . . . Yet those same brains must now swim through tsunamis of information every day.'

28. Psychologists and behavioural economists often use the terms 'automatic and reflective systems' or 'System I and System II' when they discuss these different types of human thought (Thaler and Sunstein 2008; Kahneman 2011).

29. Kogut and Zander (1992) introduced the term 'combinative capability' in the context of firm organization. In their analysis, it represented the firm's capacity to synthesize and apply knowledge from various internal and external sources to create new value for their customers. Similar combinative capability is also required from individuals in a complex knowledge society.

30. An individual's 'future consciousness' is similar to an organization's foresight: 'It is the human capacity to have thoughts, feelings, and goals about the future. It is the total integrative set of psychological abilities, processes, and experiences that humans use to understand and deal with the future' (Lombardo 2010, pp. 34–5). Future consciousness corresponds to the 'intelligence system' in a personal-level application of Stafford Beer's Viable System Model (Leonard 2012). It is intelligence for adapting to future environments.

31. The increasing life management problems have created a rapidly growing market for life-management-oriented magazines and TV programmes. Even the huge popularity of reality television can be linked to this trend. According to Filander (2007, p. 105), 'the participants of a reality TV show are scapegoats for the viewers by testing their capabilities in situations which demand extreme efforts and life management'.

32. See '100 benefits of meditation' at: http://www.ineedmotivation.com/blog/2008/05/100-benefits-of-meditation/.

33. For example, the number of potential binary connections is $n(n-1)/2$. I am grateful to Timo Lampinen for pointing out this relationship.

34. Flint-Taylor and Cooper (this volume, Chapter 9) suggest that similar governance benefits can be achieved in organizations through appropriate division of labour and cooperation.
35. See Hämäläinen and Schienstock (2001) for the original analysis of different coordination mechanisms in the organizational context.
36. The Scottish government argues that investment in early and effective interventions translates into substantial savings to the public sector. According to their review of the relevant international evidence, rates of return on investments in the early years range from 1:3 to 1:7, up to 1:17 where children have been tracked beyond the age of 21 (Scottish Government 2010, 3.2.1).
37. For a discussion of complex adaptive systems in society, the economy, nature and science, see Maturana and Varela (1998), Beer (1973), Gunderson and Holling (2002), Beinhocker (2007) and Hollingsworth and Muller (2008).

REFERENCES

Adler, Paul S. and Charles Heckscher (2007), 'Towards collaborative community', in Charles Heckscher and Paul S. Adler (eds), *The Firm as a Collaborative Community: Reconstructing Trust in the Knowledge Economy*, Oxford: Oxford University Press.

Ainslie, George (2001), *Breakdown of Will*, Cambridge: Cambridge University Press.

Antonovsky, Aaron (1987), *Unraveling the Mystery of Health: How People Manage Stress and Stay Well*, San Francisco, CA: Jossey-Bass.

Antonovsky, Aaron (1991), 'The structural sources of salutogenic strengths', in Cary L. Cooper and Roy Payne (eds), *Personality and Stress: Individual Differences in Stress Process*, New York: Wiley.

Arthur, Brian W. (1994), *Increasing Returns and Path Dependence in the Economy*, Ann Arbor: University of Michigan Press.

Ashby, Ross W. (1958), 'Requisite variety and its implications for the control of complex systems', *Cybernetica*, **1** (2), 83–99.

Baldwin, Carliss Y. and Kim B. Clark (2003), 'Managing in the age of modularity', in Raghu Garud, Arun Kumaraswamy and Richard N. Langlois (eds), *Managing in the Modular Age: Architectures, Networks, and Organizations*, Malden, MA: Blackwell.

Baumeister, Roy F. and John Tierney (2011), *Willpower: Rediscovering the Greatest Human Strength*, New York: Penguin Press.

Baumeister, Roy F., Todd F. Heatherton and Dianne M. Tice (1994), *Losing Control: How and Why People Fail at Self-regulation*, San Diego, CA: Academic Press.

Beer, Stafford (1973), 'Designing freedom', Massey Lectures, Canadian Broadcasting Corporation.

Beinhocker, Eric D. (2007), *The Origin of Wealth: Evolution, Complexity, and the Radical Remaking of Economics*, London: Random House Business Books.

Bianchi, Suzanne M. (2011), 'Family change and time allocation in American families', *Annals of the American Academy of Political and Social Science*, **638** (November), 21–44.

Bowen, Gary L., Jack M. Richman, Ann Brewster and Natasha Bowen (1998), 'Sense of school coherence, perceptions of danger at school, and teacher support among youth at risk of school failure', *Child and Adolescent Work Journal*, **15** (4) (August), 273–86.

Brown, Peter G. and Geoffrey Garver (2009), *Right Relationship: Building a Whole Earth Economy*, San Francisco, CA: Berrett-Koehler.

Burns, Harry (2012), 'Assets for health', in Elke Loeffler, Gerry Power, Tony Bovaird and Frankie Hine-Hughes (eds), *Co-production in Health and Social Care: What It Is and How to Do It*, Birmingham: Governance International.

Casti, John L. (2010), *Mood Matters: From Rising Skirt Lengths to the Collapse of World Powers*, New York: Copernicus Books, Springer Science+Business Media.

Casti, John L. (2012), *X-events: The Collapse of Everything*, New York: HarperCollins/Morrow.

Cole, Pamela M. and Kirby Deater-Deckard (2009), 'Emotion regulation, risk and psychopathology', *Journal of Child Psychology and Psychiatry*, **50** (11), 1327–30.

Csikszentmihalyi, Mihaly (2006), *Kehittyvä minuus: visioita kolmannelle vuosituhannelle* [The evolving self: a psychology for the third millennium], Helsinki: Rasalas.

David, Paul A. (1985), 'Clio and the economics of QWERTY', *American Economic Review*, **75** (2) (papers and proceedings of the Ninety-Seventh Annual Meeting of the American Economic Association, May), 332–7.

Dijksterhuis, Ap and Loran F. Nordgren (2006), 'A theory of unconscious thought', *Perspectives on Psychological Science*, **1** (2), 95–109.

Engelen, Ewald, Ismail Ertürk, Julie Froud, Sukhdev Johal, Adam Leaver, Mick Moran, Adriana Nilsson and Karel Williams (2011), *After the Great Complacence: Financial Crisis and the Politics of Reform*, Oxford: Oxford University Press.

Eurofound (2012), *Young People and NEETs in Europe: First Findings*, Dublin: European Foundation for the Improvement of Living and Working Conditions.

Fehr, Ernst and Urs Fischbacher (2005), 'The economics of strong reciprocity', in Herbert Gintis, Samuel Bowles, Robert Boyd and Ernst Fehr (eds), *Moral Sentiments and Material Interests: The Foundations of Cooperation in Economic Life*, Cambridge, MA: MIT Press.

Festinger, Leon (1957), *A Theory of Cognitive Dissonance*, Evanston, IL: Roe, Peterson and Company.

Filander, Karin (2007), 'Sosiaalipedgogiikan uusi ajankohtaisuus', in Tommi Hoikkala and Anna Snell (eds), *Nuorisotyötä on tehtävä: menetelmien perustat, rajat ja mahdollisuudet*, Helsinki: Nuorisotutkimusverkosto, Julkaisuja 76.

Frankl, Viktor E. (1978), *Elämän tarkoitusta etsimässä* [The unheard cry for meaning: psychotherapy and humanism], Helsinki: Otava.

Freeman, Christopher and Francisco Louca (2002), *As Times Go By: From the Industrial Revolutions to the Information Revolution*, Oxford: Oxford University Press.

Friedman, Milton and Rose Friedman (1990), *Free to Choose: A Personal Statement*, New York: Harcourt Brace Jovanovich.

Fromm, Eric (1976), *To Have or to Be?*, New York: HarperCollins.

Galbraith, Jay R. (2007), 'Mastering the Law of Requisite Variety with differentiated networks', in Charles Heckscher and Paul S. Adler (eds), *The Firm as a Collaborative Community: Reconstructing Trust in the Knowledge Economy*, Oxford: Oxford University Press.

Gardner, Howard (2006), *Five Minds for the Future*, Boston, MA: Harvard Business School Press.

Garud, R. and Karnøe, P. (2001), 'Path creation as a process of mindful deviation', in R. Garud and P. Karnøe (eds), *Path Dependence and Path Creation*, Mahwah, NJ: Lawrence Erlbaum, pp. 1–38.

GCPH (Glasgow Centre for Population Health) (2011), 'Asset based approaches for health improvement: redressing the balance', Briefing Paper No. 9, October.

Gerhardt, Sue (2011), *The Selfish Society: How We All Forgot to Love One Another and Made Money Instead*, London: Simon & Schuster.

Giddens, Anthony (2007), *Europe in the Global Age*, Cambridge: Polity Press.

Gintis, Herbert, Samuel Bowles, Robert Boyd and Ernst Fehr (2005), "Moral sentiments and material interests: origins, evidence, and consequences", in Gintis, Herbert, Samuel Bowles, Robert Boyd and Ernst Fehr (eds), *Moral Sentiments and Material Interests: The Foundations of Cooperation in Economic Life*, Cambridge, MA: MIT Press.

Gintis, Herbert, Samuel Bowles, Robert Boyd and Ernst Fehr (eds) (2005), *Moral Sentiments and Material Interests: The Foundations of Cooperation in Economic Life*, Cambridge, MA: MIT Press.

Gunderson, Lance H. and C.S. Holling (2002), *Panarchy: Understanding Transformations in Human and Natural Systems*, Washington, DC: Island Press.

Hakkarainen, Kai, Tuire Palonen, Sami Paavola and Erno Lehtinen (2004), *Communities of Networked Expertise: Professional and Educational Perspectives*, Amsterdam: Elsevier.

Hall, Jon, Enrico Giovannini, Adolfo Morrone and Giulia Ranuzzi (2010), *A Framework to Measure the Progress of Societies*, Statistics Directorate Working Paper No. 34, Paris: OECD.

Hämäläinen, Timo J. (2003), *National Competitiveness and Economic Growth: The Changing Determinants of Economic Performance in the World Economy*, Cheltenham, UK and Northampton, MA, USA: Edward Elgar Publishing.

Hämäläinen, Timo J. (2007), 'Social innovation, structural adjustment and economic performance', in Timo J. Hämäläinen and Risto Heiskala (eds), *Social Innovations, Institutional Change and Economic Performance: Making Sense of Structural Adjustment Processes in Industrial Sectors, Regions and Societies*, Cheltenham, UK and Northampton, MA, USA: Edward Elgar Publishing.

Hämäläinen, Timo J. (2008), 'Yhteiskunnallinen murros vaatii tulevan yhteiskuntamallin visiointia', in Juho Saari (ed.), *Sosiaaliset innovaatiot ja hyvinvointivaltion muutos*, Helsinki: Sosiaali- ja terveystyön keskusliitto.

Hämäläinen, Timo (2009), 'Yhteiskunnallinen murros ja henkinen hyvinvointi', *Tiedepolitiikka*, **4**, 43–57.

Hämäläinen, Timo J. and Gerd Schienstock (2001), 'The comparative advantage of networks in economic organization: efficiency and innovation in highly specialized and uncertain environments', in *Innovative Networks: Co-operation in National Innovation Systems*, Paris: OECD.

Hamel, Gary (2007), *The Future of Management*, Boston, MA: Harvard Business School Press.

HBR (2011), 'Embracing complexity: you can't avoid it, but your business can profit from it', *Harvard Business Review*, September, cover story.

Heckman, James (2011), 'The case for investing in disadvantaged young children', remarks at the White House Conference, 16 December, available at: www.theheckmanequation.org (accessed 2 April 2012).

Heckscher, Charles and Paul S. Adler (2007), *The Firm as a Collaborative*

Community: Reconstructing Trust in the Knowledge Economy, Oxford: Oxford University Press.

Hirsch, Fred (1977), *Social Limits to Growth*, London: Routledge & Kegan Paul.

Hirschman, Albert O. (1970), *Exit, Voice, and Loyalty: Responses to Decline in Firms, Organizations, and States*, Cambridge, MA: Harvard University Press.

Hoffren, Jukka, Inka Lemmetyinen and Leeni Pitkä (2010), *Esiselvitys hyvinvointi-indikaattoreista: mittareiden vertailu ja kehittämiskohteet*, Helsinki: Sitran selvityksiä 32.

Hollingsworth, Rogers and Karl H. Muller (2008), 'Transforming socio-economics with a new epistemology', *Socio-economic Review*, **6**, 395–426.

Huppert, Felicia A. (2009), 'Psychological well-being: evidence regarding its causes and consequences', *Applied Psychology: Health and Well-Being*, **1** (2), 137–64.

IBM (2010), *Capitalizing on Complexity: Insights from the Global Chief Executive Officer Survey*, available at: http://www-935.ibm.com/services/us/ceo/ceo study2010/index.html.

Inglehart, Ronald (1997), *Modernization and Postmodernization: Cultural, Economic, and Political Change in 43 Societies*, Princeton, NJ: Princeton University Press.

Isaacson, Walter (2011), *Steve Jobs*, New York: Simon & Schuster.

John, Peter, Sarah Cotterill, Alice Moseley, Liz Richardson, Graham Smith, Gerry Stoker and Corinne Wales (2011), *Nudge, Nudge, Think, Think: Experimenting with Ways to Change Civic Behavior*, London: Bloomsbury Academic.

Kabat-Zinn, Jon (2004), *Olet jo perillä: tietoisen läsnäolon taito* [Wherever you go there you are: mindfulness meditation in everyday life], Helsinki: Basam Books.

Kahan, Dan M. (2005), 'The logic of reciprocity: trust, collective action, and law', in Herbert Gintis, Samuel Bowles, Robert Boyd and Ernst Fehr (eds), *Moral Sentiments and Material Interests: The Foundations of Cooperation in Economic Life*, Cambridge, MA: MIT Press.

Kahneman, Daniel (2011), *Thinking, Fast and Slow*, London: Allen Lane.

Kahneman, Daniel and Richard H. Thaler (2006), 'Anomalies – utility maximization and experienced utility', *Journal of Economic Perspectives*, **20** (1), 221–34.

Kelling, George and Catherine Coles (1996), *Fixing Broken Windows: Restoring Order and Reducing Crime in Our Communities*, New York: Free Press.

Keyes, Corey (2005), 'Mental illness and/or mental health? Investigating axioms of the complete state model of health', *Journal of Consulting and Clinical Psychology*, **73** (3), 539–48.

Keyes, Corey (2006), 'Subjective well-being in mental health and human development research worldwide: an introduction', *Social Indicators Research*, **77**, 1–10.

Keyes, Corey (2007), 'Promoting and protecting mental health as flourishing: a complementary strategy for improving national mental health', *American Psychologist*, **62** (2), 95–108.

Koelen, M.A. and Bengt Lindström (2005), 'Making healthy choices easy choices: the role of empowerment', *European Journal of Clinical Nutrition*, **59**, 10–16.

Kogut, Bruce and Udo Zander (1992), 'Knowledge of the firm, combinative capabilities, and the replication of technology', *Organization Science*, **3**, 383–97.

Krugman, Paul (1991), *Geography and Trade*, Cambridge, MA: MIT Press.

Lair, Craig and George Ritzer (2009), 'Metamanagement and the outsourcing of domestic life', in Philip Hancock and Melissa Tyler (eds), *The Management of Everyday Life*, Basingstoke: Palgrave Macmillan.

Lampinen, Timo (2012), 'Avara arkiyhteisö on hyötymutaatio', Blog 25.4, available at: http://timolampinen.blogspot.com/2012/03/avara-arkiyhteiso-on-hyotymutaatio.html.

Lämsä, Anna-Liisa (2009), *Tuhat tarinaa lasten ja nuorten syrjäytymisestä: lasten ja nuorten syrjäytyminen sosiaalihuollon asiakirjojen valossa*, E 102, Oulu: Kasvatustieteiden tiedekunta, Oulun yliopisto.

Latour, Bruno (2007), *Reassembling the Social: An Introduction to Actor-Network-Theory*, Oxford: Oxford University Press.

Laszlo, Ervin (1987), *Evolution: The Grand Synthesis*, New Science Library, Boston, MA: Shambhala.

Laszlo, Ervin (2008), *Quantum Shift in the Global Brain: How the New Scientific Reality Can Change Us and Our World*, Rochester, VT: Inner Traditions.

Laszlo, Ervin (2011), 'The Akashic revolution: the new scientific worldview of the 21st century', text of the M2e-book.

Layard, Richard (2005), *Happiness: Lessons from a New Science*, London: Penguin Books.

Leonard, Allenna (2012), 'Personal Viable System Model', available at: http://www.allennaleonard.com/PersVSM.html.

Lindström, Bengt and Monica Eriksson (2005), 'Salutogenesis', *Journal of Epidemiology and Community Health*, **59**, 440–42.

Lombardo, Tom (2010), 'Wisdom facing forward: what it means to have heightened future consciousness', *Futurist*, September–October, pp. 34–42.

Lombardo, Tom (2012), 'The psychology and value of future consciousness', available at: http://www.centerforfutureconsciousness.com/FC_Readings.htm (accessed 5 January 2012).

Maslow, Abraham (1970), *Motivation and Personality*, New York: Harper & Row.

Maturana, Humberto R. (2011), lecture given at Origin: How It All Begins, Ars Electronica 2011, Linz.

Maturana, Humberto R. and Francisco J. Varela (1998), *The Tree of Knowledge: The Biological Roots of Human Understanding*, Boston, MA: Shambhala.

Michael, Donald N. (1973), 'Technology and the management of change from the perspective of a culture context', *Technology Forecasting and Social Change*, **5** (3), 219–32.

Michael, Donald N. (2000), 'Some observations with regard to a missing elephant', *Journal of Humanistic Psychology*, **40** (1), 8–16.

Mulgan, Geoff (2009), *The Art of Public Strategy: Mobilizing Power and Knowledge for the Common Good*, Oxford: Oxford University Press.

Muller, Kiti (2007), 'Työn murros haasteena aivoille – vaatiiko informaatioyhteiskunta työntekijöiksi robotteja?', *Duodecim*, **123**, 703–04.

Nesse, Randolph M. (2004), 'Natural selection and the elusiveness of happiness', *Philosophical Transactions of the Royal Society B*, **359**, 1333–47.

Noonan, Kathleen, Charles Sabel and William Simon (2009), 'Legal accountability in the service-based welfare state: lessons from child welfare reform', *Law and Social Inquiry*, **34** (3), 523–68.

Nussbaum, Martha C. (2003), 'Capabilities as fundamental entitlements: Sen and social justice', *Feminist Economics*, **9** (2–3), 33–59.

Nussbaum, Martha C. (2011), *Creating Capabilities: The Human Development Approach*, Cambridge, MA: Belknap Press of Harvard University Press.

Offer, Avner (2006), *The Challenge of Affluence: Self-control and Well-being in the USA and Britain since 1950*, Oxford: Oxford University Press.

O'Hara, Maureen (2007), 'Psychological literacy for an emerging global society:

another look at Rogers' "persons of tomorrow" as a model', *Person-centered and Experiential Psychotherapies*, **6** (1), 45–60.

Oldroyd, James B. and Shad S. Morris (2012), 'Catching falling stars: a human resource response to social capital's detrimental effect of information overload on star employees', *Academy of Management Review*, **37** (3), 396–418.

Ostrom, Elinor (2005), 'Policies that crowd out reciprocity and collective action', in Herbert Gintis, Samuel Bowles, Robert Boyd and Ernst Fehr (eds), *Moral Sentiments and Material Interests: The Foundations of Cooperation in Economic Life*, Cambridge, MA: MIT Press.

Palola, Elina, Katri Hannikainen-Ingman and Vappu Karjalainen (2012), 'Nuorten syrjäytymistä on tutkittava pintaa syvemmin', *Yhteiskuntapolitiikka*, **3**, 310–15.

Pantzar, Mika and Elisabeth Shove (2009), 'Time in practice – discussing rhythms of practice complexes', working paper.

Pugno, Maurizio (2005), 'Capabilities, the self, and well-being: a research in psycho-economics', Discussion Paper No. 18, University of Trento.

Pulkkinen, Lea, Anna-Liisa Lyyra and Katja Kokko (2011), 'Is social capital a mediator between self-control and psychological and social functioning across 34 years?', *International Journal of Behavioral Development*, **35** (6), 475–81.

Rogers, Carl R. (1995), *A Way of Being*, Boston, MA: Houghton Mifflin.

Rönkä, Anna (1999), 'The accumulation of problems of social functioning: outer, inner, and behavioral strands', Jyväskylä Studies in Education, Psychology and Social Research No. 148, University of Jyväskylä.

Rosen, Christine (2008), 'The myth of multitasking', *New Atlantis*, Spring, pp. 105–10.

Ruckenstein, Minna, Johannes Suikkanen and Sakari Tamminen (2011), *Unohda innovointi: keskity arvonluontiin*, Helsinki: Edita Publishing.

Saarinen, Esa and Raimo P. Hämäläinen (2010), 'The originality of systems intelligence', in Raimo P. Hämäläinen and Esa Saarinen (eds), *Essays on Systems Intelligence*, Espoo: Systems Analysis Laboratory, School of Science and Technology, Aalto University.

Sabel, Charles and Jonathan Zeitlin (2012), 'Experimentalist governance', in David Levi-Faur (ed.), *The Oxford Handbook of Governance*, Oxford: Oxford University Press.

Sabel, Charles, AnnaLee Saxenian, Reijo Miettinen, Peer Hull Kristensen and Jarkko Hautamäki (2011), *Individualized Service Provision in the New Welfare State: Lessons from Special Education in Finland*, Sitra Studies No. 62, Helsinki: Sitra.

Sagy, Shifra and Helen Antonovsky (2000), 'The development of the sense of coherence: a retrospective study of early life experiences in the family', *International Journal of Aging and Human Development*, **51** (2), 155–66.

Salmela-Aro, Katariina (2010), 'Koulu-uupumus sosiaalisessa kontekstissa: koulu, koti ja kaveripiiri', *Psykologia*, **45** (05–06), 448–59.

Schwartz, Barry (2005), *The Paradox of Choice: Why More Is Less*, New York: Harper Perennial.

Scottish Government (2010), *Tackling Child Poverty in Scotland: A Discussion Paper*, November, available at: http://www.scotland.gov.uk/Publications/2010/11/15103604/0 (accessed 16 September 2012).

Sen, Amartya (2001), *Development as Freedom*, Oxford: Oxford University Press.

Sen, Amartya (2009), *The Idea of Justice*, London: Allen Lane.

Siegel, Daniel J. (2009), 'Mindful awareness, mindsight, and neural integration', *Humanistic Psychologist*, **37**, 137–58.

Simon, Herbert A. (1962), 'The architecture of complexity', *Proceedings of the American Philosophical Society*, **106**, 467–82, reprinted in Raghu Garud, Arun Kumaraswamy and Richard N. Langlois (eds) (2003), *Managing in the Modular Age: Architectures, Networks, and Organizations*, Malden, MA: Blackwell.

Steel, Piers (2011), *The Procrastination Equation: How to Stop Putting Things Off and Start Getting Things Done*, London: Prentice Hall Life.

Sterman, John D. (1994), 'Learning in and about complex systems', *System Dynamics Review*, **10** (2–3) (Summer–Fall), 291–330.

Stiglitz, Joseph, Amartya Sen and Jean-Paul Fitoussi (2009), *Report by the Commission on the Measurement of Economic Performance and Social Progress*, available at: http://www.stiglitz-sen-fitoussi.fr/en/index.htm (accessed 8 January 2012).

Tainter, Joseph A. (1988), *The Collapse of Complex Societies*, Cambridge: Cambridge University Press.

Taleb, Nassim Nicholas (2007), *The Black Swan: The Impact of the Highly Improbable*, London: Penguin Books.

Thaler, Richard H. and Cass R. Sunstein (2008), *Nudge: Improving Decisions about Health, Wealth, and Happiness*, New Haven, CT: Yale University Press.

Thompson, James D. (1967), *Organizations in Action: Social Science Bases of Administrative Theory*, New York: McGraw-Hill.

Wallis, Claudia (2006), 'The multitasking generation', *Time Magazine*, 19 March.

Weehuizen, Rika (2005), *Mental Capital: An Exploratory Study of the Psychological Dimension of Economic Development*, The Netherlands: Consultative Committee of Sector Councils for Research and Development (COS).

Wilber, Ken (2011), *A Theory of Everything: An Integral Vision for Business, Politics, Science, and Spirituality*, Boston, MA: Shambhala.

Wilkinson, Richard and Kate Pickett (2010), *The Spirit Level: Why Equality Is Better for Everyone*, London: Penguin Books.

Wolff, Jonathan (2006), 'Interview with Jonathan Wolff', by Sandrine Berges, *Ethics and Economics*, **4** (2), 1–10.

Wolff, Jonathan and Avner de-Shalit (2010), *Disadvantage*, Oxford: Oxford University Press.

Wright, Georg Henrik von (1981), *Humanismi elämänasenteena*, Helsinki: Otava.

Zuboff, Shoshana and James Maxmin (2002), *The Support Economy: Why Corporations Are Failing Individuals and the Next Episode of Capitalism*, New York: Penguin Books.

3. The salutogenic framework for well-being: implications for public policy

Monica Eriksson and Bengt Lindström

INTRODUCTION

Well-being as a concept has been used in many contexts and disciplines. We would argue it is an interdisciplinary concept that needs an interdisciplinary framework. Historically, it is deeply rooted in humankind and can express, on the one hand, only a superficial momentary state of being or, on the other hand, a deep existential philosophical expression of being itself. It is dependent on culture, context and life experiences. The measurement of well-being can also be approached in different ways: objective or subjective, absolute or relative, individually or collectively, reported directly by the subject of study or reported by proxy (Diener et al. 1999, 2009; Diener 2009).

Our framework is health science. Contemporary evidence demonstrates a strong positive connection between well-being, quality of life, and perceived health which are all strongly related to objective health (Eriksson and Lindström 2006; Eriksson 2007). It is a different question about how to achieve well-being. However, there is a new health model that seems to be able to explain this, that is, the salutogenic model. Therefore, in this chapter we are approaching well-being from the salutogenic perspective. This means we are looking at systematic contextual ways whereby people can achieve the best possible well-being during their life course. Salutogenesis was originally a concept developed in sociology and public health research. Today it is the best available theoretical framework for health promotion. In the original salutogenic framework Antonovsky (1979, 1987a) operationalized a new concept called sense of coherence (SOC) that describes people's and systems' ability to use their available resources (which he named general resistance resources, GRRs) to improve health and well-being. At its heart, SOC is based on meaningfulness, comprehension and life management. Contemporary evidence demonstrates that a strong SOC leads to well-being and good quality of life far beyond the traditional disease-related perception of health.

THE SALUTOGENIC FRAMEWORK

The concept of salutogenesis was introduced by the medical sociologist Aaron Antonovsky (1979), who studied stress endurance among women who had been exposed to extreme stress. It was known that stress could have severe consequences for people's ability to manage life. Stress was seen mainly as a negative event. However, Antonovsky, much to his surprise, found a group that, in spite of severe stress exposure, did just as well as the ordinary person. Based on this finding he interviewed these women and constructed a new framework, the salutogenic approach to health. This approach sees stress as a natural part of life, and focuses on abilities and resources to develop positively rather than on the tradition of focusing only on ill health, causes of disease, risks and pathology. Looking at the evidence and effectiveness of this framework now – 30 years later – there are clear indications that salutogenesis can lead not only to better health but also to well-being in terms of mental health, perceived health and quality of life. These are what are often described as 'overall goals' in contemporary global health policies. However, few such policies describe ways of achieving the goals. This is where salutogenesis can play an important role. Evidence speaks to the fact that people who develop the salutogenic ability will live longer, perceive that they thrive in life and enjoy a good quality of life. They also manage stress and negative life events better even when facing major negative life events, disability or chronic disease (Eriksson and Lindström 2006, 2007; Eriksson 2007).

The fundamental contribution of Antonovsky was to raise the philosophical question of what creates health and search for 'the origin of health' rather than to look for the causes of disease. Health is seen as a position on a health ease–dis-ease continuum, with a focus on movement in the direction towards the health end (Antonovsky 1979, 1987a). It is a continuous movement, meaning that even if we are affected by diseases we can to some extent still be healthy. Further, the health ease–dis-ease continuum (Figure 3.1) challenges the existence of a dichotomy between health and disease. A technical and theoretical description of the core concepts and outcomes can be found in Antonovsky's books (1979, 1987a) and more recently in other authors (Eriksson 2007; Lindström and Eriksson 2010a).

The salutogenic model of well-being is based on two concepts: the sense of coherence and generalized resistance resources.

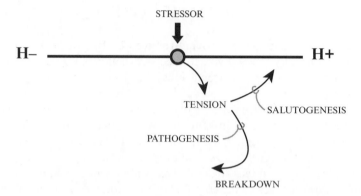

Source: Lindström and Eriksson (2010a). © Bengt Lindström, Monica Eriksson and Peter Wikström.

Figure 3.1   The health ease–dis-ease continuum

Sense of Coherence

The sense of coherence is a resource that enables people to manage tension, to reflect about their external and internal resources, and to identify and mobilize them in order to promote effective coping. SOC is a life orientation, a way of viewing the world as comprehensible, manageable and meaningful (Antonovsky 1987a). The basic assumption is that things will go well: one has the confidence and trust that whatever happens life can be managed; one has the ability to learn from one's life experiences and manage, either by oneself or by trusting one will get the support needed from one's close environment. The SOC is defined as:

> a global orientation that expresses the extent to which one has a pervasive, enduring though dynamic feeling of confidence that (1) the stimuli from one's internal and external environments in the course of living are structured, predictable, and explicable; (2) the resources are available to one to meet the demands posed by these stimuli; and (3) these demands are challenges, worthy of investment and engagement. (Antonovsky 1987a, p. 19)

A crucial element in the salutogenic orientation is to view stimuli as challenges, not as threats leading to breakdown, and to view challenges as being a natural part of everyday life (Antonovsky 1985). The SOC construct indicates it is a question of synergy between the individual and the context in an ongoing lifelong learning process reflecting the success people have in dealing with and managing their life experiences. Antonovsky stated that people's SOC is mainly developed in childhood and early adulthood. However, this seems not to be the case. New research points to the fact it is a continuous process throughout life (Feldt et al. 2003; Lindmark et al. 2009; Eriksson and Lindström 2011). There is a two- way effect of SOC: first, on the individual level regarding psycho-emotional confidence; and second, a synergy between actions in societies, that is, policies, and an interaction between the individual and his or her context. It is a question of a confident and trusting health-promoting dialogue between the individual and the context, a reciprocal 'attachment'. The detailed development of a dialogue based on salutogenic principles has been described elsewhere (Lindström and Eriksson 2010a).

Generalized Resistance Resources

The generalized resistance resources are of both an external and an internal character. As Antonovsky explained, people have at their disposal resources of both internal and external characteristics which make it easier for them to manage life (Antonovsky 1979, 1987a). The GRRs are of any character, such as material, knowledge or intelligence, ego identity, coping strategy, social support, ties, commitment, cultural stability, philosophy or a stable set of answers; in other words, they range from material to virtual spiritual dimensions of the mind, processes and psychological mechanisms. The main thing is that people are able to use the GRRs for their own good and for health development. Common to all GRRs are that they facilitate making sense out of the countless number of stressors with which we are constantly bombarded. In so doing the GRRs give the prerequisites for the development of a strong SOC. Equally important for the development of a strong SOC is the balance between underload and overload of stress, participation in shaping the outcome (empowerment), consistency and emotional closeness (Sagy and Antonovsky 1999). The salutogenic model of well-being corresponds to some extent with the dynamic model of well-being of the new economics foundation (nef). While the nef model focuses on external conditions (e.g. material, work, income) and personal resources (e.g. health, resilience, self-esteem, optimism), the salutogenic model uses generalized resistance resources as the prerequisites for the development of a strong SOC. The outcome in Antonovsky's model was health and well-being, which, in turn, are here expanded by the authors to well-being and quality of life.

Measuring Sense of Coherence

The Orientation to Life Questionnaire is the original name of the instrument for measuring sense of coherence, and it consists of 29 items (SOC-29). A shorter form of 13 items (SOC-13) was later developed (Antonovsky 1987a). The SOC Questionnaire uses seven-point Likert scales summed into a score ranging from 13 to 91 points (SOC-13) or 29 to 203 points (SOC-29). High scores are analogous with a strong SOC, indicating a better coping capacity. The items relate to the dimensions of the SOC, for example: 'When you talk to people, do you have the feeling that they don't understand you?' (comprehensibility), 'Do you have the feeling that you don't really care about what goes on around you?' (meaningfulness) and 'Do you have the feeling that you're being treated unfairly?' (manageability) (Antonovsky 1987a, appendix). A detailed description of the questionnaire is found elsewhere (Antonovsky 1987a). The SOC Questionnaire has been translated into at least 49 languages and used in 45 countries all over the world, in all continents, in varying cultures, on different sample populations, such as healthy populations, several groups of patients and disabled people, and among professionals (Eriksson and Lindström 2005; Eriksson, forthcoming). Most of the studies used one of the original scales, the SOC-29 or the SOC-13. However, besides the original SOC questionnaires there are some modified questionnaires that can be found, modified in the sense that the questions are the same as in the original scales but with different scoring alternatives or varying numbers of items included (from a range of 3 to 28 items). In addition, two SOC scales for measuring SOC in families are in use (Sagy and Antonovsky 2000): a questionnaire especially adjusted for children (Margalit and Efrati 1996) and the sense of school coherence instrument (Bowen et al. 1998).

Other Concepts Explaining Well-being

Salutogenesis is much more than only the measurement of the SOC; it is a much broader concept focusing on resources, competencies, abilities and assets on different levels – individual (Eriksson 2007), group (Antonovsky and Sourani 1988), organization (Feldt 2000; Graeser 2011; Mayer 2011), society (Eriksson et al. 2007; Lindström and Eriksson 2009). Today we can talk about salutogenesis as an umbrella concept, here visualized in Figure 3.2, which also shows other concepts contributing to the explanation of well-being. We do not claim the SOC covers the entire spectrum of personal resources, but instead utilize it to open up a reflection of other resource-oriented constructs than the SOC. We will next describe three of them: resilience, flourishing and empowerment. All three of them are important for good functioning and well-being. However, to scrutinize all of them fully is not possible within the space of this chapter. We illuminate only resilience and empowerment, since there is a common misunderstanding that salutogenesis is the same concept as each of these. Flourishing is highlighted because this is a new expression of mental health from a resource-oriented perspective.

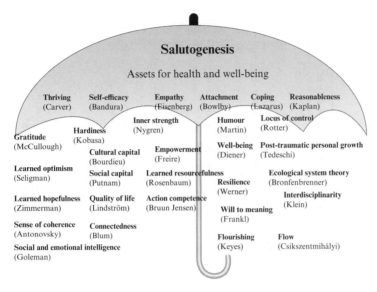

Figure 3.2   The salutogenic umbrella

Resilience

We begin with the concept of resilience. To many, this is a familiar concept related to coping with adversities (Werner and Smith 1982, 2001; Rutter 1985; Garmetzy and Rutter 1988; Luthar 2003). Do resilience and SOC describe the same concept? In our opinion the answer is 'no'. However, there are similarities and differences between the two concepts (see Table 3.1) (Eriksson and Lindström 2011).

First, the starting points for these two concepts are completely different. While Antonovsky (1979, 1987a) refers to a positive outcome independent of stress under certain conditions, research on resilience starts by recognizing the risk for a negative health outcome. Both concepts are process oriented (on a continuum), not part of personal characteristics. The salutogenic theory describes generalized resistance resources, factors that create the prerequisites for the development of the SOC. Resilience research follows a similar reasoning, but calls them protective factors for a positive health and well-being outcome. Both the SOC concept and resilience can be applied to different levels: the individual, group (families) or society.

Table 3.1 A theoretical comparison between salutogenesis and resilience

Approach indicators	Salutogenesis (Antonovsky 1979)	Resilience (Garmetzy and Rutter 1988)
The frameworks:		
Attention on	Stress	Risk
Approach	Contextual, situational, systems	Contextual, situational, systems
Orientation	Life orientation, a dynamic process in a continuum of ease–dis-ease	A dynamic process of recovery in a continuum
	Health promotion	Health protection
The core question	The origin of health: what creates health? Who are the people staying well? What can their experience tell us about health resources?	Why do some people stay healthy and others do not, regardless of severe hardships and adversities?
The theoretical foundation:		
Definition	The original definitions of salutogenesis and the sense of coherence (Antonovsky 1979) are generally accepted as defining the concepts under discussion. Salutogenesis is a much broader concept than only the measurement of the SOC. There are many other theories and concepts with salutogenic elements available for explaining health	Hard to get a hold of the complete content of resilience. Many different definitions of the concept, because of different available applications on different levels
Key concepts	Sense of coherence (SOC), a multidimensional construct	Resilience, 'bouncing back', beating the odds, multidimensional construct

		Protective factors
Prerequisites	General resistance resources	
Status	Coherent theoretical framework, extensively and empirically examined, systematically and analytically synthesized, evident (Eriksson 2007)	Lack of a coherent theory base, many theories depending on the level and dimensions explored Conceptually diffuse, 'slippery' concept, principle, evidence
The operationalization:		
The measurement	The Orientation to Life Questionnaire. The original SOC-29 and SOC-13 item scales, some modified versions with the *same questions* but with differing scoring alternatives	Different questionnaires with *different items* depending on the level and dimensions explored
The implementation:		
Applicability	Individual, group (families), organizational and societal level	Individual, group (families) and societal level
Outcome	Good perceived health (mental, physical, social) and quality of life (spiritual health)	Survival, perceived good health and quality of life
Effectiveness	The global evidence base proves the health model works	Lack of coherent and comprehensive evidence

Source: Adapted from Eriksson and Lindström (2011).

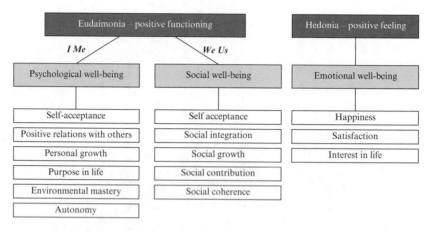

Source: Corey Keyes (2010).

Figure 3.3   Mental health as flourishing

Flourishing

Flourishing can be seen as an expression of mental health, that is, being and functioning well in life (Keyes 2002, 2006, 2007). According to Keyes, flourishing is described as the presence of mental health, whereas the absence of mental health is characterized as languishing (Keyes 2002, p. 208). Two dimensions of flourishing have emerged, a hedonic well-being dimension (i.e. positive emotions toward life) and a eudaimonic well-being dimension (i.e. positive psychological and social functioning in life) (see Figure 3.3) (Keyes 2010). Signs of hedonic well-being are feelings of being happy with life, finding interest in life and being satisfied with life. Signs of eudaimonic well-being are feelings that one is able to contribute to society and of being socially integrated, as well as feelings of social growth and potential, acceptance of others, social interest and *coherence* (being able to make meaning of what is happening in society) (Keyes 2002, 2005; Westerhof and Keyes 2010). Mental health as flourishing is a concept and framework having a clear salutogenic approach, focusing on people's potentials and strengths while also taking into account the prevalence of mental illnesses.

When combined, these concepts (psychological, social and emotional well-being) mean we are talking about a mental health continuum, derived from the salutogenic framework of health, which posits an ease–dis-ease continuum, where ease signifies health, and dis-ease signifies less health. They are further complemented with the pathogenic paradigm, which looks at well-being as the absence of diseases and poor functioning.

Findings from research which used this mental health continuum demonstrated that flourishing individuals reported the fewest missed days of work, the healthiest psychosocial functioning (i.e. low level of helplessness, having clear goals in life, high resilience and high intimacy), the lowest risk of cardiovascular disease, the lowest number of chronic physical diseases with age, and good functioning in daily life activities (Keyes 2007, p.95). This is a valuable approach for mental health promotion and practice, having many salutogenic elements.

Empowerment

The concept of empowerment has raised considerable interest, involving researchers from many different fields such as social psychology, community psychology, the social sciences, education and public health and health promotion (Freire 1970; Eklund 1999; Askheim and Starrin 2007; Laverack 2009). Paolo Freire, whose original work is in many ways a foundation for work on this concept, aimed to reduce inequity through the learning process and mobilize the uneducated. The core of this theory is centred on the creation of a respectful dialogue, thereby enhancing a sense of social community, that is, building social capital. Empowerment is about giving people control and mastery over their lives, and is similar to the enabling process in health promotion. It is about the development of abilities and coping skills and endowing people with the ability to work for active critical consciousness-raising. It is also a democratic concept looking at the structure of power between the individual life and the structure of the society. It is about the transformation of power from politicians, policy makers and professionals to the individual. Today the concept is used in many different contexts, for example by civil rights movements, the women's movement and the health promotion movement.

According to Koelen and Lindström (2005) empowerment is still conceptualized as a principle or an idea rather than a solid theory. This makes it difficult to operationalize and measure (Rissel 1994; Koelen and Lindström 2005; Aujoulat et al. 2007). Empowerment has increasingly been given the meaning of a multilevel construct that evolves upwards from an individual, group, organization or society rather than coming down from a top-down hierarchy. There is a consensus, independent of the level of implementation (individual, group or society), that empowerment is the process that enables people to be more aware of health-promoting strategies, which, in turn, leads to a higher level of well-being (Rappaport 1987; Rissel 1994). Some attempts to capture the essence of empowerment are related to the salutogenic construct. Koelen and Lindström (2005) defined individual empowerment 'as a process by which people gain mastery (control) over their lives, by which they learn to see a closer correspondence between their goals and a sense of how to achieve these goals, and by which people learn to see a relationship between their efforts and the outcomes thereof' (ibid., p.512). In this salutogenic definition of the concept, the focus is on resources, both internal and external, and on the learning process in order to create a sense of coherence. Findings from an ongoing review of the SOC and empowerment showed that empowerment is something more than only a feeling of sense of coherence. Conceptually, the two constructs differ (see Table 3.2) (Eklund and Eriksson 2011). However, further research is needed to theoretically and conceptually examine the associations between the salutogenic theory and the concept of empowerment.

THE EVIDENCE BASE OF SALUTOGENIC RESEARCH

Today there is an extensive research synthesis, referring to hundreds of articles on the SOC at individual, group and population level demonstrating the strength of the salutogenic concept (Eriksson and Lindström 2005, 2006, 2007; Eriksson 2007). In general, a strong SOC is associated with good functioning, well-being and health, particularly mental health. The SOC protects against anxiety, depression, burnout and hopelessness, and is strongly and positively related to health resources such as optimism, hardiness, control and coping. The SOC buffers against stress during the whole life cycle from adolescence through adulthood to old age (Eriksson and Lindström 2005, 2006, 2007; Lindström and Eriksson 2010a). Moreover, the SOC increases with age. It seems to be relatively stable over time, but not as stable as Antonovsky initially assumed. He stated that the SOC develops until the age of 30, and then is stable until retirement, after which it decreases. This assumption has not been empirically supported. Findings show that the SOC shows a lifelong development (Eriksson and Lindström 2011).

There has been much concern about health of adolescents because of their increasing exposure to stress in everyday life, particularly in schools. A strong SOC also seems to modify stress among adolescents (Nielsen and Hansson 2007; Moksnes 2011). A cross-sectional study of about 3000 Danish adolescents demonstrated that girls with a strong SOC perceive less stress and reported illness than those with a weak SOC (Nielsen and Hansson 2007). Further, behavioural problems at the age of 3 years predicted a poor SOC at the age of 18 years. That was the main finding from a study on Finnish 12-year-old schoolchildren (n = 1231). A poor SOC

Table 3.2 *A theoretical comparison between salutogenesis and empowerment*

Approach indicators	Salutogenesis (Antonovsky 1979, 1987a)	Empowerment (Freire 1970; Rappaport 1987; Rissel 1994; Zimmerman 2000)
The frameworks:		
Attention on	Stress	Power relations between laypeople, professionals and policy or decision makers
Orientation	Life orientation, a dynamic process in a continuum of ease–dis-ease Health promotion	Historical process in a society. The foundation for the new public health and health promotion
The core question	The origin of health: what creates health? Who are the people staying well? What can their experience tell us about health resources?	How can power relations be changed? How can individuals and groups be strengthened to gain power in decisions affecting them?
The theoretical foundation:		
Definition	The original definitions of salutogenesis and the sense of coherence (Antonovsky) are generally accepted. Salutogenesis is a much broader concept than only the measurement of the SOC	Consensus on the original definition of empowerment. After this, complementary definitions from various authors
Key concepts	Sense of coherence (SOC), a multidimensional construct consisting of comprehensibility, manageability and meaningfulness	Psychological empowerment: personality, motivational, cognitive and contextual dimensions. Community empowerment: cognitive, affective, behavioural and actual environmental change dimensions
Prerequisites	General resistance resources	Critical consciousness of injustice in society and in distribution of decision-making power
Status	Coherent theoretical framework, extensively and empirically examined, systematically and analytically synthesized, evident (Eriksson 2007)	No consensus on a coherent theory base. Many theories depending on the level and dimensions explored. Concept, model, principle

Table 3.2 (continued)

Approach indicators	Salutogenesis (Antonovsky 1979, 1987a)	Empowerment (Freire 1970; Rappaport 1987; Rissel 1994; Zimmerman 2000)
The operationalization: The measurement	The Orientation to Life Questionnaire. The original SOC-29 and SOC-13 item scales, some modified versions with the *same questions* but with differing scoring alternatives	Different questionnaires with different items depending on the level and dimensions explored
The implementation: Applicability, development direction and target levels	Individual, group (families) and societal level	Society, group (families, neighbours, peer group)
Outcome	Good perceived health (mental, physical, social) and quality of life (spiritual health)	Feeling of being empowered, strengthened self-esteem, improved coping strategies and managing problems in life, shift in power relations, actual changes in the community environment, participation in decision making
Evaluation	The key concepts of salutogenesis, the sense of coherence	Hard to evaluate, dependent on different theories and instruments related to the level examined. Several instruments and approaches
Political approach	Implicit	Explicit

Source: Adapted from Eklund and Eriksson (2011).

was associated with psychological symptoms and behavioural problems in adolescence (Honkinen et al. 2009). A strong SOC, in turn, is associated with a positive school performance, achievement, success, the ability to manage conflicts and transcultural competences and well-being (Mayer and Boness 2011a).

The results raise the critical question of how to strengthen the SOC during adolescence in order to promote well-being later in life. One way could be to create 'supportive environments' in schools in order to make the learning process conducive to health (Lindström and Eriksson 2011). Supportive environments in the school context are environments with social and physical features characterized by clear structures where pupils understand themselves as parts of a broader whole, which makes it easier to manage daily stress and stay well. It is most important to create learning situations that make sense and have meaning for young people. Here we have to take into consideration the importance of different kinds of learning and varying didactic methods. However, the crucial condition for creating a healthy learning process is the participation of pupils (Reid et al. 2008).

A practical application of the salutogenic model is exemplified by the 'salutogenic dialogue' that promotes health. Characteristics of such dialogue are, *inter alia*, an atmosphere of sincere willingness to understand each other, respect for the other's knowledge and experiences as different but of equal value, a strong ethical foundation where both are respectfully treated, and a context where both feel empowered and strengthened (Lindström and Eriksson 2010b, p. 46). Mayer and Boness (2011a) propose the 'team ombuds model (tOm)', a new educational model that aims at promoting transcultural competencies and well-being in students and educational professionals. It aims to strengthen the generalized resistance resources of learners and teachers as well as the SOC components: comprehensibility, manageability and meaningfulness (Mayer and Boness, 2011a, p. 519). Personal resources such as self-worth and a sense of belonging are fundamental health factors in an educational context (Krause 2011). Another example of practical realization of salutogenesis in an educational context is the 'I am I programme' developed and successfully implemented in kindergartens (Krause 2009). The most important aspect here is the participation of the parents and their support by the professional educators.

According to Antonovsky (1987b) the theoretical model of health and well-being is also a model appropriate for the analysis of working conditions. Today there are a large number of studies demonstrating that a strong SOC among employees and managers has an impact on well-being in workplaces. A strong SOC buffers against workplace stress (Albertsen et al. 2001; Holmberg et al. 2004; Hogh and Gemzoe Mikkelsen 2005; Bildt et al. 2006; Kinman 2008; Olsson et al. 2009). SOC has a main (direct) effect, a moderating effect and a mediating effect on workplace stress (Feldt 2000). In a longitudinal study exploring the health-promoting impact of the SOC in combination with exposure to adverse working conditions the findings showed an association between the SOC and work-related psychosocial factors (Holmberg et al. 2004). The main finding was that the SOC was strongly related to job demand control – a concept, introduced in the Karasek model (Karasek 1979), of a balance between job demands and being able to control one's work. This suggested that SOC is correlated with psychosocial work characteristics.

Precariousness is one of the most common characteristics of the working life today. How do employees manage these kinds of negative factors for well-being? Do they really manage? Ciairano and colleagues examined the role of the SOC on well-being (life satisfaction) among young Italian adults (Ciairano et al. 2010). The results showed that youths with a precarious job perceived reality as less controllable, man-ageable and meaningful. Manageability was positively related with their satisfaction with close relationships, and meaningfulness was, in turn, related with life satisfaction in general. Meaningfulness also buffered the effect of job precariousness on satisfaction for close relationships. In work settings and organizations, the salutogenic factors for mental health promotion included: (a) participation and comprehensibility within the organization (i.e. to being part of and understanding the organization), (b) social cohesion and social climate on the social level, and (c) recog-nition at the individual level (i.e. feeling one belongs and is accepted) (Graeser 2011).

The salutogenic approach has been applied in an organizational context. Mayer and Boness (2011b) assessed concepts used by organizations to promote the well-being of managers. This multi-method research study, conducted in an international organization in South Africa, showed that the manager's concepts of health and well-being mainly refer to physical and mental health concepts. When managers seemed to have a salutogenic rather than a pathogenic approach to health, they reported a high degree of comprehensibility, manageability and meaningfulness: that is, a strong SOC.

Organizational changes such as mergers usually influence the work environment in an organization and may affect employees' well-being. Findings from the Still Working Study, a longitudinal population study (n = 4279) on Finnish employees, showed that a stronger SOC decreased the adverse effects of a negative appraisal of change on mental health and seemed to be a protective factor for mental health (Pahkin et al. 2011).

Long-term sick leave often leads to difficulties with returning to work. There is a substantial amount of research on this issue that demonstrates how the SOC is a significant resource needed for the successful return to work of the employee. The SOC predicts work presence (Hansen et al. 2005, 2006). In a longitudinal study with a two-year follow-up, with the main purpose of finding predictors of individual resources for a return to work after long-term leave, Hansen et al. (2005) found that persons with stronger SOC tended to return to work to a greater extent than people with a weak SOC. A strong SOC was here associated with a higher level of coping resources (measured by the Coping Resources Inventory), which in turn could be the explanation for a faster return to work. Similar findings were found in a study on the Swedish workforce (n = 3139) (Engström and Janson 2009). A strong SOC was found to counteract short- as well as long-term sickness absences. However, opposite findings are also reported. Such a positive effect of the SOC could not be recognized in a sample of Norwegian patients affected by musculoskeletal pain (Lillefjell and Jakobsen 2007). No significant association was found between SOC and work re-entry.

We have above briefly described the evidence base of the SOC on well-being in adolescence and in adulthood and also as particularly related to working life. As earlier stated, a strong SOC is a protective factor for well-being, and this also applies in old age, by making it possible for the elderly to reconstruct their daily lives and coherence (Rennemark and Hagberg 1999; Holmgren and Söderhamn 2005; Schneider et al. 2006). Further, a strong SOC is a coping resource reducing stress related to caregiving for relatives (Andrén and Elmståhl 2008). Healthy active ageing is an overall goal in the EU, which designated 2012 to be the 'European Year for Active Ageing'. Evidence on factors maintaining well-being among older people becomes important, because policies and programmes have to be designed differently depending on different target groups. There is an emerging body of research on how a strong SOC can counteract difficulties and affect well-being in old age. In a study of subjective well-being as an indicator for successful ageing, a strong SOC seemed to be an important factor for psychological adaptation among elderly Germans (Wiesmann and Hannich 2008). It was found that resistance resources (such as age, education, physical health, activity level and social support) co-varied with the SOC and subjective well-being. The SOC clearly mediated the relationship between resources and well-being. Wiesmann and Hannich (2008) conclude that the SOC creates, or maintains, a form of psychological integrity as represented by subjective well-being. In other words, being psycho-emotionally integrated creates a sense of overall well-being. This suggests that the promotion of a strong SOC should be a major aim of gerontological interventions. Similar results were reported by Holmgren and Söderhamn (2005) among physically active older Swedes. Here the SOC was a significant determinant of well-being. An example of how promotion of health and well-being could gain from the salutogenic theory and principles can also be found in the Netherlands (Lezwijn et al. 2011). This framework supports intersectoral collaboration built upon three interrelated concepts: the SOC, resources for health and well-being.

DEFINING WELL-BEING

This chapter adopts a salutogenic approach to well-being. This concept of health integrates physical, mental, social and spiritual health on the individual (micro), group (meso) or societal (macro) level, that is, the quality of one's entire life (Lindström 1994). Health in salutogenic terms underlines the importance of structured and empowering environments, where people are able to identify their internal and external resources and use and reuse them in order to realize aspirations, satisfy needs, perceive meaningfulness and cope with changes in a health-promoting manner (Eriksson 2007). Well-being is here defined in terms of health, mental health and quality of life. It is the process where people perceive a good life based on their own merits. Although health today can be defined in terms of well-being and the absence of disease (according to WHO) it is usually described and measured in terms of risk, negative determinants and disease. However, if health was approached from a resource perspective and utilizing indicators from a well-being perspective, we could construct broader systems for well-being. To give a concrete example, vital national statistics mainly describe the disease and risk burden of a population rather than health or resources and indicators for health.

The concept of *well-being* is hard to define. There are many different definitions, and also an abundance of theories emanating from different perspectives, such as hedonic theories, desire theories, theories of happiness and eudaimonic theories (Eid and Larsen 2008). The field of subjective well-being has been strongly influenced by the work of Ed Diener (Diener et al. 1999, 2009; Diener 2009). According to Diener subjective well-being is a broad category of phenomena that include people's emotional responses, domain satisfactions, and global judgements of life satisfaction. Diener and colleagues, who have reviewed evidence of subjective well-being and discussed modern theories of subjective well-being that stress dispositional influences, adaptation, goals, and coping strategies, conclude that:

The next steps in the evolution of the field are to comprehend the interaction of psychological factors with life circumstances in producing SWB [subjective well-being], to understand the causal pathways leading to happiness, understand the processes underlying adaptation to events, and develop theories that explain why certain variables differentially influence the different components of SWB. (Diener et al. 1999, p. 276)

Here the salutogenic framework corresponds very well to the concept of well-being and contributes to the explanation of well-being. In his first book, *Health, Stress and Coping: New Perspectives on Mental and Physical Well-being*, Antonovsky (1979) discussed the concepts of health and well-being 'by defining health as coextensive with the many other dimensions of well-being'. The nature of this relationship is one that must be subjected to theoretical clarification and empirical investigation (Antonovsky 1979, p. 68). However, since his death in 1994, a substantial body of research has been published which links the SOC to well-being.

In studying well-being there are two different points of departure (Figure 3.4). The first is to study how people manage hardships and risks and develop resilience to adverse conditions. Within psychology, resilience research and practice have a long tradition, but conceptually resilience is still not clearly defined. Therefore the measurement of resilience is rather difficult. The other point of departure is to study how well-being is

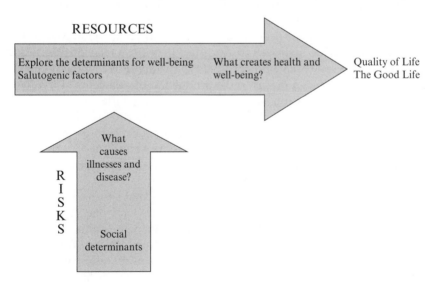

Source: © Bengt Lindström and Monica Eriksson.

Figure 3.4   Well-being in the context of health research

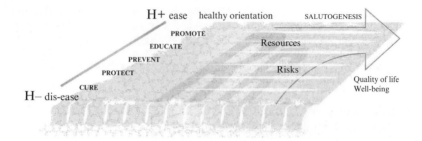

Source: © Bengt Lindström, Monica Eriksson and Peter Wikström.

Figure 3.5 The river of life

developed and what key resources are needed to create contexts for people to maintain well-being. This is what salutogenesis does, and from a salutogenic framework one would argue for synergy and coherence between systems. Rather than focusing on finding differences, the salutogenic approach emphasizes the synergies and similarities in and between systems which can generate well-being (Eriksson and Lindström 2008; see also Hämäläinen, this volume, Chapter 2).

To clarify our standpoint we want to add a metaphor to describe well-being in the context of health integrating the two approaches. The image of a river has often been used to describe the development of health, but mainly using disease or death and health as end points. However, if we use the salutogenic approach instead, health will be related directly to *life*, where the salutogenic process leads to quality of life and well-being. Health thus becomes a means to the production of well-being. Therefore the exploration of health and well-being needs a different image (see Figure 3.5). Here the flow of the river is in the direction of life (horizontally in this image). Health is seen as a continuum between un-health and health (vertical). The process of life (horizontal) can lead to well-being if supported by health-promoting mechanisms and processes such as described in the salutogenic approach to health.

Conceptually well-being is closely related to mental health and the good life, where health is an important piece but not the only one. A good life, or well-being, is a much broader concept than only health. Therefore it becomes crucial to clarify what we mean by well-being. *Health* is a complex concept with different contents dependent on different perspectives of health. Historically the understanding of health has developed through the understanding of mechanisms that oppose death and disease. The underlying assumption has been that the absence of diseases is the same as being healthy. This can be the case, but not necessarily. There are people with diagnosed diseases who still perceive they are in good health and, on the other hand, people without any disease who are in poor health and low well-being. *Mental health* has been described as 'a state of well-being in which the individual realises his or her own abilities, can cope with the normal stresses of life, can work productively and fruitfully, and is able to make a contribution to his or her community' (WHO 2001). Mental health is not only the absence of mental illnesses (Patel et al. 2007). According to Antonovsky (1985):

> mental health refers to the location, at any point in the life cycle, of a person on a continuum which ranges from excruciating emotional pain and total psychological malfunctioning at one extreme to a full, vibrant sense of psychological *wellbeing* at the other. It is about understanding how people move from the use of unconscious psychological defense mechanisms toward the use of conscious coping mechanisms; from the rigidity of defensive structures to the capacity for constant and creative inner readjustment and growth; from a waste of emotional energy toward its productive use; from emotional suffering toward joy; from exploitation of others toward reciprocal interaction. (ibid., p. 274)

We have now explained what we mean by health and especially mental health. Some further clarification is needed before reaching the concept of well-being, which we defined earlier as 'the process where people perceive a good life based on their own merits'.

The concept of *quality of life* (QoL) is equally complex to those of health and mental health. There is no universally accepted definition, but a general understanding of the concept is multidimensional and hard to capture (Bowling 1997; Fayers and Machin 2000; Rapley 2003). QoL can be viewed from the perspective of various sciences, such as philosophy (good life), sociology (intangible welfare and well-being), the economy (economic standard), behavioural science (well-being) and medicine (normality) (Lindström 1994). QoL has been defined as personal well-being or satisfaction with life (Fayers and Machin 2000), as well as physical and material well-being, relations with other people, social, communal or civic activities, personal development and fulfilment (Flanagan 1982), positive mental health (Kovess-Masfety et al. 2005), a degree of goodness (Bowling 1997), and being related to health (HRQOL). Functional status, often actually functional limitations, and health are two dimensions of HRQOL. A salutogenic interpretation of the QoL concept combines the global, external, interpersonal and personal resources of an individual, group or society (Lindström 1994). These four dimensions form a holistic definition of the QoL based on the salutogenic theory as follows: 'QoL is the total existence (being) of an individual, a group or a society describing the essence of existence as measured objectively and perceived subjectively by the individual, group or society' (Lindström 1994, p. 43).

POLICY IMPLICATIONS

In this chapter we have shown that there is a strong link between health and well-being, where well-being is described in terms of quality of life, mental health and perceived health. It is also evident that well-being can be obtained through a health process based on salutogenesis. However, well-being is often an individual perception, while policies are made on the basis of what is best for the collective. Based on the founding principles of the UN we argue that policies have to be based on equity, sustainability and human rights perspectives, as also specified in the UN Millennium Goals (UN 2011). This implies that individual happiness cannot be achieved at the cost of other people's happiness. Therefore the UN resolution on the pursuit of happiness needs to be interpreted on a collective level.

Implementing what we know about the evidence on the salutogenic model to health in practical policy development would increase the mean SOC of the population and simultaneously well-being. We have shown that people who develop a strong sense of coherence will in general manage most of the challenges of life better than others and at the same time be well and feel life as meaningful. Again it must be understood that a strong SOC as such only implies that a person or a system is able to manage its life challenges successfully. To meet the above Millennium Goals we further need to complement the SOC with human rights, again underlying the fact that success and well-being cannot be achieved at the cost of others.

Within the field of public health policy there was a change in the early 1980s from an exclusive focus on the health sector towards a new emphasis on an overall 'global health' that involves all sectors in society. This took place in 1981 when the WHO actively created its global 'Health For All' (HFA) policy (WHO 1981), which later incorporated the UN Millennium Goals. The HFA policy also directly formulated goals aimed at well-being. Policy efforts should attempt not only to prolong life (adding years to life, AYL) but also to create conditions for well-being and quality of life (adding life to years, ALY) and, at the same time, find sustainable and equitable conditions for health. Two years later the implementation strategy was ready, formulating the principles for health promotion through the Ottawa Charter. This also meant a different view on the concept of health, which no longer was seen as a complete state of well-being but a process where people learn to identify and use their health determinants, thereby improving their health, which again would enable an active and productive life, that is, a high quality of life.

Looking at the salutogenic model we can identify strong similarities, although this framework was not known to the HFA policy makers at that time. The tools and the evidence of the salutogenic framework would give

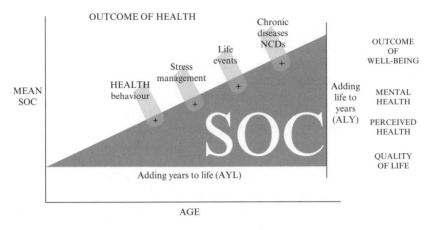

Source: © Bengt Lindström, Monica Eriksson and Peter Wikström.

Figure 3.6   The impact of the SOC in a lifetime perspective

the HFA policy instruments to accomplish its overall goals. Figure 3.6 describes these HFA policy opportunities during people's life course as their SOC accumulates.

The perception of coherence is based on cognitive, behavioural and motivational factors, which can be improved by raising the consciousness of the population, empowering them, and providing policy support for meaningful activities (Lindström and Eriksson 2009). We know from research that people (and organizations) who have developed skills to use the available resources, and focus on problem solving and positive outcomes, tend to have a stronger sense of coherence (SOC), better perceived health, adjustment to chronic disease, positive health behaviours, a longer life span and a better general well-being, mental health and quality of life (Eriksson and Lindström 2006, 2007; Eriksson 2007). This knowledge can be transferred to policy making (Lindström and Eriksson 2009). The key question is: what has to be considered in order to make health and other policies more supportive to salutogenic processes? What salutogenic questions have to be addressed and how can public policies best support comprehensibility, manageability and meaningfulness to all involved?

Based on the evidence of salutogenic research presented in this chapter we want to emphasize three issues where salutogenesis could guide policy makers constructing public policies. These are: (a) theory-driven policies, (b) indicators for well-being, and (c) coherence for decision making.

Theoretical accounts of well-being support policy making by providing useful information about the quality of people's life. They are useful for policy making only when three crucial conditions are satisfied: they must be theoretically rigorous, policy relevant and empirically robust (Dolan et al. 2011). Dolan et al. distinguish three types of well-being measures that are relevant to policy making: evaluation (monitoring life satisfaction, including domains of relationships, health, work, finances, time, children and satisfaction with services); experience (monitoring happiness and worries, or affect associated with particular activities); and 'eudaimonic measures' (reports of purpose and meaning, and worthwhile things in life and reward from activities). To continue on this track, we propose that a fourth assessment should be added about the sense of coherence. The SOC, as a global orientation and a view of life as coherent, manageable and meaningful, catches the essence of well-being. The salutogenic theory is conceptually sound, and the SOC has been empirically examined and found to be a valid and reliable measure of well-being. Finally, the research on the salutogenic theory has been extensively analysed and synthesized (Eriksson and Lindström 2005, 2006, 2007; Eriksson 2007).

Despite its potential, the SOC has not yet been applied as an indicator for the positive development of well-being. The European Health Promotion Indicator Development model (EUHPID) has been developed as the basis for establishing a set of European indicators for monitoring health promotion interventions. However, the SOC has not yet been included in the model (Bauer et al. 2006). Korkeila et al. (2003) considered the SOC as an indicator of well-being, but it was not mentioned on their list of indicators, which included socio-demographic factors, social networks, life events, factors of mental health and well-being, subjective experience of the individual including health and QoL, morbidity and disability.

It is important for any policy maker to understand how the principles of promoting well-being, health and quality of life guide the development of policies, and in turn form programmes and interventions. The question of effectiveness is delicate (McQueen and Jones 2007). As Jané-Llopis et al. (2011) state:

> Evidence from effect studies will be only one of a number of factors that will need to be taken into account in the decision-making processes. Equally important for policymakers will be the use of different types of evidence including implementation essentials and other decision-making principles such as social justice, political, ethical, equity issues, reflecting public attitudes and the level of resources available, rather than be based on health outcomes alone. (p.i140)

We totally agree with the authors; we need new approaches for healthy public policy and health in all policies (Ståhl et al. 2006; Kickbusch et al.

2008; Lindström and Eriksson 2009). We have the evidence; what do we do with it? The salutogenic theory can be understood and used in at least two ways:

1. Implement the resource-oriented (salutogenic) principles in all policies, not only in health policies, in different policy documents, in strategies for improving well-being on the national level and in planning for general programmes on well-being, and as an indicator for measuring well-being in populations. In a long-term perspective this leads to the creation of healthy societies where people feel well and perceive they lead the good life.
2. Implement the principles in activities and programmes for well-being at an individual and group level by creating such conditions that people perceive the situation as comprehensible, manageable and, most importantly, meaningful, and hence experience a high sense of coherence. In salutogenic terms, it is an empowerment process where people become aware of their strong motivators (meaning); they understand their situations and the arguments presented (comprehensibility); and the most sensible chain of activities is clear to them (manageability). This requires the right language and good communication skills from professionals (Lindström and Eriksson 2009).

The lifelong well-being process that enables a good quality of life is achieved through intersectoral or interdisciplinary community- and population-oriented *coherent* actions which create *synergy* between actions (Eriksson and Lindström 2008). This means creating synergy in and between action arenas in order to increase the overall effectiveness for health promotion. The way people are able to perceive structures, create coherence and keep everything together has a central impact on health.

Lerner and Benson (2003) discuss a framework for developing theory-driven asset building in communities that raises some critical questions. We apply here their thinking in the salutogenic framework and raise some key questions for an applied public policy where well-being is an essential goal for all policies:

1. What is meant by well-being? Are health and the quality of life of individuals integrated? Are individuals seen as resourceful and competent, contributing to the development of the society?
2. What creates well-being? How do gender, age, culture and other social determinants affect well-being?
3. What are the sources and resources for well-being? Who has the capacity to influence the well-being of individuals? What is the quality

of relationships with adults, peers, family, neighbours, schoolmates and the community?

4. Is evidence-based policy making focusing on salutary factors? What kind of intervention is effective in a short- and long-term perspective?
5. How is the humanity behind the policy described and expressed? Are people considered as resources? What are the values behind the policy?
6. Is a participatory approach adopted? Are people able to affect the policy? Are people empowered by the policy? In what way are the policies communicated?

CONCLUSIONS

Research consistently shows that interventions directed to systems in the community are more efficient than individually oriented programmes (Keleher et al. 2007; Kickbusch 2009). We strongly emphasize a systematic implementation of the findings from the research described in this chapter.

We described the integration of Antonovsky's salutogenic theory and model of health and well-being to the core principles of the Ottawa Charter and exemplified how healthy public policy can be formulated in the salutogenic way (Lindström and Eriksson 2009). In addition, we introduced a theoretical, process-oriented and coherent health promotion model that integrates the salutogenic and resiliency approaches. The objective of this theoretical model was to bring together the whole spectrum of risk factors, protective factors and promotion factors in one model. Finally, the individual, group and societal implications were considered.

REFERENCES

Albertsen, K., M.L. Nielsen and V. Borg (2001), 'The Danish psychosocial work environment and symptoms of stress: the main, mediating and moderating role of sense of coherence', *Work and Stress*, **15**, 241–53.

Andrén, S. and S. Elmståhl (2008), 'The relationship between caregiver burden, caregivers' perceived health and their sense of coherence in caring for elders with dementia', *Journal of Clinical Nursing*, **17**, 790–99.

Antonovsky, A. (1979), *Health, Stress and Coping: New Perspectives on Mental and Physical Well-being*, San Francisco, CA: Jossey-Bass.

Antonovsky, A. (1985), 'The life cycle, mental health and the sense of coherence', *Israel Journal of Psychiatry and Related Sciences*, **22**, 273–80.

Antonovsky, A. (1987a), *Unraveling the Mystery of Health: How People Manage Stress and Stay Well*, San Francisco, CA: Jossey-Bass.

Antonovsky, A. (1987b), 'Health promoting factors at work: the sense of coherence', in M. Kalimo, M. Eltatawi and C. Cooper (eds), *Psychosocial Factors at Work and Their Effects on Health*, Geneva: World Health Organization, pp. 153–67.

Antonovsky, A. and T. Sourani (1988), 'Family sense of coherence and family adaptation', *Journal of Marriage and the Family*, **50** (1), 79–92.

Askheim, O.P. and B. Starrin (eds) (2007), *Empowerment in Theory and Practice* [in Swedish], Malmö: Gleerups.

Aujoulat, I., W. d'Hoore and A. Deccache (2007), 'Patient empowerment in theory and practice: polysemy or cacophony?', *Patient Education and Counseling*, **66**, 13–20.

Bauer, G., J.K. Davies and J. Pelikan, on behalf of the EUHPID Theory Working Group and the EUHPID Consortium (2006), 'The EUHPID Health Development Model for the classification of public health indicators', *Health Promotion International*, **21**, 153–9.

Bildt, C., L. Backstig and I.-L. Andersson Hjelm (2006), 'Work and health in Gnosjö: a longitudinal study', *Work*, **27**, 29–43.

Bowen, G.L., J.M. Richman, A. Brewster and N. Bowen (1998), 'Sense of school coherence, perceptions of danger at school, and teacher support among youth at risk of school failure', *Child and Adolescence Social Work Journal*, **15**, 273–86.

Bowling, A. (1997), *Measuring Health: A Review of Quality of Life Measurement Scales*, Maidenhead: Open University Press.

Ciairano, S., E. Rabaglietti, A. Roggero and T.C. Callari (2010), 'Life satisfaction, sense of coherence and job precariousness in Italian young adults', *Journal of Adult Development*, **17**, 177–89.

Diener, E. (ed.) (2009), *The Science of Well-being: The Collected Works of Ed Diener – General Reviews and Theories of Subjective Well-being*, New York: Springer.

Diener, E., E.M. Suh, R.E. Lucas and H.L. Smith (1999), 'Subjective well-being: three decades of progress', *Psychological Bulletin*, **125**, 276–302.

Diener, E., R.E. Lucas and U. Schimmack (2009), *Well-being for Public Policy*, Oxford: Oxford University Press.

Dolan, P., R. Layard and R. Metcalfe (2011), *Measuring Subjective Wellbeing for Public Policy*, Special Paper No. 23, March, London: Centre for Economic Performance.

Eid, M. and R.J. Larsen (eds) (2008), *The Science of Subjective Well-being*, New York: Guilford Press.

Eklund, L. (1999), 'From citizen participation towards community empowerment: an analysis on health promotion from citizen perspective', doctoral thesis, Faculty of Medicine, University of Tampere.

Eklund, L. and M. Eriksson (2011), 'Salutogenesis and empowerment as prominent approaches for a sustainable health promotion: some theoretical comparisons', presentation at HTAi 2011: HTA for Health Systems Sustainability, 27–29 June, Rio de Janeiro, Brazil.

Engström, L.-G. and S. Janson (2009), 'Predictors of work presence – sickness absence in a salutogenic perspective', *Work*, **33**, 287–95.

Eriksson, M. (2007), 'Unravelling the mystery of salutogenesis: the evidence base of the salutogenic research as measured by Antonovsky's Sense of Coherence Scale', doctoral thesis, Åbo Akademi University Vasa, Research Report 2007:1, Folkhälsan Research Centre, Turku.

Eriksson, M. (forthcoming), 'The salutogenic framework for health promotion and disease prevention', in D.I. Mostofsky (ed.), *Handbook of Behavioral Medicine*, Hoboken, NJ: Wiley.

Eriksson, M. and B. Lindström (2005), 'Validity of Antonovsky's Sense of Coherence Scale – a systematic review', *Journal of Epidemiology and Community Health*, **59**, 460–66.

Eriksson, M. and B. Lindström (2006), 'Antonovsky's Sense of Coherence Scale and the relation with health – a systematic review', *Journal of Epidemiology and Community Health*, **60**, 376–81.

Eriksson, M. and B. Lindström (2007), 'Antonovsky's Sense of Coherence Scale and its relation with quality of life: a systematic review', *Journal of Epidemiology and Community Health*, **61**, 938–44.

Eriksson, M. and B. Lindström (2008), 'A salutogenic interpretation of the Ottawa Charter', *Health Promotion International*, **23**, 190–99.

Eriksson, M. and B. Lindström (2011), 'Life is more than survival: exploring links between Antonovsky's salutogenic theory and the concept of resilience', in K.M. Gow and M.J. Celinski (eds), *Wayfinding through Life's Challenges: Coping and Survival*, New York: Nova Publishers, pp. 31–46.

Eriksson, M., B. Lindström and J. Lilja (2007), 'A sense of coherence and health: salutogenesis in a societal context: Åland – a special case?', *Journal of Epidemiology and Community Health*, **61**, 689–94.

Fayers, P.M. and D. Machin (2000), *Quality of Life: Assessment, Analysis and Interpretation*, New York: John Wiley & Sons.

Feldt, T. (2000), 'Sense of coherence: structure, stability and health promoting role in working life', Jyväskylä Studies in Education, Psychology and Social Research, doctoral thesis, University of Jyväskylä.

Feldt, T., E. Leskinen, U. Kinnunen and I. Ruoppila (2003), 'The stability of sense of coherence: comparing two age groups in a 5-year follow-up study', *Personality and Individual Differences*, **35**, 1151–65.

Flanagan, J.C. (1982), 'Measurement of quality of life: current state of the art', *Archives on Physical Medicine and Rehabilitation*, **63**, 56–69.

Freire, P. (1970), *Pedagogy of the Oppressed*, New York: Herder and Herder.

Garmetzy, N. and M. Rutter (eds) (1988), *Stress, Coping, and Development in Children*, Baltimore, MD: Johns Hopkins University Press.

Graeser, S. (2011), 'Salutogenic factors for mental health promotion in work settings and organizations', *International Review of Psychiatry*, **23** (6), 508–15.

Hansen, A., C. Edlund and I.-B. Bränholm (2005), 'Significant resources needed for return to work after sick leave', *Work*, **25**, 231–40.

Hansen, A., C. Edlund and M. Henningsson (2006), 'Factors relevant to a return to work: a multivariate approach', *Work*, **26**, 179–90.

Hogh, A. and E. Gemzoe Mikkelsen (2005), 'Is sense of coherence a mediator or moderator of relationships between violence at work and stress reactions?', *Scandinavian Journal of Psychology*, **46**, 429–37.

Holmberg, S., A. Thelin and E.-L. Stiernström (2004), 'Relationship of sense of coherence to other psychosocial indices', *European Journal of Psychological Assessment*, **20**, 227–36.

Holmgren, L. and O. Söderhamn (2005), 'Perceived health and well-being in a group of physically active older Swedish people', *Vård i Norden*, **25** (77), 39–42.

Honkinen, P.-L., M. Aromaa, S. Suominen, P. Rautava, A. Sourander, H. Helenius and M. Sillanpää (2009), 'Early childhood psychological problems predict a poor sense of coherence in adolescents: a 15-year follow-up study', *Journal of Health Psychology*, **14**, 587–600.

Jané-Llopis, E., H. Katschnig, D. McDaid and K. Wahlbeck (2011), 'Supporting decision-making processes for evidence-based mental health promotion', *Health Promotion International*, **26**, i140–46.

Karasek, R.A. (1979), 'Job demands, job decision latitude, and mental strain: implications for job redesign', *Administrative Science Quarterly*, **24**, 285–307.

Keleher, H., C. MacDougall and B. Murphy (eds) (2007), *Understanding Health Promotion*, New York: Oxford University Press.

Keyes, C.L. (2002), 'The mental health continuum: from languishing to flourishing in life', *Journal of Health and Social Research*, **43**, 207–22.

Keyes, C.L. (2005), 'Mental illness and/or mental health? Investigating axioms of the complete state model of health', *Journal of Consulting and Clinical Psychology*, **73**, 539–48.

Keyes, C.L.M. (2006), 'Subjective well-being in mental health and human development research worldwide: an introduction', *Social Indicators Research*, **77**, 1–10.

Keyes, C.L.M. (2007), 'Promoting and protecting mental health as flourishing', *American Psychologist*, **62**, 95–108.

Keyes, C.L. (2010), 'Mental health as flourishing', guest lecture, University West, Trollhättan, Sweden, 8 December.

Kickbusch, I. (ed.) (2009), *Policy Innovation for Health*, New York: Springer.

Kickbusch, I., W. McCann and T. Sherbon (2008), 'Adelaide revised: from healthy public policy to Health in All Policies', *Health Promotion International*, **23**, 1–4.

Kinman, G. (2008), 'Work stressors, health and sense of coherence in UK academic employees', *Educational Psychology*, **28**, 823–35.

Koelen, M.A. and B. Lindström (2005), 'Making healthy choices easy choices: the role of empowerment', *European Journal of Clinical Nutrition*, **59**, 10–16.

Korkeila, J., V. Lehtinen, R. Bijl, O.S. Dalgard, V. Kovess, A. Morgan and H. Salize (2003), 'Establishing a set of mental health indicators for Europe', *Scandinavian Journal of Public Health*, **31**, 451–9.

Kovess-Masfety, V., M. Murray and O. Gureje (2005), 'Positive mental health', in H. Herrman, S. Saxena and R. Moodie (eds), *Promoting Mental Health: Concepts, Emerging Evidence, Practice*, Geneva: World Health Organization, pp. 35–45.

Krause, C. (2009), *The I Am I Programme: Improving the Self-worth in Kindergarten with Pauline and Emil* [in German], Berlin: Cornelsen Scriptor.

Krause, C. (2011), 'Developing sense of coherence in educational contexts: making progress in promoting mental health in children', *International Review of Psychiatry*, **23** (6), 525–32.

Laverack, G. (2009), *Public Health: Power, Empowerment and Professional Practice*, New York: Palgrave Macmillan.

Lerner, R.M. and P. Benson (eds) (2003), *Developmental Assets and Asset-building Communities: Implications for Research, Policy, and Practice*, New York: Kluwer Academic/Plenum Publishers.

Lezwijn, J., L. Vaandrager, J. Naaldenberg, A. Wagemakers, M. Koelen and C. van Woerkum (2011), 'Healthy ageing in a salutogenic way: building the HP 2.0 framework', *Health and Social Care in the Community*, **19** (1), 43–51.

Lillefjell, M. and K. Jakobsen (2007), 'Sense of coherence as a predictor of work reentry following multidisciplinary rehabilitation for individuals with chronic musculoskeletal pain', *Journal of Occupational Health Psychology*, **12** (3), 222–31.

Lindmark, U., U. Stenström, E. Wärnberg Gerdin and A. Hugoson (2009), 'The distribution of "sense of coherence" among Swedish adults: a quantitative cross-sectional population study', *Scandinavian Journal of Public Health*, doi: 10.1177/1403494809351654.

Lindström, B. (1994), 'The essence of existence: on the quality of life of children in the Nordic countries – theory and practice in public health', doctoral thesis, Nordic School of Public Health.

Lindström, B. and M. Eriksson (2009), 'The salutogenic approach to the making of HiAP/healthy public policy: illustrated by a case study', *Global Health Promotion*, **16**, 17–28.

Lindström, B. and M. Eriksson (2010a), *The Hitchhiker's Guide to Salutogenesis: Salutogenic Pathways to Health Promotion*, Helsinki: Folkhälsan IUHPE Global Working Group on Salutogenesis.

Lindström, B. and M. Eriksson (2010b), 'Salutogeeninen lähestymistapa terveyteen', in A.-M. Pietilä (ed.), *Terveyden edistäminen: Teorioista toimintaan*, Porvoo: WSOY.

Lindström, B. and M. Eriksson (2011), 'From health education to healthy learning: implementing salutogenesis in educational science', *Scandinavian Journal of Public Health*, **39**, 85–92.

Luthar, S.S. (ed.) (2003), *Resilience and Vulnerability: Adaptation in the Context of Childhood Adversities*, Cambridge: Cambridge University Press.

McQueen, D. and C. Jones (2007), *Global Perspectives on Health Promotion Effectiveness*, New York: Springer.

Margalit, M. and M. Efrati (1996), 'Loneliness, coherence and companionship among children with learning disorders', *Educational Psychology*, **16**, 69–80.

Mayer, C.-H. (2011), *The Meaning of Sense of Coherence in Transcultural Management*, Internationale Hochschulschriften Series, vol. 563, Münster: Waxmann.

Mayer, C.-H. and C. Boness (2011a), 'Interventions to promoting sense of coherence and transcultural competences in educational contexts', *International Review of Psychiatry*, **23** (6), 516–24.

Mayer, C.-H. and C. Boness (2011b), 'Concepts of health and well-being in managers: an organizational study', *International Journal of Qualitative Studies on Health and Well-being*, **6**, doi: 10.342/qhw.v6i4.7143.

Moksnes, U.K. (2011), 'Stress and health in adolescents: the role of potential protective factors', doctoral thesis, Norwegian University of Science and Technology, Trondheim.

Nielsen, A.M. and K. Hansson (2007), 'Associations between adolescents' health, stress and sense of coherence', *Stress and Health*, **23**, 331–41.

Olsson, G., Ö. Hemström and J. Fritzell (2009), 'Identifying factors associated with good health and ill health: not just opposite sides of the same coin', *International Journal of Behavioral Medicine*, **16**, 323–30.

Pahkin, K., A. Väänänen, A. Koskinen, B. Bergbom and A. Kouvonen (2011), 'Organizational change and employees' mental health: the protective role of sense of coherence', *Journal of Occupational and Environmental Medicine*, **53**, 118–23.

Patel, V., A.J. Flisher, S. Hetrick and M. Patrick (2007), 'Mental health of young people: a global public-health challenge', *Lancet*, **369**, 1302–13.

Rapley, M. (2003), *Quality of Life Research: A Critical Introduction*, London: Sage.

Rappaport, J. (1987), 'Terms of empowerment/exemplars of prevention: toward a theory for community psychology', *American Journal of Community Psychology*, **15**, 121–48.

Reid, A., B. Bruun Jensen, J. Nikel and V. Simovska (eds) (2008), *Participation and Learning: Perspectives on Education and the Environment, Health and Sustainability*, New York: Springer.

Rennemark, M. and B. Hagberg (1999), 'What makes old people perceive symptoms of illness? The impact of psychological and social factors', *Aging and Mental Health*, **3**, 79–87.

Rissel, C. (1994), 'Empowerment: the holy grail of health promotion?', *Health Promotion International*, **9**, 39–47.

Rutter, M. (1985), 'Resilience in the face of adversity', *British Journal of Psychiatry*, **147**, 598–611.

Sagy, S. and H. Antonovsky (1999), 'Factors related to the development of the sense of coherence (SOC) in adolescents: a retrospective study', *Polish Psychological Bulletin*, **30**, 255–62.

Sagy, S. and H. Antonovsky (2000), 'The development of the sense of coherence: a retrospective study of early life experiences in the family', *Journal of Aging and Human Development*, **51**, 155–66.

Schneider, G., G. Driesch, A. Kruse, H.-G. Nehen and G. Heuft (2006), 'Old and ill and still feeling well? Determinants of subjective well-being in ≥60 year olds: the role of the sense of coherence', *American Journal of Geriatric Psychiatry*, **14**, 850–59.

Ståhl, T., M. Wismar, E. Ollila, E. Lahtinen and K. Leppo (eds) (2006), *Health in All Policies: Prospects and Potentials*, Helsinki: Ministry of Social Affairs and Health Finland.

UN (2011), *Happiness: Towards a Holistic Approach to Development*, available at: http://www.un.org/en/mdg/summit2010/pdf/mdg%20outcome%20document.pdf.

Werner, E. and R. Smith (1982), *Vulnerable but Invincible: A Longitudinal Study of Resilient Children and Youth*, New York: McGraw-Hill.

Werner, E. and R. Smith (2001), *Journeys from Childhood to Midlife: Risk, Resilience, and Recovery*, Ithaca, NY: Cornell University Press.

Westerhof, G.J. and C.L. Keyes (2010), 'Mental illness and mental health: the two continua model across the lifespan', *Journal of Adult Development*, **17**, 110–19.

WHO (1981), *Global Strategy for Health for All by the Year 2000*, Geneva: World Health Organization.

WHO (2001), 'Mental health: strengthening our response', available at: http://www.who.int/mediacentre/factsheets/fs220/en/ (accessed 9 December 2011).

Wiesmann, U. and H.-J. Hannich (2008), 'A salutogenic view on subjective well-being in active elderly persons', *Aging and Mental Health*, **12**, 56–65.

Zimmerman, M. (2000), 'Empowerment theory: psychological, organizational and community levels of analysis', in J. Rappaport and E. Seidman (eds), *Handbook of Community Psychology*, New York: Plenum Press.

4. Well-being and well-becoming: reauthorizing the subject in incoherent times

Maureen O'Hara and Andrew Lyon

INTRODUCTION

Writing this chapter has been an interesting challenge. This is partly because as authors we are separated by 6000 miles and eight time zones. But mainly it has been a conceptual challenge created by the same conditions of incoherence and complexity that we hope to highlight in what follows. Initiatives to make enhancement of human well-being the explicit focus of social policy rather than a hoped-for side effect to economic success are a welcome shift in emphasis. To do it well and to avoid unwanted consequences requires some reflection on deeper meta-theoretical and contextual issues that influence how we think and act to forward that agenda. Our aim is to consider the question of well-being against a larger story of cultural transition in which many of the conceptual and institutional assumptions that have underpinned Western culture for nearly 400 years are losing their coherence and explanatory power, with no new coherence having emerged to replace it. Contemporary conversations about human well-being, variously defined, straddle a gap between a culture that promotes a way of life that is no longer sustainable and the possibility of a new cultural story that supports a transformed relationship between humanity and our home planet. In the words of California state senator John Vasconcellos, we are called to be simultaneously 'hospice workers for a dying culture and midwives for the new' (quoted in Leicester and O'Hara, 2009).

As others in this volume have said, over the last two decades interest in happiness and well-being and efforts to create measures of happiness within populations has exploded. Major factors in this rise have been the availability of large databases and advanced analytics, and the development of new fields within psychology such as behavioural economics, subjective well-being and happiness studies, and positive psychology. The

Report by the Commission on the Measurement of Economic Performance and Social Progress (referred to subsequently as Stiglitz–Sen–Fitoussi) examines the strategies and methods available for linking economic and social indicators (Stiglitz et al. 2009). The Happy Planet Index (HPI) (Marks et al. 2006) links measures of subjective well-being with objective economic and environmental indicators. Hämäläinen (this volume, Chapter 2) reports that a 2010 study found 15 different indices being used to measure various aspects of well-being, and a cursory search of the World Wide Web reveals more checklists and self-measures coming online all the time, created by NGOs, social service agencies, think tanks, management consulting firms and individual entrepreneurs. Another contributing factor has been the interest in positive psychology by government agencies as the basis for interventions to solve social ills, especially in the US, Scotland and the wider UK.

The positive effect of all this work is that questions about the good life, well-being and happiness have become an explicit focus of conversation in all sectors of public life, particularly in advanced Western democracies; and assumptions inherited from the Enlightenment[1] about free market capitalism's ability to ensure human happiness are also under scrutiny.

But in the search for ways to measure well-being there are reasons to consider the limits of current studies and, even more importantly, their usefulness in a global context where the basic conceptual frames and narratives that hold societies together are changing. Since the mid-twentieth century, social indicators have been used to reduce complex science-based data to relatively simple algorithms to aid those responsible for developing social and economic policy. Where intentions are clear and explicit, parameters are appropriate, and categories are clearly delineated and realistic, indicators can be effective tools for monitoring the progress and effectiveness of programmes that must operate at scale (Noll 2002). But, as Stiglitz–Sen–Fitoussi states, 'what we measure affects what we do; and if our measurements are flawed, decisions may be distorted' (Stiglitz et al. 2009, p. 7). Looking back over the twentieth century one can see many examples of large-scale schemes that were intended to improve lives which have not helped the people they were intended to help, and benefits that have been unequally distributed and short-lived and have inadvertently brought disruption (Jacobs 1961; Bardhan 1995; Scott 1998). Schemes frequently fail because they attempt to impose order and apply an overly simplistic, mechanistic causal logic upon complex human interdependencies which they do not and *cannot* fully comprehend or control (Scott 1998). The degree to which persons are reduced to abstract categories that exclude their personhood, interiority, sovereignty and historical, relational and contextual particularities as 'being-for-themselves' risks turning people into objects and raises the danger of contributing further to the alienated social and psycho-spiritual pathologies of the modern world (Fromm 1955; Levin 1987a) – in other words, exacerbating the conditions we hope to improve.

PART ONE: METHODOLOGY, EPISTEMOLOGY AND REALITY

Standard Science in Well-being Studies

Any plan to use indicators of well-being or to apply happiness science to drive public policy raises concerns about ontology (what kinds of reality do our data represent?), method (what assumptions about research design do we use?) and epistemology (what kind of knowledge claims can we make on the basis of our studies?). All human activity including scientific research goes on within specific psychospheres.[2] The research most prominent in today's policy-level discussions about well-being and happiness across multiple disciplines reflects the psychosphere of modernity in which the 'standard view' of social science (Scheffler 1967) predominates. Inherited from the Enlightenment, core concepts are that: human beings are individual, autonomous agents; social progress is obtained by ordering society and nature through top-down application of scientific methods; there are regular, reliably predictable causal relationships between independent and dependent variables; and new knowledge and productivity will yield to probabilistic, quantitative and reductionist methods of inquiry.

Many researchers acknowledge that their categories and models are not the 'thing itself', but are constructions to permit simple measurement and theory building. For example, the new economics foundation (nef) report on the HPI (Marks et al. 2006) identifies (but does not resolve) some of these issues. But citizens and policy makers who consume research are mostly unaware of the tacit, culture-specific assumptions embedded in studies, or that 'subjective well-being' as a numerical abstraction stripped of its contextual nuances and interdependencies might have very little connection to subjective well-being as a holistic lived experience. They may also be unaware that the frames that direct survey construction, category formation, choice of variables and interpretation of data reflect a priori moral, cognitive and emotional commitments of the scientists and the discipline. For example, as American evolutionary biologist Steven Jay Gould (1996) pointed out, white supremacist social agendas permeated intelligence studies that claimed to show differences in IQ between American racial groups.

The goal of the standard view in behavioural science has been to establish laws of human behaviour that are as reliable as the laws of physics, which when applied will produce predictable outcomes, but, as Csikszentmihalyi (this volume, Chapter 10), Maslow ([1966] 1999), Rogers (1964), Fromm (1955) and Bateson (1972) have argued, this project has largely failed. Standard science relies on models and abstractions that leave out too much of the deeper existentially nuanced knowledge of our selves and the world. Mulgan (this volume, Chapter 11) notes that much social research derives its power from abstraction from large data sets. Such studies may make some things easier but at the same time run the risk of excluding important particularities such as individual differences and relational contingencies such as family and social context.

To the extent that policy makers take their cues from a limited range of sources of information that represent too narrow a set of assumptions about human reality, their grasp of the issues remains impoverished and may lead down false and dangerous trails (consider, for example, the design of the city of Brasilia, China's Great Leap Forward, Stalinist Russia and South African apartheid).

Other paradigms of research and intervention are available that both allow for significantly more granularity and nuance and offer a more faithful understanding of human lives as they are actually lived. Philosophy, the arts, humanities, and religious and moral investigations also provide insights and practices that have stood the test of time, sustaining humankind for all but the last 300 years. But the dominance of standard science in social thought through editorial policies of prominent journals, professional organizations, regulatory bodies, national research institutes, and foundation funding priorities over many years has resulted in marginalization of non-standard research, with its knowledge base ignored or denigrated.[3] Recent moves towards an ecological approach to public health research and intervention (Trickett et al. 2011), the recovery movement in mental health (Davidson et al. 2010), post-positive human science (Polkinghorne 1983), soft-systems design (Tsivasou 2004) and the 2012 adoption of a Qualitative Science division by the American Psychological Association all point to important correctives to the dominance of the standard science culture in social science. But so far very little of these more holistic paradigms is visible in the well-being field.[4]

Considering Orders of Consciousness

In standard science, survey research respondents are the unit of analysis or object of study, and any difference among them is presumed to be the result of external causes. In the Gallup World Poll (GWP) a standard question asks 'Thinking about your own life and personal circumstances, how satisfied are you with what you are achieving in life?' and offers a score between 0 and 10 (Cummins and Lau 2006). An assumption is that a difference in score correlates with differences in an inner state, 'satisfaction', which is taken to be a measure of well-being. A distinguishing feature of human consciousness, however, is that people vary in cognitive style, complexity of thought, levels of self-integration and relational considerations along a developmental continuum (Maslow 1971; Kegan 1982; Loevinger 1982; Kohlberg et al. 1983; Belenky et al. 1997; Wilber 2000). At a non-reflective first-order level of psychological process, 'satisfaction' may be based on achievement of self-indulgent desires and may be empty of moral considerations, whereas, at higher levels of psychological integration and relatedness, 'satisfaction' may be part of a complex set of dynamically connected meanings including compassion, empathy and a sense of justice. Differences in psychological development – which is to some degree a function of educational formation – affect how respondents answer poll questions, but when survey results are compiled these important differences in how people construe their world are invisible.

Measuring Reality or Creating It?

Answering a researcher's question is a formative experience in which both the researcher's and the respondent's entire consciousness is involved. The phrasing of a question primes respondents to adopt categories offered by the researcher and through the process of anchoring may unconsciously reinforce the assumptions of the questions (Bowers and Marsolek 2003). The GWP question above prompts respondents to link satisfaction with achievement and to think of their experience on a linear numerical scale. Such a construal would be foreign to most of the world's people (Geertz 1979; Hofstede 1980).

Researchers create their own psychospheres, adopting framing which is assumed to represent an 'objective reality'. This process is well documented in medicine (Rosenberg 1989), where what were once 'ailments' or 'afflictions' requiring 'care' are now 'diseases' needing 'treatment'. Creation and reification of happiness and well-being categories are well under way.[5] Consistency in definitions and terminology may be a boon for those looking to conduct statistical manipulations on large data sets, but in the social sciences the methods we use may actually construct the phenomena we are trying to measure (Polanyi 1957; C. Taylor 1973; Manicas and Secord 1983). In short, questions tend to reflect the preoccupations of the scientist rather than the subject.

Cultural Bias

Western bias in well-being and happiness research is also well documented (Lu et al. 2001; Collinge et al. 2002; Ng et al. 2003; Sundararajan 2005). The Chinese language, for instance, did not have a word for happiness until recently, nor does it have an equivalent to 'self-esteem' (Lu et al. 2001), and many languages have no direct equivalent to 'achievement' (Hofstede 1980). There is wide variability in ways of life, worldview, expectations, metaphysics, perception, reasoning, values, motivation and moral priorities across the world's cultures (Shweder 1991; Ishii et al. 2003; Nisbett 2003). Bjørnskov (2008) identifies potentially 'severe' (p. 43) problems created by the ways questions in the different well-being polls are framed so that answers 'are not fully comparable across individuals, and less so across countries' (p. 44).

Scientific Neutrality and Moral Inversion

A long-standing concern about the standard science paradigm in the social sciences is its claim of objectivity and moral neutrality. As critical theorists have demonstrated, science is never neutral and inevitably serves particular human interests (Habermas 1971). A league table of national happiness scores has social and political consequences. Proponents of positive psychology, which plays a large role in the current well-being conversation, insist on its 'scientific' status and its moral neutrality, while at the same time describing positive psychology as a 'movement' aiming to articulate an empirically based path to a 'good life' in a 'good society' (Sundararajan 2005). Sundararajan (2005) questions 'whether any form of life that is considered "good" ... can be devoid of a moral map' (p. 36). Though Csikszentmihalyi (this volume, Chapter 10) considers the goals of the US Army's Comprehensive Soldier Fitness Program, which aims to apply positive psychology techniques to reduce the traumatic effects of combat, 'laudable' (and up to a point so do we[6]), he raises important concerns about the relationship between positive psychology and the military. Csikszentmihalyi is worried about the scientists losing their objectivity. We are worried about citizens losing their moral standing. When any social programme – even one to improve the level of happiness or resilience – is justified in the name of 'science', while other positions are dismissed as 'unscientific', there is the danger of moral inversion (Polanyi 1957). In Polanyi's view Stalinism and Nazism are extreme examples of the use of claims made in the name of scientific objectivity to further political ends. Urban renewal schemes of the post-Second World War period that relocated poor but vibrant communities into soulless housing projects, the introduction of 'scientific management' (F.W. Taylor 1919) into modern factories, and the labelling of opposition to authority in adolescents as a treatable 'disease' are others. Social scientists in non-Western and indigenous societies have described how imposition of projects justified as 'scientific truth' by Western colonists upon indigenous populations, whose traditional moral systems and cultural wisdom were deemed superstitions, decimated local ways of life and cultural resilience (Nandy 1983; Duran and Duran 1995). A substantial literature exists of similar observations with regard to gender, race, religion, class, disability and immigration status.

Requisite Diversity of Viewpoints

None of the foregoing is meant to argue against the importance of social science as an essential source of information, or to doubt the validity of many well-crafted behavioural studies of well-being and happiness that take pains to address the issues we have raised. Nor are we suggesting that indicators based on large survey data can never or should never aid policy considerations at the macro level. But we do wish to raise concerns that if the findings from such research are to be applied at scale through top-down interventions within real communities their limitations be acknowledged and that we exercise critical judgement, requisite caution, as much granularity as is feasible, and more than a little humility about what we don't know. And, more importantly in our view, studies must start and end with the affirmation that each subject is a unique, irreducible, self-authorizing and sovereign *person* who lives within complex, multi-layered particular relationships to other such subjects. As the notable British systems science pioneer Sir Geoffrey Vickers famously said, 'human systems are different' (Vickers 1983). If our metrics and methods exclude the qualities of Being that, as Robert F. Kennedy said, 'make living a human life worthwhile' (1968), not only do we dehumanize those whom our data exclude but, at the end of the day, we dehumanize the entire culture.

PART TWO: WELL-BEING IN UNCERTAIN AND INCOHERENT TIMES

Questions regarding the adequacy of the conceptual frames of modernity in the well-being discourse have more than academic importance. What was deemed essential to the 'good life' by Enlightenment thinkers depended on progress, industrialism and economies of scale that are no longer sustainable – ecologically, economically, politically or psychologically. Though the fruits of modern science have enabled unprecedented increases in material wealth, health and longevity for those in the developed world, at the same time they have contributed to the 'wicked' problems (Churchman 1967) that now bear down on every major human system and threaten the entire planetary socio-ecosystems. Humanity is experiencing what many now describe as a crisis of culture – even a crisis of civilization (Diamond 2005; Homer-Dixon 2006; D.M. Taylor and Taylor 2007; Beddoe et al. 2009; Ahmed 2010) – in which certainties that have guided modern societies for 400 years no longer hold, but as yet no new certainties have emerged to replace them.

Social psychologist Donald N. Michael was among the first to point out the psychological and social costs of complexity and uncertainty, and he identified epistemological, social and psychodynamic incoherence as primary factors contributing to the deepening insecurity of the times (Michael 1973). Bauman (2010) refers to our times as 'liquid modernity', in which scientific theories, cultural narratives, identities, values, social norms and social policies are in play and all social processes must be understood within the context of rapidly changing and incoherent patterns of life. For any social entity – from bowling club to civilization – to remain stable and cohesive there needs to be a coherent set of narratives that gives satisfactory answers to a small set of existential questions. Agreements are needed on origins (where we come from), identity (who 'we' are and who 'they' are), relationship to the natural world (whether we are part of it, in charge of it or at the mercy of it), distribution of wealth (why some have more than others), what the nature of reality is (random, intentional, material, divine) and what is 'taboo' (what we cannot do and remain human) (Shweder 1991). Where agreements remain constant, or changes occur incrementally, explanatory frames from within the existing psychosphere will be used to address challenges. Voting rights for women and then blacks, for example, could be understood in terms of principles already established without any necessity for reordering deeper understandings. Such 'first-order' changes can be assimilated into existing frameworks, evaluated by agreed-upon standards and executed through respected institutional structures and create relatively little cognitive dissonance (Festinger 1957; Yankelovich 1991; Hämäläinen 2007).

But times are no longer characterized by incremental changes. Radical shifts are under way – futurist Willis Harman (1998) dubbed it a 'new Copernican revolution' that brings into question bedrock assumptions upon which Western civilization is built at every level from conceptual frames to governance. At the same time these assumptions are increasingly in conflict with those of other worldviews (such as Islamic and Buddhist societies) where the European Enlightenment has had less of an influence on the psychosphere. Complexity increases exponentially as worldviews intersect, boundaries become fluid, contradictions mount, social consensus fragments, agreements or priorities are harder to come by, morale drops and the effectiveness of collective action diminishes. This in turn generates more frustration, anxiety and uncertainty, which leads to more disorder and even more uncertainty in a vicious cycle until navigating the incoherent world becomes overwhelming.

There are signs of serious distress in cultural, psychological, spiritual and environmental spheres (see Hämäläinen, this volume, Chapter 2; Bartolini, this volume, Chapter 6) even in affluent societies. The demands of our times may already be beyond current mental, organizational and structural capacities to cope and we are 'over our heads' (Beer 1973; Kegan 1994), with some developmental psychologists estimating that less than 25 per cent of adults reach a level of mental capacity needed to deal easily with the complexity of contemporary life (Kegan 1994). This shows up in many walks of contemporary life. The World Health Organization estimates that 450 million people globally suffer from a mental disorder at any one time. This accounts for 13 per cent of the global burden of all disease. The WHO also suggests that many more than this are suffering mental health problems which are not addressed (WHO 2011). One in four people globally will develop a mental health problem at some point in their life. These data represent the tip of a considerable iceberg, which includes increasing self-harm, suicide and relationship breakdown, which are rising as the conditions of life become more pressing for increasing numbers of people and the demands of everyday life outstrip our cultural capacity to generate the mental capacity to keep up. The rising chaos, relentless bad news, ineffectiveness of institutions and governments, and ecological overload are seen by some as signalling the coming collapse of Western civilization and decline into another dark age (Stavrianos 1976; Dror 2001; Diamond 2005; Homer-Dixon 2006; Gilding 2011).

Dystopic and apocalyptic themes (and their nostalgic and escapist antidotes) show up in films, poems, novels and video games as artists tap into the cultural anxiety, and the collapse theme features prominently in academic conferences in many disciplines. Major institutions such as the financial sector, health care, education and environmental management are under extreme strain and nearing collapse, and the people in them are increasingly troubled by a cascade of interlocking difficulties for which solutions are scarce (Kelly 2005; Hanlon et al. 2012). Problems of obesity and drug and alcohol abuse in high-income societies of the West and middle- and low-income societies across the globe, rapidly rising rates of mental distress and disorder (WHO 2004; Layard 2006; Alexander 2008), diminishing or flat scores on individual and social well-being scales (Lane 2000; Layard 2006; Offer 2006), and increasing health and social inequalities (CSDH 2008; Wilkinson and Pickett 2009) are well documented. Other looming problems, which at first glance may seem unrelated to the above but put increasing strain on minds and resources, include anthropogenic climate change (McMichael et al. 2006), peak oil (Roberts 2005), exponential population growth (Bartlett 1997) and the continuing global economic crises (Elliott and Atkinson 2009). Recent uprisings in Arab societies, street riots in the UK and other parts of Europe, and Occupy events have been linked to the psychic impacts of these pressures (Korten 2011). The uncertainty produced by the combined effects of all this contributes to the febricity of the times.

Coherence as Primary Need

In his theory of motivation Maslow includes stability, certainty and the need for coherence, as primary safety needs as basic as food, water and shelter. When coherence is disturbed, anxiety rises and psychological and social resources are mobilized in efforts to bring anxiety to tolerable levels and restore the sense of mental equilibrium (Maslow [1954] 1970). Antonovsky (1979) first described the salutogenic effects of coherence (SOC), as well as the pathogenic effects of incoherence. This model, further developed by Eriksson and Lindström (this volume, Chapter 3) and Hämäläinen (this volume, Chapter 2), documents the social and individual effects of incoherence, uncertainty and information overload created by the conditions of life in affluent advanced societies.

Studies from multiple psychological perspectives identify three qualitatively different kinds of responses to incoherence, each with its own distinct process and impact on well-being.[7] These responses either reduce complexity through increased control or collapse or reduce incoherence by enlarging capacity and arriving at a larger, more integrated coherence.

Reducing Complexity

Defensive strategies reduce incoherence and lower anxiety by mobilizing mechanisms to reduce complexity and simplify what needs to be dealt with. The most common defences are part of the twentieth-century lexicon: denial – failing to acknowledge some new experience; projection – ascribing to others an unacceptable thought or impulse of one's own; rationalization – making up an alternative, more palatable explanation for an action; reaction formation – overreacting negatively to something one unconsciously desires so as to keep it from getting too close; and distortion – misreading a situation so as to create an alternative meaning that does not challenge one's existing sense of order. All serve to maintain the view that things are not as bad as they seem, and that problems are amenable to existing frameworks if only we can specify the right targets, improve our execution and redouble our efforts.

Defensive strategies are necessary manoeuvres in situations that might otherwise overwhelm, but, if a defence becomes chronic or filters out information needed to thrive, consequences can become problematic. As a chronic strategy for managing incoherence it may lead to mental health issues. Avoidance of anxiety is a factor in attention deficit, obsessive and compulsive disorders, phobias, depression, narcissism, post-traumatic stress disorder and addictions. In organizations, defence manifests itself in rigid cultures, ritualistic management procedures, resistance to change even in the face of evidence that things are not working as intended, micro-management, overreliance on standardization and measurement, risk avoidance and groupthink (Schein 1992; Pauchant 1994; Alpaslan and Mitroff 2011). Authoritarianism, fundamentalism, distraction (bread and circuses), nostalgia, identity politics, segregation, conformity and compliance, anti-intellectualism, paranoia, heightened security, apathy and disengagement, backlash, scapegoating and polarization offer cultural-level defences against too much uncertainty (May 1950; Fromm 1955; Freud 1959; Levin 1987a; C. Taylor 1992). What these diverse strategies have in common is that they reduce complexity by excluding from awareness information that would require significant change. Though anxiety is contained it is by creating a false sense of coherence.

Breakdown

When threats can no longer be met with existing resources, individual or collective coherence systems become unmanageable and may collapse altogether. Without structures and constraints provided by mutually maintained boundary conditions (identities, values, social norms, laws, constitutional agreements) these become chaotic and swing wildly from one extreme to another, causing further incoherence. In individuals this may result in decompensation, psychosis, despair, self-destruction, suicide, catatonia or violent acting out. At societal levels extreme incoherence may lead to social disorder, lack of solidarity, internecine conflicts, mob violence, genocide (Dutton 2007), failed states, the fall of empires and civilization collapse (Diamond 2005).

Transformation and Growth in Capacity

If resistance and collapse were the only possible outcomes of rising incoherence we would likely all still be hunter-gatherers. In sufficiently

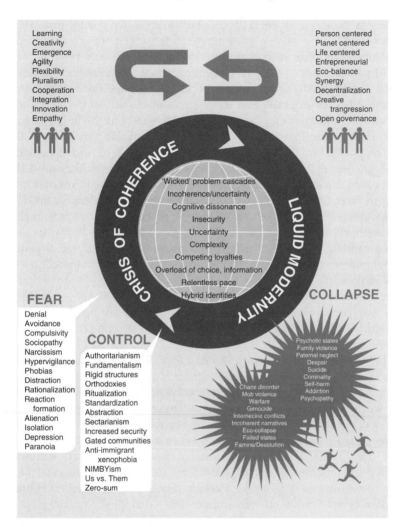

Figure 4.1 Transformation

resilient systems, however, a certain amount of anxiety, incoherence and threat may actually spur growth and learning. When enough mental and physical resources are available to do more than maintain, human imagination and creativity may result in a transformative process (see Figure 4.1). If it does, consciousness may undergo a holistic creative reordering into more highly developed frameworks with greater capacity to cope and transcend the current situation (Festinger 1957; Schön 1973; Kegan 1982; Csikszentmihalyi 1993; Torbert 2004). This does not appear to be an incremental process but rather a step change in capacity. Observations of complex dynamic systems suggest that, once incoherence reaches a critical level, though collapse is certainly possible, so is self-organization into a higher-order coherence (Maguire and McKelvey 1999; Kosse 2000). Observations of human groups show that human systems also self-organize and transformational shifts in the direction of increased complexity and capacity occur (Bowen et al. 1979; O'Hara and Wood 1984; Kauffman 1992; Banathy 2000; Alpaslan and Mitroff 2011; March 2011). For the new states to become stabilized and sustained at the higher levels, in individuals, groups and populations, they must then be worked through (Yankelovich 1991). This process requires that innovations have time to be discussed, tested, put into practice, reconsidered and modified through the social learning process until multiple anchoring connections on multiple levels are established. In this way a new psychosphere – either local or global – emerges with cognitive, organizational and governance structures in place that are better adapted to meet new challenges.

We are mindful of the human propensity to impose one's own hopes and fears upon inchoate signals (from which we are not exempt). We nevertheless believe that, along with clear signs of general defensiveness and localized collapse, a transformational process may be discernible in the 'Cambrian explosion' of human ingenuity under way worldwide. The WiserEarth database (www.wiserearth.org) now lists over a million different non-profit and social entrepreneurial groups worldwide that are working to bring about positive change, many of them operating at small scale outside the large aid agencies (Hawken 2007). While many bring a modernist, technology-focused agenda, Hawken reports that over 30 000 focus on community issues. A keyword search on values and mission descriptors used by these groups suggests that a new consciousness is at work. 'Participation', 'personal and community empowerment', 'authentic communication', 'dialogue', 'mutual respect', 'collective deliberation', 'talking across differences', 'active listening', 'empathy', 'decentralized governance', 'transformative conversation', 'collective intelligence', 'respectful relationships' and 'non-violent communication' show up frequently (O'Hara 2013). This is not a coordinated movement directed from anywhere in particular but rather a decentralized, loosely coupled ecology of people doing what humans do when faced with challenges that go beyond existing ways of addressing them: inventing new ways to advance human well-being – their own and other people's.

PART THREE: POLICY IMPLICATIONS OF AN EMERGING NEW CONTEXT

The theory we are advancing is that we are not simply in an era of change, but in a change of eras. Business as usual will not merely be inadequate in supporting human well-being, but might also be destructive, supporting ways of life that are psychologically, culturally and environmentally unsustainable. As the level of uncertainty and turbulence continues to mount, pressure will increase on policy makers and anxious citizens – in the words of the once again popular poster from Second World War Britain – to 'stay calm and carry on', that is, to redouble their efforts, employ tried-and-true strategies, and use resources within existing institutional and conceptual frameworks, and familiar forms of structural power to reduce anxiety, restore order and keep things from collapsing. This maintenance activity is necessary and in the short run useful where lowering volatility is essential and where the challenges faced are amenable to first-order solutions. But it is unlikely to be sufficient even in the medium let alone longer run. We see the need to direct at least some policy attention to the call of the longer-term future. As Michael (1997) puts it, we must plan to learn our way into an unknown, uncertain future and focus not only on individual and organizational learning, but on societal and cultural learning.

Policy makers today are well aware that mega-crises are looming and that new skills are required by today's citizens if they are to participate in the advanced economies of the twenty-first century. But so far the emphasis is on science, technology, engineering and mathematics (STEM), as if better technologies and more nimble business strategies will save us. Though advances in STEM skills will surely be necessary and policies to train more scientists and experts are clearly needed, unless the fundamental ways of being and understanding the world evolve beyond existing capacities this will not be enough.[8] Driven by expanded sources of information, 'big data'[9] and the speeded-up pace at which decisions must be made, the level of complexity of any situation outstrips existing mental, social, structural capacities (Hämäläinen 2007). This is a cultural problem not a technical one (Harrison and Hunter 2001). If the mindsets, which include deep psychic structure, levels of consciousness, ethics and logics that people bring to twenty-first-century challenges are those which evolved to address the challenges of the nineteenth, the chances of paradigmatic breakthrough are low. When faced with problems that are intractable at the current level, what we need is 'second-order' learning that not only changes what we know, but changes the grounds on which we know it, and changes who humans are as twenty-first-century persons.

'Third-order' reflective learning (Argyris and Schön 1978), which reviews its own assumptions as it goes forward, will be required by leaders and policy makers, and they too will have to become learners.

Towards a Learning Culture

So, how do we change a culture while still embedded in it?

When in unknown and confusing territory a compass is more useful than a map. In our view such a compass is not located in our abstractions, algorithms, models, ideology, objectivity, machines or even skills, but in Being that finds its expression in the bodies, hearts and minds of men and women who are fully alive and awake and are engaged in concrete challenges. So we turn our focus to how we might *learn to create a new cultural context* that will enable more fulfilling lives. This less travelled path has in our view the best chance of reducing suffering and enhancing well-being in sustainable ways. This is the path of *humanization* that puts persons as human 'beings-for-themselves' in the centre of social policy, and the living planet (including our place in it) at the centre of the emerging global psychosphere.

Accepting the extent of our ignorance is a first step. Otherwise we will continue to see outdated ways of doing things as the only options. Some help from people and groups experienced at deep learning might be useful. Transformative learners are to be found in many walks of life – among artists, scientists, entrepreneurs, the marginalized and even those straining to keep current systems from collapsing – but they are not usually asked for help. The responsibility for learning does not rest only with the experts but must include a requisite variety of viewpoints to match the scope and complexity of the task ahead.

Because second-order learning disrupts the status quo, spaces need to be developed that operate outside the culture, institutions and personalities of established expertise. For example, in a recent policy conversation about a Scottish city's transport infrastructure for cyclists, one citizen exemplified a reflective second-order move when he said:

> We are obsessed by providing an extra strip of tarmac for cyclists. *This is a product of how we are taught to think. We would do better to consider how we might reconceive the public realm so that the experience of using it evokes well-being.* It gives the message you are welcome here; sit; walk; talk; pass through; enjoy. (Emphasis added)

Once the second-order reframing was made by this one participant other participants were able to make the same frame-changing leap. Hämäläinen (2007) proposes that transformative learning spaces can be developed by 'institutional entrepreneurs' who see the need and will take risks that established institutions cannot. Omer (2005) suggests that in order to learn how to take successful action that is both transgressive *and* generative we look to those who live successfully on the margins and have come to understand the dynamics of their relationship to the centre. Omer uses Gandhi's salt march of 1930, part of his Free India movement, to illustrate the point. The Salt Act of 1882 made it illegal for Indians to freely collect salt – a basic necessity of similar meaning to a diverse range of social groups. Instead, they had to buy it as a heavily taxed commodity. Gandhi led a small group from his ashram to Dandi, where they picked up naturally occurring salt, thus breaking the law. Eighty thousand Indians were imprisoned for this transgressive action, which attracted worldwide attention to injustice in India and drew significant concessions from the colonial government. Artists, playwrights, public intellectuals and Occupy heretics may fulfil similarly transgressive roles, opening up spaces for imagination and new forms of action not predictable from within existing frames.

Cultural Learning

Several models for human-centred cultural learning have been developed. In our work in the International Futures Forum we draw on the I-Space model (Boisot et al. 2007), which follows a cyclical process that moves from holistic embodied knowing – hunches, intuitions and rules of thumb which arise uniquely and creatively from concrete experiences in the world – to codification into generalizations, theories, models and schemata which can be articulated.[10] Though the move from inchoate awareness to consolidation and explication involves a reduction and some loss of resolution, it gains in communicability and can be shared through TED talks, scientific publications, Hollywood movies, university lectures and public policy documents. Once diffused to become part of a now altered psychosphere it becomes a new contextual basis for concrete experiences.

Cultural capacity for authentic well-being that honours the aspirations of persons-for-themselves starts with public participation in multiple forms of discourse about each person's particular meaning of a well-lived life within particular contexts. This diversity of individual perspectives informs the process of insight and consensus development, policy formulation and action. In absorbing the implications of new insights, human networks transform their perspectives and the cycle regenerates itself through learning. The new sustaining narratives emerge from the combined voices of fully expressed personal truths and gain validity not from statistical significance but from freedom and fullness of participation in a context of mutual respect and care (O'Hara 1997; O'Hara and Wood 2004).

The iterative nature of the process, wherein holistic and interpretative modes of knowing including embodied and non-textual knowing are combined with focused analytics, provides a non-reductionist model for a postmodern knowledge-generating process. Abstractions can be checked against subjective lived experience, and individual experience can be informed by generalizations and models developed within one's own community, thereby encouraging integration of abstract and embodied knowledge into an evolving cycle of learning.

Promising paradigms for new non-reductionist learning include dialectical synthesis of agency and communion by integrating concepts from East and West (Ng et al. 2003), complexity science (González et al. 2010), second-order learning theory (Bohm 2004; Brown and Sice 2005), phenomenology (Küpers 2005), transformative soft-systems design (Reason 1994; Banathy and Jenlink 2004; Tsivasou 2004), action inquiry (Reason 1994; Torbert 2004) and appreciative inquiry (Cooperrider and Whitney 2000). The policy dialogues developed by Rosell and Yankelovich (Yankelovich 1991), Bohmian dialogues (Isaacs 1999; Bohm 2004; Scharmer 2007), Theory U (Scharmer 2007), World Cafe (Brown and Isaacs 2005), emancipatory education based on the work of Paulo Freire (1973), and the praxis of the International Futures Forum with communities in transition and education leaders in the US and UK are among a burgeoning plenitude of participatory social learning processes that have shown promise in complex situations with multiple stakeholders where creative ideas and contributions as well as felt needs are included in the co-creation of the emerging but as yet unknown future.

CONCLUSION

Faced with the fundamental uncertainty and complexity which multiple unknown unknowns bring we have two main choices: reduce complexity or increase capacity. We have argued that, in an interregnum where the guiding narratives inherited from the Enlightenment no longer serve, but before any more adaptive narratives have coalesced, policy makers must seek to do both and they must be clear about which is maintenance work and which is future facing.

We should not view well-being as a measurable commodity but as an integral dimension of the holistic capacity for life, a resource through which a good life is made more possible. As the chapters in this volume collectively demonstrate, well-being is *a function of whole systems where each element is a participant in the interconnected whole*. If we are serious about supporting happiness and well-being through policy, the goal should be to reduce unnecessary defensive procedures that, though they reduce complexity, do so by imposing a false coherence. We consider the rampant standardization, simplistic causal logic applied to complex emergent messy systems, reliance on outdated paradigms, over-regulation of human systems where freedom and improvisation are needed, and under-regulation of automated systems that avoid human responsibility to be in this category. At the same time, policy should nurture the emergence of a new learning society that offers authentic coherence and creates opportunities for the expansion of collective and individual capacity for a fully human life and always with global intent.

One of the greatest assets of our species is that we are not blocks of identical biological material which if manipulated in the same way will yield the same result every time. There is more likelihood of increased subjective well-being by any measure if the subject is allowed in the act. In the search for happiness we should not mistake it for an abstraction, nor separate it from biography and culture, nor seek it outside the history of a well-lived life nor our species' relationship to the planet upon which all else depends.

NOTES

1. The Enlightenment heritage is explicit in the work of Daniel Kahneman, who recommends that we go 'back to Bentham' and utilitarianism in behavioural economics (Kahneman et al. 1997).
2. O'Hara (2009) uses the term 'psychosphere' to refer to the holistic, 'interconnected, interpenetrated mutually influential system of narratives, symbols, images, representations, languages, metaphors, patterns of life, values, epistemologies, cognitive habits, rituals, religions, power relationships, sports, forms of commerce, governance, metaphysics, art, and technologies' that delineates the psychological context of individual and group life.
3. Seligman and Csikszentmihalyi (2000) for instance dismiss the earlier positive psychology of Maslow, Rogers and humanistic psychology, claiming it has 'failed its science examination' because phenomenology and case study are 'sloppy'.
4. Notable exceptions are the work of Ryff and Keyes, who include humanistic–existential models of well-being in their seminal paper (1995), and Hämäläinen (this volume, Chapter 2).
5. The use of 'subjective' in 'subjective well-being' (SWB) is illustrative. In the history and philosophy of psychology, 'subjective' refers to a multi-layered process of knowledge production that weighs feelings, cognitions, perception, interpretation, moral reasoning, insight and intuition (Manicas and Secord 1983). In SWB research it refers only to the fact that the data originates in direct questions to people and not to indirect assessments based on factors such poverty statistics or GDP.
6. We are concerned, though, that this project involves over a million service members, and was adopted by the US military before any evidence was available that showed that positive psychology was effective in this application (Eidelson et al. 2011).
7. This schematic is based on contemporary psychodynamic (Stolorow 2007), existential humanistic (May 1950; Cooper 2003), cognitive-neuropsychology (Bishop et al.

2006) and cognitive development (Kegan 1982; Markus and Zajonc 1985) theories. Description of collective anxiety processes draws from classic research on prejudice (Allport 1958), genocide and sectarian violence (Dutton 2007), social pathology (Fromm 1955; Levin 1987a, 1987b), organizational culture change (Schein 1992), large 'mega-messes' in society (Alpaslan and Mitroff 2011) and studies in the behaviour of complex dynamic human systems (Maguire and McKelvey 1999).

8. The Lumina Foundation Degree Qualifications Profile (DQP) (Lumina Foundation for Education 2011), which is being piloted in universities in the US, identifies five knowledge areas that they propose be the focus of all US degrees from associate to master's level. These are intellectual skills, civic learning, specialized knowledge, applied learning and integrative knowledge. The DQP explicitly excludes 'fostering personal growth and helping students examine their values and commitments' (Lumina Foundation for Education 2011, p. 2), because, although many universities consider these as part of their mission, they do not include them as requirements for awarding degrees.

9. The term 'big data' is used in information technology circles as a shorthand for increasingly large, interconnected, abstract data sets which are becoming increasingly difficult to manipulate, store and understand.

10. The I-Space model, which embraces a duality of holism and focus, seeing one within the context of the other, has much in common with Nonaka and Konno's (1998) concept of 'ba' in the SECI model for knowledge generation and dissemination within organizations.

REFERENCES

Ahmed, N.M. (2010), *A User's Guide to the Crisis of Civilization: And How to Save It*, London: Pluto, Macmillan.

Alexander, B. (2008), *The Globalisation of Addiction: A Study in the Poverty of the Spirit*, Oxford: Oxford University Press.

Allport, G.W. (1958), *The Nature of Prejudice*, New York: Doubleday.

Alpaslan, C.A. and I.I. Mitroff (2011), *Swans, Swine, and Swindlers: Coping with the Growing Threat of Mega-crises and Mega-messes*, High Reliability and Crisis Management, Stanford, CA: Stanford Business Books.

Antonovsky, A. (1979), *Health, Stress and Coping: New Perspectives on Mental and Physical Well-being*, San Francisco, CA: Jossey-Bass.

Argyris, C. and D. Schön (1978), *Organizational Learning*, Reading, MA: Addison-Wesley.

Banathy, B.H. (2000), *Guided Evolution of Society: A Systems View*, New York: Kluwer.

Banathy, B. and P. Jenlink (eds) (2004), *Dialogue as a Means of Collective Communication*, New York: Kluwer/Plenum.

Bardhan, P. (1995), *Poverty Alleviation*, Occasional Paper No. 1, New York: Overseas Development Council.

Bartlett, A.A. (1997), 'Is there a population problem?', *Wild Earth*, **7** (3) (Fall), 88–90.

Bateson, G. (1972), *Steps to an Ecology of Mind*, New York: Ballantine.

Bauman, Z. (2010), *Letters from the Liquid Modern World*, Cambridge: Polity.

Beddoe, R., R. Costanza, J. Farley, E. Garza, J. Kent, I. Kubiszewski, L. Martinez, T. McCowen, K. Murphy, N. Myers, Z. Ogden, K. Stapleton and J. Woodward (2009), 'Overcoming systemic roadblocks to sustainability: the evolutionary redesign of worldviews, institutions and technologies', *Proceedings of the National Academy of Sciences of the United States of America*, **106** (8), 2483–9.

Beer, S. (1973), 'Designing freedom', Massey Lectures, Canadian Broadcast Corporation.

Belenky, M., B.M. Clinchy, N. Goldberger and J.M. Tarule (1997), *Women's Ways of Knowing: The Development of Self, Voice and Mind*, New York: Basic Books.

Bishop, S.J., R. Jenkins and A.D. Lawrence (2006), 'Neural processing of fearful faces: effects of anxiety are gated by perceptual capacity limitations', *Cerebral Cortex*, **17** (7), 1595–1603.

Bjørnskov, C. (2008), 'How comparable are the Gallup World Poll life satisfaction data?', *Journal of Happiness Studies*, **11**, 41–60.

Bohm, D. (2004), *On Dialogue*, London: Routledge.

Boisot, M.H., I.C. MacMillan and K.S. Han (2007), *Explorations in Information Space: Knowledge, Agents and Organizations*, Oxford: Oxford University Press.

Bowen, M.V., M. O'Hara, C.R. Rogers and J.K. Wood (1979), 'Learnings in large groups: implications for the future', *Education*, **100** (2), 108–17.

Bowers, J.S. and C.S. Marsolek (2003), *Rethinking Implicit Memory*, Oxford: Oxford University Press.

Brown, J. and D. Isaacs (2005), *The World Cafe: Shaping Our Futures through Conversations That Matter*, San Francisco, CA: Berrett-Koehler.

Brown, J. and P. Sice (2005), 'Towards a second order research methodology', *Electronic Journal of Business Research Methodology*, **3** (1), 25–36.

Churchman, C.W. (1967), Guest editorial, *Management Science*, **14** (4).

Collinge, A., K. Rudell and K. Bhui (2002), 'Quality of life assessment in non-Western cultures', *International Review of Psychiatry*, **14** (3), 212–18.

Cooper, M. (2003), 'Between freedom and despair: existential challenges and contributions to person-centered and experiential therapy', *Person-Centered and Experiential Psychotherapies*, **2** (1), 43–56.

Cooperrider, D. and D. Whitney (2000), *Collaborating for Change: Appreciative Inquiry*, San Francisco, CA: Berrett-Koehler.

CSDH (Commission on Social Determinants of Health) (2008), *Closing the Gap in a Generation: Health Equity through Action on the Social Determinants of Health – Final Report of the Commission on Social Determinants of Health*, Geneva: World Health Organization.

Csikszentmihalyi, M. (1993), *The Evolving Self: A Psychology for the Third Millennium*, New York: Harper Perennial.

Cummins, R.A. and A. Lau (2006), *Personal Wellbeing Index: International Wellbeing Group Manual 2005*, 4th edn, Melbourne: Australian Centre on Quality of Life, Deakin University, available at: http://www.deakin.edu.au/research/acqol/instruments/wellbeing_index.htm.

Davidson, L., J. Takfeldt and J. Strauss (2010), *The Roots of the Recovery Movement in Psychiatry*, New York: Wiley.

Diamond, J. (2005), *Collapse: How Societies Choose to Fail or Succeed*, New York: Viking.

Dror, Y. (2001), *The Capacity to Govern*, Portland, OR: Frank Cass.

Duran, E. and B. Duran (1995), *Native American Postcolonial Psychology*, Albany: State University of New York Press.

Dutton, D.G. (2007), *The Psychology of Genocide, Massacres, and Extreme Violence: Why 'Normal' People Come to Commit Atrocities*, Westport, CT: Praeger Security International.

Eidelson, R., M. Pilisuk and S. Soldz (2011), 'The dark side of comprehensive soldier fitness', *American Psychologist*, **66** (7), 643–4.

Elliott, L. and D. Atkinson (2009), *The Gods That Failed and How Blind Faith in the Markets Has Cost Us the Future*, New York: Nation Books.

Festinger, L. (1957), *A Theory of Cognitive Dissonance*, Stanford, CA: Stanford University Press.

Freire, P. (1973), *Education for Critical Consciousness*, New York: Continuum.

Freud, S. (1959), *Group Psychology and the Analysis of the Ego*, trans. J. Strachey, New York/London: Liveright/International Psychoanalytic Press.

Fromm, E. (1955), *The Sane Society*, New York: Henry Holt.

Geertz, C. (1979), 'From the native's point of view: on the nature of anthropological understanding', in P. Rabinow and W.M. Sullivan (eds), *Interpretive Social Psychology*, Berkeley: University of California Press, pp. 225–41.

Gilding, P. (2011), *The Great Disruption*, New York: Bloomsbury.

González, M., G. Coenders, M. Saez and F. Casa (2010), 'Non-linearity, complexity and limited measurement in the relationship between satisfaction with specific life domains and satisfaction with life as a whole', *Journal of Happiness Science*, **11**, 335–52.

Gould, S.J. (1996), *The Mismeasure of Man*, rev. edn, New York: Norton.

Habermas, J. (1971), *Knowledge and Human Interests*, trans. J.J. Shapiro, Boston, MA: Beacon.

Hämäläinen, T.J. (2007), 'Social innovation, structural adjustment and economic performance', in T.J. Hämäläinen and R. Heisakala (eds), *Social Innovations, Institutional Change and Economic Performance*, Cheltenham, UK and Northampton, MA, USA: Edward Elgar Publishing.

Hanlon, P., S. Carlisle, M. Hannah and A. Lyon (2012), *The Future Public Health*, London: Open University Press.

Harman, W. (1998), *Global Mind Change: The Promise of the 21st Century*, 2nd edn, San Francisco, CA: Berrett-Koehler.

Harrison, L.E. and S.P. Hunter (2001), *Culture Matters*, New York: Free Press.

Hawken, P. (2007), *Blessed Unrest: How the Largest Movement in History Is Restoring Grace, Justice, and Beauty to the World*, New York: Penguin.

Hofstede, G. (1980), 'Motivation, leadership and organization: do American theories apply abroad?', *Organizational Dynamics*, **9** (1), 42–63.

Homer-Dixon, T. (2006), *The Upside of Down: Catastrophe, Creativity and the Renewal of Civilization*, Toronto: Knopf Canada.

Isaacs, W. (1999), *Dialogue: The Art of Thinking Together*, New York: Doubleday/Currency.

Ishii, K., A.J. Reyes and S. Kitayama (2003), 'Spontaneous attention to word content versus emotional tone: differences among three cultures', *Psychological Science*, **14** (1), 39.

Jacobs, J. (1961), *The Death and Life of Great American Cities*, New York: Random House.

Kahneman, D., P. Wakker and R. Sarin (1997), 'Back to Bentham? Explorations of experienced utility', *Quarterly Journal of Economics*, **112**, 375–406.

Kauffman, S.A. (1992), 'The sciences of complexity and "Origins of Order": principles of organization in organisms', in J.E. Mittenthal and A.B. Baskin (eds),

Proceedings of the SFI Studies in the Sciences of Complexity, Reading, MA: Addison-Wesley.

Kegan, R. (1982), *The Evolving Self: Problem and Process in Human Development*, Cambridge, MA: Harvard University Press.

Kegan, R. (1994), *In over Our Heads: The Mental Demands of Modern Life*, Cambridge, MA: Harvard University Press.

Kelly, E. (2005), *Powerful Times: Rising to the Challenge of Our Uncertain World*, Philadelphia, PA: Wharton School Publishing.

Kennedy, R.F. (1968), Address to the University of Kansas, 18 March, available at: http://www.jfklibrary.org/Research/Ready-Reference/RFK-Speeches/Remarks-of-Robert-F-Kennedy-at-the-University-of-Kansas-March-18-1968. aspx.

Kohlberg, L., C. Levine and A. Hewer (1983), *Moral Stages: A Current Formulation and a Response to Critics*, New York: Karger.

Korten, D. (2011), 'Occupy: A new conversation', *Yes Magazine*, 16 November, available at: http://www.yesmagazine.org/issues/the-yes-breakthrough-15/occupy-a-new-conversation.

Kosse, K. (2000), 'Some regularities in human group formation and the evolution of social complexity', *Complexity*, **6** (1).

Küpers, W. (2005), 'Phenomenology and integral pheno-practice of embodied well-be(com)ing in organizations', *Culture and Organization*, **11**, 221–32.

Lane, R.E. (2000), *The Loss of Happiness in Market Democracies*, New Haven, CT: Yale University Press.

Layard, R. (2006), 'The case for psychological treatment centres', *British Medical Journal*, **332**, 1030–32.

Leicester, G. and M. O'Hara (2009), *Ten Things to Do in a Conceptual Emergency*, Axminster, Devon: Triarchy Press.

Levin, D.M. (1987a), 'Psychopathology in the epoch of nihilism', in D.M. Levin (ed.), *Pathologies of the Modern Self: Postmodern Studies on Narcissism, Schizophrenia, and Depression*, New York: New York University Press.

Levin, D.M. (ed.) (1987b), *Pathologies of the Modern Self: Postmodern Studies on Narcissism, Schizophrenia, and Depression*, New York: New York University Press.

Loevinger, J. (1982), *Ego Development*, San Francisco, CA: Jossey-Bass.

Lu, L., R. Gilmour and S.F. Kao (2001), 'Cultural values and happiness: an East–West dialogue', *Journal of Social Psychology*, **141** (4), 477–93.

Lumina Foundation for Education (2011), *Degree Qualifications Profile*, Indianapolis, IN: Lumina Foundation.

McMichael, A.J., R.E. Woodruff and S. Hales (2006), 'Climate change and human health: present and future risks', *Lancet*, **367**, 859–69.

Maguire, S. and B. McKelvey (1999), 'Complexity management: moving from fad to firm foundations', *Emergence*, **1** (2), 19–61.

Manicas, P.T. and P.F. Secord (1983), 'Implications for psychology of the new philosophy of science', *American Psychologist*, **33**, 399–413.

March, K. (2011), 'Sociality, from an ecological, dynamical perspective', in G.R. Semin and G. Echterhoff (eds), *Grounding Sociality*, New York: Taylor & Francis, pp. 53–81.

Marks, N., S. Abdallah, A. Simms and S. Thompson (2006), *The Happy Planet Index*, London: new economics foundation.

Markus, H. and R.B. Zajonc (1985), 'The cognitive perspective in social psychology', in G. Lindzey and E. Aronson (eds), *Handbook of Social Psychology*, vol. 1, New York: Random House, pp. 225–305.

Maslow, A.H. ([1954] 1970), *Motivation and Personality*, New York: Harper & Row.

Maslow, A. ([1966] 1999), *Towards a Psychology of Being*, New York: Wiley.

Maslow, A.H. (1971), *The Farther Reaches of Human Nature*, New York: Penguin.

May, R. (1950), *The Meaning of Anxiety*, New York: Ronald Press.

Michael, D.N. (1973), 'Technology and the management of change from the perspective of a culture context', *Technology Forecasting and Social Change*, **5** (3), 219–32.

Michael, D.N. (1997), *Learning to Plan and Planning to Learn*, Alexandria, VA: Miles River Press.

Nandy, A. (1983), *The Intimate Enemy: Loss and the Recovery of Self under Colonialism*, New Delhi: Oxford University Press.

Ng, A.K., D.Y.F. Ho, S.S. Wong and I. Smith (2003), 'In search of the good life: a cultural odyssey in the East and West', *Genetic, Social and General Psychology Monographs*, **29** (4), 317–63.

Nisbett, R.E. (2003), *The Geography of Thought: How Asians and Westerners Think Differently . . . and Why*, New York: Free Press.

Noll, H.H. (2002), 'Social indicators and quality of life research: background, achievements and current trends', in N. Genov (ed.), *Advances in Sociological Knowledge over Half a Century*, Paris: International Social Science Council.

Nonaka, I. and N. Konno (1998), 'The concept of "ba": building a foundation for knowledge creation', *California Management Review*, **40** (3) (Spring).

Offer, Avner (2006), *The Challenge of Affluence: Self-control and Well-being in the United States and Britain since 1950*, Oxford: Oxford University Press.

O'Hara, M. (1997), 'Relational empathy: from egocentric modernism to sociocentric postmodernism', in A.C. Bohart and L.S. Greenberg (eds), *Empathy Reconsidered: New Directions in Psychotherapy*, Washington, DC: American Psychological Association, pp. 295–320.

O'Hara, M. (2009), 'Another inconvenient truth and the developmental role for psychology in a threatened world', *Humanistic Psychologist*, **38** (2), 101–19.

O'Hara, M. (2013), 'Person-centred approach as cultural leadership', in M. Cooper, M. O'Hara, P.F. Schmid and A.H. Bohart (eds), *The Handbook of Person-centred Psychotherapy and Counselling*, 2nd edn, Basingstoke: Palgrave.

O'Hara, M. and J.K. Wood (1984), 'Patterns of awareness: consciousness and the group mind', *Gestalt Journal*, **6** (2), 103–16.

O'Hara, M. and J.K. Wood (2004), 'Transforming communities: person-centered encounters and the creation of integral conscious groups', in B. Banathy and P. Jenlink (eds), *Dialogue as a Means of Collective Communication*, New York: Kluwer Academic/Plenum, pp. 95–126.

Omer, A. (2005), 'The spacious center: leadership and the creative transformation of culture', *Shift*, **6**, 30–33.

Pauchant, T.C. (ed.) (1994), *In Search of Meaning: Managing for the Health of Our Organizations, Our Communities and the Natural World*, San Francisco, CA: Jossey-Bass.

Polanyi, M. (1957), 'Scientific outlook: its sickness and its cure', *Science*, **125**, 480–84.

Polkinghorne, D. (1983), *Methodology for the Human Sciences*, Albany: State University of New York Press.

Reason, P. (1994), 'Three approaches to participative inquiry', in N.K. Denzin and Y.S. Lincoln (eds), *Handbook of Qualitative Research*, Thousand Oaks, CA: Sage, pp. 324–39.

Roberts, P. (2005), *The End of Oil: On the Edge of a Perilous New World*, New York: Houghton Mifflin.

Rogers, C.R. (1964), 'Towards a science of the person', in T.W. Wann (ed.), *Behaviorism and Phenomenology: Contrasting Bases for Modern Psychology*, Chicago, IL: University of Chicago Press, pp. 109–40.

Rosenberg, C.E. (1989), 'Disease in history: frames and framers', *Milbank Quarterly*, **67**, 1–15.

Ryff, C.D. and C.L.M. Keyes (1995), 'The structure of psychological well-being revisited', *Journal of Personality and Social Psychology*, **69** (4), 719–27.

Scharmer, C.O. (2007), *Theory U: Leading from the Future as It Emerges*, Cambridge, MA: Society for Organizational Learning.

Scheffler, I. (1967), *Science and Subjectivity*, New York: Bobbs-Merrill.

Schein, E.H. (1992), *Organizational Culture and Leadership*, San Francisco, CA: Jossey-Bass.

Schön, D.A. (1973), *Beyond the Stable State*, New York: W.W. Norton.

Scott, J.C. (1998), *Seeing like a State: How Certain Schemes to Improve the Human Condition Have Failed*, London: Yale University Press.

Seligman, M.E.P. and M. Csikszentmihalyi (2000), 'Positive psychology: an introduction', *American Psychologist*, **55** (1), 5–14.

Shweder, R.A. (1991), *Thinking through Cultures: Expeditions in Cultural Psychology*, Cambridge, MA: Harvard University Press.

Stavrianos, L.S. (1976), *The Promise of the Coming Dark Age*, New York: W.H. Freeman.

Stiglitz, J.E., A. Sen and J.-P. Fitoussi (2009), *Report by the Commission on the Measurement of Economic Performance and Social Progress*, available at: http://www.stiglitz-sen-fitoussi.fr/documents/rapport_anglais.pdf.

Stolorow, R. (2007), *Trauma and Human Existence: Autobiographical, Psychoanalytic, and Philosophical Reflections*, New York: Analytic Press.

Sundararajan, L. (2005), 'Happiness donut: a Confucian critique of positive psychology', *Journal of Theoretical and Philosophical Psychology*, **25**, 35–60.

Taylor, C. (1973), 'Peaceful co-existence in psychology', *Social Research*, **40**, 55–82.

Taylor, C. (1992), *Multiculturalism and the 'Politics of Recognition'*, Princeton, NJ: Princeton University Press.

Taylor, D.M. and G.M. Taylor (2007), 'The collapse and transformation of our world', *Journal of Futures Studies*, **11** (3), 29–46.

Taylor, F.W. (1919), *Principles of Scientific Management*, New York: Harper.

Torbert, B. (2004), *Action Inquiry*, San Francisco, CA: Berrett-Koehler.

Trickett, E.J., S. Beehler, C. Deutsch, L.W. Green, P. Hawe, K. McLeroy, R.L. Miller, B.D. Rapkin, J.J. Schensul, A.J. Schulz and J.E. Trimble (2011), 'Advancing the science of community-level interventions', *American Journal of Public Health*, **101** (8), 1410–1719.

Tsivasou, I. (2004), 'Designing communities of ideas for human well-being', in B. Banathy and P. Jenlink (eds), *Dialogue as a Means of Collective Communication*, New York: Kluwer/Plenum, pp. 41–70.

Vickers, G. (1983), *Human Systems Are Different*, London: Harper & Row.

WHO (World Health Organization) (2004), *Promoting Mental Health: Concepts,*

Emerging Evidence, Practice – Summary Report, report from the World Health Organization, Department of Mental Health and Substance Abuse in collaboration with the Victorian Health Promotion Foundation (VicHealth) and the University of Melbourne, Geneva: WHO.

WHO (World Health Organization) (2011), *World Mental Health Atlas*, Geneva: WHO.

Wilber, K. (2000), *Integral Psychology: Consciousness, Spirit, Psychology, Therapy*, Boston, MA: Shambhala.

Wilkinson, R.G. and K. Pickett (2009), *The Spirit Level: Why Greater Equality Makes Societies Stronger*, New York: Bloomsbury Press.

Yankelovich, D. (1991), *Coming to Public Judgment: Making Democracy Work in a Complex World*, Syracuse, NY: Syracuse University Press.

PART II

Restoring the centrality of the social

5. Understanding and improving the social context of well-being

John F. Helliwell*

INTRODUCTION

Most theory and practice aimed at understanding and improving human well-being deals with individuals, and largely ignores their social interactions. Likewise, both theory and practice tend to focus on individual problems and how they can be fixed. This chapter attempts to fill these gaps, first by showing the fundamental importance of the social context, and then by showing how well-being can be improved by changing the focus from repair of damage to building happier lives. Both of these new directions are based on recent theoretical and empirical advances in the study of subjective well-being. Treating people's self-assessments of the quality of their lives as valid measures of well-being exposes the importance of the social context and suggests new ways to design better policies.

The chapter starts with demonstrations of the fundamental importance of the social context, building on the unexpectedly great well-being consequences of social and pro-social behaviour. In addition, evidence is advanced to show an evolutionary fitness for social and pro-social behaviours above and beyond those flowing through their direct consequences for subjective well-being. This is followed by discussion of specific measures of the social context, and of the fundamental importance of trust as social glue.

Turning then to policy applications, the chapter deals with valuing the social context, building the evidence base for improving the social context, and demonstrating a variety of policy applications.

HUMANS ARE SOCIAL BEINGS

Seen in evolutionary context, brains are expensive, occupying only 2 per cent of adult human body weight but requiring 20 per cent of total energy intake (Aiello and Wheeler 1995). Early comparative studies argued that this costly brain was needed to survive and prosper in complex feeding and foraging environments (Clutton-Brock and Harvey 1980). It has since been argued that primate brains are larger than required by the relative complications of their ecologies (Dunbar 1998), and that this extra size is located in the prefrontal cortex, that recently evolved part of the brain devoted to the computational demands of complex social systems. This was first labelled Machiavellian intelligence (Bryne and Whitten 1988), reflecting its original focus on strategies of deception and dominance, but was later set in a broader context as the social brain hypothesis (Dunbar 1998). Using several sorts of data, Dunbar argues that the evolution of large human prefrontal cortices was required by the complexities of managing social groups, and was justified, despite its substantial resource cost, by the great benefits from these more complex social interactions. The evidence includes data showing that across genetically quite separate primate species there is a strong correlation between prefrontal cortex size and the existence, size and intensities of social groups (Schultz and Dunbar 2007). A further link between prefrontal cortex size and social groupings is that the adult cortex size across primate species correlates not with the duration of gestation, lactation or life, but with the length of the juvenile period, during which social learning is concentrated (Joffe 1997).

Contemporary evidence of the power and fundamental nature of social activities is provided by two recent experiments. E.E.A. Cohen et al. (2010) found that pain thresholds were much higher for rowers doing an ergometer workout in synchrony, compared to doing the identical work alone. In a lighter vein, laughing together (while watching comedy) significantly increased pain thresholds compared to watching and laughing alone (Dunbar et al. 2011). Hence social activities, even of a fairly basic sort (as with simple synchrony), significantly increase physical and presumably mental capacities to deal with challenges.

Much of this evolutionary analysis is done in narrowly utilitarian terms: expensive brain developments were evolutionarily successful because the social activities thereby increased group fitness and survival powers. The notion of group fitness as sufficient grounds for evolutionary success was challenged strongly by Williams (1966) and more famously by Dawkins (1976). Both emphasized that fitness at the individual gene level was required for evolutionary success. Dawkins's 'selfish gene' description was taken by many to suggest not just that the evolutionary success of genes was dependent only on their own fitness, but that individuals were by some parallel reason selfish. At the very least, this forced evolutionists to be more clear about the channels through which social and pro-social behaviour could achieve evolutionary fitness. West et al. (2007) advocate a four-way classification of behaviours that have been selected for by natural selection, scored by their effects on the actor and the recipient, respectively: mutual benefit $(+/+)$, altruism $(-/+)$, selfishness $(+/-)$ and spite $(-/-)$. To keep the altruistic category conceptually clean, they recommend doing the accounting long-term rather than immediately (to permit what is often called 'reciprocal altruism' to be treated as mutually beneficial) and making 'weak altruism' only ambiguously altruistic. Weak altruism is defined as action that leads to negative direct benefits for the actor relative to other members of the group. But, if the group as a whole benefits from the action, then the actor can have negative effects relative to the group but possibly even larger positive effects flowing from membership in the group thereby benefited (perhaps the boy with his finger in the dyke?). Thus some models that have been described as altruistic because individuals contribute when they could have been free riders might actually increase fitness even at the individual level, and hence might better be described as mutually advantageous or ambiguous cases.

However the edges of the categories are drawn, the prevalence of mutual advantage situations, and hence the evolutionary advantages of social and pro-social behaviour, are likely to be larger if social and pro-social behaviour increases subjective well-being. Why might this be the case?

First, the difficulty of assembling and motivating groups of sufficient size and community of interests to meet effective environmental challenges is bound to be less if members of the species in question have and enjoy good social relations. For example, the strength of social ties has been shown to predict increased cooperation in a social network (Harrison et al. 2011), and many studies have shown that even modest amounts of face-to-face connection significantly increase willingness to cooperate (see the meta-analysis by Balliet 2010).

Second, in addition to all these practical advantages, social engagement makes people happy. Such a happiness bonus would itself produce an evolutionary advantage for the species, because that part of the prefrontal cortex used for problem-solving but energy-using (Kahneman 2011) thinking[1] works more effectively, and suffers less fatigue, when people are happy (Diamond 2007). If social activity in and of itself makes people happy, then effective groups are less costly (in terms of the required size and energy use of the prefrontal cortex) to create and manage. Hence there is likely to be an overall efficiency gain when, as is the case for modern humans, people simply enjoy each other's company. Thus, in the model of Gintis (2000), any enjoyment-driven costly cooperative behaviour will increase the chances that a community will cohere and survive in bad times.

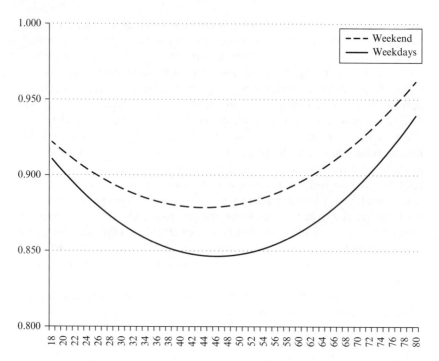

Figure 5.1   Happiness by age, on weekdays and weekends

Figure 5.1 provides one example drawn from a vast range of data showing the links between social activity and happiness. For each age, average happiness scores are reported separately for weekends and weekdays. Over half a million respondents to the Gallup Healthways US daily poll were asked how happy they were yesterday. As shown in Helliwell and Wang (2011b) the only significant day-of-the-week patterns were between weekdays and weekends (where the latter includes all statutory holidays). For all ages, but especially for those ages when full-time work is the norm, weekends are happier than weekdays. By itself, this finding is interesting, but not a convincing demonstration of the importance of the social context, because leisure is usually assumed to be happier than work. But when the results are analysed in more detail the correlates of the extra weekend happiness are exposed to be social.

Across individuals, the number of hours of social activity the day before is a strong correlate of the happiness reported for that day, and average number of daily hours spent in social activities is one-third larger on weekends. Most of the rest of the weekend effect is determined by the relative quality of the social context at home and at work. For example, the weekend effect is less than half as large for those who regard their immediate work supervisor as a partner as it is for those who see the supervisor as a boss (Helliwell and Wang 2011b, fig. 3.3). Differences in the time available for social activities are also likely to be a major part of the reason for the U-shapes of Figure 5.1, which show that happiness is lowest in midlife, where the competing time pressures from work and home are greatest, thereby reducing the time available for, and the pleasures derived from, social interactions. For example, the happiness effects of having children are more frequently positive on weekends than on weekdays, and for those who are not in full-time employment.

Many other studies have shown that life satisfaction is higher for those who have larger networks of both family and friends, and who are able to spend more time with them. Thus both the existence and the use of social networks are important supports for well-being, even when other factors are taken into account. People with supportive social networks feel more sense of belonging in their communities, which adds even more to their satisfaction with life. For example, a strong sense of belonging to one's community has the same association with life satisfaction as would a trebling of household income (Helliwell and Barrington-Leigh 2011, table 4.1).

HUMANS ARE PRO-SOCIAL BEINGS

We have seen that people are happier when they are with other people. This already provides a stronger basis for individuals to want to build and use their social linkages, and these linkages in turn increase the prospects of finding collaborative solutions to community problems. The evolutionary advantage of sociability would be even greater if humans enjoyed doing things not just with others, but also for others (Batson and Shaw 1991). This makes the study of pro-social behaviour important for the theory of evolution, for the prediction of human behaviour and for the design of public policies.

What does the evidence show? First, when people are in bilateral social relationships that involve one person helping the other, it is often, or perhaps usually, the giver who receives the bigger boost in subjective well-being. For example, Schwartz and Sendor (1999) find that in patient-based peer-to-peer counselling of multiple sclerosis patients the subjective well-being benefits are larger and more prolonged for givers than for receivers. What is especially telling about the example is that the original study only looked at the benefits for recipients, reflecting the standard assumption that the values of kindness flow to the recipients rather than the donors. Only afterwards did researchers think to assess the well-being consequences for the givers. Hence there are still relatively few studies that even try to compare the well-being benefits for givers and receivers. One prospective study (Brown et al. 2003) showed that subsequent mortality experiences were better for givers than receivers of help. A more recent qualitative study of the consequences for supporters in peer-to-peer counselling among female cancer patients (Pistrang et al. 2013) showed that, while the givers were sometimes apprehensive about possible ill-effects on their own recovery and ability to cope, they instead found the process very rewarding in several ways, and most especially in subjective well-being.[2]

Second, comparative cross-cultural experiments have been combined with international survey data from more than 130 countries to suggest that the happiness effects of pro-social acts have claims to be universal features of human behaviour. Although the form and purpose of giving differ from country to country, depending upon needs and customs, those who give are happier than those who do not (Aknin et al. 2010). This is consistent with experimental results from 15 different societies showing that cooperative behaviour in experimental games is greater everywhere than would be predicted using selfish assumptions (Henrich et al. 2001).

Third, although their pro-social acts make them happier, many people appear to underestimate the extent of this effect (Dunn et al. 2008), just as they tend to overestimate the subjective well-being they will get from higher incomes and consumption. One possible, although somewhat convoluted, rationale for this might be that the so-called 'warm glow' obtained by doing things for others might be less warm if it were foreseen, and hence open to be seen as a more sophisticated form of selfishness. Perhaps it is no coincidence that almost every religion has a version of the golden rule as a primary tenet. It has been documented that the existence of such advisory rules has a significant effect on behaviour, and hence can provide a way for unselfish benevolence to get its full happiness reward. For example, student subjects showed some modest tendency to give themselves higher grades than they had earned (self-awarded scores exceeded the true scores by just under 7 per cent, on average; Mazar et al. 2008, experiment 1), but had no such tendency if they had previously been asked to write down as many as they could remember of the Ten Commandments. This is in contrast to the dishonest marking of the unprimed control group and another comparison group asked instead to write down the names of ten books they had read in high school. External reputation also matters. Tirole and Benabou (2010) survey studies showing not just that people want to do the right thing, but that they also want to be seen to do so.

HEALTH FEEDBACKS STRENGTHEN THE EVOLUTIONARY CASE FOR THE PRO-SOCIAL BRAIN

There is a positive feedback loop running from happiness induced by social behaviour back into better health outcomes, which in their turn support happiness. There is a large and growing literature showing that greater happiness predicts better health (S. Cohen and Pressman 2006; Diener and Chan 2011). Through a variety of processes (e.g. Steptoe et al. 2005) positive affect reduces the onset and seriousness of diseases, from the common cold (S. Cohen et al. 2003) to suicide (Koivumaa-Honkanen et al. 2000) and all-cause mortality (Danner et al. 2001; Chida and Steptoe 2008). In addition to these general links from happiness to better health, there is evidence of direct links from social nurturing to better health and reproductive fitness (Huppert 2005, p. 312). For example, social support early in life is a strong predictor of health in adulthood, mediated in part by the quality of social relationships during adulthood (Shaw et al. 2004).

Finally, another large literature (surveyed by Lyubomirsky et al. 2005) shows a number of feedbacks from positive affect to marital and other social successes likely to support evolutionary fitness.

WHAT, ME WORRY?

If the positive feedback loop linking sociality, pro-sociality, happiness and health is so powerful in evolutionary terms, why is there so much unhappiness about? Is there an evolutionary downside to happiness that requires periodic doses of unease and distrust to make a viable evolutionary package? In his research into the evolutionary fitness of moods, Nesse (2004) argues that, even though a moderately high baseline mood is likely to be evolutionarily successful, for reasons like those outlined above, defence against threats requires negative emotions to spur hard thinking and timely action. An attitude of 'What, me worry?' poses an evolutionary disadvantage in the face of obstacles, whether physical or social in origin, requiring effective planning and actions if they are to be surmounted. Thus, for Nesse, negative emotions play an essential role as spurs to effortful actions needed to ensure survival. Of course, too much or misplaced anxiety may be counterproductive. And evolutionary lags may leave some unnecessary fears intact (fear of snakes is his example) while not yet instilling sufficiently immediate responses to the impending danger of a speeding car.

Kahneman (2011) makes the same point in a quite different way, using his distinction between System 1 (fast) and System 2 (slow) thinking. If people are either tired or happy, they are more likely to use their fast System 1 responses. System 1 thinking is less likely to see threats for what they are, and hence may be in trouble if the actual environment poses serious threats. Effortful System 2 analysis is required to assess risks, especially if they are novel or complicated, and to develop smart strategies for dealing with them. Being too mellow may leave System 2 powers switched off just when they are needed most.

Do these lines of thought threaten the evolutionary effectiveness of the pro-social brain? I think not. But they do require a more sophisticated interpretation. The Nesse and Kahneman analysis argues that a positive feedback loop linking sociality, happiness and health may threaten survival power if anxiety and defensive actions cannot be triggered when they are needed. That is a very important qualification.

The saving grace for the evolutionary power of social and pro-social behaviour, even including their happiness bonuses, is that effective social networks are better both at sounding appropriate alarms and at responding to them. What makes a socially connected community agile and effective in responding to threats is that its members do not have to waste their scarce System 2 resources, or be unduly anxious, about watching their backs. Since they are pro-social, and members can trust each other, the required watchfulness can be shared and delegated, and the best brains drawn upon for the design of fast action plans when the community faces new threats or challenges. Indeed, in terms of survival power, the evolutionary advantage of social and pro-social attributes is probably most in evidence not in times of happy rest, but when the group needs to act fast to deal with existential threats. That does require the capacity for bouts of watchful anxiety, and purposeful thinking, plus the capacity to act in concert when the need arises. It is not an accident that environmental or other crises can provide occasions for communities with high social capital to test their mettle and help each other. Examples where communities were drawn together under external threats include the Finnish experience during the Winter War (Kivimäki and Tepora 2009) and that of Aceh, Indonesia, in response to the 2004 tsunami (Deshmukh 2009). Less well endowed communities may at least be spurred to press the reset button eventually to develop a strategy to rebuild, as shown by Kusago's (2011) analysis of the destruction and eventual rebuilding of the community in Minamata, Japan, after many lives were lost through poisoning from a chemical plant. He illustrates how social connections were eventually rebuilt, enabling people to recover better lives from a disastrous starting point.

MEASURING THE SOCIAL CONTEXT

How is the social context to be defined and measured? One practical definition might be that any aspect of the social context is important in so far as it impinges on subjective well-being. This may leave out linkages of fundamental importance solely because they have not been isolated and studied enough for their importance to be revealed. In these relatively early years of attempting to define and assess the importance of different elements of the social context, the total importance of the social context has probably been understated, because of the lack of relevant measures for aspects of the social context that theory suggests are likely to be important.

Early empirical work on the social context of well-being was designed to value those aspects of the social context that had been identified and measured as part of social capital (see especially Putnam 2000). These initially included social trust (often seen as a measure of the efficacy of social capital) and a range of measures of social ties to friends, family and neighbours.

Soon after, surveys were extended to produce separate measures of the size and extent of use of various social networks. Both size and use were found to be important supports for overall measures of happiness and life satisfaction (Helliwell and Putnam 2004 for comparable Canadian and US estimates; and Helliwell and Barrington-Leigh 2011 for joint and separate estimates of the well-being effects of social network size and use).

More recently, measures of social identity have been used to mediate between social interactions and subjective well-being. One Canadian finding is that local belonging is more important than, but does not diminish or replace, more encompassing social identities. In particular, evidence from the Canadian General Social Survey shows that community-level, provincial and national senses of belonging are all important supports for life satisfaction, with the local effects being twice as large as those of provincial or national belonging (Helliwell and Barrington-Leigh 2011, table 4.1).

TRUST IS SPECIAL

Trust provides at once a fundamental measure of the quality of the social context and a key ingredient for successful collaborations. Interactions build trust, and vice versa. Trust appears to be more readily destroyed than rebuilt, although related evidence from well-being studies is not readily to hand. This asymmetry suggests that extra attention needs to be paid to maintaining the fabric of trust, since its subsequent re-establishment may be difficult to achieve. Where trust is low, but not too low, then an external threat can provide a spur to cooperation that would otherwise have been impossible to achieve.

Thus it was in the case already mentioned of the 2004 tsunami death and damage in Aceh, Indonesia. The shock was sufficient to break the long-established and even more damaging cycle of conflict that had previously existed. The well-being effects of ending the long conflict – the peace dividend – were so great that surveys showed subjective average life satisfaction to be higher after than before the tsunami. But trust levels can be so low, and conflicts so ingrained, that a natural disaster can make them even worse, and external relief efforts can deliver more grounds for conflict. Such was the case in Sri Lanka, where the direct tsunami damage was of the same magnitude as in Aceh, but the long-standing conflict was made even worse, and life satisfaction was much lower after than before the disaster (for a comparison of the two cases, see Deshmukh 2009). Where trust is high, or at least recoverable, then an external threat or physical disaster can create opportunities for trust and healthy social connections to be exercised and celebrated. Where trust is too low, then an external crisis provides one more thing to fight over, and more evidence of dysfunctional community life.

Where actual and expected trustworthiness differ, it is the expected level that dominates when people assess the quality of their lives. Analysis based on national surveys of the past and expected future incidence of property crimes shows a significant negative cross-country correlation ($r = -0.37$, $p = 0.05$) between subjective well-being and expected future rates of crime. No such relation shows up for variations in the actual incidence, even though both past occurrences and future prospects are derived from the same respondents in the same victimization surveys (Helliwell and Wang 2011a, pp. 55–6).

Although trust in neighbours and strangers delivers large happiness benefits, people underestimate the chances of their lost wallets being returned. Less than 25 per cent of the population of Toronto think that their cash-bearing wallets would be returned, but, when the *Toronto Star* dropped 20 cash-bearing wallets around town, 16 were returned, all but one with cash intact (Helliwell and Wang 2011a, p. 55).

Within workplaces, the importance of trust dwarfs the impact of salary and bonuses: to work where trust in management is one point higher, on a ten-point scale, has the same relation to life satisfaction as a one-third-higher income (Helliwell and Huang 2010). Yet many public and private workplaces have seen income disparities grow and trust levels fall over the past 30 years.

Trust is built by frequent chances to interact with strangers and neighbours, whether in lifts, buses, libraries or public spaces. Yet buildings are designed for looks and streets to move traffic, with scant thought for shared public spaces in which to build the trust needed to let children walk to school, workers collaborate for innovation, and passers-by smile. One example of such innovation is provided by the surge of interest in community gardens. Although these are usually undertaken to increase the availability and quality of locally grown food, they increase trust-building frequent social contacts that can sprout and sustain vibrant local social communities (Ladner 2011).

USING SUBJECTIVE WELL-BEING DATA TO VALUE THE SOCIAL CONTEXT

Experimental and survey evidence developed over the past 15 years now permits at least some aspects of the social context to be valued in ways that enable a possible revolution in the techniques used to assess public policies. Although benefit–cost analysis has become a standard tool for evaluating changes in government policies and many investment projects, the calculations are usually limited to outcomes for which a monetary value can be assigned. Other outcomes, including changes in the social context, were often recognized to be important. Yet as 'intangibles' they were frequently relegated to the footnotes. From there they would emerge only if two projects were more or less tied in terms of the calculated benefit–cost ratios.

All of this has now changed. Analysis of subjective well-being can now deliver estimates of the well-being contributions of income and various aspects of the social context. These in turn permit estimates of the income-equivalent values of different aspects of the social context. These are often described as 'compensating differentials', since they represent the amount of income sufficient to match the value of some aspect of the social context. These compensating differentials can be used to attach income-equivalent values to the social context, thereby lifting social capital and the quality of community life from the footnotes to the centre of benefit–cost analysis.

A Canadian study (Gyarmati et al. 2008) recruited people in six communities who were receiving either income assistance or employment insurance, and randomly selected those who were to receive instead a comparable income for working in community projects chosen and managed by each of the communities. Their subsequent conventional benefit–cost analysis took direct account only of the subsequent income and employment experience of those chosen for the programme, compared to the control group. Changes in community-level social trust were noted, but did not enter the conventional analysis explicitly. An extended benefit–cost analysis, making use of life satisfaction equations to attach values to improvements in the quality of community life, lifted the social context benefits from the footnotes into the central analysis. The resulting benefit–cost ratios were much higher, showing clearly the advantages of income maintenance programmes designed to increase the social capital of the participants and their communities.

BUILDING THE EVIDENCE BASE FOR BETTER POLICIES

Much of the early evidence on the value of the social context was based on cross-sectional survey data. While these results showed many important patterns, there was every indication of two-way relationships, with better social interactions leading to greater subjective well-being, and vice versa. The most convincing way of unravelling the underlying causal structures is to find some form of experimental intervention that can be treated as a trigger for a cascade of subsequent changes. If the intervention is a natural event, and researchers are fast-moving enough, then the consequences of the same changes playing out in different communities can be assessed. Thus it was possible to assess the consequences of new political powers in Italian regions with differing initial amounts of social capital (Putnam 1993; Helliwell and Putnam 1995). Alternatively, if the change affects some but not all communities, then the effects of the change can be established by comparison with otherwise similar communities that did not face the change (Gyarmati et al. 2008).

Where random-assignment tests of changes have been undertaken, they have typically operated at the individual level, often for reasons of cost or simplicity, usually without any consideration of variations in the social context. Thus there has been little experimental assessment of how differing social contexts alter the consequences of interventions. In the light of the importance of the social context, more of such research is badly needed. A UK experiment showed that starting a water club in a residential care facility, with increased water consumption as the central aim, produced significant health benefits. These were initially attributed to a lower incidence of dehydration, the frequency of which provided the impetus for creating the water club. Yet, when researchers subsequently decomposed the experiment into its club and water-drinking components (by comparison with an alternative social club that did not involve drinking water or anything else), it was found that it was the club rather than the water that increased health and well-being (Gleibs et al. 2011).

To broaden the evidence base for policy applications requires imaginative interplay between large surveys capturing population-level linkages, natural experiments, lab experiments, small-scale interventions and larger field trials.

BROADENING THE SCOPE OF POLICY APPLICATIONS

Discussions of policy uses of well-being research, whether pro or con, usually focus on national policies of conventional sorts, often relating to the use of taxation to redistribute income or expenditure, based on estimated relations between income and subjective well-being (e.g. Layard 2005). The importance of the social context of well-being, as documented in this chapter, suggests a much wider range of policy implications and applications.

The social circumstances underpinning subjective well-being are influenced by how all institutions are set up and managed. The 'how' of policy delivery is as important as the 'what' (Frey et al. 2004). As argued in this chapter, and more fully in Helliwell (2011b), there are clear implications for the management of institutions ranging from schools and hospitals (Haslam et al. 2008) to prisons (Helliwell 2011a; Leong 2011), workplaces (Helliwell and Huang 2011b), communities (Bacon et al. 2010; Halpern 2010) and elder care (Haslam et al. 2010). The elder care example helps to show why 'how' trumps 'what'. Elder care residents near Exeter, in the UK, were being transferred to a new facility, and the researchers set up an experiment to test the effects of what seemed a modest change in 'how' the move was done. There were two floors of residents in the facility, and they were treated as the control and treatment groups for the move to the new facility. The (initially) less happy floor was made the treatment group. Both groups had the same budget for the decoration of the common social areas in the new facility. The control group had their social spaces designed by professionals, while the residents of the unhappy floor were invited to work together to choose their own decor. This simplest possible change in the 'how' of service delivery led the previously unhappy floor to 50 per cent greater use of their new social spaces, compared to the happy floor. These effects were both significant and sustained. The previously unhappy floor became the happier floor, with more social connections and fewer health problems requiring a doctor's attention. Social context experiments like this are costly to administer, given the need for group intervention with comparable control groups, and this may help to explain why there has been so little research of this type into the possible gains from changing how public and private services are designed and delivered. Yet the results are so striking, and their applicability to many other contexts so obvious, that it is right to recommend and expect much more future attention to the 'how'.

The quality of government institutions has direct linkages to life satisfaction, with efficiency and trustworthiness likely to be more important than how the government is elected (Helliwell and Huang 2008).

Diverse policy innovations, each capable of being copied by others, can help to create better social contexts and more sustainable environments, in firms, neighbourhoods, NGOs and nations.

In the macroeconomic context, happiness equations have been used to estimate the comparable well-being values of national inflation and unemployment rates (Di Tella et al. 2001; Di Tella and MacCulloch 2009) and to compare the direct and indirect well-being consequences of unemployment (Helliwell and Huang 2011a). More direct macro policy implications of well-being findings are illustrated by the South Korean approach to macroeconomic policies designed to maintain income, employment, investment and fiscal balance following the 2008 global financial crisis (Helliwell 2011b, pp. 298–300). Recognizing the high subjective well-being costs of unemployment, the government acted to encourage both public and private employers to maintain employment, and to use their temporarily spare capacity to design and implement industrial changes for a Green Korea. 'The "grand social compact" which was agreed to in February 2009 set a guideline according to which the social partners should negotiate employment retention as a quid-pro-quo for wage concessions' (OECD 2010, p. 2). South Korea chose policies that could be argued to enhance subjective well-being, above and beyond any economic consequences, but still left Korea at the top of the international league table for crisis and post-crisis economic outcomes. The 'social compact' nature of the policy package almost surely contributed additional subjective well-being, according to the evidence reported elsewhere in this chapter. By redirecting activities rather than increasing unemployment, the policy strategy enabled all parties to see themselves not as competitors for fractions of a shrinking pie, but as collaborative contributors to outcomes designed to benefit all. Thus more recognition of what motivates behaviour, and what delivers better lives, can lead to policies that simultaneously deliver better economic and non-economic outcomes.

CONCLUSION

Research on the determinants of subjective well-being has already produced insights useful for governments, NGOs, communities, firms and families. The results confirm that sufficient income is a strong support for happiness, but that the social context is even more important. This is too often forgotten in the race for higher incomes and consumption.

Income matters less than the chance to connect with others, thereby improving our own lives and especially the lives of others. There is even evolutionary evidence that bulging human brains, and especially the prefrontal cortices, have been crucial in allowing humans to be the most social beings, living better lives through cooperation.

Within workplaces, the importance of the social context dwarfs the impact of salary and bonuses. To work where trust in management is one point higher, on a ten-point scale, has the same relation to life satisfaction as a one-third-higher income. Yet many public and private workplaces have seen income disparities grow and trust levels fall over the past 30 years.

Experiments in elder care facilities show that residents given the chance to do things together, to help themselves and others, live healthier and happier lives. Other experiments show that, although everybody gains from peer support groups among disease sufferers, the caregivers gain even more health and happiness than do the recipients.

Although trust in neighbours and strangers delivers huge happiness benefits, people overestimate the risks of future burglaries and underestimate the chances of their lost wallets being returned. Trust is built by frequent chances to interact with strangers and neighbours, whether in lifts, buses, libraries or public spaces. Yet buildings are designed for looks and streets to move traffic, with scant thought for the public spaces needed to build the trust needed to let children walk to school.

Other examples, ranging from delivery of health care and management of prisons and schools, to macroeconomic policies, show how governments can learn from happiness research to make lives better for all. Individuals and neighbours can lead the way, improving lives while showing governments better paths to follow.

NOTES

* An earlier version of this chapter was presented at the 15–16 December 2011 Helsinki meeting of the Sitra–nef project New Theories and Policies for Well-being. I am very grateful for subsequent helpful suggestions from Roland Benabou, Adele Diamond, Timo Hämäläinen, Alex and Cath Haslam, Danny Kahneman, Juliet Michaelson, Randy Nesse and Nancy Pistrang.
1. Kahneman (2011) contrasts this more reflective slow thinking with the fast instinctive reactions that are initially deployed in response to unfolding events. He refers to the latter as System 1 thinking, because of its first-responder role, while he refers to the more reflective and energy-using process as System 2 thinking.
2. Two examples are: 'It's been a very, very positive thing. I've walked away feeling really

happy that my very bad experience has benefited somebody else' and 'It was very nice to feel that you may have shone a bit of light into the corners of somebody else's dark room' (Pistrang et al. 2013, table 2).

REFERENCES

Aiello, L.C. and P. Wheeler (1995), 'The expensive tissue hypothesis', *Current Anthropology*, **36**, 184–93.

Aknin, L.B., C.P. Barrington-Leigh, E.W. Dunn, J.F. Helliwell, R. Biswas-Diener, I. Kemeza, P. Nyende, C.E. Ashton-James and M.I. Norton (2010), *Prosocial Spending and Well-being: Cross-cultural Evidence for a Psychological Universal*, NBER Working Paper No. 16415, Cambridge, MA: National Bureau of Economic Research.

Bacon, N., M. Brophy, N. Mguni, G. Mulgan and A. Shandro (2010), *The States of Happiness: Can Public Policy Shape People's Wellbeing and Resilience?*, London: Young Foundation.

Balliet, D. (2010), 'Conversation and cooperation in social dilemmas: a meta-analytic review', *Journal of Conflict Resolution*, **54**, 39–57.

Batson, C.D. and L.L. Shaw (1991), 'Evidence for altruism: toward a pluralism of prosocial motives', *Psychological Inquiry*, **2** (2), 107–22.

Brown, S.L., R.M. Nesse, A.D. Vinokur and D.M. Smith (2003), 'Providing social support may be more beneficial than receiving it: results from a prospective study of mortality', *Psychological Science*, **14** (4), 320–27.

Bryne, R. and R. Whitten (eds) (1988), *Machiavellian Intelligence*, Oxford: Oxford University Press.

Chida, Y. and A. Steptoe (2008), 'Positive psychological well-being and mortality: a quantitative review of prospective observational studies', *Psychosomatic Medicine*, **70**, 741–56.

Clutton-Brock, T.H. and P.H. Harvey (1980), 'Primates, brains and ecology', *Journal of Zoology*, **190** (3), 309–23.

Cohen, E.E.A., R. Ejsmond-Frey, N. Knight and R.I.M. Dunbar (2010), 'Rowers' high: behavioural synchrony is correlated with elevated pain thresholds', *Biology Letters*, **6** (1), 106–08.

Cohen, S. and S.D. Pressman (2006), 'Positive affect and health', *Current Directions in Psychological Science*, **15** (2), 22–5.

Cohen, S., W.J. Doyle, R.B. Turner, C.M. Alper and D.P. Skoner (2003), 'Emotional style and susceptibility to the common cold', *Psychosomatic Medicine*, **50**, 652–7.

Danner, D.D., D.A. Snowdon and W.D. Friesen (2001), 'Positive emotions in early life and longevity: findings from the nun study', *Journal of Personality and Social Psychology*, **80**, 804–13.

Dawkins, R. (1976), *The Selfish Gene*, Oxford: Oxford University Press.

Deshmukh, Y. (2009), 'The "hikmah" of peace and the PWI: impact of natural disasters on the QOL in conflict-prone areas: a study of the tsunami-hit transitional societies of Aceh (Indonesia) and Jaffna (Sri Lanka)', ISQOLS World Congress, Florence, July.

Diamond, A. (2007), 'Interrelated and interdependent', *Developmental Science*, **10** (1), 152–8.

Diener, E. and M.Y. Chan (2011), 'Happy people live longer: subjective well-being contributes to health and longevity', *Applied Psychology: Health and Well-Being*, **3** (1), 1–43.

Di Tella, R. and R. MacCulloch (2009), 'Happiness, contentment and other emotions for central bankers', in C.L. Foote, L. Goette and S. Meier (eds), *Policymaking Insights from Behavioral Economics*, proceedings of a conference held September 2007, Boston, MA: Federal Reserve Bank of Boston, pp. 311–73.

Di Tella, R., R. MacCulloch and A. Oswald (2001), 'Preferences over inflation and unemployment: evidence from surveys of happiness', *American Economic Review*, **91** (1), 335–41.

Dunbar, R.I.M. (1998), 'The social brain hypothesis', *Evolutionary Anthropology*, **6** (5), 178–90.

Dunbar, R.I.M., R. Baron, A. Frangou, E. Pearce, E.J.C. van Leeuwen, J. Stow, G. Partridge, I. MacDonald, V. Barra and M. van Vugt (2011), 'Social laughter is correlated with elevated pain threshold', *Philosophical Transactions of the Royal Society B*, published online 14 September in advance of the print edition.

Dunn, E.W., L.B. Aknin and M.I. Norton (2008), 'Spending money on others promotes happiness', *Science*, **319**, 1687–8.

Frey, B.S., M. Benz and A. Stutzer (2004), 'Introducing procedural utility: not only what but how matters', *Journal of Institutional and Theoretical Economics*, **160**, 377–401.

Gintis, H. (2000), 'Strong reciprocity and human sociality', *Journal of Theoretical Biology*, **206**, 169–79.

Gleibs, I.H., C. Haslam, S.A. Haslam and J.M. Jones (2011), 'Water clubs in residential care: is it the water or the club that enhances health and well-being?', *Psychology and Health*, **26** (10), 1361–77.

Gyarmati, D., S. de Raaf, B. Palameta, C. Nicholson and T. Hui (2008), *Encouraging Work and Supporting Communities: Final Results of the Community Employment Innovation Project*, Ottawa: Social Research and Demonstration Corporation.

Halpern, D. (2010), *The Hidden Wealth of Nations*, Cambridge: Polity Press.

Harrison, F., J. Sciberras and R. James (2011), 'Strength of social tie predicts cooperative investment in a human social network', *Plos One*, **6** (3), e18338, doi: 10.1371/journal.pone.0018338.

Haslam, C., A. Holme, S.A. Haslam, A. Iyer, J. Jetten and W.H. Williams (2008), 'Maintaining group memberships: social identity continuation predicts well-being after a stroke', *Neuropsychological Rehabilitation*, **18** (5/6), 671–91.

Haslam, C., S.A. Haslam, J. Jetten, A. Bevins, S. Ravenscroft and J. Tonks (2010), 'The social treatment: the benefits of group interventions in residential care settings', *Psychology and Aging*, **25** (1), 157–67.

Helliwell, J.F. (2011a), 'Institutions as enablers of well-being: the Singapore Prison case study', *International Journal of Wellbeing*, **1** (2), 255–65, available at:http://www.internationaljournalofwellbeing.org/index.php/ijow/article/view/28.

Helliwell, J.F. (2011b), 'How can subjective well-being be improved?', in F. Gorbet and A. Sharpe (eds), *New Directions for Intelligent Government in Canada*, Ottawa: Centre for the Study of Living Standards, pp. 283–304, available at: http://www.csls.ca/festschrift/Helliwell.pdf.

Helliwell, J.F. and C.P. Barrington-Leigh (2011), 'How much is social capital worth?', in J. Jetten, C. Haslam and A. Haslam (eds), *The Social Cure: Identity, Health and Well-Being*, London: Psychology Press, pp. 55–71.

Helliwell, J.F. and H. Huang (2008), 'How's your government? International evidence linking good government and well-being', *British Journal of Political Science*, **38**, 595–619.

Helliwell, J.F. and H. Huang (2010), 'How's the job? Well-being and social capital in the workplace', *Industrial and Labor Relations Review*, **63**, 205–28.

Helliwell, J.F. and H. Huang (2011a), *New Measures of the Costs of Unemployment: Evidence from the Subjective Well-being of 2.3 Million Americans*, NBER Working Paper No. 16829, Cambridge, MA: National Bureau of Economic Research.

Helliwell, J.F. and H. Huang (2011b), 'Well-being and trust in the workplace', *Journal of Happiness Studies*, **12**, 747–67.

Helliwell, J.F. and R.D. Putnam (1995), 'Economic growth and social capital in Italy', *Eastern Economic Journal*, **21** (3), 295–307.

Helliwell, J.F. and R.D. Putnam (2004), 'The social context of well-being', *Philosophical Transactions of the Royal Society B*, **359**, 1435–46, reprinted in F.A. Huppert, B. Keverne and N. Baylis (eds) (2005), *The Science of Well-being*, London: Oxford University Press, pp. 435–59.

Helliwell, J.F. and S. Wang (2011a), 'Trust and well-being', *International Journal of Wellbeing*, **1** (1), 42–78, available at: www.internationaljournalofwellbeing. org/index.php/ijow/article/view/3/85.

Helliwell, J.F. and S. Wang (2011b), *Weekends and Subjective Well-being*, NBER Working Paper No. 17180, Cambridge, MA: National Bureau of Economic Research.

Henrich, J., R. Boyd, S. Bowles, C. Camerer, E. Fehr, H. Gintis and R. McElreath (2001), 'In search of Homo economicus: behavioral experiments in 15 small-scale societies', *American Economic Review*, **91** (2), 73–8.

Huppert, F. (2005), 'Positive mental health in individuals and populations', in F.A. Huppert, B. Keverne and N. Baylis (eds), *The Science of Well-being*, London: Oxford University Press, pp. 307–40.

Joffe, T.H. (1997), 'Social pressures have selected for an extended juvenile period in primates', *Journal of Human Evolution*, **32**, 593–605.

Kahneman, D. (2011), *Thinking, Fast and Slow*, Toronto: Doubleday.

Kivimäki, V. and T. Tepora (2009), 'War of hearts: love and collective attachment as integrating factors in Finland during World War II', *Journal of Social History*, **43** (2), 285–305.

Koivumaa-Honkanen, H., R. Honkanen, H. Viinamäki, K. Heikkilä, J. Kaprio and M. Koskenvuo (2000), 'Self-reported life satisfaction and 20-year mortality in healthy Finnish adults', *American Journal of Epidemiology*, **152** (10), 983–91.

Kusago, T. (2011), 'A sustainable well-being initiative: social divisions and the recovery process in Minamata, Japan', *Community Quality of Life Indicators: Best Cases V*, **3**, 97–111.

Ladner, P. (2011), *The Urban Food Revolution*, Vancouver: New Society.

Layard, R. (2005), *Happiness: Lessons from a New Science*, New York: Penguin.

Leong, Lena (2011), 'The story of the Singapore Prison Service: from custodians of prisoners to captains of life', in J. Bourgon (ed.), *A New Synthesis of Public Administration*, Kingston: Queen's School of Policy Studies, McGill-Queen's University Press, pp. 139–54.

Lyubomirsky, S., L. King and E. Diener (2005), 'The benefits of positive affect: does happiness lead to success?', *Psychological Bulletin*, **131** (6), 803–55.

Mazar, N., O. Amir and D. Ariely (2008), 'The dishonesty of honest people: a theory of self-concept maintenance', *Journal of Marketing Research*, **45**, 633–44.

Nesse, R. (2004), 'Natural selection and the elusiveness of happiness', *Philosophical Transactions of the Royal Society B*, **359**, 1333–47, reprinted in F.A. Huppert, B. Keverne and N. Baylis (eds) (2005), *The Science of Well-being*, London: Oxford University Press, pp. 3–32.

OECD (2010), *Employment Outlook 2010: How Does Korea Compare?*, Paris: OECD, available at: http://www.oecd.org/dataoecd/13/42/45603966.pdf.

Pistrang, N., Z. Jay, S. Gessler and C. Barker (2013), 'Telephone peer support for women with gynaecological cancer: benefits and challenges for supporters', *Psycho-oncology*, **44** (4), 886–94.

Putnam, R.D. (1993), *Making Democracy Work: Civic Traditions in Modern Italy*, Princeton, NJ: Princeton University Press.

Putnam, R.D. (2000), *Bowling Alone: The Collapse and Revival of American Community*, New York: Simon & Schuster.

Schultz, S. and R.I.M. Dunbar (2007), 'The evolution of the social brain: anthropoid primates contrast with other vertebrates', *Proceedings of the Royal Society B*, **274**, 2429–36.

Schwartz, C.E. and M. Sendor (1999), 'Helping others helps oneself: response shift effects in peer support', *Social Science and Medicine*, **48**, 1563–75.

Shaw, B.A., N. Krause, L.M. Chatters, C.M. Connell and B. Ingersoll-Drayton (2004), 'Emotional support from parents early in life, aging, and health', *Psychology and Aging*, **19** (1), 4–12.

Steptoe, A., J. Wardle, M. Marmot and B.S. McEwen (2005), 'Positive affect and health-related neuroendocrine, cardiovascular, and inflammatory processes', *Proceedings of the National Academy of Sciences of the United States of America*, **102** (18), 6508–12.

Tirole, J. and R. Benabou (2010), 'Individual and corporate social responsibility', *Economica*, **77**, 1–19.

West, S.A., A.S. Griffin and A. Gardner (2007), 'Social semantics: altruism, cooperation, strong reciprocity and group selection', *Journal of Evolutionary Biology*, **20** (2), 415–32.

Williams, G.C. (1966), *Adaptation and Natural Selection: A Critique of Some Current Evolutionary Thought*, Princeton, NJ: Princeton University Press.

6. Buying alone: how the decreasing American happiness turned into the current economic crisis

Stefano Bartolini

INTRODUCTION

Capitalism is an unstable economic system. Although it often generates economic growth over the long term, this growth does not take place in a continuous fashion, but rather in a cyclical manner, that is, alternating periods of economic boom and stagnation and, at times, deep recession.

Many argue that the crisis that began in the summer of 2007 is one of the typical cyclical crises of capitalism. In its extraordinary dimension it is a 'black swan', an extremely unlikely event. The message implied by these interpretations of the crisis is: we do not need to change things. The party is simply on hold for the moment, because the jukebox is broken. But it will be mended and the dancing will start again, as thrilling and fun as before.

The thesis I contend, instead, is that the present crisis is not simply a cyclical one and it does not merely signal the instability of capitalism. It is the entire type of capitalism that became dominant, especially in the US in the last few decades, that is in crisis. My message is: the music is, after all, not that great at this party, even when the jukebox works and, in any case, if we don't change the music, the jukebox will break down over and over again.

In fact, the current crisis is the epilogue of the type of capitalism that I have called NEG (negative endogenous growth) capitalism. The economic growth generated by NEG capitalism is fraught with dangers to our well-being, our interpersonal relationships and the way we use our time, not to speak of the environment. In my explanation of this crisis, certain well-known long-term trends peculiar to US society – the decline in social capital and happiness and the increase in materialism and working hours – will appear as intertwined aspects of a social crisis that laid the foundations of the economic crisis. These foundations, under certain financial market conditions, can lead to global instabilities and recessions. Such conditions had matured enough in the summer of 2007 to trigger the explosion of the crisis.

The chapter is organized as follows. The section that follows underlines the extraordinary dimension of American consumerism, despite the fact that – in the past few decades – powerful forces were driving the American economy towards a limitation of its consumption potential. The chapter continues by emphasizing that American consumerism led to an enormous debt for American households. The global crises grew out of this indebtedness of American consumers. The chapter next discusses the most popular current explanations of this debt, underlining their limitations. The chapter then exposes a theory of consumerism – NEG – based on the decline of common goods, particularly interpersonal relationships, which forces people to buy private goods to compensate for the declining common ones. The chapter goes on to concentrate on the causes of the decline of relationships, identified in the modern evolution of cities and in the diffusion of materialistic values. In turn, the spread of materialism is fostered both by the diffusion of market relationships and by the media, in particular by advertising. After that, the chapter examines whether the US showed any evidence of economic growth of the NEG type over the past few decades. Comparisons with Europe suggest that the rooting of NEG processes appears to be much stronger in the US. The explanation of this difference is considered. Unlike in Europe, materialism has spread greatly in the US over the past few decades. This can be explained by the comparatively much greater pressure exerted on Americans by the advertising industry and by the relatively large penetration of market relationships into American society. In addition to these factors, the remarkable expansion of American cities in the past 20 years followed an urban model – the low-density city – that has a particularly damaging impact on social relationships. The chapter then discusses the financial mechanism that transformed an American crisis into a global infection, before it summarizes and concludes.

PROLOGUE: THE FORMIDABLE AMERICAN CONSUMER

The current crisis originated in the US, and from there it spread rapidly to the rest of the world. The premises for the crisis accumulated progressively during the decades preceding the crisis and are to be found in American consumerism. Let us first consider its extraordinary dimensions.

The formidable American consumer has been the engine of the global economy over the past two decades. Indeed, the American market absorbed a great mass of consumer goods produced in Europe and particularly in Asia. Yet there were powerful forces which tended towards containing the level of American consumption.

First of all was the loss of competitiveness of the American economy. The competition of Asian manufacturers brought about a sharp worsening in the US trade balance over the past 20 years. US imports progressively outstripped exports. From 1996 to 2007, an invasion of foreign products – in particular Chinese – caused an increase of more than 600 per cent in the trade deficit.[1] As a consequence of the foreign competition, the US industry was forced either to delocalize abroad or to downsize. This means that a portion of the incomes of US manufacturers were transferred to foreign manufacturers.

Secondly, the increase in income inequality might have been expected to depress the consumption potential of the US economy.[2] In an economy that had allocated increasingly larger shares of its GDP to those who were already affluent, the rise in wages had been relatively slow and the middle class had thinned. Other things being equal, this should have depressed actual consumption, given that the driving force of mass consumption is the middle class. Instead, as illustrated in Figure 6.1, US consumption grew at a faster rate than that of wages.

In short, US consumption continued to grow at a substantial pace, even though income was being redistributed from US workers to foreign ones and to owners of capital. This increase in consumption is mirrored in the decline in the personal saving rate since the 1980s (see Figure 6.2).

Figure 6.3 clarifies the peculiarity of the American attitude towards consumption by showing that not only did the US experience a period of increasing consumption, in particular since the second half of the 1990s, but also that its private consumption-to-GDP ratio remained persistently and remarkably higher than in major countries of mainland Europe.

The patterns in Figure 6.3 are certainly affected by the fact that public consumption has typically constituted a smaller portion of GDP in the US compared to mainland Europe. However, even when adding public to private consumption, total US (private plus public) consumption results in a substantially larger share of GDP than in European countries, as can be seen in Figure 6.4.

Why did average Americans continue in their frenzied race to increase their consumption? And how did they finance this spending spree? In the next sections, I will attempt to give some answers to these questions.

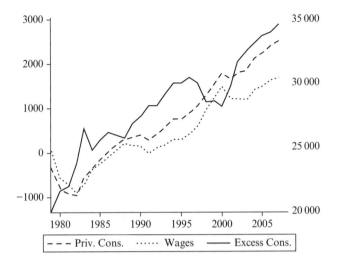

Note: Private consumption ('Priv. Cons.'), measured on the right axis, grew more than wages including benefits (right axis). Excess consumption ('Excess Cons.') is calculated as private consumption less total wages (left axis). All numbers are in 1980 dollars per household.

Source: Jagannathan et al. (2009).

Figure 6.1 Private consumption, wages and excess consumption

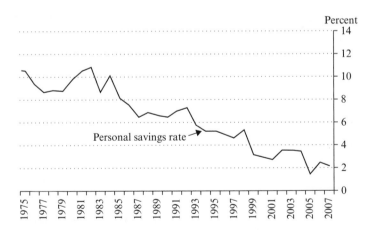

Source: McCully (2011).

Figure 6.2 Personal saving rate as a percentage of disposable personal income

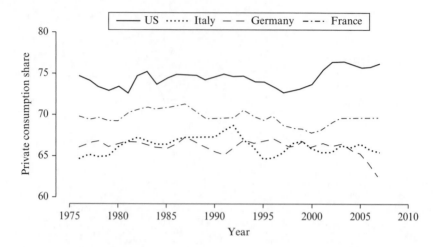

Note: Consumption is expressed in PPP GDP per capita (2005 constant prices).

Source: Heston et al. (2011).

Figure 6.3   Private consumption-to-GDP ratio across countries

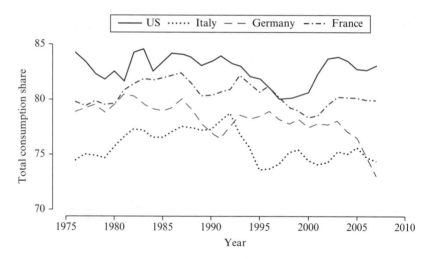

Note: Total consumption is the sum of private and government consumption expressed in PPP GDP per capita (2005 constant prices).

Source: Heston et al. (2011).

Figure 6.4   Total consumption-to-GDP ratio across countries

THE FORMIDABLE DEBT OF THE AMERICAN CONSUMER

The answer to the second question is simple and well known: the consumer spending binge was financed by accumulating an enormous debt. American households bought larger and nicer houses, and more consumer goods, than they could actually afford. Credit cards and mortgages allowed millions of Americans to spend beyond their means.

Given that a growing share of the American incomes were flowing to the more affluent and that, consequently, the salary of Ms or Mr Jones – the average American – was rising at a rather weak rate, Americans financed their feverish consumption race by falling deeper and deeper into debt. As a result, the US household debt grew much faster than wages, more than doubling the ratio of total debt to wages in less than 30 years (Figure 6.5).

The weakening of Ms or Mr Jones's income, owing to the loss of competitiveness of the American economy, provoked the same type of reaction – to borrow more and more. Figure 6.6 shows how the indebtedness of US households rose in parallel to the increase in the current account deficit.

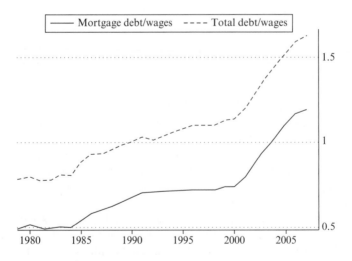

Source: Jagannathan et al. (2009).

Figure 6.5   Ratio between US household debt (mortgage debt and total debt) and wages

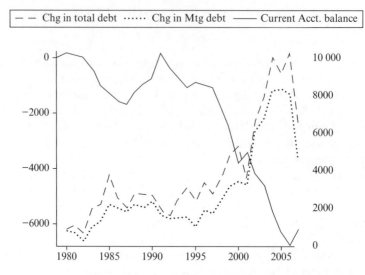

Note: Change in US household total debt ('Chg in total debt') and in mortgage debt ('Chg in Mtg debt'), both on the right axis: they increase, while the current account balance ('Current Acct. balance') worsens its deficit (left axis). The current account balance figures are mainly affected by the trade deficit. Figures are in US dollars per household.

Figure 6.6   Change in US household total debt, mortgage debt and current account balance

WHY DID AMERICANS BECOME INCREASINGLY INDEBTED?

This huge US private debt is at the base of the crisis that began in the summer of 2007 with the default of sub-prime mortgages. In fact, everything that happened afterwards – the collapse of the US financial system, the contagion passed on to the rest of the world, the credit crunch – was caused, as we shall see in the section 'Epilogue: the implosion of NEG capitalism' below, by the spread of a disease that grew out of the indebtedness of American consumers.

Accordingly, to explain the crisis one must begin by explaining the existence of this debt. And the explanation is not obvious, because it is caused by an urge to consume. We are not talking about a population that we would expect to be burdened by unsatisfied basic needs. Although poverty does of course exist, the average American consumer is one of the most affluent in the world. It is not clear why Ms or Mr Jones should feel the need to borrow more and more to finance consumption that goes far

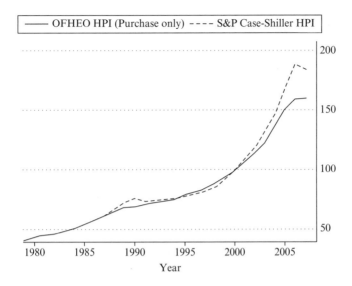

Note: HPI = home price index.

Source: Jagannathan et al. (2009).

Figure 6.7 Home price indexes

beyond his or her means. So, to explain the current crisis, we must first explain the consumption spree of an opulent economy. What induced affluent consumers to fall deeply in debt in order to buy more and more?

A possible answer lies in the myopic nature of human beings, in particular in the short-sightedness of their decisions (Hämäläinen, this volume, Chapter 2). Another popular answer – which tries to reconcile the evidence with the assumption of rationality of human beings typical among economists – is based on the illusion of wealth created by the inflation of real estate values. Figure 6.7 illustrates the constant increase in the price of US homes over the past 30 years.

According to this explanation, the constant increase in the prices of homes induced their owners to believe that they were growing richer and that, therefore, they could afford to borrow more and more. In reality, they were dealing with a real estate bubble, which ultimately burst. However, US mortgage debt grew much faster than real estate values (Figure 6.8), with mortgage debt used also to finance non-housing consumption. This suggests that the consumerism was largely fuelled by something other than the illusion of wealth created by the residential bubble.

A further widespread explanation focuses on the exceptional abundance

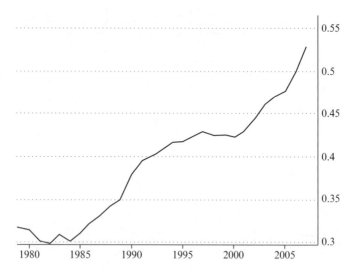

Source: Jagannathan et al. (2009).

*Figure 6.8   Ratio between the value of US residential mortgages and
residential home values (primary residence only)*

of low-cost credit available in the US, an explanation I will discuss later.
But neither this nor any of the other explanations examined so far reveal
why the credit demand was motivated by the need to consume. Instead of
using it to support their consumption spree, Americans could have used
their access to credit to replace, in part, their labour income and so to
diminish their working time and increase their leisure time. Yet they continued to buy. Why? These explanations offer no answers to this question.

BUYING ALONE: NEG CAPITALISM

My answer is that this debt is the result of the strong pressure for consumption exerted by the American socio-economic structure and culture.
According to a theory which my co-authors and I have presented elsewhere (Bartolini and Bonatti 2002, 2003, 2008; Antoci and Bartolini 2004),
consumerism is generated by a societal model called NEG capitalism. In
this and in the following section, I summarize the general features of NEG
capitalism, while in the section 'NEG capitalism in America' below I focus
on the US, arguing that the type of capitalism that took root there over the
past 30 years is precisely the NEG capitalism referred to above.

To understand how NEG capitalism works one must consider first that there are common goods that are important for our well-being which we cannot buy. I refer, first of all, to the quality of social and emotional relationships and of the environment. We can think of relationships as a common good, such as air quality, that we share with someone else. In a city, everyone breathes the same air, and this air cannot be privately appropriated. Similarly, a city incorporates a network of relationships between people. And both of these, relationships and air quality, are free goods.

Interpersonal relationships are generally treated in social sciences by using the concept of social capital. More precisely, the latter is a measure of one's networks, personal connections, social involvement, civic engagement and attitudes, such as honesty, solidarity and trust, towards others (Helliwell, this volume, Chapter 5).

The decline in these common goods forces us to buy private goods. As I have said elsewhere:

> In fact, money offers many forms of protection – real or illusory – from the poverty of relationships. If the elderly are alone and ill, the solution is a caregiver. If our children are alone, the solution is a baby-sitter. If we have few friends and the city has become dangerous, we can spend our evenings at home, fulfilled by all kinds of home entertainment. If our frenzied lives and the unliveable climate of our cities distresses us, we can lift our spirits with a holiday in some tropical paradise. If we quarrel with our neighbours, we can hire a lawyer to defend ourselves from their harassment. If we don't trust someone, we can pay to have him monitored. If we are afraid, we can protect our possessions with alarm systems, security doors, private guards, etc. If we are alone, or if we have difficult and unsatisfying relationships, we can seek a form of identity-making redemption in consumption, success or our work.
>
> Advertising has charged itself with the task of obsessively reminding us that if we are afraid of not being members of this society, of being losers, the reassurance for all our fears is to buy: 'I consume, therefore I am.' And besides, in advertising, products are perfect substitutes for love. In the rose-colored world of advertising, products require our love. But in the real world, they obstinately refuse to exhibit any emotion.
>
> All these private goods protect us from the decay of things that were once common and free: a liveable and low-crime city, with more trust and communication among neighbors, with a social fabric made of neighborhoods, of communities, one that provided company to children and the elderly. Or, at least, they promise to protect us, as does the advertising industry with respect to our fears of exclusion, fears which flourish in a world of rarified and difficult relationships . . . The same argument applies to the quality of the environment. Vacations in unspoiled environments offer us the clean air, seas and rivers that we can no longer find in our unlivable cities. (Bartolini, forthcoming)

In sum, we have the possibility of defending ourselves from the degradation of the environmental or social conditions that surround us by buying something. In other words, we can offset the deterioration of what we have in common with private wealth. This contrast is a typical characteristic of 'affluent societies' (Galbraith 1962).

Naturally, to be able to sustain these 'defensive expenditures', we need to work and produce more, which increases GDP. In other words, our reactions to the decay of the environment and of our relationships generate economic growth. Such reactions are a driving force of the economy. When social ties and the environment decline, the economy of solitude, fear and evasion thrives.

But what fuels the decline of common goods? Growth itself can have this effect. As far as the environment is concerned, this takes place as a result of the increase in pollution related to higher levels of production and consumption.

Growth can also tend to 'pollute' our relationships, although it doesn't necessarily have to have this effect. It may do so, if the social, economic and cultural organization exhibits certain characteristics. It is these characteristics which define NEG capitalism, and I will discuss them in more detail later.

If growth has a negative effect on common goods, then a self-feeding mechanism is generated where environmental decay and the deterioration of our relationships produce economic growth and this, in turn, produces an even greater environmental decay and a further deterioration of our relationships. This is the catch-22 of growth that is generated by NEG capitalism. The result of this self-feeding process, based on the substitution of common goods with private goods, is growing economic affluence associated with poorer relationships and environmental deterioration.

This mechanism creates formidable consumers, because it creates expensive lives. In fact, under these conditions, growth generates an ever rising need to consume. Instead of creating consumers who are increasingly satiated because of the greater amount of goods purchased, growth drives them towards a consumption spree fed by the desire to defend themselves from the degraded conditions of the relationships and the environment around them. This generates a pressure to consume even in opulent economies.

NEG capitalism creates individuals whose motivation to consume is fuelled by the fact that they live in a society in which less and less can be accessed free. In a society in which opportunities for well-being that do not pass through the market are increasingly scarce and in which well-being can only be bought, individuals are thrust into a feverish pursuit of money and consumption. This is a possible explanation of the surprisingly unbridled consumerism of opulent societies. Yet this opulence is purely one of private goods. The other side of the coin is the poverty of common goods. It is the need to compensate this poverty which nourishes the urge for private opulence.

In addition to creating formidable consumers, this mechanism creates also formidable workers. Lives where a great deal of time and effort are dedicated to one's job are the other face of the growing need to consume.

In a world – such as the NEG one – in which the affluence of private goods is based on the desertification of common goods, economic growth has predictably disappointing effects on well-being. The increase in GDP misleads us on the evolution of well-being over time, since GDP measures private goods but not free commons. In a world of people who buy more and more, because they feel increasingly alone and have increasingly difficult relationships, well-being cannot increase.

As I have said:

> This is why the traditional view of growth tells only one part of the story, the bright part. The one according to which the luxury goods of one generation become the standard goods of the next generation and these, in turn, become the basic needs of the successive one. The history of economic growth obviously abounds with examples of this kind. But there is a dark side to this story that remains untold. It is the story of goods that are free for one generation, which become scarce and costly for the next generation and luxury goods for the one following that. The history of growth is full of these examples as well. Goods that were available for free, or almost so, to our grandparents and often to our parents, but that now have a cost, goods such as, for example, clean natural environments or simply human curiosity. (Bartolini, forthcoming)

WHAT CAUSES THE DECLINE OF RELATIONSHIPS?

Given that the decline of relationships plays such a crucial role in the growth process described above, it is natural to question its causes. In the following sections I will focus on the evolution of modern cities and the change in the values of individuals.

The Modern City: Economic Prosperity versus Social Poverty

Cities were originally conceived as places of social bonding. For 5000 years, social aggregation was at the core of the urban project. But the evolution of the modern city has drastically worsened the quality of those spaces that promote the creation of relationships. This kind of development has made our cities an aggregation point solely for production and consumption. At present, our cities are environments designed for working and buying, and not for meeting people. In fact, they provide a scarcity of opportunities for building relationships and very few low-cost meeting places, while simultaneously offering a wealth of costly pastimes for one's leisure time. Yet, to indulge in these, one needs money. Therefore the urban environment is the emblematic example of the motivation to make money generated by the scarcity of our relationships.

The cornerstones of this type of urbanization are the organization of space and mobility. Relationships require, first of all, good-quality common spaces. The town square around which European cities were originally built was *the* place for human relationships. For a long time, cities slowly expanded by adding new neighbourhoods around new squares. In such a fashion, good-quality public pedestrian areas continued in their function of offering opportunities for creating relationships that can offset, at least in part, income inequalities.

The problem is that the quality of common spaces has worsened in Western cities, with the result of making the opportunities for creating relationships – in particular during one's leisure time – dependent on income. The impact of the automobile played a decisive role in this process. Up to a short while ago, cities were intended for people. All city streets were pedestrian. Then, all of a sudden (a very short time in historical terms) cars appeared, transforming the most human of all environments into a dangerous place for humans. The automobile is a menace for pedestrians: each year, all over the world, tens of thousands of people are run over on city streets.

The decline in the quality of common spaces due to private traffic has had the effect of weakening the social fabric (Peñalosa 2008; Montgomery 2013). This destruction forces us to sustain expenses, such as, for example, those for raising children. The increase in traffic brought an end to children's freedom to move around alone in their neighbourhoods, a possibility that was generally widespread in European cities up to the 1950s or 1960s. This radically changed the children's way of life, making it more costly for their parents. Today's children spend a lot more time at home, and when they are outside they have to be constantly supervised by adults. Their chances for independent social experiences have been reduced and have become dependent on the decisions of adults. To what extent is the money we spend on toys aimed at providing entertainment and companionship to children who are increasingly alone? To what extent has the use of babysitters become a necessity for families, because it has become impossible for our children to move independently around cities?

A recent academic paper about urban environments became immediately well known, because it supplied the most compelling evidence to date linking the different degrees of walkability of various neighbourhoods to the social capital and well-being of their inhabitants (Rogers et al. 2010).

Using a case study approach, the authors argued that the generation and maintenance of social capital are facilitated by living in a walkable community. Residents of three communities in New Hampshire, living in neighbourhoods of varying built forms and, thus, varying levels of walkability, were surveyed about their levels of social capital and well-being. Comparisons between the more and the less walkable neighbourhoods showed that the more walkable a neighbourhood, the higher the levels of social capital and well-being.

The authors concluded that the land-use design and the physical infrastructure of a neighbourhood or a region are what provide the conduits for individuals to meet, thereby increasing their social capital. A neighbourhood that provides residents with easy access to municipal infrastructure, such as post offices, town parks and playgrounds, coffee shops, restaurants, barber's shops and club meeting venues, will have high values of social capital.

The results of Rogers et al. (2010) support the view according to which communities are more resilient if they have a physical infrastructure that supports the interaction of residents. Walkability enhances social capital by providing the means and locations for individuals to connect, share information and interact with those whom they otherwise might not meet.

Rogers et al. captured something that has recently become the focus of political debate in many cities. Indeed, a growing awareness of the importance of the quality of public spaces has given rise to remarkable political novelties in local elections. In the last decade, mayors of important cities, such as Bogotá, Paris and Mexico City, won elections following electoral campaigns that emphasized the need for radical reform of the quality of public spaces and transport.

Rogers et al. (2010) brought to light one of the many ways in which the urban environment affects our relationships and well-being. These aspects go far beyond walkability. The impressive review provided by Basu et al. (this volume, Chapter 7) includes: shared green spaces, small setbacks, front porches, common shared areas, parking spaces behind houses, community gardens, proximity of housing and services through mixed use, ample pavements, the possibility of watching nature from one's window and even the aesthetics of one's environment.

These aspects of living environments have received little or no attention in the way our cities have been designed in modern times. This is the reason why urban life has become the paradigmatic example of NEG processes: the modern city has become a powerful destroyer of goods such as relationships and the environment and, precisely for this reason, a powerful producer of economic growth.

A world in which silence, clean air, clean seas or rivers and pleasant walks have become the privilege of exclusive or uncontaminated locations and tropical paradises is a world in which people tend to expend considerable resources to escape from the unlivable environments they have created. It is a world in which escape has become a need. According to conventional economic wisdom, our expenditures for these evasions are a sign of economic progress. Yet it could be that those cyclical mass migrations we call summer holidays are not only signs of an increased living standard, but also a response to the deterioration in the quality of our life.

This is how cities have lost their original function of social bonding, inhibiting the formation of social networks and turning into centres of exclusion through the creation of profound inequalities. For these reasons, modern cities have become the pillar of a social organization that produces economic wealth, on the one hand, and poverty of relationships, environment and time, on the other.

Materialism Generates Poor Relationships

The diffusion of materialistic values is another plausible culprit for the decline of social relationships. Materialism is defined as a system of personal values ascribing great importance in life to extrinsic motivations and low priority to intrinsic motivations. The distinction between extrinsic and intrinsic motivations refers, respectively, to the instrumentality or lack thereof of the motivations for acting (Deci 1971). In fact, the term 'extrinsic' refers to motivations that are external to an activity, such as money or success, whereas 'intrinsic' refers to internal motivations, such as self-actualization, affection, human relationships, solidarity, civic engagement, and pro-social behaviours more generally.

The influence of materialistic values on the quality of our relationships is the focus of a vast number of social psychology studies. These studies show that the more materialistic an individual, the poorer the quality of his or her relationships.

Individuals with materialistic inclinations develop attitudes that form the basis of their poorer relationships with friends and loved ones. In particular, the tendency to 'objectify' the other, in other words the tendency to consider others as objects, does not favour the creation of fulfilling relationships. Objectification refers to the low levels of generosity, empathy, cooperation and genuineness (non-instrumentality) and the high levels of cynicism and mistrust that more materialistic individuals put into their relationships (Belk 1985; Kasser et al. 1995; Cohen and Cohen 1996; McHoskey 1999; Kasser and Sheldon 2000; Sheldon et al. 2000; Kasser 2002).

In other words, more materialistic individuals can be expected to have a reduced capacity to build satisfying relationships, that is, the capacity to build social capital. This makes the diffusion of materialism – which will be discussed later – a plausible culprit for the decline in social relationships.

Poor Relationships Generate Materialism

Materialism generates poor relationships, but the causality works in the opposite direction as well. Indeed, materialism thrives and finds nourishment when our relationships become scarce.

Many studies in social psychology support the view that the experiences of children in their relationships with their parents are important in determining their values as adults (Kasser et al. 1995; Cohen and Cohen 1996; Williams et al. 2000). These studies document that children with less caring and nurturing parents will tend more towards materialism as adults. The reason seems to be that less nurturing parents bring forth more insecure children, who, therefore, are more receptive to social messages that promise security and social approval through consumption.

In short, a poor emotional relationship with parents during infancy is associated with higher levels of materialism during adolescence and adulthood. Indeed, a lack of affection generates insecurity, and materialism is an answer to insecurity.

Remarkable evidence concerning the causality running from insecurity to materialism is provided by a study concerning 'terror management' (Kasser and Sheldon 2000). In this type of experiment, participants are asked to write about their own death (the condition of terror), whereas the control group is asked to write about music. The result is that the first group later exhibits significantly higher levels of materialism. Materialism is, therefore, a form of terror management, an answer to the insecurities generated by fear.

The researchers concluded that there is a circular effect that leads materialism and the scarcity of relationships to nourish each other. Materialism leads individuals to organize their lives in ways that do not allow them to fulfil their need for relationships, and this, in turn, leads these individuals to greater materialism.

The Market Economy Spreads Materialism

My thesis is that the main factors responsible for the dissemination of materialistic values are the economic system and the media.

The role of the economic system can be understood in the light of the theory of the crowding out of motivations (Frey and Jegen 2001; Thompson et al. 2010; Fang and Gerhart 2012). This theory was developed by social psychologists to explain those situations in which incentives have an opposite effect to that expected by economists.

Classic examples of this type of behaviour concern the unintended effects of the introduction of monetary compensations. If compensation is paid for donating blood, the amount of blood donated falls, instead of rising (Titmuss 1970). The establishment of fines for parents who pick up their children late from day care centres actually increases the number of latecomers, rather than reduces it (Gneezy and Rustichini 2000). Offering compensation for people willing to accept a toxic waste dump in their area in fact reduces the percentage of those in favour, instead of increasing it (Frey 1997).

In all these examples, the introduction of a monetary incentive reduces the willingness of people to behave in the way that is being encouraged, contrary to the expectations of economists.

The explanation advanced by the theory of the crowding out of motivations is that monetary compensation crowds out intrinsic motivations (Deci 1971; Deci et al. 1999). Donating blood for money is different from donating blood out of solidarity: the introduction of a monetary motivation for a donation replaces the motivation of solidarity and is not added to it. Establishing fines for latecomers undermines the motivation to pick up one's children on time out of a sense of responsibility. An offer of compensation for a waste dump undermines the motivation to accept it out of civic engagement.

In other words, the different motivations are not added together, but tend to replace each other. Extrinsic motivations tend to substitute for intrinsic motivations. The researchers believe that the reason why monetary compensation undermines intrinsic motivations is that it changes people's own perception of why they behave the way they do. To do something out of solidarity or civic-mindedness is different from doing it for money, and the two motivations cannot be added. Individuals do not add the 'whys' instrumental and non-instrumental of their actions. They tend to focus on a predominant 'why' when doing things.

This theory emphasizes important aspects of the way our brain functions. Indeed, the underlying issue for the crowding out of motivations is the need of human beings to give a sense to what they do. Thus, giving a motivation to an action actually means giving it a sense.

The market economy creates an economic organization that relies only on extrinsic motivations. It is an organization that sets instrumental motivations as the basis for relationships between individuals. In other words, market relationships affect our perception of why we are in a relationship. They suggest that it is based on personal and material advantage.

Since the different motivations tend to replace each other the emphasis on extrinsic motivations obscures all those aspects of social life that depend on intrinsic motivations, above all that of relationships. The appeal to personal advantage as a motivation for relationships redefines the motivations for the relationships themselves, not sparing even intimate ones.

Given that materialism assigns a high priority to extrinsic motivations, the organization of economic relationships on the basis of these motivations tends to generate a system of materialistic values.

This is the principal dark side of the market. While it provides benefits in terms of economic prosperity, it also disseminates its disadvantages in terms of changes in people's values. And the extent to which it does this varies with the degree of penetration of market relationships into the social sphere. In short, the amount of market we inject into our social relationships has significant collateral effects, because it affects the diffusion of materialism.

The Media Promote Materialistic Values

The media, and in particular advertising, play a central role in stimulating the diffusion of materialistic values. This is pointed out by Juliet Schor (2005) – a leading scholar of advertising – in her book *Born to Buy*, on which this section largely draws.

Advertising has become increasingly sophisticated, heading towards the marketing of a lifestyle. This growing sophistication embraces the total awareness of the importance of non-material needs by those who work to promote the sale of material objects. In fact, advertisements are increasingly aimed at convincing people that buying provides them with non-material benefits, such as social inclusion, good relationships and, ultimately, well-being. This is why the creed of advertising people is not that of providing information on products, but that of creating an association between a product and positive emotions.

In order for the advertisement of a product to work, it must call to mind something other than the product itself. To be precise, it must call up an identity. The attempt to link personal traits to consumption has become the beacon of marketing research. An enormous amount of resources have been expended to discover what type of person buys a certain brand of soap instead of another, or what type of person is sitting inside a certain car instead of another. The predominant belief of adverting professionals is that consumption is a form of individual expression. The philosophy imparted is 'I buy, therefore I am'; the things we own are our 'extended self'.

The result of this obsessive stimulus to possess is the internalization of an existential message with the following import: 'If you feel insecure, inadequate, excluded, in short a loser, you'll feel better if you increase your consumption. The reassurance for your fears of exclusion, the guarantee of the fact that you are a member of this society, lies in buying.' Other types of solutions to this disaffection – such as buying less in order to have to work less and so be able to better nurture one's relationships – could probably work better, but they are not those suggested by the world created by advertising. Advertising touts what can be sold, and no one sells time or affection.[3]

NEG CAPITALISM IN AMERICA

Many signs indicate that NEG capitalism may have put down solid roots in the United States and that it may have guided American growth over the past few decades. In comparison, NEG capitalism in Europe seems less entrenched.

The signs of NEG capitalism can be seen in the evolution of certain features of society over time. The NEG approach suggests that the more a society acts in a destructive fashion with regard to social capital, that is, the worse the trend of social capital, the worse the trend observed in well-being, and the higher the growth rates of GDP, of consumption and of work hours. Let us examine the trends of these variables in the United States:

- *Social capital.* Putnam (2000) pointed to a decline in social capital in the decades prior to his study, and evidence suggests that the trend continued for at least a few years after he published.[4] A series of indicators point, on the one hand, to an increase in solitude and communicative difficulties, in the sense of fear and isolation, in mistrust and in the instability of families and, on the other, to a decline in solidarity, honesty, civic engagement and participation in social networks (see Table 6.1).
- *Expenditures.* Economic growth rates have been greater in the US compared to the major Western countries over the past two decades, right up to the beginning of the current crisis. This growth was driven by the formidable dynamics of US consumption. Within this consumption, the trend of those expenditures used as a defence against the deterioration of relationships signalled a remarkable increase over the past decades. For example, the home entertainment sector experienced an impressive boom. At the same time,

Table 6.1   Trends of US social capital 1975–2004, General Social Survey data

Marriages	−	Confidence in companies	−
Separations	+	Confidence in religious organizations	−
Divorces	0	Confidence in education	−
People are trustworthy	−	Confidence in the executive	−
People are fair	−	Confidence in universities	−
People are helpful	−	Confidence in the press	−
Monthly with relatives	0	Confidence in medicine	−
Monthly with neighbours	−	Confidence in television	−
Monthly with friends	+	Confidence in the Supreme Court	0
Monthly in a bar	−	Confidence in science	−
Associational activities	−	Confidence in Congress	−
		Confidence in the army	−
		Confidence in banks	−

Note: Data includes marital status, trust in others, the perception of other people as fair or helpful, the frequency of interactions with relatives, neighbours, friends and people in bars and taverns, associational activities and trust in various kinds of institutions; '+' means that the indicator showed an increasing trend over the period, '−' means that the trend was decreasing, '0' means that the trend was non-significant.

Source: Bartolini et al. (2011).

US expenditures in formal activities of social control and dispute resolution also exhibited an explosive increasing trend during the last decades of the twentieth century. Putnam (2000) attributes such an explosion to the decline in social trust over that same period. He observes that, since the 1980s, spending on security rose rapidly as a share of US GDP. The upsurge of this trend is reflected by a 40 per cent increase in police and guards and by a 150 per cent increase in lawyers and judges over the levels that would have been projected in 1970 (Putnam 2000, p. 146). In other words, the erosion of social capital (trust, work ethics, honesty) boosted the expansion of those sectors of the economy that provide the goods and services, which individuals and organizations employ to defend themselves from rising opportunism.[5] The growth of these sectors must be framed within the secular trend to expand the 'transaction cost sector'[6] documented by Wallis and North (1986) for the US economy. They estimated that the (private plus public) transaction cost sector was 26.1 per cent of US GDP in 1870 and 54 per cent in 1970.[7] However, this growth – paralleled by the decline in peer monitoring and informal sanctioning provided by social capital – has accelerated since

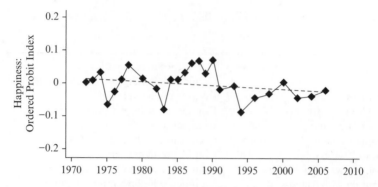

Note:

Note: The ordered probit index on the vertical axis indicates the variation of the average happiness with respect to the initial year.

Source: Stevenson and Wolfers (2008).

Figure 6.9   Trend of self-reported happiness in the US

the 1970s. According to Jayadev and Bowles (2006), work supervisors and guards (police, corrections officials and security personnel) grew from 10.8 per cent of the US labour force in 1966 to 13.4 per cent in 1979 and to 17.9 per cent in 2002. Conversely, this share had remained stable between 1948 and 1966. The astonishing figure of a US jail population of 2 million during the 2000s – risen from 0.3 per cent of the total labour force in 1979 to 1.8 per cent in 2002 – mirrors these disquieting numbers.

- *Well-being.* Despite their increasing consumption, Americans have been feeling progressively worse over the last few decades. Self-reported happiness declined in the United States over the course of more than 30 years (see Figure 6.9). The diminishing self-reported happiness in the US is paralleled by a rampant diffusion of mental illnesses (Twenge 2000; Diener and Seligman 2004; Wilkinson and Pickett 2009). In short, available measures of well-being, both subjective and objective, point to a decrease in well-being in the US over the last few decades. Increasing inequality may have contributed to this decline, both by generating a slower growth of median income than per capita GDP[8] and by exacerbating the 'positional arms race' implied by social comparisons.[9] However, a study by Bartolini et al. (2013) shows that, consistent with the NEG approach, the decline of social capital played a fundamental role. In fact, a large portion of the decline in happiness of the average American is predicted by the decline of his/her social capital.

- *Work hours.* Working hours increased in America over the past 30 years, and this is surprising in an increasingly wealthy country. Bartolini and Bilancini (2011) have shown that individuals with fewer and poorer relationships tend to work more. The causality seems to run both ways. People seem to find, in money and work, compensation for the poverty of relationships in their lives. At the same time, those individuals who work more tend to have fewer and poorer relationships, because work takes away time and energy that could instead be dedicated to relationships. This study confirms the NEG view that decline of relationships and increase in working hours are connected by a bi-directional causality. This suggests that American society may be trapped in a vicious circle, in which a lack of relationships causes a greater number of working hours and these, in turn, cause a greater lack of relationships.

Summarizing, while Americans have consumed and worked more and more – despite the fact that they have lived in a very prosperous economy – they have also experienced a decline in their happiness and the quality of their relationships. The signs of NEG capitalism are evident in the US.

AND EUROPE?

Over a similar time period, continental European economies grew less quickly (Table 6.2).

Working hours diminished compared to the US. In the mid-1970s, British, German and French men worked on average 5 to 10 per cent longer hours than American men. Yet 30 years later they were working

Table 6.2 Growth rates of GDP 1980–2005 in the US and in some big European economies

	Total growth rate 1980–2005	Average annual growth rate 1980–2005
France	47%	1.8%
Germany	48%	1.8%
Italy	49%	1.9%
United States	69%	2.7%

Note: PPP converted GDP per capita (Laspeyres), at 2005 constant prices.

Source: Heston et al. (2011).

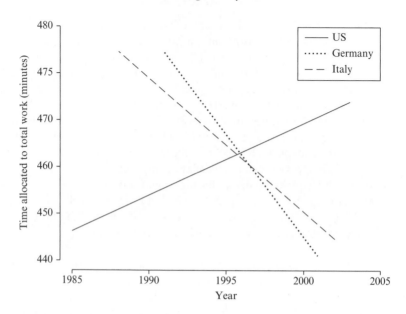

Note: In average minutes per day, person aged 20–74.

Source: Burda et al. (2007).

Figure 6.10   Trends in total working time across countries

only 70–75 per cent as long as the average American (Prescott 2004; see also Alesina et al. 2005; and Stiglitz 2008). Figure 6.10 illustrates the trends of work time for the US, Germany and Italy.

This difference in the trends of work hours between Europe and the US is mitigated by the different trends in home work, that is, unpaid work in the home, which dropped more sharply in the US. Indeed, Europeans self-produced part of those services, which Americans, instead, bought (Davis and Henrekson 2004; Freeman and Schettkat 2005; Aguiar and Hurst 2007; Burda et al. 2007; Rogerson 2008; Olovsson 2009). But the parable of German mothers cooking more at home compared to their American counterparts – who more often go out to eat at restaurants (Gordon 2006) – is not sufficient to overturn the evidence that Europeans do indeed have more free time, as shown in Figure 6.11.

Moreover, one should not attach 'much weight to those studies emphasising that because the number of hours of home work has been reduced true leisure has increased' in the US (Stiglitz 2008, p. 46). The reason is that home work is often not a cost. 'For a farmer to toil in his field is work but for a middle-class American or European to toil in his garden is pleasure.

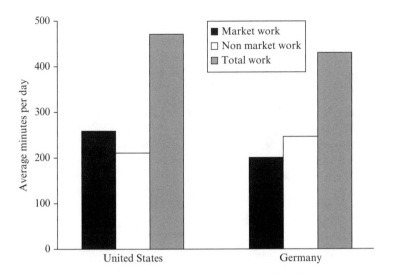

Source: Bonatti (2008).

Figure 6.11 Differences in the use of time between Germany and the US

Cooking may be toil but for many individuals . . . on occasion cooking is a pleasure' (Stiglitz 2008, p. 46). Lastly, home work tends to strengthen family relations. Homes that are empty for the greater part of the day are obviously not fertile ground for nurturing relationships.

If the trend of social capital really is a contributing factor in explaining these differences, then we should expect to find that social assets had a better trend over the period in Europe than in the United States. The same should be true for the happiness trend. This is exactly what seems to have happened. In general, social capital and well-being grew in Europe. Drawing from World Values Survey/European Values Study data, Sarracino (2011) shows that the levels of social trust, associational activities and happiness grew (albeit weakly) in 11 Western European countries in the past few decades. Figure 6.12 indicates the trend of subjective well-being in Western Europe, drawn from another source, Eurobarometer.

In short, international comparisons suggest that NEG capitalism finds its most extreme example in the United States. Such capitalism seems to be less rooted in Europe where the evolution over time of social relationships seems less disappointing, and this contributes to the result of a slower growth rate of the economy, of a reduction in working hours and of a less disappointing trend of well-being. The home of NEG capitalism is America.

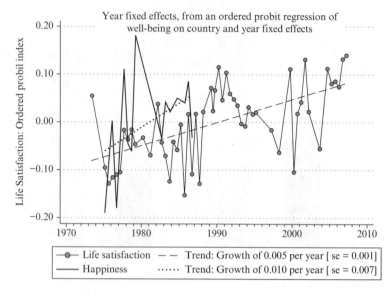

Note: The ordered probit index on the vertical axis indicates the variation over time of the average life satisfaction or happiness.

Source: Stevenson and Wolfers (2008), based on Eurobarometer data 1973–2007.

Figure 6.12   Trends in European well-being

These international differences find further confirmation in cross-country comparisons of an important component of the expenditures generated by the erosion of trust on the workplace – the work supervisors' share of the labour force – which show that the US ranks at the top (see Table 6.3).

WHY DOES NEG CAPITALISM THRIVE IN AMERICA?

One may conclude that there are strong signs indicating that America has become the temple of NEG capitalism. These findings support the thesis that the decline of social capital in America lies at the root of the rampant consumerism that has guided American growth over the past decades and that has created the premises for the current economic crisis. The destruction of social relationships seems to have been stronger in the United States than in Europe and has had an impact on the differences observed in the trends of happiness, working hours and growth.

*Table 6.3   Work supervisors as a percentage of the total labour force: 18
advanced economies in 2002*

Country	Supervisors
United States	14.9
United Kingdom	13.4
New Zealand	11.9
Netherlands	11.6
Australia	11.1
Ireland	10.6
Belgium	10.3
Greece	9.1
Canada	8.5
Iceland	7.9
Norway	7.3
Denmark	6.9
Austria	6.8
Portugal	6.7
Spain	6.7
Switzerland	5.8
Sweden	4.4
Italy	2.9

Source: Jayadev and Bowles (2006).

But how did America turn into the temple of NEG capitalism? I highlight
here two key causes of decline in American social relationships, relating to
materialism and the urban features previously discussed.

The Growth of Materialism

The materialistic culture has spread very fast in the US over recent
decades. The percentage of university students who believed that an outstanding economic condition is an essential goal in life stood at 39 per cent
in 1970. But in 1995 this percentage had risen to 74 per cent, becoming the
students' main goal in life and overtaking any other ambition (Myers and
Diener 1997). From 1975 to 1991, the percentage of Americans who felt
it was important to have 'a lot of money' rose from 38 per cent to 55 per
cent. The percentage of those who considered it important to have 'a job
that pays much more than the average' grew from 45 per cent to 60 per
cent. On the other hand, non-materialistic ambitions for a happy marriage
and an interesting job fell in importance (Schor 1998).

These findings are not surprising if one takes into account the enormous increase in Americans' exposure to the media in this period. Time dedicated to the media increased across all social categories and age cohorts, starting with children (Schor 2005).

And it is even less surprising if one considers the huge increase in market relationships in American social life. In fact, since the 1980s, America has been the scene of a large-scale experiment inspired by a free market philosophy, aimed at increasing the penetration of the market into society. Market mechanisms were extended into spheres of social life from which they had previously been excluded or limited, that is to say, health care, education and pensions. The labour market was made totally flexible, giving companies complete freedom in firing. Companies were 'restructured' to promote a work organization based on more incentives, more stress, more controls, more pressure, more competition and more tension (Harrison and Bluestone 1990).

From the viewpoint of risk, these changes narrowed the gap between the middle class with comfortable incomes and the poor. Sudden downturns in life can drive a family from middle-class status to poverty in a short time (Hacker 2006).

The American experience shows that these changes have the effect of promoting a sense of collective insecurity that pushes a vast part of the middle class into a state of precariousness. For this reason, these changes may have contributed to the increase in materialism. As we saw earlier, materialism is, in fact, a reaction to insecurity. In other words, a reason why the changes introduced into the American economy generate materialism is that they stimulate the fear of exclusion. They create individuals who fear being marginalized with respect to something as fundamental as, say, health care or a good education for their children. The possibility of finding reassurance through consumption seduces these individuals. And there is an entire propaganda apparatus set to convince them that consumption is the answer to their fears of exclusion.

Here again, differences emerge with respect to European societies. The per capita advertising expenditure in the US is four times that of continental Europe (Mulgan, this volume, Chapter 11). The trends of materialism are different as well. Bartolini and Sarracino (2013), using internationally comparable data over the last 25 years, find that, while materialism increased in the US, it decreased in the six major countries of Western Europe.

The Expansion of the Low-density City

American growth over the past 20 years was driven by an extraordinary and prolonged real estate boom. Cities expanded, and the new neighbourhoods were built according to the low-density-city model – in other words, suburbs of single-family detached homes, often surrounded by a garden. This is a city model with a great destructive effect on relationships and environmental resources.

From the point of view of relationships, the historical core of European cities has, in general, a potential advantage compared to American cities, which is that of not having been built for cars. Low-density cities are not an environment designed for pedestrians, because their homes are separated from points of interest, such as shops, by great distances. Many suburbs in the United States don't even have any pavements, so that pedestrians, especially children, feel insecure on the streets (Peñalosa 2008).

American suburbs present, therefore, an extreme example of the problems of human relationships arising in cities dominated by cars. If there are few inhabitants per acre, and if the environment is not designed for pedestrians, few people will be found walking around on suburban streets. Suburbs become solitary places, and shopping malls tend to become the only public meeting places. Moreover, people who live in the suburbs go less often to city-centre theatres, restaurants or museums, and so low-density cities also have reduced cultural activities. In addition, the scarcity of public transport prevents members of weaker groups from reaching city centres (Peñalosa 2008).

The lesson of American suburbs is that transport based on cars produces social disruption even in cities designed for cars. In addition, low-density cities make it impossible to realize an efficient public transport system. In scarcely populated suburbs, it is impossible to offer a low-cost and high-frequency public transport service. Indeed, in very large cities, the average distance between two points of interest becomes longer, and the low population density around the bus or train stop areas implies that the means of transport would circulate almost empty.

Putnam (2000, Chapter 12) spoke up against the suburbanization because of its damaging effects in terms of the reduction of social connectedness and civic engagement and the increase in social segmentation. Lewis Mumford defined the suburbanization trend over 70 years ago as 'a collective effort to lead a private life' (quoted by Putnam 2000, p. 210).

It is also difficult to overestimate the environmental damage of suburbanization. Suburbs are strongly energy-consuming for two reasons. The first is that they require an individual to cover great distances to go to work, to go shopping or to spend some leisure time outside of the home. This implies an abundant use of cars. The second reason is 'thermal'. In the US, suburban homes are exposed to the weather on all sides and built with thin walls that generally provide poor thermal insulation, in the sense that they are very hot when it is hot and very cold when it is cold. The climate in America varies from desert heat to extreme cold. But the build-ing materials of these homes do not substantially change. In these homes, it is necessary to use large amounts of energy for a greater part of the year not to suffer from the heat or the cold, because of an extensive use of heating or cooling systems (Kahn 2000).

This type of urban expansion has contributed to create the formidable profile of the American consumer, because it created the needs of costly lives. One must have a great deal of energy, a lot of money for one's leisure time, a comfortable home that is large and well appointed, a large and fully accessorized car, many status-symbol goods – and even lawyers, who seem to have almost become an essential need in an increasingly conflict-ridden society.

EPILOGUE: THE IMPLOSION OF NEG CAPITALISM

Why did the American crisis infect the world? The aspect of the current crisis that surprised most observers is that it originated out of a relatively small and localized default crisis, that of sub-prime mortgages in the United States. How is it possible that such a small crisis was able to trigger the greatest global financial crisis of the past 80 years?

And yet the international financial system had basically withstood a series of violent crises (Mexico, Argentina, Brazil, Russia, South-East Asia, etc.) over the past 20 years. These crises had disastrous effects in the stricken countries, but the contagion effects on the global financial system were essentially limited and transitory. Instead, a small default crisis in the US brought this system to its knees. Why?

The World Financed American Consumption

As previously mentioned, the root of the crisis lies in the huge size of the debt of American households. Everything else is the financial transmission of this debt crisis to the rest of the world. In the mechanics of this transmission, bulimia, greed and the lack of ethics all play a significant role. Let us see how.

At the start of the crisis, the American financial system was heavily indebted to the rest of the world. Indeed, most countries in the world had been buying bonds, especially private ones, on Wall Street for at least 15 years. As an example, China had increased its financial investments in the United States by a factor of 10, from $92 million in 1994 to $922 million in 2007. In addition, while in 1994 these investments were restricted to treasury bonds, in 2007 they were aimed largely towards assets issued by private companies (Jagannathan et al. 2009).

Particularly over the past ten years, this flood of money flowing into the United States had been increasingly channelled towards financing the credit of the average American. In short, it was the extraordinary inflows of capital into the United States that had financed the easy credit of American households. In practice, the American financial system financed the loans it granted to the average American mostly by borrowing capital from the world.

Since American households resorted to borrowing in order to increase their consumption expenditures, the world was financing American consumption. This financing mechanism was based on a certain type of derivatives, currently known as 'toxic assets'. These structured assets, derived from the securitization of mortgages and loans, pool together high- and low-quality debts, generating opacity concerning their 'true' risk of default (Jagannathan et al. 2009).

Figure 6.13 illustrates the dramatic growth in the volume of toxic assets in the United States over the past 30 years.

While the American private debt increased and the world was being flooded by assets based on this debt, the freedom to move capital internationally – which followed the collapse of Bretton Woods in the

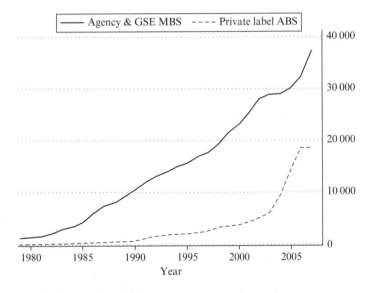

Note: In US dollars per household.

Source: Jagannathan et al. (2009).

Figure 6.13   Outstanding mortgage-backed securities by issuer

1970s – had profoundly changed the habits of savers all over the world.[10] The liberalization of the export of capital had created a world of financial opportunities. Suddenly, it was possible to invest in any stock, anywhere in the world. In this new era, where did capital from all over the planet predominantly flow? Obviously, towards the most reliable countries and the largest financial markets – in other words, towards the United States.

If countries were financially similar, international mobility would distribute capital all over. But, in a world in which there is a country that is considered more reliable than others and which has a very large financial market, a globalized financial system takes on the role of provider of capital for that country.

If we consider this in conjunction with the securitization of the debt of American households, the financial system that emerges possesses two traits: it creates a strong global demand for American assets, because the markets trust in the solvency of Americans, and it creates a strong supply of assets, through financial engineering applied to the debt of Americans.

This is how Wall Street came to absorb a large part of the capital of the world. This way, the extreme inequalities, with regard to solvency and the size of financial markets, among the countries of the world resulted in the financing of consumption in the country that was already the biggest consumer of all. Wall Street became the meeting ground of the willingness of the world to finance Americans and the willingness of the formidable American consumer to become indebted. In this fashion, Wall Street transmitted the massive debt that Americans had been accumulating on to the rest of the world.

Exporting the Crisis: The Credit Crunch

The default of the sub-prime mortgages was triggered by a decline in the real estate market. In fact, when the price of homes falls, many mortgage holders prefer not to pay or cannot find the means to do so.

Having first hit sub-prime mortgages, the crisis spread to the rest of the American financial system, leading to a series of bankruptcies of large banks and insurance companies. Americans, to put it bluntly, had stopped repaying their debts. This drove the global financial system into a crisis. A surge in interbank rates following the sub-prime mortgage crisis was the consequence of spreading mistrust among banks, all more or less laden with toxic assets, the world over. Banks feared the bankruptcy of other banks and stopped lending each other money if not at high interest rates. Credit tightened, and the credit crunch arrived. The latter passed the financial collapse on to the real economy, triggering the recession.

In this way, the American crisis was transmitted to the rest of the world, because the entire world was holding assets on the debt of American households, assets that lacked transparency concerning their default risk.

SUMMARY: THE DESERT BEHIND, THE ABYSS AHEAD

Why did the crisis originate in the US? And why did the American crisis infect the entire planet? I first underlined two powerful forces that in the past few decades drove the US economy towards a limitation of its consumption potential: the increase in income inequality and the worsening of the trade balance. However, despite these forces, the enormous push to consumption exerted by the US economy did not halt. Rather, consumption grew faster than wages. US households financed this consumption rush by going deeply into debt. The important question is: what motivated this urgent need to consume in an affluent economy? In other words, the issue is to find an explanation for American hyper-consumerism.

I first exposed a theory of consumerism and then turned to the US to check whether the evidence supports an explanation of American consumerism based on such a theory. The main features of this theory of consumerism are the following. There are common free goods that cannot be bought and that are important for people's well-being, such as the quality of human relationships or of the environment. Households can defend themselves from the decline of these common goods by buying consumer goods as substitutes for declining free goods. In order to finance these expenditures, households have to work and produce more, thereby supporting economic growth. In turn, growth can further deplete these common goods, generating a self-feeding mechanism whereby the deterioration of the environment and of human relationships produces economic growth and this, in turn, produces an even greater environmental decay and a further deterioration of relationships. This is the engine of the diffusion of consumption- and work-oriented lifestyles.

I give the label of NEG (negative endogenous growth) capitalism to the economic, social, cultural and institutional features that produce this self-reinforcing process. What are these features? Why can economic growth generate this decline in common goods? Regarding the environment, the answer obviously lies in greater amounts of pollution. As far as the decline of interpersonal relationships is concerned, I argue that it may be due to:

1. The way modern cities are designed and organized. In particular, the modern decline in the quality of urban public spaces damages the social fabric.
2. The spread of materialistic values. Indeed, materialism is related to the poverty of relationships by means of a bi-directional causation. On the one side, materialistic individuals tend to develop certain attitudes in their relationships with other people which disfavour positive experiences in such relationships. On the other side, individuals who experience poor relationships tend to develop materialistic values. Indeed, materialism is a response to insecurity, and poor relationships, especially during infancy, tend to produce insecurity. The conclusion is that there is a circular effect that leads materialism and the scarcity of relationships to nourish each other.
3. In turn, materialism is promoted by market relationships. In particular, the higher the penetration of market relationships into social relationships, the greater their impact in promoting materialistic values.
4. The media, especially advertising, play a role in spreading materialism as well.

The NEG approach suggests that the better the evolution over time of social capital, the lower the growth rate of the economy, of work hours and of consumption and the better the trend of well-being. I then turned to the US to examine whether it showed any evidence of an economic growth of the NEG type over the past few decades. I found this evidence in the decline of US social capital, in the remarkable increase in expenditures as a defence against the deterioration of social capital, in the decrease of average well-being and in the increase in work hours. The roots of NEG capitalism appear to be much stronger in the US compared to Europe. Indeed, in Europe, in the past few decades, social capital and well-being increased slightly, whereas work hours fell and growth was weaker compared to the US.

These differences between Europe and the US find a plausible explanation in the different dynamics of the factors affecting the evolution of social capital over time. In a different trend from that seen in Europe, materialism spread greatly in the US over the past few decades. This, in turn, may have been affected by the comparatively much greater pressure exerted on Americans by the advertising industry. Moreover, in the past 30 years the US has experienced economic reforms that brought the penetration of market relationships into the society to unprecedented levels in human history. Finally, the remarkable expansion of American cities in the past 20 years followed the model of the low-density city, a model that has a particularly harmful effect on social assets.

To conclude, the economic growth produced by NEG capitalism is fraught with the risk of crises and, under certain financial market conditions, can produce global crises. When the crisis exploded, these financial market conditions had matured enough to allow the contagion to be exported to the rest of the planet. In fact, the expansion of American private debt had been facilitated by the abundance of credit in the United States, fuelled by the funding of the American debt which the world had carried out by flooding Wall Street with its capital for decades. It is precisely for this reason that the American crisis infected the rest of the planet: the contagion vectors were the toxic assets on the American private debt. The abundance of credit in the United States and the export of the American crisis are two sides of the same coin.

The explanation for American consumerism proposed here is not intended as exhaustive. It could easily coexist with other explanations, in particular with that based on the role of increasing income inequality within a context of social comparisons. In any case, whatever its explanation, American consumerism stands at the core of this crisis.

This approach emphasizes that what happened in the credit market is the flip side of the coin of what happened in the labour market. Americans plundered every accessible resource to support their consumption: credit and their own time. A society that produces people who are increasingly lonely and more and more willing to consider 'buying' as the solution to their problems tends to live systematically beyond its means, if the conditions of the credit market allow it to do so. The crisis was triggered by an extremely dangerous combination of two factors: the willingness of a people to live beyond its means and the willingness of the rest of the world to provide it with the resources to do so. In turn, the willingness to live beyond one's means stems from the world – created by NEG capitalism – in which material satisfaction is used as compensation for social dissatisfaction. This material–social imbalance, by way of the credit market, can be transformed into global economic imbalances that lead to profound planetary crises.

This is why the goal of promoting happiness coincides with that of promoting economic stability. Both require the construction of a world that is more attentive to that dimension of life which concerns social relationships. In other words, the antidote to NEG capitalism lies in policies for social capital (Bartolini, forthcoming; Helliwell, this volume, Chapter 5).

NOTES

1. In 1996, the trade deficit was $1006 per household; in 2000, it had increased to $3787 per household; it finally exploded to $6194 per household in 2007 (Jagannathan et al. 2009).

2. The share of wages and salaries as a percentage of American GDP was 49 per cent in 2000, but it had dropped to 46 per cent in 2007. Adding proprietors' income to this share, it dropped to 54 per cent of GDP in 2007 compared to 57 per cent of GDP in 2000 (Jagannathan et al. 2009). All indicators of income inequality – e.g. the Gini index – point to a worsening of income distribution in the US over the past 30 years (see Atkinson et al. 2009).
3. An example of advertising conveying a different existential message is 'The Impossible Ad' (http://www.youtube.com/watch?v=OvfWGlzFVDw). It is impossible because it advertises products that are not sold by anyone: time and affection. Contrary to commercial advertising, 'The Impossible Ad' suggests that the remedy to dissatisfaction lies in having more time and in nurturing more one's affective relations, which arguably implies working (and consuming) less.
4. Putnam's findings were criticized (i.e. Ladd 1996) and carefully scrutinized, but in the end they proved to be substantially correct (Paxton 1999; Robinson and Jackson 2001; Costa and Kahn 2003; Bartolini et al. 2013).
5. Opportunism is the practice – motivated by self-interest – of exploiting circumstances without regard to moral principles or others' interests.
6. The concept of transaction cost covers a range of costs associated with the exchange of goods or services and the protection of private property. Transaction costs importantly include those costs related to protection from opportunism. Examples are provided in the text and include police, guards, lawyers and judges.
7. Wallis and North (1986) mainly attributed the growth of the transaction cost sector to the increasing division of labour and number of transactions in the US economy. However, according to Putnam's thesis, the decline in social trust have played a role in the expansion of the transaction cost sector.
8. Fischer (2008) shows that, while per capita GDP is not correlated to happiness over the last few decades in the US, happiness and median income are correlated. However, a large part of the happiness trend remains unexplained by median income.
9. 'Additional spending by the rich shifts the frame of reference that defines what the near-rich consider necessary or desirable, so they too spend more. In turn, this shifts the frame of reference for those just below the near-rich, and so on, all the way down the income ladder' (Frank 2009, p. 13).
10. In 1944, the powers that were close to winning the Second World War negotiated in Bretton Woods (US) an agreement concerning the rules that had to regulate the monetary and financial relationships among countries in the after-war period. The main feature of the Bretton Woods system was an obligation for each country to keep its exchange rate fixed – through proper monetary policy – with respect to the US dollar, whose value was established in terms of gold. The member states were encouraged to use capital controls (limitations to international capital flows) to maintain external balance in the face of potentially destabilizing capital flows. In the early 1970s, the collapse of the Bretton Woods system opened up the new era – in which we still live – of full freedom of international capital movements.

REFERENCES

Aguiar, M. and E. Hurst, (2007), 'Measuring trends in leisure: the allocation of time over five decades', *Quarterly Journal of Economics*, **122** (3), 969–1006.

Alesina, A., E.L. Glaeser and B. Sacerdote (2005), 'Work and leisure in the US and Europe: why so different?', CEPR Discussion Paper No. 5140.

Antoci, A. and S. Bartolini (2004), 'Negative externalities, defensive expenditures and labor supply in an evolutionary context', *Environment and Development Economics*, **9**, 591–612.

Atkinson, A.B., T. Piketty and E. Saez (2009), *Top Incomes in the Long Run of History*, NBER Working Paper No. 15408, Cambridge, MA: National Bureau of Economic Research.

Bartolini, S. (forthcoming), *Manifesto for Happiness: Shifting Society from Money to Well-being*, Philadelphia: Pennsylvania University Press.

Bartolini, S. and E. Bilancini (2011), 'Social participation and hours worked', Quaderni del Dipartimento di Economia Politica e Statistica, Università di Siena, No. 620.

Bartolini, S. and L. Bonatti (2002), 'Environmental and social degradation as the engine of economic growth', *Ecological Economics*, **41**, 1–16.

Bartolini, S. and L. Bonatti (2003), 'Endogenous growth and negative externalities', *Journal of Economics*, **79**, 123–44.

Bartolini, S. and L. Bonatti (2008), 'Endogenous growth, decline in social capital and expansion of market activities', *Journal of Economic Behavior and Organization*, **67** (3), 917–26.

Bartolini, S. and F. Sarracino (2013), 'Twenty-five years of materialism: do the US and Europe diverge?', Quaderni del Dipartimento di Economia Politica e Statistica, Università di Siena, No. 689.

Bartolini, S., E. Bilancini and M. Pugno (2013), 'Did the decline in social connections depress Americans' happiness?', *Social Indicators Research*, **110** (3), 1033–59.

Belk, R.W. (1985), 'Materialism: trait aspects of living in the material world', *Journal of Consumer Research*, **12**, 265–80.

Bonatti, L. (2008), 'Evolution of preferences and cross-country differences in time devoted to market work', *Labour Economics*, **15** (6), 1341–65.

Burda, M., D.S. Hamermesh and P. Weil (2007), 'Total work, gender and social norms', Institute for the Study of Labor (IZA) Discussion Paper No. 2705.

Cohen, P. and J. Cohen (1996), *Life Values and Adolescent Mental Health*, Mahwah, NJ: Lawrence Erlbaum.

Costa, D.L. and M.E. Kahn (2003), 'Understanding the decline in social capital, 1952–1998', *Kyklos*, **56**, 17–46.

Davis, S.J. and M. Henrekson (2004), *Tax Effects on Work Activity, Industry Mix and Shadow Economy Size: Evidence from Rich-country Comparisons*, NBER Working Paper No. 10509, Cambridge, MA: National Bureau of Economic Research.

Deci, E. (1971), 'Effects of externally mediated rewards on intrinsic motivations', *Journal of Personality and Social Psychology*, **18**, 105–15.

Deci, E., R. Koestner and R.M. Ryan (1999), 'A meta-analytic review of experiments examining the effects of extrinsic rewards on intrinsic motivation', *Psychological Bulletin*, **125**, 627–68.

Diener, E. and M. Seligman (2004), 'Beyond money: toward an economy of well-being', *Psychological Science in the Public Interest*, **5** (1), 1–31.

Fang, M. and B. Gerhart (2012), 'Does pay for performance diminish intrinsic interest?', *International Journal of Human Resource Management*, **23** (6), 1176–96.

Fischer, C.S. (2008), 'What wealth–happiness paradox?', *Journal of Happiness Studies*, **9**, 219–26.

Frank, R. (2009), 'Post-consumer prosperity: finding new opportunities among the economic wreckage', *American Prospect*, **20** (3).

Freeman, R. and R. Schettkat (2005), 'Marketization of household production and the EU–US gap in work', *Economic Policy*, **20** (41), 6–50.

Frey, B.S. (1997), *Not Just for the Money: An Economic Theory of Personal Motivation*, Cheltenham, UK and Lyme, NH, USA: Edward Elgar Publishing.

Frey, B.S. and R. Jegen (2001), 'Motivation crowding theory', *Journal of Economic Surveys*, **15** (5), 589–611.

Galbraith, J.K. (1962), *The Affluent Society*, Harmondsworth: Penguin Books.

Gneezy, U. and A. Rustichini (2000), 'A fine is a price', *Journal of Legal Studies*, **29**, 1–17.

Gordon, R.J. (2006), 'Issues in the comparison of welfare between Europe and the United States', paper presented at the Venice Summer Institute, Isola di San Servolo, Venice.

Hacker, J. (2006). *The Great Risk Shift*, New York: Oxford University Press.

Harrison, B. and B. Bluestone (1990), *The Great U-turn: Corporate Restructuring and the Polarizing of America*, New York: Basic Books.

Heston, A., R. Summers and B. Aten (2011), 'Penn World Table version 7.0', Center for International Comparisons of Production, Income and Prices, University of Pennsylvania.

Jagannathan, R., M. Kapoor and E. Schaumburg (2009), *Why Are We in a Recession? The Financial Crisis Is the Symptom, Not the Disease!*, NBER Working Paper No. 15404, Cambridge, MA: National Bureau of Economic Research.

Jayadev, A. and S. Bowles (2006), 'Guard labor', *Journal of Development Economics*, **79** (2), 328–48.

Kahn, E.M. (2000), 'The environmental impact of suburbanization', *Journal of Policy Analysis and Management*, **19**, 569–86.

Kasser, T. (2002), *The High Price of Materialism*, Cambridge, MA: MIT Press.

Kasser, T. and K.M. Sheldon (2000), 'Of wealth and death: materialism, mortality salience, and consumption behaviour', *Psychological Science*, **11**, 352–5.

Kasser, T., R.M. Ryan, M. Zax and A.J. Sameroff (1995), 'The relations of the maternal and social environments to late adolescents' materialistic and pro-social values', *Developmental Psychology*, **31**, 907–14.

Ladd, E. (1996), 'The data just don't show erosion of America's social capital', *Public Perspective*, **7**, 1–30.

McCully, C.P. (2011), 'Trends in consumer spending and personal saving, 1959–2009', *Survey of Current Business*, **91** (6), 14–23.

McHoskey, J.W. (1999), 'Machiavellianism, intrinsic vs. extrinsic goals, and social interest: a self-determination theory', *Motivation and Emotion*, **23**, 267–83.

Montgomery, C. (2013), *Happy City: Transforming Our Lives through Urban Design*, Toronto: Doubleday Canada.

Myers, D. and E. Diener (1997), 'The science of happiness', *Futurist*, **31** (5), 1–7.

Olovsson, C. (2009), 'Why do Europeans work so little?', *International Economic Review*, **50** (1), 39–61.

Paxton, Pamela (1999), 'Is social capital declining in the United States? A multiple indicator assessment', *American Journal of Sociology*, **105** (1), 88–127.

Peñalosa, E. (2008), 'A more socially and environmentally sustainable city', in Ilka and Andreas Ruby (eds), *Urban Transformation*, Berlin: Ruby Press.

Prescott, E. (2004), 'Why do Americans work so much more than Europeans?', *Federal Reserve Bank of Minneapolis Quarterly Review*, **28**, 2–14.

Putnam, R.D. (2000), *Bowling Alone: The Collapse and Revival of American Community*, New York: Simon & Schuster.

Robinson, R.V. and E.F. Jackson (2001), 'Is trust in others declining in America? An age–period–cohort analysis', *Social Science Research*, **30**, 117–45.

Rogers, S.H., J.M. Halstead, K.H. Gardner and C.H. Carlson (2010), 'Examining walkability and social capital as indicators of quality of life at the municipal and neighborhood scales', *Applied Research in Quality of Life*, doi: 10.1007/s11482-010-9132-4.

Rogerson, R. (2008), 'Structural transformation and the deterioration of European labor market outcomes', *Journal of Political Economy*, **116** (2), 235–59.

Sarracino, F. (2011), 'Money, sociability and happiness: are developed countries doomed to social erosion and unhappiness?', *Social Indicators Research*, 7 July, pp. 1–54, doi: 10.1007/s11205-011-9898-2.

Schor, J. (1998), *The Overspent American: Why We Desire What We Don't Need*, New York: Basic Books.

Schor, J. (2005), *Born to Buy: The Commercialized Child and the New Consumer Culture*, New York: Scribner.

Sheldon, K.M., M.S. Sheldon and R. Osbaldiston (2000), 'Prosocial values and group assortation in an N-person prisoner dilemma', *Human Nature*, **11**, 387–404.

Stevenson, B. and J. Wolfers (2008), 'Economic growth and subjective well-being: reassessing the Easterlin paradox', IZA Discussion Paper No. 3654.

Stiglitz, J.E. (2008), 'Towards a general theory of consumerism', in L. Pecchi and G. Piga, *Revisiting Keynes*, Cambridge, MA: MIT Press.

Thompson, G.D., S.V. Aradhyula, G. Frisvold and R. Tronstad (2010), 'Does paying referees expedite reviews? Results of a natural experiment', *Economic Journal*, **76** (3), 678–92.

Titmuss, R. (1970), *The Gift Relationship: From Human Blood to Social Policy*, London: Routledge.

Twenge, J. (2000), 'The age of anxiety? The birth cohort change in anxiety and neuroticism, 1952–1993', *Journal of Personality and Social Psychology*, **79** (6), 1007.

Wallis, J.J. and D. North (1986), 'Measuring the transaction sector in the American economy, 1870–1970', in S.L. Engerman and R.E. Gallman (eds), *Long-term Factors in American Economic Growth*, Cambridge, MA: National Bureau of Economic Research, pp. 95–162.

Wilkinson, R. and K. Pickett (2009), *The Spirit Level: Why More Equal Societies Almost Always Do Better*, London: Allen Lane.

Williams, G., R. Frankell, T. Campbell and E. Deci (2000), 'Research on relationship-centred care and healthcare outcomes from the Rochester Biopsychosocial Program: a self-determination theory integration', *Families, Systems and Health*, **18**, 79–90.

7. Creating supportive environments to foster reasonableness and achieve sustainable well-being

Avik Basu, Rachel Kaplan and Stephen Kaplan

Well-being depends on others and the environment. Our capacity to meet our needs and pursue a meaningful life is affected by the actions of other people as well as the shared environmental resources on which we all depend. These impacts play out unequally across socio-economic, geographic and political boundaries. Excessive resource use by industrialized nations leads to exploitation, both human and natural, in underdeveloped yet resource-rich nations. On a smaller scale, how farmers care for a shared pasture can have an impact on the well-being of those with whom they share it. Inequalities range across temporal boundaries as well – the well-being of future generations depends on the decisions and actions of the current generation, just as ours has depended on those of past generations.

If our goal is to improve the well-being of all people, then maximizing the individual well-being of some at the cost of others and the environment cannot be an adaptive solution. Consequently, policies aimed at improving the well-being of current as well as future generations must simultaneously address individual well-being and the larger good (Kjell 2011). To promote this more egalitarian well-being, we address the needs for reasonableness and coexistence that can foster the well-being of others as well as ourselves.

We begin by describing our conceptualization of reasonableness, its commonalities with and differences from current notions of well-being (in particular, subjective well-being) and the centrality of information in understanding ways to foster reasonableness. This leads to a brief overview of the Reasonable Person Model, a theoretical framework which casts reasonableness in terms of human informational needs. To fulfil these needs, in turn, it is important to consider how environments can support reasonableness. One category of needs relates to functioning effectively in a world that readily undermines our mental resources. How can environments sustain and restore our inherently limited mental capacity? The second category concerns the need for community, in terms both of ways to promote social interaction and of opportunities for acting meaningfully. Implicitly we take the position that reasonableness is strengthened by sharing perspectives, learning from others and feeling that one is a useful member of the species. We close with the suggestion that small experiments are an effective means for testing some of these ideas while creating environments that can bring out the best in people.

REASONABLENESS

Reasonableness addresses the issues that help (or hinder) us in being civil and sociable, developing trust, and cooperating with one another in the face of shared challenges. More simply, it refers to the way in which people, at their best, deal with one another and the resources on which we all rely. While humans have evolved to have pro-social inclinations (Tomasello and Herrmann 2010), the frequent examples of unreasonableness in modern life suggest that all too often people are not at their best. Irritability, intolerance, incivility, lack of respect, and a sense of hopelessness are but a few instances of a reasonableness deficit in managing oneself and interacting with others. Greed, waste and pollution are examples of unreasonableness that have an impact on our shared resources. By contrast, achieving sustainability relies on regard for others and appreciation of what sustains us.

Subjective Well-being and Reasonableness

The notion of reasonableness focuses strongly on humankind's mutual dependencies and less on the personal aspects of subjective well-being (SWB). Whereas SWB is primarily a measure of one's own state, reasonableness also reflects how we treat others. While research supports that cooperation can enhance well-being, there are also ample examples of people whose well-being is not reflected in their civility towards others. It is also possible that consideration of the larger good may not permit maximizing individual well-being. For example, people often take on challenges that may compromise their own well-being in order to achieve a larger purpose (e.g. raising children, helping others, learning about oneself). While such challenges may diminish one's autonomy or pleasure in the short term, the realization of a long-term achievement can benefit overall well-being. We propose, therefore, that reasonableness may provide a useful standard for addressing the issues of interdependence that are pivotal to both the individual and the societal aspects of well-being.

While reasonableness does place a greater focus on interdependence, there are several themes that reasonableness and research linked to SWB have in common. For example, Helliwell's analysis of SWB (this volume, Chapter 5) includes findings supporting the human inclination for pro-social behaviour that resonate strongly with the notion of reasonableness. Likewise, there are some interesting parallels between Antonovsky's sense of coherence (Hämäläinen, this volume, Chapter 2; Eriksson and Lindström, this volume, Chapter 3), consisting of comprehensibility, manageability and meaningfulness, and factors related to reasonableness. Deci and Ryan's (2000) notions of autonomy, competence and relatedness are characteristics that connect well with reasonableness. Also, among Peterson and Seligman's (2004) list of character strengths and virtues, many – e.g. wisdom and knowledge, courage, justice, transcendence, temperance, humanity – are in concordance with the characteristics of a reasonable person.

Information and Reasonableness

What are the reasons behind reasonable behaviour? We suspect that an underlying issue is our relationship with information. For a species whose survival has hinged on wits rather than speed or strength, it should not be surprising that we are greatly motivated by and concerned about information. Our survival toolkit depends on mechanisms for gathering information from our surroundings to recognize existing dangers or opportunities and to anticipate future outcomes. Yet our relationship with information is anything but straightforward. We seek it and share it, even horde it, and struggle to make sense of it. At the same time, we hide it, get bored with it and become overwhelmed by it. The joys and pains of this relationship suggest that we care deeply about making sense of our world and, accordingly, would go to great lengths to avoid confusion. When we are unable to do so, we are more likely to find ourselves in an unreasonable state.

For example, being in a state of confusion can easily make us irritable. Our patience is tested when our expectations of others are not met (consider, for example, a law-abiding driver who might develop road rage at someone skirting the rules). Impatience can be quickly exacerbated in contexts where we do not know what is going on or why things are happening a certain way. O'Hara and Lyon (this volume, Chapter 4) assert that an uncertain, rapidly changing global context now leads to an incoherent worldview with concomitant psychological costs. Lack of clarity at many scales can thus readily lead to expressions of unreasonableness.

The information we absorb from and about others colours the way we perceive and interact with them. How we understand others and their circumstances can thus play an important role in developing trust, achieving tolerance and respect, and countering stereotypes that easily lead to unthinking reactions. Developing such understanding requires community and social interaction, yet as people are increasingly isolated (Helliwell and Putnam 2004; Bartolini, this volume, Chapter 6) such opportunities are less frequent. Furthermore, inequality exacerbates feelings of resentment towards others (Oishi et al. 2011).

Reasonableness, however, requires more than having needed information and a sense of clarity. We must also have the mental capacity to use the information effectively. For example, we may know that saying something is impolite or inappropriate, but may not have the mental resources necessary to refrain from doing so. Von Hippel and Gonsalkorale (2005) exemplified this in an amusing cuisine-related study which showed that people with a depleted capacity for self-restraint are more likely to make culturally insensitive comments. By contrast, listening and showing respect to others depend on our ability to control the urge to interrupt and jump to conclusions. In short, civility depends a great deal on self-restraint.

Even when we have the needed information and can competently utilize the knowledge, reasonableness may still founder. Taking action and then realizing it has made little difference can lead to distrust, a sense of helplessness and hopelessness, and inappropriate behaviour. On the other hand, getting positive feedback about the difference we've made can have the opposite effect.

Supportive Environments as Conditions to Foster Reasonableness in Policy

Given the breadth of issues associated with reasonableness, improving it may seem like an intractable problem, particularly from the vantage point of policy initiatives. We propose that focusing on the impact *environments* can have in fostering reasonableness and well-being may offer some fresh insights.

Environments can be thought of as patterns of information that their human occupants must process. They can take many forms. They can be created by people (houses, office buildings, streets) or products of natural forces (forests, streams). Both cities and forests provide information that is essential to human knowledge, wayfinding, prediction and action. Similarly, many other contexts, circumstances and situations can be considered as patterns of information that serve human functioning.

Our analysis thus broadens the environment concept to include not only physical settings, but programmes, interventions and virtual environments. For example, what we see on our computers and smartphones can be a captivating or confusing environment. Classrooms, boardrooms and courtrooms are characterized not only by the design of physical space, but also by the rules, customs, formalities and informalities which govern how people share information, respect one another and work together.

Environments, in this broad sense, can have a dramatic effect on physical and emotional states as well as behaviour. One can get into the driver's seat of a car and become a very different person. Zimbardo (1973) famously put innocent people into a prison context, some as prisoners and others as guards. The 'guards', who had no previous experience as such, treated the 'prisoners' so badly that the experiment had to be terminated. Similarly, being lost in an unfamiliar neighbourhood can lead to frustration and fear. Attending some lectures can produce sufficient confusion or boredom to make one head for the door.

While there are plenty of negative examples, our focus here is on the kinds of environments that can bring out the best in people. The next section presents a framework that builds on these notions.

THE REASONABLE PERSON MODEL

The Reasonable Person Model (RPM) (S. Kaplan and Kaplan 2003, 2009) posits that reasonableness and well-being depend greatly on meeting informational needs. From an RPM perspective, environments are patterns of information that people want to make sense of, utilize effectively and engage with meaningfully. Since information patterns serve as the common coin, institutional or cultural arrangements can be analysed through the same RPM lens as physical environments. For example, people in more individualistic societies are regularly exposed to information, through media and through others' actions, that promotes selfish behaviour. Thus, cultural values and norms can be framed as information that influences reasonableness.

RPM breaks these informational needs into three interdependent domains that have already been hinted at in the previous discussion (Figure 7.1). While RPM does not address every cause of unreasonableness, the basic premise of the model is that we are more likely to be reasonable when all three domains of needs are addressed.[1]

Model Building

The first domain of RPM concerns our need to build mental models. These models take the form of neural structures that represent ideas and objects in the real world as well as the relationships between them. Constructing such mental models (i.e. learning) is a relatively slow process that requires multiple and varied experiences. The resulting maplike structures (also

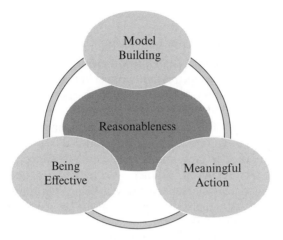

Figure 7.1   Three interrelated domains of the Reasonable Person Model

known as cognitive maps) allow us to store information and to use it to anticipate forthcoming events and evaluate possible outcomes (S. Kaplan 1973). Our mental models permit us to parse an otherwise incoherent mass of information and pick up on salient patterns, ignore the superfluous, and make predictions of what might come next. Because of our ubiquitous reliance on mental models, we are hard-wired to want to extend our maps. At the same time, however, given the effort put into building them, we are often inclined to cling to the mental models we already have, sometimes despite evidence to the contrary. Like most products of evolution, it is by no means a perfect system, but it has helped the species carve out a large and often comfortable niche.

Undermining our capacity to build mental models undermines our reasonableness. Research in environmental preference has shown strong commonalities in the kinds of environments that people prefer. These are settings we can understand and that offer us the opportunity to learn something new (S. Kaplan and R. Kaplan 1982). On the other hand, environments that are consistently less preferred are ones where our models cannot grow (e.g. boredom) or where they are not useful (e.g. confusion). Extending our models is facilitated when new knowledge connects sensibly to what we already know and grows mostly incrementally. While innovation sometimes comes from 'thinking outside the box', more commonly being able to explore in a realm not too far away from one's expertise is more comforting. Being able to do so at one's pace fosters the model-building process. RPM emphasizes that addressing these needs for understanding and exploration is a critical component of enhancing reasonableness.

Being Effective

The second domain of RPM deals with the need to function effectively. First, doing so requires more than knowing what to do – it also requires a sense of competence. This means cultivating skills for how to do things. It also requires knowing how things work in the world and finding opportunities to apply one's skills.

Second, developing this competence is dependent on thinking with a clear head, yet we often find our thoughts muddled (see also Hämäläinen, this volume, Chapter 2). Not only is such a state disconcerting, but it can impair learning, cooperation, problem solving, civility, and many other activities central to reasonableness and well-being. This unfortunate state of mind is a result of a depleted mental resource known as directed attention (DA) (S. Kaplan 1995).

In technical terms, DA is an inhibitory neural mechanism used for self-regulation, self-control and executive functions (Baumeister 2004; S. Kaplan and Berman 2010). More simply, it is what people depend upon to pay attention, block out distractions, resist temptations and stay focused on goals. Thus, DA is essential for coping with the environment. The demands on attention in modern environments are rapidly increasing, but the evolution of our brains has not kept pace (Grinde 2009a). Yet those same brains must now swim through tsunamis of information every day. In some respects technology has helped where evolution has not; in other respects, however, it has exacerbated the situation by the sheer volume of added information to which attention must be paid. In other words, more information is not always helpful.

All of this would not be a problem if DA were boundless. Alas, it is a limited resource, meaning that we cannot pay attention indefinitely. The depletion of this resource – resulting in directed attention fatigue (DAF) – can have serious effects on functioning effectively and our sense of competence. It can increase the likelihood of incivility and aggression, as well as decrease the capacity to face challenges (Kuo and Sullivan 2001a). These and other factors combine to reduce our overall effectiveness. In light of the far-reaching implications of human attentional capacities it is important to consider ways not only to restore DA but to reduce the likelihood of DAF.

Meaningful Action

The third domain of RPM addresses our need to make a difference in the world around us. Such meaningful action is far different in the modern world than it was for our Stone Age ancestors. For them, foraging for food was clearly linked to survival and quality of life. In our modern times the relationship between one's actions and the outcome is often more murky. Nevertheless, our desire to make a difference remains a strong motivating factor. Feeling that our actions make no difference can be a tremendous detriment to our self-worth and lead to a sense of helplessness (Seligman 1975). On the other hand, knowing that we have had an impact can make us feel accomplished and useful, bolstering respect for ourselves and also garnering the respect of others.

Meaningful action can find expression in a multitude of common activities that permit us to have a sense that we make a difference, are heard and respected, and may be part of something bigger than ourselves. Participating in plans that may affect our communities is a chance to act meaningfully. It is hardly surprising that when participation is solicited but the outcomes show little trace of its impact the consequences are distressing to those who were involved. The desire to be respected and to be heard is a key motivation that when undermined can be detrimental to reasonableness. Yet, while the desire to be heard is strong, the challenge is often to listen to others. Listening, however, is critical for developing shared mental models, and such models are needed for groups to work together and achieve mutually beneficial outcomes.

Helping fellow members of our species can be a meaningful experience. While such pro-social behaviour is by no means guaranteed, creating conditions of familiarity and trust between people makes such behaviour more likely (Helliwell, this volume, Chapter 5). Grinde's (2009b) comparison of social units (e.g. families, tribes) in Palaeolithic versus modern times suggests that, while the species has relied heavily on social relationships for survival, modern contexts and environments are often detrimental to such relationships (see also Bartolini, this volume, Chapter 6).

The desire to be needed and to be useful creates an enormous, and often underutilized, human talent pool. While this talent can be used for anti-social causes (e.g. gangs, terrorism), the meteoric rise of the NGO sector (Hawken 2007) suggests that pro-social outlets are not only possible but widespread (see also O'Hara and Lyon, this volume, Chapter 4). NGO projects and similar opportunities could foster well-being both at an individual level by meaningfully engaging human talents and at a societal level by dealing with problems that are salient enough to attract that talent.

The discussion of each of the RPM domains separately may obscure their strong interrelationships. From a policy perspective especially it is the connections among the domains that must be considered. For example, working together requires sharing knowledge with others (i.e. model building) as well as patience and self-restraint (i.e. being effective). It also demands a capacity for treating others with respect and recognizing a universal desire to make a difference (i.e. meaningful action). While not specifically addressed, the necessity of model building is intrinsic to the issues raised in the next two sections. These sections discuss supportive environments in terms of ways they can sustain and restore our limited capacity for attention, and ways they can contribute to developing social capital and community.

REASONABLENESS, MENTAL CAPACITY AND EFFECTIVE FUNCTIONING

Acting reasonably is particularly challenging when it is important to inhibit counterproductive inclinations. Such self-regulation requires directed attention. In this section we turn first to ways that environments can help sustain this finite resource and then consider the role the environment can play in restoring it.

Environments to Sustain Directed Attention

An environment that sustains DA would reduce unnecessary pressures on it. For example, noise has been shown to have a strong negative effect on student performance (Haines et al. 2002; Clark et al. 2006). Children's inability to concentrate on their tasks in such an environment is presumably a contributing factor to the performance decrement. Siting noisy land uses (such as airports) away from schools and locating schools in quiet areas (e.g. through zoning regulations or other land-use policies) may be a fruitful way to preserve DA. Likewise, certain kinds of green roofs, because they have soft surfaces which absorb noise instead of reflecting it, can reduce sound by 5–50 decibels (Dunnett and Kingsbury 2004; Getter and Rowe 2006). Many other distractions are endemic in the local environment. Policy makers may find the knowledge of local citizens a rich source of suggestions for ameliorating some of these situations.

Dealing with daily annoyances can also deplete DA. Commutes, traffic, and reliance on cars provide examples for many people. The hallmark of driving is its fast pace of travel that prohibits communication with others and often raises uncertainty and frustration (e.g. it is hard to know whether the other driver is honking at you or someone else). Dealing with this uncertainty does more than put one in a bad mood; it also uses up precious DA. Other means of transport – walking, biking, trains, sharing rides, and buses – circumvent many annoyances. Changing the reliance on driving necessitates numerous policy decisions with respect both to the availability of reliable, convenient and efficient alternative means of transport and to work patterns which reduce the need for it (e.g. telecommuting) (Goldman and Gorham 2006; Zielinski 2006). The resulting changes not only serve to sustain DA; they can also benefit everyone's daily well-being as well as preserve environmental resources for future generations.

Getting lost, and even concern about getting lost, is another drain on DA. Finding one's way around can be challenging within buildings, campuses, neighbourhoods and many urban settings. Signage can be helpful in such situations. Unfortunately, it can also add to the confusion. Street mazes with incoherent directions, maps that are counterintuitive (e.g. north need not always point to the top of the map) or have lengthy complex legends, and systems that add to the memory load (e.g. remembering the colour associated with where one parked most recently) all exacerbate wayfinding problems. Designs that facilitate wayfinding, by contrast, may reduce the need for signage. For example, grid-based street designs are more navigable than cul-de-sacs (Tasker-Brown and Pogharian 2000). Furthermore, if people and their travel destinations (e.g. work, shopping) were closer to each other, both the need to drive and the likelihood of getting lost would be reduced. This has benefits not only for mental resources but for environmental resources as well.

Yet another drain on DA is the consequence of the difficulties of weighing among alternative decisions that need to be made. While choice is seen as a hallmark of freedom, having too many choices can have psychological costs. This is the primary insight from Schwartz's *Paradox of Choice* (2004), in which he argues that having too many choices leads both to an inability to make a decision and to feeling less satisfied with the outcome. Vohs et al.'s (2008) work on *decision fatigue* makes the link more explicitly to DAF, showing that making decisions expends a limited resource (i.e. DA) for self-regulation and thereby impairs one's subsequent capacity to regulate behaviour. Therefore another way to sustain DA is to reconsider environments in which choice may be overbearing (see also Hämäläinen, this volume, Chapter 2). For example, as exemplified by many software programs, default options may minimize the user's need to consider a multitude of possibilities, although these can still be available for those who wish to use them.

Environments to Restore Directed Attention

We have explored a variety of ways to sustain DA by reducing the many daily occasions that call upon these precious and finite attentional resources. Even if many culturally ingrained patterns that assault DA could be diminished, however, DA can be depleted through concerted and intended effort. It is necessary, therefore, to permit DA to replenish or become restored. Here again, environments can be more or less helpful.

Attention restoration theory (R. Kaplan and Kaplan 1989; S. Kaplan 1995) provides an analysis of the kinds of experiences that lead to recovery from the fatigue of DA. It relies on an attentional mechanism that does not require the effort-driven and fatigable DA, but rather one that is more automatic, centring our focus on attributes of the environment that are inherently fascinating. This alternative kind of attention – proposed long ago by William James (1898) – requires minimal effort (e.g. watching the antics of wildlife in a nearby tree), and, while people are fascinated in this way, their DA can rest and replenish.

In addition, when the environment softly holds our attention (e.g. wind blowing through leaves), it frees the remaining mental space to reflect on difficult events or ideas that don't make sense (R. Kaplan and Kaplan 2011). It also allows the unconscious mind to work on unresolved issues. Such opportunities can help reduce the impact of mental stresses, as well as the cognitive dissonance issues raised by O'Hara and Lyon (this volume, Chapter 4). Thus, creating environments that engage our senses effortlessly and provide opportunities for reflection can help to restore DA.

Restorative benefits of nature

Many kinds of environments and activities have this restorative potential. In particular, a growing body of literature on restorative environments has focused on the beneficial impact of exposure to natural environments that contain trees, plants and other greenery (Pretty 2004; Frumkin 2005; Velarde et al. 2007; Abraham et al. 2010). Studies have consistently found that exposure to natural settings can reduce DAF and lead to various benefits, whether one is physically in the environment or otherwise engaged with it.

Taking a walk in nature has been shown to improve the capacity for directing one's attention. For example, Berman et al. (2008) compared walking in a serene natural setting to a walk of the same duration on a busy street and found that participants who walked in nature performed better on several attention-related measures. The authors attribute the improvement in attention to environmental factors; while the natural environment provided walkers with a multitude of fascinating objects to softly engage the senses, the busy street required walkers to maintain a constant vigilance (e.g. to avoid being hit by a car).

A substantial empirical literature has shown that opportunities to view nature from the window not only is restorative (Tennessen and Cimprich 1995), but also improves satisfaction and well-being (R. Kaplan 2001). Views can also have a range of health benefits, as evidenced by Moore's

(1981) study which showed that prison inmates in cells with views of a nearby farm field visit the infirmary less than inmates whose cells face a barren inside courtyard. In a more virtual environment, Berto (2005) showed that even viewing photographs of natural settings can restore DA.

Chicago's public housing projects presented a remarkable opportunity to test the effects of nature exposure in a gritty and challenging context. The layout of the project buildings provided some residents with views of some trees and green areas, while others had little if any nature available. In a series of studies, Kuo and Sullivan reported that residents with views of nature exhibited less aggression (Kuo and Sullivan 2001a), committed fewer crimes (Kuo and Sullivan 2001b) and felt more capable taking on challenges (Kuo 2001). The researchers attribute these benefits to restored attentional capacity amongst the residents who had nature views.

Matsuoka's (2010) study extended the context to high school students. He related the nature views at 101 high schools in south-east Michigan to student performance and behaviour measures. After controlling for socio-economic factors, he found that schools that have cafeterias with nature views are linked to better student performance. The author interprets this in terms of students' opportunity during break time to deal with their internal thoughts and recover from mental fatigue, which then increases their capacity in class for learning. This is corroborated by a study of students with attention deficit hyperactivity disorder (ADHD) which found that those who spend their break time exposed to green outdoor settings are less symptomatic than students who spend their break in built environments (Kuo and Faber Taylor 2004; Faber Taylor and Kuo 2011).

In a caregiving context, Canin's (1991) study found that in the demanding world of HIV caregivers those who reported walking, hiking, biking and other nature-based activities scored higher on measures of effective functioning and well-being. Nature walks and gardening have also been shown to improve the recovery of post-surgery breast cancer patients by reducing the mental fatigue that comes from the stresses of chemotherapy and the uncertainty associated with concerns about mortality (Cimprich 1993; Cimprich and Ronis 2003).

A large-scale study in the Netherlands compared the amount of green space near citizens' residences (based on GPS data) to various measures of the residents' health as collected in a national health survey. They found that those who live closer to natural areas such as gardens, neighbourhood parks or larger green spaces (what they call 'Vitamin G') are healthier on a wide range of measures (Groenewegen et al. 2006). This not only suggests that the benefits of nature exposure go beyond the realm of attention restoration, but also underscores the importance of creating environments in which nature is equitably distributed such that all citizens can benefit from having easy access. Similarly, Stigsdotter et al. (2010) have shown, in a large-scale study based on a random sample, that the proximity of the natural environment is significantly related to reduced stress and enhanced quality of life.

Having nature nearby can be particularly beneficial to children. Louv's (2005) *Last Child in the Woods* bemoans the diminishing time children spend in the outdoors and describes the multiple benefits children receive from having time to play outside. It may be beyond the purview of policy to dictate what can or cannot be shown on television, even though many forms of programming can have a detrimental effect on attention level (Christakis 2011; Lillard and Peterson 2011), but having nature nearby can give children at least an option to do something other than sit in front of the television.

Policy opportunities
Population growth and the concomitant urbanization of natural lands continue to dramatically change landscapes around the world. The desire to retain some aspects of nature in these increasingly human-built environments is now more than an expression of nostalgia or Luddism. Severing our connection to nature has substantial psychological costs; it impairs our capacity to think clearly and function effectively, which in turn diminishes the collective well-being. For policies geared towards improving well-being, the mandate then should be to preserve nature where it exists, revitalize nature where it has been disregarded, and integrate nature into the fabric of cities and neighbourhoods.

Preserve   Creating nationally protected parklands or wilderness areas is certainly a desirable way to preserve nature and protect it from future development. Even when this is feasible, however, such areas are likely to be inaccessible to many people. Using a smaller-scale approach would provide benefits for more people, more readily and more frequently. An example of such an approach is to preserve smaller pieces of nature such as street trees, pavement shrubs and corner parks (R. Kaplan et al. 2007).

Arendt's (1996, 2004) conservation developments have provided a way of preserving existing nature in a residential neighbourhood, adopted in many parts of the US and in Canada. Such developments commit to preserving sensitive and desirable natural areas on a land parcel before it is divided into residential parcels. The resulting lot sizes of the houses are smaller; however, because the residents have access to, and views of, the common natural area, they receive both psychological (R. Kaplan et al. 2004) and economic (Mohamed 2006) benefits. In several rural communities in the United States, local governments have voted to require a certain percentage of new residential building be conservation developments.

Revitalize Overgrown lots and abandoned buildings, found in many urban areas, are linked to lower levels of well-being for nearby residents (Evans 2006). Reclaiming these derelict lands through brownfield redevelopment, urban greening and community gardens allows for the restoration of natural elements in the environment. New York City's MillionTreesNYC programme (PLANYC, n.d.) is an excellent example of a high-level policy geared towards this end. More generally, ecological restoration efforts can help to create not only more functional but also aesthetically pleasing areas in which people may be more likely to linger and build community. They can also have the further advantage of providing local residents with opportunities to participate in the stewardship of the natural settings they cherish (Ryan and Grese 2005).

Integrate The evidence discussed earlier has many policy implications for public institutions such as public housing, schools, hospitals and prisons. In each of these contexts, policy makers can have a direct impact on the well-being of residents, students, patients and even the incarcerated – who are less likely to commit crimes again if their well-being is improved in prison (Helliwell 2011a) – by integrating nearby nature into the design and management of the physical environments of such institutions.

The urban greening movement showcases many exemplary strategies of integrating nature into urban spaces (Rubin 2008). Green roofs, which transform building roofs by covering them with growing vegetation, are an excellent example of utilizing unused space to create a green space that has restorative potential and ecological benefits (Getter and Rowe 2006; Dvorak and Volder 2010). Across the urban greening movement, one of the most noteworthy patterns is that integrating nature need not require excessive time, space or financial resources; even small windowsill gardens, flower pots near doorways, or ivy on buildings can have a restorative effect.

Interventions like these may actually lower future costs. For example, hospitals can reduce the length of patient stays, and states can reduce the costs of prison health care. Costs of maintaining nature areas can also be reduced if local citizens are given the opportunities to participate in their care. In addition to cost savings, this promotes an engagement with nature, with all of its restorative benefits, and enhances the well-being of the community through opportunities for social interaction, which is a central theme of both Helliwell's chapter (this volume, Chapter 5) and our next section.

REASONABLENESS AND COMMUNITY

As an information-based species, we are necessarily dependent on each other. To the extent that reasonableness concerns how we trust and treat others and share knowledge with them, it is important to consider ways to foster community and enhance social capital. Central to social capital are social resources, networks and relationships (Field 2003). It is through these that our social fabric can develop and people can gain a sense of belonging.

The lack of social ties, furthermore, has been shown to relate to mortality rates (Whitehead and Diderichsen 2001) and social well-being. The correlates of subjective well-being include the size and use of one's social network (Helliwell and Barrington-Leigh 2010), level of trust in others (Helliwell and Wang 2010), and ties to friends, neighbours and work colleagues (Helliwell and Putnam 2004). While these studies take an individual perspective, the factors also address the needs for reasonableness. They may also have a self-reinforcing effect in that communities with higher social capital and sense of community can better convey similar values to newcomers, who can perpetuate the cycle.

Developing these connections requires getting to know people in one's community as well as the environment which one shares with them. Aung San Suu Kyi, the 1991 Nobel Peace laureate and democracy activist in Burma, has said that democracy requires broad-mindedness and acceptance of people of different cultures and backgrounds (Aung San Suu Kyi 1991). This in turn requires developing empathy and respect for the needs, values, cultures and expectations of others. What we know about others can greatly influence how we treat them. Treating others better (being civil, helping, listening) enhances mutual trust and good will; it is also a source of individual satisfaction (Peterson 2006). In this way, developing mental models of others can enhance the communal capacity for coexistence and reasonableness.

Developing such mental models draws on a variety of social skills. As Drayton (2011, p. 37) notes: 'Whoever has not mastered the complex, learned skill of empathy will hurt others and disrupt groups – and will be marginalized regardless of the computer science or other knowledge they have.' Drayton also recognizes that empathy is essential for learning how to listen: 'People typically tend to hear only 20 or 30 percent of the words of the person they are conversing with. You can improve that dramatically . . . Listening is understanding. The skill of empathy is a must to be able to listen!' (Bagchi 2011).

Becoming familiar with other people, especially those very different from oneself, requires multiple and diverse ways to learn about them and interact with them. Knowing others means being able to anticipate their behaviours and trust them, feel safe around them, relate to them and communicate with them. The process may also require changing some of the mental models we rely upon without realizing it. Despite these challenges and the time developing them may take, with increased familiarity our sense of being lost and confused is reduced and we can, therefore, feel more secure and capable of coping and acting.

These characteristics and benefits of familiarity apply not only to social contexts but to physical environments as well. Familiar contexts enable us to be more reasonable and function more effectively. Furthermore, the comfort of the familiar makes it safer to venture into the unknown – to explore new ways, perspectives and places. Conversely, feeling lost or unsafe can quell one's motivation to take a chance to explore a new place or learn something about a stranger. Over the long term such feelings can overwhelm the capacity for reasonableness.

Familiarity with one's neighbours, however, does not in itself address the meaningful action component of RPM and the sense of purpose that various researchers have found to be important to overall well-being (Antonovsky 1979; Deci and Ryan 2000; Helliwell 2011b; S. Kaplan and Kaplan 2009). Putting our knowledge and networks to use in order to make a difference for oneself and one's community is likely to enhance subjective well-being (Helliwell and Putnam 2004), while also improving community cohesion by developing mutual respect and increasing the expectation to give help to and receive help from others.

Here we consider two sets of environmental factors that aim to improve sense of community. The first examines the kinds of environments that help people get to know each other by promoting social interaction. This relies not only on building mental models of others but also on having opportunities to help others and receive help. The second explores environments that foster shared experiences and civic engagement, both of which address the need for meaningful action.

Environments to Promote Social Interaction and Model Building

Pruitt Igoe, the infamous public housing project in St Louis, was demolished in the 1970s because of issues of crime, poverty and segregation. One explanation for this failure was a lack of spaces for people to safely get to know each other, develop mutual trust, and value their shared resources (Yancey 1971; Newman 1995). This analysis suggested that the lack of social ties was partly responsible for the rampant vandalism of shared resources as well as for burglaries and rapes that occurred even amongst neighbours. In the words of one resident, there was 'nobody to

help' (Fisher et al. 1984, pp. 259–60). In a less dramatic but no less important context, Putnam (2000) connects the decline of membership in social
organizations to an undermining of civic engagement and consequently
the lack of a strong democracy. He attributes this in part to 'individual-
izing' environments; the time spent on our mobile phones, watching television, playing video games and browsing the internet reduces opportunities
for quality face-to-face relationships (Bartolini, this volume, Chapter 6).

By contrast, our focus here is on the opposite kinds of environments,
those that enhance connection amongst community members by creating places and contexts that offer opportunities for social interaction and
relationship building. Social ties are formed through repeated face-to-face
contact and short-duration conversations (Greenbaum 1982). How many
neighbours one can identify by name has been positively linked to sense of
community (Glynn 1986). Contact may or may not be planned and could
occur between close friends or complete strangers. In any case, environments can offer the opportunity for positive social interactions, thereby
building familiarity, trust and social cohesion. Policy mechanisms, often
at a relatively local level, can foster the creation and stability of these kinds
of places.

Mixed use, front porches and pedestrianism

Enhancing social connectivity is one of the principal motivations for
the Smart Growth and New Urbanist movements (Duany et al. 2000;
Calthorpe and Fulton 2001). These approaches to urban design promote
pedestrianism, ample pavements, small setbacks, front porches, common
shared spaces, parking behind the houses, and proximity between housing
and services through mixed-use neighbourhoods. Studies of the impacts
of such designs on social interaction and the overall sense of community
suggest that the hypotheses posed by Calthorpe, Duany and others have
significant merit (Litman 2011).

Mixed use – for example, a building with a storefront at the street level
with housing above – can have a positive impact on sense of community.
Wood et al. (2010) discuss the benefits afforded by creating retail areas
that are set closer to the kerb and have limited surface parking. Jane
Jacobs (1961) famously argued that mixed use was one of the main reasons
for the vibrancy of Boston's North End neighbourhood. Even though it
was considered a slum at the time, she claimed that residents' ability to
talk to each other and keep an eye out for one another created a tight-knit
neighbourhood.

Being able to watch what is going on in your neighbourhood is a key
to developing the mental models necessary to build trust. A study of
elderly Hispanics living in Florida found that residents with front porches

reported higher levels of perceived social support and lower levels of psychological distress (Brown et al. 2009). The authors' interpretation is that porches provide visual access to the thoroughfares and opportunities to meet neighbours.

In communities where people are able to walk to stores or parks, they are more likely to chance upon one another and share a greeting or a conversation. The link between pedestrianism and social interaction is supported by Kim and Kaplan's (2004) study. They found that, in the New Urbanist neighbourhood, which promotes pedestrianism through mixed use, grid-based street designs, and parking at the back of the houses, residents have a higher likelihood of social interaction than in a nearby traditional subdivision.

Similarly, Leyden (2003), in a comparison of eight neighbourhoods in Ireland that ranged from pedestrian-oriented mixed use to car-dependent suburban subdivisions found that residents of the more walkable neighbourhoods were more likely to know their neighbours and had higher levels of social capital, trust and social engagement. Lund (2002) showed similar improvements in sense of community in Portland, Oregon.

Gallimore et al. (2011) studied how easily children could walk to school in New Urban versus suburban neighbourhoods. They found that New Urban residents perceived their neighbourhoods to be more walkable and to offer greater traffic safety and crime safety. They also found that, if as little as 10 per cent of a walking route is perceived to be unwalkable, it acts as a barrier to walking at all.

Shared green spaces
Shared spaces offer community members opportunities to get to know one another through planned gatherings or serendipitous events where they may meet others and be exposed to ideas and cultures they might not otherwise experience. The presence of trees and greenery enhances common spaces by making them more preferred, reducing the fear associated with barren treeless spaces, encouraging people to spend time in them, and thereby promoting more social activity, building social relationships and enhancing sense of belonging (Kweon et al. 1998). Residents of subdivisions with green open spaces tend to have a higher sense of community than residents of subdivisions that do not incorporate natural areas (Kim and Kaplan 2004). Sense of community has also been shown to be enhanced in apartments with inside courtyards that have trees (Nasar and Julian 1995).

Studies at the Robert Taylor Homes, a low-income public housing project in Chicago, found that common spaces with more trees and greenery attract residents to the outdoors and provide more opportunities for interaction, thereby developing stronger social connections (Coley et al. 1997; Kuo et al. 1998; Kweon et al. 1998). These effects are particularly noteworthy in light of the wariness of one's neighbours that often accompanies living in these housing projects. The advantages of nearby green spaces in reducing fear, crime and aggression levels (Kuo and Sullivan 2001a) suggest that policy initiatives that emphasize green common space will be beneficial on multiple accounts.

Safety and aesthetics

The safety and aesthetics of environments play an important role in determining their use. Whereas crowded, noisy and dangerous settings promote social withdrawal and inhibit the formation of social connections (Evans 2006), safe and aesthetically pleasing environments encourage people to linger, develop social connections (Wood et al. 2008; Sullivan and Chang 2011) and enhance place attachment (Low and Altman 1992).

Broken window theory (Kelling and Wilson 1982) links aesthetics and crime levels, stating that visible signs of disorder and petty crimes alter social norms and are self-reinforcing – that is, they lead to more crime. Explaining this phenomenon, Cialdini (2007) says that, 'if a lot of people are doing this, it's probably a wise thing to do'. From a mental model standpoint, it makes sense that repeatedly experiencing such disorder may diminish one's perception of place, how safe one feels in it and how much one cares for it. In a series of studies Keizer et al. (2008) demonstrated the effect of a disorderly environment on the propensity for not returning shopping carts, littering and stealing. The authors suggest that minimizing visible signs of lack of care is key to reducing the development of negative social norms.

Third places

In *The Great Good Place* (1989), Oldenburg contrasts the two core centres of American life – home and work – with 'third places' which provide 'the core settings of informal public life'. Coffee shops, general stores, post offices, community libraries, pubs and dog parks are all examples of third places. Oldenburg describes the capacity of third places to 'promote social equality by leveling the status of guests, provide a setting for grassroots politics, create habits of public association, and offer psychological support to individuals and communities'. In short, such places present a lively hub of social interaction while, at the same time, decreasing the social segregation associated with many neighbourhoods and workplaces.

The description that Ewing et al. (2005, p. 273) provide of 'main streets' as 'highways and streets whose adjacent land uses require accommodation of pedestrians and bicyclists, serious consideration of street aesthetics, and a degree of traffic calming' exemplifies the third place. A study by Pendola and Gen (2008) provides useful insights based on a comparison of four San Francisco neighbourhoods differing in whether or not they had a single main street. The presence of such central gathering places was related to residents' perceptions of shared values, ability to get help if needed, knowing more people by name, and feeling that neighbourhood problems could be handled without external help.

Creating third places in the commercial sector depends on many factors that are at the discretion of individual and corporate owners. However, design guidelines and land-use policies can also have an impact on decisions about offering opportunities for informal encounters. Policy, such as mixed-use zoning, can create the conditions that reduce the distance between home and work to third places. Policies to enhance the attractiveness and safety of public spaces can also be effective approaches. Reducing parking fees, creating pedestrian-only main streets and having town fairs are further ways to bring people and their vitality to third places.

Wayfinding and exploration

Being lost or confused is not a desirable state, yet disorienting and confusing environments are not a rare occurrence. The feasibility of enjoying nearby nature spaces or third places depends on being able to find one's way there. Familiarity and connections to place occur through repeated experiences that will not happen when people cannot find their way around. Such environments can enhance social interaction and sense of community.

In *The Image of the City*, Lynch (1960) identified a variety of physical features that can make places more legible and help people build mental maps of them. Landmarks can help distinguish one place from the next and give locals and travellers alike waypoints to recognize and use in finding their way back again. Unique city districts with clear boundaries can also serve to distinguish one area from the next. Since our cognitive apparatus tends to store objects of some significance and ignores what comes in between, having such distinguishing characteristics is important. Well-designed signage can also be helpful for anticipating people's navigational needs and point them in the right direction.

Legible cities and neighbourhoods, where things are familiar and people know their way around, create a sense of security and familiarity. Yet this familiarity grows slowly and incrementally. From a familiar home base, people feel safe enough to explore new parts, extending their range of comfort. Over repeated experiences, this self-initiated, self-paced exploration helps to extend one's mental maps. At the same time the process of discovery can lead to finding new places and opportunities for interacting with others.

Knowledge of an environment also increases people's attachment to it (Low and Altman 1992). From a sustainability perspective, what we know about our environment can influence how we care for it (Walker and Ryan 2008). Moreover, people who know their way around may feel more comfortable walking and are more likely to receive physical health benefits (Frank et al. 2007). It also warrants repeating that a legible environment reduces the mental resources required for navigating and thus sustains our precious DA. Given our reliance on the mental maps of environments that we need to navigate, investment in creating legible environments can have multiple rewards, at the individual as well as social level.

Environments to Promote Meaningful Action

The desire to cooperate with others is part of our genetic make-up, and our species is one of the few that helps non-kin members (Pennisi 2009; Helliwell, this volume, Chapter 5). Our ancestors survived wars, floods, famines and plagues because they were predisposed to help each other. Yet this inherent motivation often goes unrealized because opportunities to help others are inadequate, foiled or not readily apparent. Put another way, people want to help others and engage in meaningful activities (Antonovsky 1979; Deci and Ryan 2000; R. Kaplan and Kaplan 2008) but too often find themselves in situations where it is difficult to take actions. The resulting sense of helplessness can be debilitating and demoralizing. Here we consider a few environments that help people work with others, develop a sense that they can make a difference, and benefit the larger good. While the previous subsections have focused on physical characteristics of the environment, this subsection also applies the broader notion of environment with examples of social mechanisms that create opportunities for oft-marginalized groups to be heard and make a difference.

Community gardens

Few contexts offer the richness of benefits and opportunities that community gardens have provided in many countries and diverse populations. These settings have served, among others, low-income and homeless groups, where they not only increase food security but also serve to teach about nutrition (Schmelzkopf 1995). Such gardens have served recent immigrant groups, offering opportunities for maintaining and sharing cultural patterns (Baker 2004). Stuart (2005) discusses community gardening programmes in the context of domestic violence shelters, where 1500 women and children in a number of California cities participated. Community gardens have been incorporated in school settings and after-school programmes to encourage young people to diversify and improve their diet (Boden 2009).

A common attribute of community gardens is the diversity of psycho-logical and social benefits that they afford. This parallels the psychological benefits associated with nature settings that were previously discussed. Community gardens, however, bestow additional benefits that are the consequences of their being communal. Stuart (2005, p. 80) shows that for the women and children in the shelters the gardens 'helped to boost morale, create a stronger shelter community, and build stronger ties to the surrounding neighborhood'. Schukoske (2000, p. 352) speaks of the gardens as enhancing intergenerational and multi-racial collaboration and 'foster[ing] a spirit of community cooperation'. Blair et al. (1991) found that, in comparison to a control group, randomly selected urban gardeners were significantly more likely to participate in neighbour-hood improvement and social events and to consider their neighbours as friendly. Similarly, residents who spend more time caring for lawns, flowers or trees have stronger social networks (Brunson et al. 1998). Twiss et al. (2003) specifically mention the role of community gardens in build-ing and nurturing community capacity.

Community gardens exemplify a diversity of ownership and manage-ment patterns. In some cases they are a feature of a residential community or housing complex, so the land is mutually owned by the residents or by the management corporation. In many cases, however, community gardens occupy urban 'open space', often the consequence of neglected vacant lots. Such areas lead to blighted communities and demoralized citizens. Using community gardens or other projects such as tree plant-ing programmes can transform the area, reduce the stigma of living there and bring people together (Schukoske 2000; Austin and Kaplan 2003; Semenza and March 2009). Management of these areas has taken many forms, including land trusts, conservation easements and public–private partnerships.

New York City's GreenThumb programme is fascinating for its origin and the success it has achieved. Initiated more than 40 years ago as a result of the city's widespread abandonment of public and private land, it now claims to be the largest community gardening programme in the United States, with over 500 gardens all over the city (US Forest Service, Northern Research Station 2009, p. 122). While a partnership with the city's Parks and Recreation Department, it is managed entirely by com-munity members; they design, plan and govern the gardens. Nearly 90 per cent of GreenThumb gardens offer consistent public programming aimed at improving quality of life for residents of all ages ('GreenThumb community gardens', n.d.).

Given their capacity for neighbourhood and community development and role in food security, it is not surprising that cities around the world have formulated policies related to community gardens. There are numerous examples of land-use and planning policies (Public Health Law and Policy 2008), and resources available to help frame policies to promote community gardens (Wooten and Ackerman 2011). From a policy perspective, ceding control of lots to local citizens represents a way to simultaneously reduce management costs and foster participation. An important benefit of such an approach is that locals tend to have a greater knowledge of the unique needs of their territory and also have more invested in its upkeep than professional hired help.

Youth involvement

In the eyes of their elders and communities, youth are sometimes considered lacking in reasonableness. They can be rash and risky in their behaviour; they can also be unwilling to do what they are told. From the youth perspective, however, adults may also seem unreasonable in a variety of ways, certainly including their expectations of youth. Countering such stereotypes and perceptions are frequent examples of young people whose efforts have made remarkable contributions. Such stories are so pervasive that drawing on the energy, insights, creativity and talents of local youth could reap many benefits both to them and to their communities.

Growing Up in Cities is a UNESCO-funded project involving research at 14 sites around the world. Chawla (2002) and Driskell (2002) document the potential of participatory processes in creating environments that bring out the best in local youth. When children are free to explore and their involvement is sought and accepted by the community, not only are they more satisfied, but the benefits spread to their families and communities. Children's perspective and their knowledge can greatly enrich community planning and development. Driskell's book is intended to be a practical manual for making such participation useful.

Earth Force ('Earth Force', n.d.) is a US non-profit organization dedicated to enabling youth to make positive environmental change in their worlds. Its efforts are noteworthy not only for the process of engaging youth but also for the approaches it uses to situate the children's efforts within their communities. Thus their efforts extend beyond the youth and their projects to diverse community-based organizations as well as the corporate partners. The young people's projects entail a six-step process, Community Action and Problem Solving (CAPS), that guides students to

identify and democratically select a problem that is of both local importance and sufficient interest to them, to learn and analyse existing conditions and policies that relate to the problem as well as ways to influence
a decision, and to plan potential solutions and ways to take action. This
problem-solving process guides each project; it also teaches the young
people steps that are applicable in many other contexts (Bardwell and
Kaplan 2008).

Youth advisory boards and youth serving on boards of community
organizations have become more common. In the context of their schools,
children and youth may also have opportunities to raise issues and participate in activities that effect change. It would be misleading, however,
to assume that it is only the exceptional young person who has the ability
to make a difference. Both the Growing Up in Cities projects and Earth
Force reach diverse groups, often in underserved communities. There are
countless other examples that document that children's talent, vitality and
willingness to engage are widespread.

Positive outcomes, however, depend on some key ingredients. An often-
repeated theme is the importance of how youth are treated. Perhaps even
more than older members of the community, young people are sensitive to
token efforts to invite their involvement; they know when they are talked
down to and when their input is ignored. Listening to their perspectives
and permitting their involvement are ways to show respect and establish
trust, qualities that are likely to foster reasonable behaviour, meaningful
action and future positive engagement.

Microcredit and gifts that multiply

Now widely adopted, especially in the developing world, the microcredit
movement offers a compelling story of the power of making a difference
on multiple levels. The Grameen Bank (Yunus 1999), which in Bengali
means 'village bank', has to date loaned over $10 billion, in very small
amounts, to nearly 8.5 million poor people in Bangladesh. The approach,
initiated by Grameen and subsequently followed by various microcredit
institutions around the world, not only fulfils a need of many for working
capital but also features some noteworthy social mechanisms both to
keep the institutions sustainable (i.e. maximize loan repayment) and to
empower the populations they serve.

First, since the recipients have neither possessions nor credit history, the
banks do not require any collateral for their loans, nor is there any written
contract for the loan. For the poorest of the poor, the interest rate for the
loans is zero. Moreover, the loan recipients become part owners of the
Grameen Bank. Such policies are a sign of trust and respect to people who
would simply be turned away from traditional banks. Given the typically

large income and trust gap between loan officers and loan recipients, this exchange of dignity could well serve to bridge two very different classes of a community and foster a sense of shared purpose.

Second, 97 per cent of Grameen loans go to women. Heifer International, an organization that provides 'living loans' in the form of livestock, also directs its resources towards impoverished women (Heifer International, n.d.). Both organizations find that, because women tend to make the majority of household decisions, particularly with respect to the care and education of children, they have a greater influence on the long-term well-being of the community.

Third, the Grameen Bank utilizes 'solidarity lending', which requires borrowers to be part of a group. If any member of the group fails to pay, all of the members risk losing their line of credit. This ingenious use of peer pressure improves repayment rates for the bank and also provides a context in which people must work together towards a common purpose. Also, because Grameen promotes a culture where successful entrepreneurs help bring up those in need, there is a multiplier effect for each investment Grameen makes. Similarly, Heifer requires that recipients 'pass on the gift' by giving offspring of the livestock to others in their community who could use it. These contexts create an opportunity for respect building – those who can successfully utilize their loans can both earn the respect of their peers and develop a sense of self-respect.

Finally, the distributed nature of the microcredit model means that many would-be entrepreneurs receive small loans to try out their ideas. Having a large number of diverse, small experiments running in parallel leads to an ecosystem of ideas that can address a variety of community needs (Lindblom 1959; Irvine and Kaplan 2001). By spreading resources across the community, it not only increases the chances of success for difference-making endeavours but also creates a sense of possibility in communities that might otherwise feel hopeless. As Bornstein and Davis (2010, p. 17) point out, 'Rather than implement preset policies through bureaucracies in a top-down fashion, they grew solutions from the bottom in a process characterized by trial and error, continuous iteration, and a sharp focus on results.'

Kiva, which was founded in 2005, offers a relatively recent addition to the microcredit movement. According to its website (kiva.org) the organization has made over a million loans in more than 200 countries, with a 98.9 per cent repayment rate. What makes the Kiva example particularly striking in terms of our discussion here, however, is the source of the funds for the loans. Over 750 000 individuals have participated in Kiva's online system, which requires a minimum of a $25 loan. What is the return on investment for these lenders? Certainly meaningful action has to be a major explanation for making loans that are repaid without interest.

Moreover, although there is some effort to personalize the relationship in as much as the lender identifies a person or group, there is no personal contact between individual lenders and the recipients. This lack of a social bond between lender and recipient differentiates this example from the other community-oriented examples in the chapter. The success of these organizations in spite of such barriers shows the powerful motivation of meaningful action and suggests a wide range of institutional arrangements that can provide people with meaning and motivation.

Goldschmidt (1990) describes the desire for respect as one of the primary motivations for human action. In other words, one is more likely to engage in an activity from which one derives respect. Grameen and similar institutions are examples of environments that not only provide opportunities for people to pull themselves out of poverty but also convey trust and respect to those who would normally not receive it. While escaping poverty is by no means straightforward (Chavan and Ramakumar 2002), the modest resources provided by microcredit institutions – a few dollars and a little dignity – are small differences that have made big differences in bringing meaning and well-being to the recipients and their communities (Hossain and Knight 2008).

Enabling community participation

Town halls, envisioning meetings and public forums are environments meant to foster citizen participation, yet they often fail to do so. There are many reasons. Meetings can be dominated by a small number of strong personalities whose views do not always reflect the needs of the general public. Despite good intentions, facilitators may be condescending, talking over the heads of participants or conveying a lack of respect for their knowledge and concerns. Participants too often feel that their needs are ignored and that their involvement is pro forma, making little difference to the ultimate outcome in the current situation, thus also diminishing motivation for future participation. These patterns can be reversed by creating contexts that engage the help of an able and willing public.

Enabling participation by a large, diverse set of people in the participatory process (e.g. different ages, cultures, political sensibilities, socioeconomic backgrounds) requires multiple means (e.g. newspapers, blogs, social media) for informing them about the opportunity. Many venues for citizen input do not depend on the traditional public meeting. For example, public spaces (e.g. libraries, meeting rooms in civic buildings) can facilitate the preparation and dissemination of ideas. Virtual spaces (e.g. e-democracy.org, idealist.org) can also be used to help people discuss and share their ideas. Furthermore, opportunities such as volunteer days can direct participants towards specific community needs. When public meetings are utilized, vital issues include building trust and communicating that public input is valued. For example, a readily accessible location for public meetings, timing them early enough in the process to signal that input can inform critical decisions, and sensitivity to cultural differences are all crucial for achieving satisfying outcomes.

Many deficiencies of the participatory process derive from the difficulties of conveying information to the public as well as permitting the public to convey their knowledge and perspective to the experts. Ignoring the differing mental models of the citizens and the policy makers, planners and other professionals can result in frustration and a sense of futility for all concerned. The differing experiences, familiarity with local conditions, perspectives regarding policy, and perceptions of risk (Slovic 1987) all have an impact on effective information sharing. Participants can be overwhelmed by the quantity of information and confused by the jargon. The experts' reactions may be that the public is incompetent, since they assume the information is elementary. The process can be more satisfying if the leaders see their role as facilitating an exploration of existing conditions and possible solutions rather than to educate the public. Therefore sensitivity to the challenges associated with absorbing new information and providing opportunities to study and explore it are crucial characteristics of an effective participatory process.

Such exploration also provides opportunities for two-way exchanges. While public meetings often involve informing the public, listening is a crucial and often missing component. Listening, however, does not depend on public meetings. For example, photo questionnaires, which involve rating pictures of different kinds of environments, provide an effective way to inform participants while also gaining insight into their perspective (R. Kaplan 1979; R. Kaplan et al. 1998, pp. 58–66). Internet-based tools can also be used to gather public input (Snyder n.d.; Snyder and Herman 2003). For example, Allourideas.org presents two ideas side by side and asks users which one they like better. The process repeats as long as people want to continue. Participants can also submit new ideas to the voting process. This innovative process allows local governments to easily gather and act on the collective knowledge and preferences of thousands of people (Emery 2010). The diverse knowledge of the public is an essential resource for taking on local problems; at the same time, the global aggregation of that diversity is pivotal for societal learning, innovation and ultimately transformation (O'Hara and Lyon, this volume, Chapter 4).

ENVIRONMENTS AS SMALL EXPERIMENTS

Our focus has been on creating the conditions, contexts and environments that foster reasonableness and well-being by helping people function effectively and work with others to make a difference in personal and community-oriented challenges. Creating environments is also the subject of Alexander et al.'s classic *Pattern Language* (1977), in which they propose a variety of architectural elements designed to meet human needs. While the designs are quite detailed, the authors make explicit that the ideas presented are hypotheses meant to be tested. Although there is substantially more empirical evidence to support the claims in this chapter, we share the environments and contexts presented here in the same spirit.

We expect that our conceptualization applies broadly, but the realizations of the concepts will necessarily differ. Given the enormous diversity of communities, a universal solution is neither likely nor desirable. Environments which improve well-being in one community may be less effective in others. And solutions that are viable at a given time may need to be rethought as communities change. In order to account for a variety of circumstances, it is necessary to try things out at a manageable scale. Such small experiments (R. Kaplan 1996; Irvine and Kaplan 2001) are intended to have relatively modest aims and require modest resources. Engagement of local people is fundamental, since they have on-the-ground knowledge that is often invisible to officials. In cases where policies may require significant change, the small experiment approach proposes limiting the scale of changes initially. Finally, experiments involve keeping track of what worked, what did not work and the circumstances that led to positive changes. Thus, rather than failure being debilitating, the process permits learning and adjustment. It can also foster reasonableness. As the efforts to assess and improve well-being through policy are still quite new, it would be prudent to take an approach that is both cautious and enlightening.

Policy makers at the state and national level have the influence to improve many lives through well-crafted policies. However, since local issues are often more central to well-being than those at higher levels (Helliwell 2011b), local officials may have an even more powerful impact. Their decision making with regard to planning systems, design standards and participatory processes can directly affect how supportive the environment is on a daily basis. As many of the examples presented in this chapter and throughout this volume show, these decisions have an effective impact on individual well-being while simultaneously benefiting communities.

This chapter has shown how environments can bring out the best in human behaviour. It is interesting to consider whether such behaviour might also foster taking better care of the Earthly environments that sustain us. One could imagine a virtuous cycle in which environments support human reasonableness and humans, in turn, care for the planet's well-being.[2] Such a cycle could serve as one potential pathway towards sustainable well-being.

NOTES

1. Although RPM evolved independently from Antonovsky's sense of coherence (SOC) (see Hämäläinen, this volume, Chapter 2; Eriksson and Lindström, this volume, Chapter 3) and the two frameworks draw on different empirical bases, they offer many parallels, especially with respect to some similarities between their domains: *model building* and *comprehensibility*, *being effective* and *manageability*, and *meaningful action* and *meaningfulness*. SOC focuses on utilizing one's resources to confidently navigate life experiences and improve one's well-being. RPM addresses informational needs that have an impact on both individual and communal well-being, and these, in turn, help identify ways in which environments are more likely to foster reasonableness.
2. We thank Andrew Lyon for suggesting this notion of a virtuous cycle after reviewing an early draft of this chapter.

REFERENCES

Abraham, A., K. Sommerhalder and T. Abel (2010), 'Landscape and well-being: a scoping study on the health-promoting impact of outdoor environments', *International Journal of Public Health*, **55** (1), 59–69.

Alexander, C., S. Ishikawa and M. Silverstein (1977), *A Pattern Language: Towns, Buildings, Construction*, New York: Oxford University Press.

Antonovsky, A. (1979), *Health, Stress, and Coping*, San Francisco, CA: Jossey-Bass.

Arendt, R. (1996), *Conservation Design for Subdivisions: A Practical Guide to Creating Open Space Networks*, Washington, DC: Island Press.

Arendt, R. (2004), 'Linked landscapes: creating greenway corridors through conservation subdivision design strategies in the northeastern and central United States', *Landscape and Urban Planning*, **68**, 241–69.

Aung San Suu Kyi (1991), *Freedom from Fear: And Other Writings*, ed. M. Aris, London: Penguin Group.

Austin, M.E. and R. Kaplan (2003), 'Identity, involvement and expertise in the inner city: some benefits of tree planting projects', in S. Clayton and S. Opotow (eds), *Identity and the Natural Environment: The Psychological Significance of Nature*, Cambridge, MA: MIT Press, pp. 205–25.

Bagchi, S. (2011), 'The change maker – Bill Drayton on empathy and leadership', *Forbes India Magazine*, 8 June, available at: http://www.business.in.com/article/zen-garden/the-change-maker-bill-drayton-on-empathy-and-leaderhip/25642/1.

Baker, L.E. (2004), 'Tending cultural landscapes and food citizenship in Toronto's community gardens', *Geographical Review*, **94** (3), 305–25.

Bardwell, L.V. and S. Kaplan (2008), 'Creating a generation of problem-solvers: a cognitive perspective on service-learning', *Information for Action: A Journal for*

Research on Service-Learning for Children and Youth, available at: http://www.
service-learningpartnership.org/ifa_journal/winter_2008/CreatingaGeneration
ofProblemSolvers.pdf.

Baumeister, R.F. (2004), *Handbook of Self-regulation: Research, Theory, and Applications*, New York: Guilford Press.

Berman, M.G., J. Jonides and S. Kaplan (2008), 'The cognitive benefits of interacting with nature', *Psychological Science*, **19** (12), 1207–12.

Berto, R. (2005), 'Exposure to restorative environments helps restore attentional capacity', *Journal of Environmental Psychology*, **25** (3), 249–59.

Blair, D., C.C. Giesecke and S. Sherman (1991), 'A dietary, social and economic evaluation of the Philadelphia urban gardening project', *Journal of Nutrition Education*, **23** (4), 161–7.

Boden, L.F. (2009), *Growing School and Youth Gardens in New York City: A Guide to Resources 2009*, New York: GreenThumb, City of New York Parks and Recreation Department, available at: http://www.nycgovparks.org/sub_about/partners/greenthumb/school_garden_resource_guide.pdf.

Bornstein, D. and S. Davis (2010), *Social Entrepreneurship: What Everyone Needs to Know*, Oxford: Oxford University Press.

Brown, S.C., C.A. Mason, J.L. Lombard, F. Martinez, E. Plater-Zyberk, A.R. Spokane, F.L. Newman, H. Pantin and J. Szapocznik (2009), 'The relationship of built environment to perceived social support and psychological distress in Hispanic elders: the role of "eyes on the street"', *Journals of Gerontology Series B: Psychological Sciences and Social Sciences*, **64B** (2), 234–46, doi: 10.1093/geronb/gbn011.

Brunson, L., F.E. Kuo and W.C. Sullivan (1998), 'Sowing the seeds of community: greening and gardening in inner-city neighborhoods', University of Illinois, Urbana-Champaign.

Calthorpe, P. and W. Fulton (2001), *The Regional City: Planning for the End of Sprawl*, Washington, DC: Island Press.

Canin, L.H. (1991), 'Psychological restoration among AIDS caregivers: maintaining self-care', unpublished dissertation, University of Michigan, Ann Arbor.

Chavan, P. and R. Ramakumar (2002), 'Micro-credit and rural poverty: an analysis of empirical evidence', *Economic and Political Weekly*, **37** (10), 955–65.

Chawla, L. (ed.) (2002), *Growing Up in an Urbanising World*, London: Earthscan.

Christakis, D.A. (2011), 'The effects of fast-paced cartoons', *Pediatrics*, **128** (4), 772–4, doi: 10.1542/peds.2011-2071.

Cialdini, R.B. (2007), 'Descriptive social norms as underappreciated sources of social control', *Psychometrika*, **72** (2), 263–8.

Cimprich, B. (1993), 'Development of an intervention to restore attention in cancer patients', *Cancer Nursing*, **16** (2), 83–92.

Cimprich, B. and D.L. Ronis (2003), 'An environmental intervention to restore attention in women with newly diagnosed breast cancer', *Cancer Nursing*, **26** (4), 284–92.

Clark, C., R. Martin, E. van Kempen, T. Alfred, J. Head, H.W. Davies, M.M. Haines, I. Lopez Barrio, M. Matheson and S.A. Stansfeld (2006), 'Exposure–effect relations between aircraft and road traffic noise exposure at school and reading comprehension', *American Journal of Epidemiology*, **163** (1), 27–37.

Coley, R.L., W.C. Sullivan and F.E. Kuo (1997), 'Where does community grow?', *Environment and Behavior*, **29** (4), 468–94.

Deci, E.L. and R.M. Ryan (2000), 'The "what" and "why" of goal pursuits: human needs and the self-determination of behavior', *Psychological Inquiry*, **11** (4), 227–68.

Drayton, B. (2011), 'Collaborative entrepreneurship: how social entrepreneurs can tip the world by working in global teams', *Innovations: Technology, Governance, Globalization*, **6** (2), 35–8.

Driskell, D. (2002), *Creating Better Cities with Children and Youth: A Manual for Participation*, Growing Up in Cities, London: Earthscan.

Duany, A., E. Plater-Zyberk and J. Speck (2000), *Suburban Nation: The Rise of Sprawl and the Decline of the American Dream*, New York: North Point Press.

Dunnett, N. and N. Kingsbury (2004), *Planting Green Roofs and Living Walls*, Portland, OR: Timber Press.

Dvorak, B. and A. Volder (2010), 'Green roof vegetation for North American ecoregions: a literature review', *Landscape and Urban Planning*, **96** (4), 197–213.

Earth Force (n.d.), available at: http://www.earthforce.org/ (accessed 20 November 2011).

Emery, C. (2010), 'Computers intersect with sociology to sift through "all our ideas"', *News at Princeton*, 19 July, available at: http://www.princeton.edu/main/news/archive/S27/92/93G66/index.xml?section=featured.

Evans, G.W. (2006), 'Child development and the physical environment', *Annual Review of Psychology*, **57**, 423–51.

Ewing, R., M.R. King, S. Raudenbush and O.J. Clemente (2005), 'Turning highways into main streets', *Journal of the American Planning Association*, **71** (3), 269–82.

Faber Taylor, A. and F.E. Kuo (2011), 'Could exposure to everyday green spaces help treat ADHD? Evidence from children's play settings', *Applied Psychology: Health and Well-being*, **3** (3), 281–303.

Field, J. (2003), *Social Capital*, London: Routledge.

Fisher, J.D., P.A. Bell and A. Baum (1984), *Environmental Psychology*, New York: Holt, Rinehart and Winston.

Frank, L.D., B.E. Saelens, K.E. Powell and J.E. Chapman (2007), 'Stepping towards causation: do built environments or neighborhood and travel preferences explain physical activity, driving, and obesity?', *Social Science and Medicine*, **65**, 1898–1914.

Frumkin, H. (2005), 'The health of places, the wealth of evidence', in P.F. Barlett (ed.), *Urban Place: Reconnecting with the Natural World*, Cambridge, MA: MIT Press, pp. 253–70.

Gallimore, J.M., B.B. Brown and C.M. Werner (2011), 'Walking routes to school in New Urban and suburban neighborhoods: an environmental walkability analysis of blocks and routes', *Journal of Environmental Psychology*, **31** (2), 184–91, doi: 10.1016/j.jenvp.2011.01.001.

Getter, K.L. and D.B. Rowe (2006), 'The role of extensive green roofs in sustainable development', *HortScience*, **41** (5), 1276–85.

Glynn, T.J. (1986), 'Neighborhood and sense of community', *Journal of Community Psychology*, **14** (4), 341–52.

Goldman, T. and R. Gorham (2006), 'Sustainable urban transport: four innovative directions', *Technology in Society*, **28** (1–2), 261–73.

Goldschmidt, W. (1990), *The Human Career: The Self in the Symbolic World*, Cambridge, MA: Basil Blackwell.

Greenbaum, S.D. (1982), 'Bridging ties at the neighborhood level', *Social Networks*, **4**, 367–84.

'GreenThumb community gardens' (n.d.), available at: http://www.nycgovparks. org/sub_about/partners/greenthumb/greenthumb.html (accessed 20 November 2011).

Grinde, B. (2009a), 'Can the concept of discords help us find the causes of mental diseases?', *Medical Hypotheses*, **73** (1), 106–09.

Grinde, B. (2009b), 'An evolutionary perspective on the importance of community relations for quality of life', *Scientific World Journal*, **9**, 588–605, doi: 10.1100/ tsw.2009.73.

Groenewegen, P., A. van den Berg, S. de Vries and R. Verheij (2006), 'Vitamin G: effects of green space on health, well-being, and social safety', *BMC Public Health*, **6** (149), doi: 10.1186/1471-2458-6-149.

Haines, M.M., S.A. Stansfeld, J. Head and R.F.S. Job (2002), 'Multilevel modelling of aircraft noise on performance tests in schools around Heathrow Airport London', *Journal of Epidemiology and Community Health*, **56** (2), 139–44.

Hawken, P. (2007), *Blessed Unrest: How the Largest Movement in the World Came into Being, and Why No One Saw It Coming*, New York: Viking Press.

Heifer International (n.d.), 'Empowering women', available at: http://www.heifer. org/give/empowering-women (accessed 20 November 2011).

Helliwell, J.F. (2011a), 'Institutions as enablers of wellbeing: the Singapore Prison case study', *International Journal of Wellbeing*, **1** (2), 1–11.

Helliwell, J.F. (2011b), 'How can subjective well-being be improved?', New Directions for Intelligent Government in Canada, Canadian Institute for Advanced Research and University of British Columbia.

Helliwell, J.F. and C.P. Barrington-Leigh (2010), *How Much Is Social Capital Worth?*, NBER Working Paper Series No. 16025, Cambridge, MA: National Bureau of Economic Research, available at: http://www.nber.org/papers/w16025.

Helliwell, J.F. and R.D. Putnam (2004), 'The social context of well-being', *Philosophical Transactions of the Royal Society B: Biological Sciences*, **359**, 1435–46, doi: 10.1098/rstb.2004.1522.

Helliwell, J.F. and S. Wang (2010), 'Trust and well-being', *International Journal of Wellbeing*, **1** (1), 42–78.

Hippel, W. von and K. Gonsalkorale (2005), 'That is bloody revolting!', *Psychological Science*, **16** (7), 497–500.

Hossain, F. and T. Knight (2008), 'Can micro-credit improve the livelihoods of the poor and disadvantaged? Empirical observations from Bangladesh', *International Development Planning Review*, **30** (2), 155–75.

Irvine, K.N. and S. Kaplan (2001), 'Coping with change: the small experiment as a strategic approach to environmental sustainability', *Environmental Management*, **28**, 713–25.

Jacobs, J. (1961), *The Death and Life of Great American Cities*, New York: Random House.

James, W. (1898), *Psychology: The Briefer Course*, New York: Holt.

Kaplan, R. (1979), 'A methodology for simultaneously obtaining and sharing information', General Technical Report No. RM 68, Assessing Amenity Resource Values, USDA Forest Service.

Kaplan, R. (1996), 'The small experiment: achieving more with less', in J.L. Nasar and B.B. Brown (eds), *Public and Private Places*, Edmond, OK: Environmental Design Research Association, pp. 170–74.

Kaplan, R. (2001), 'The nature of the view from home', *Environment and Behavior*, **33** (4), 507–42.

Kaplan, R. and S. Kaplan (1989), *The Experience of Nature: A Psychological Perspective*, Cambridge: Cambridge University Press.

Kaplan, R. and S. Kaplan (2008), 'Bringing out the best in people: a psychological perspective', *Conservation Biology*, **22**, 826–9.

Kaplan, R. and S. Kaplan (2011), 'Well - being, reasonableness, and the natural environment', *Applied Psychology: Health and Well - being*, **3** (3), 304–21, doi: 10.1111/j.1758-0854.2011.01055.x.

Kaplan, R., S. Kaplan and R.L. Ryan (1998), *With People in Mind: Design and Management of Everyday Nature*, Washington, DC: Island Press.

Kaplan, R., M.E. Austin and S. Kaplan (2004), 'Open space communities: resident perceptions, nature benefits, and problems with terminology', *Journal of the American Planning Association*, **70**, 300–312.

Kaplan, R., J.E. Ivancich and R. De Young (2007), *Nearby Nature in the City: Preserving and Enhancing Livability*, Ann Arbor: School of Natural Resources and Environment, University of Michigan, available at: http://deepblue.lib.umich.edu/bitstream/2027.42/48784/3/Nearby_Nature_in_the_City_2007a.pdf.

Kaplan, S. (1973), 'Cognitive maps in perception and thought', in R.M. Downs and D. Stea (eds), *Image and Environment*, Chicago, IL: Aldine, pp. 63–78.

Kaplan, S. (1995), 'The restorative benefits of nature: toward an integrative framework', *Journal of Environmental Psychology*, **15**, 169–82.

Kaplan, S. and M.G. Berman (2010), 'Directed attention as a common resource for executive functioning and self-regulation', *Perspectives on Psychological Science*, **5** (1), 43–57, doi: 10.1177/1745691609356784.

Kaplan, S. and R. Kaplan (1982), *Humanscape: Environments for People*, Ann Arbor, MI: Ulrich's Books.

Kaplan, S. and R. Kaplan (2003), 'Health, supportive environments, and the Reasonable Person Model', *American Journal of Public Health*, **93**, 1484–9.

Kaplan, S., and R. Kaplan (2009), 'Creating a larger role for environmental psychology: the Reasonable Person Model as an integrative framework', *Journal of Environmental Psychology*, **29** (3), 329–39.

Keizer, K., S. Lindenberg and L. Steg (2008), 'The spreading of disorder', *Science*, **322** (5908), 1681–5, doi: 10.1126/science.1161405.

Kelling, G.L. and J.Q. Wilson (1982), 'Broken windows', *Atlantic Monthly*, **249** (3), 29–38.

Kim, J. and R. Kaplan (2004), 'Physical and psychological factors in sense of community: New Urbanist Kentlands and nearby Orchard Village', *Environment and Behavior*, **36**, 313–40.

Kjell, O.N.E. (2011), 'Sustainable well-being: a potential synergy between sustainability and well-being research', *Review of General Psychology*, **15**, 255–66, doi: 10.1037/a0024603.

Kuo, F.E. (2001), 'Coping with poverty', *Environment and Behavior*, **33** (1), 5–34.

Kuo, F.E. and A. Faber Taylor (2004), 'A potential natural treatment for attention-deficit/hyperactivity disorder: evidence from a national study', *American Journal of Public Health*, **94** (9), 1580–86, doi: 10.2105/AJPH.94.9.1580.

Kuo, F.E. and W.C. Sullivan (2001a), 'Aggression and violence in the inner city', *Environment and Behavior*, **33** (4), 543–71.

Kuo, F.E. and W.C. Sullivan (2001b), 'Environment and crime in the inner city', *Environment and Behavior*, **33** (3), 343–67.

Kuo, F.E., W.C. Sullivan, R.L. Coley and L. Brunson (1998), 'Fertile ground for community: inner-city neighborhood common spaces', *American Journal of Community Psychology*, **26** (6), 823–51.

Kweon, B.S., W.C. Sullivan and A.R. Wiley (1998), 'Green common spaces and the social integration of inner-city older adults', *Environment and Behavior*, **30** (6), 832–58.

Leyden, K.M. (2003), 'Social capital and the built environment: the importance of walkable neighborhoods', *American Journal of Public Health*, **93** (9), 1546–51.

Lillard, A.S. and J. Peterson (2011), 'The immediate impact of different types of television on young children's executive function', *Pediatrics*, **128** (4), doi: 10.1542/peds.2010-1919.

Lindblom, C.E. (1959), 'The science of "muddling through"', *Public Administration Review*, **19** (2), 79–88.

Litman, T. (2011), *Evaluating Criticism of Smart Growth*, Victoria, BC: Victoria Transport Policy Institute, available at: www.vtpi.org/sgcritics.pdf.

Louv, R. (2005), *Last Child in the Woods: Saving Our Children from Nature-deficit Disorder*, Chapel Hill, NC: Algonquin Books.

Low, S.M. and I. Altman (1992), 'Place attachment: a conceptual inquiry', in S.M. Low and I. Altman (eds), *Place attachment*, New York: Plenum Press, pp. 1–12.

Lund, H. (2002), 'Pedestrian environments and sense of community', *Journal of Planning Education and Research*, **21** (3), 301–12.

Lynch, K. (1960), *The Image of the City*, Cambridge, MA: MIT Press.

Matsuoka, R.H. (2010), 'Student performance and high school landscapes: examining the links', *Landscape and Urban Planning*, **97**, 273–82.

Mohamed, R. (2006), 'The economics of conservation subdivisions: price premiums, improvement costs, and absorption rates', *Urban Affairs Review*, **41**, 376–99.

Moore, E.O. (1981), 'A prison environment's effect on health care service demands', *Journal of Environmental Systems*, **11**, 17–34.

Nasar, J.L. and D.A. Julian (1995), 'The psychological sense of community in the neighborhood', *Journal of the American Planning Association*, **61**, 178–184.

Newman, O. (1995), 'Defensible space: a new physical planning tool for urban revitalization', *Journal of the American Planning Association*, **61** (2), 149–55, doi: 10.1080/01944369508975629.

Oishi, S., S. Kesebir and E. Diener (2011), 'Income inequality and happiness', *Psychological Science*, **22** (9), 1095–1100, doi: 10.1177/0956797611417262.

Oldenburg, R. (1989), *The Great Good Place: Cafes, Coffee Shops, Community Centers, Beauty Parlors, General Stores, Bars, Hangouts, and How They Get You through the Day*, New York: Paragon House.

Pendola, R. and S. Gen (2008), 'Does "main street" promote sense of community? A comparison of San Francisco neighborhoods', *Environment and Behavior*, **40** (4), 545–74.

Pennisi, E. (2009), 'On the origin of cooperation', *Science*, **325** (5945), 1196–9.

Peterson, C. (2006), *A Primer in Positive Psychology*, New York: Oxford University Press.

Peterson, C. and M.E.P. Seligman (2004), *Character Strengths and Virtues: A Handbook and Classification*, New York: Oxford University Press.

PLANYC (n.d.), 'MillionTreesNYC', available at: http://www.milliontreesnyc.org/ (accessed 28 November 2011).

Pretty, J. (2004), 'How nature contributes to mental and physical health', *Spirituality and Health International*, **5** (2), 68–78.

Public Health Law and Policy (2008), 'Land use and planning policies to support community and urban gardening', available at: http://norcalheal.cnr.berkeley. edu/docs/CommunityGardenPolicyInventory_PHLP.pdf.

Putnam, R.D. (2000), *Bowling Alone: The Collapse and Revival of American Community*, New York: Simon & Schuster.

Rubin, V. (2008), 'The roots of the urban greening movement', *Growing Greener Cities: Urban Sustainability in the Twenty-first Century*, Philadelphia: University of Pennsylvania Press, pp. 187–206.

Ryan, R.L. and R.E. Grese (2005), 'Urban volunteers and the environment: forest and prairie restoration', in P.F. Barlett (ed.), *Urban Place: Reconnecting with the Natural World*, Cambridge, MA: MIT Press.

Schmelzkopf, K. (1995), 'Urban community gardens as contested space', *Geographical Review*, **85** (3), 364–81.

Schukoske, J.E. (2000), 'Community development through gardening: state and local policies transforming urban open space', *NYU Journal of Legislative and Public Policy*, **3**, 351–92.

Schwartz, B. (2004), *The Paradox of Choice: Why More Is Less*, New York: HarperCollins.

Seligman, M.E.P. (1975), *Helplessness: On Depression, Development, and Death*, San Francisco, CA: Freeman.

Semenza, J.C. and T.L. March (2009), 'An urban community-based intervention to advance social interactions', *Environment and Behavior*, **41** (1), 22–42, doi: 10.1177/0013916507311136.

Slovic, P. (1987), 'Perception of risk', *Science*, **236** (4799), 280–85.

Snyder, K. (n.d.), 'PlaceMatters', available at: http://www.smartgrowthtools.org/ (accessed 20 November 2011).

Snyder, K. and J. Herman (2003), 'Visualization tools to improve community decision making', *PAS Memo*, November.

Stigsdotter, U.K., O. Ekholm, J. Schipperijn, M. Toftager, F. Kamper-Jørgensen and T.B. Randrup (2010), 'Health promoting outdoor environments: associations between green space, and health, health-related quality of life and stress based on a Danish national representative survey', *Scandinavian Journal of Public Health*, **38**, 411–17, doi: 10.1177/1403494810367468.

Stuart, S.M. (2005), 'Lifting spirits: creating gardens in California domestic violence shelters', in P.F. Barlett (ed.), *Urban Place: Reconnecting with the Natural World*, Cambridge, MA: MIT Press, pp. 61–88.

Sullivan, W.C. and C.-Y. Chang (2011), 'Mental health and the built environment', in A.L. Dannenberg, H. Frumkin and R.J. Jackson (eds), *Making Healthy Places: Designing and Building for Health, Well-being, and Sustainability*, Washington, DC: Island Press, pp. 106–16.

Tasker-Brown, J. and S. Pogharian (2000), *Learning from Suburbia: Residential Street Pattern Design*, Ottawa: Canada Mortgage and Housing Corporation.

Tennessen, C.M. and B. Cimprich (1995), 'Views to nature: effects on attention', *Journal of Environmental Psychology*, **15**, 77–85.

Tomasello, M. and E. Herrmann (2010), 'Ape and human cognition: what's the difference?', *Current Directions in Psychological Science*, **19** (1), 3–8, doi: 10.1177/0963721409359300.

Twiss, J., J. Dickinson, S. Duma, T. Kleinman, H. Paulsen and L. Rilveria (2003),

'Community gardens: lessons learned from California Healthy Cities and Communities', *American Journal of Public Health*, **93** (9), 1435–8.

US Forest Service, Northern Research Station (2009), *Restorative Commons: Creating Health and Well-being through Urban Landscapes*, General Technical Report No. NRS-P-39, Newtown Square, PA: USDA Forest Service, Northern Research Station.

Velarde, M.D., G. Fry and M. Tveit (2007), 'Health effects of viewing landscapes: landscape types in environmental psychology', *Urban Forestry and Urban Greening*, **6** (4), 199–212.

Vohs, K.D., R.F. Baumeister, B.J. Schmeichel, J.M. Twenge, N.M. Nelson and D.M. Tice (2008), 'Making choices impairs subsequent self-control: a limited-resource account of decision making, self-regulation, and active initiative', *Journal of Personality and Social Psychology*, **94** (5), 883–98, doi: 10.1037/0022-3514.94.5.883.

Walker, A.J. and R.L. Ryan (2008), 'Place attachment and landscape preservation in rural New England: a Maine case study', *Landscape and Urban Planning*, **86**, 141–52.

Whitehead, M. and F. Diderichsen (2001), 'Social capital and health: tip-toeing through the minefield of evidence', *Lancet*, **358** (9277), 165–6.

Wood, L., T. Shannon, M. Bulsara, T. Pikora, G. McCormack and B. Giles-Corti (2008), 'The anatomy of the safe and social suburb: an exploratory study of the built environment, social capital and residents' perceptions of safety', *Health and Place*, **14** (1), 15–31.

Wood, L., L.D. Frank and B. Giles-Corti (2010), 'Sense of community and its relationship with walking and neighborhood design', *Social Science and Medicine*, **70** (9), 1381–90.

Wooten, H. and A. Ackerman (2011), *Seeding the City: Land Use Policies to Promote Urban Agriculture*, National Policy and Legal Analysis Network to Prevent Childhood Obesity, Public Health Law and Policy, available at: http://www.phlpnet.org/childhood-obesity/products/urban-ag-toolkit.

Yancey, W.L. (1971), 'Architecture, interaction, and social control: the case of a large-scale public housing project', *Environment and Behavior*, **3** (1), 3–21, doi: 10.1177/001391657100300101.

Yunus, M. (1999), 'The Grameen Bank', *Scientific American*, **281** (5), 114–19.

Zielinski, S. (2006), 'New Mobility: the next generation of sustainable urban transportation', *Bridge Magazine of the National Academy of Engineers*, **36**, 33–8.

Zimbardo, P.G. (1973), 'On the ethics of intervention in human psychological research: with special reference to the Stanford prison experiment', *Cognition*, **2** (2), 243–56.

PART III

Revising economic principles

8. What implications does well-being science have for economic policy?

Charles Seaford

It is now very widely agreed that the intermediate objective that has dominated economic policy for the last 40 years and more – maximizing GDP – no longer does the job. Over the last three to four years it has become clear to a steadily widening group that growth on its own cannot deliver what a broad coalition now wants: sustainability, social justice and improved well-being.

Instead, we need to ask how efficient different forms of economic and other societal activity are at delivering what we really want, that is, well-being, or the good life. Well-being may be a function of economic activity, but it is clearly not a simple one: there are many other variables involved as well. In addition, if we also ask what impact these forms of activity have on the environment, we can start to manage the trade-off between well-being now and well-being in the future, that is, delivering well-being in a way that is sustainable.

In this chapter I try to set out some of the implications for economic policy of making well-being efficiency a central objective – that is, of trying to maximize the well-being generated by each unit of output. The chapter presents some of the key empirical findings from the literature, and draws together the implications of these findings for policy objectives. This is followed by an illustrative deep dive into what two or three of these objectives might mean for economic policy in the UK at the moment. The chapter concludes with an attempt to draw out the implications for an overall approach to economic policy making. This is work in progress: research and analysis on this topic by the new economics foundation (nef) and others are ongoing.

WHAT DOES THE EVIDENCE SHOW ABOUT THE KIND OF ECONOMY WE WANT?

I believe the evidence supports the following eight propositions which are relevant to economic policy. In some cases the support from the evidence is very direct; in others the proposition is the best explanation of complex or even apparently paradoxical data:

1. Income is important to well-being, but only up to a certain level, which varies from society to society.
2. Equality is positively associated with well-being, although the relationship is complex.
3. Unemployment is very damaging to well-being.
4. Economic instability is damaging to well-being.
5. The various components of a 'good job' (in addition to income) are strongly associated with well-being; this includes the right amount of work – not too much but not too little either.
6. The way we consume does not optimize our well-being, and advertising may contribute to this.
7. Some types of personal debt are associated with low levels of personal well-being.
8. There are other features of society, such as the strength of personal relationships and social capital, which are strongly associated with well-being and which, while themselves 'non-economic', are influenced by the design of the economy.

1.   Income Is Important to Well-being, but only up to a Certain Level, Which Varies from Society to Society

There is a myth about well-being science that it shows that 'money doesn't matter' once people have escaped from poverty. This is not true. There is a positive relationship between an individual's income and his or her level of well-being when measured at any given time in a particular country (developing or developed), but the relationship weakens as income rises. This is as predicted by standard economic theory, which posits declining marginal utility of income. The shape and position of the curve describing the relationship vary with the measure of well-being used and the country.[1]

At the time of writing, the study based on the largest data set was conducted in 2010 in the US, with over 450 000 respondents.[2] This showed that when well-being is defined in terms of affect (positive feelings and a relative absence of negative feelings) increases in household income have no impact on well-being above $75 000 (this is an average across households – clearly you would expect variations depending on household type). In addition there is a clear inflection point in the curve at around $50 000 where the marginal impact of an extra dollar falls sharply, suggesting that income may be relatively unimportant above this level (relatively as compared with say quality of personal relationships, social capital or the local environment). However, when the well-being score is defined as an assessment of one's life as compared with the best possible life, the study picked up no real limits to the impact of more money (at least up to its top income category of above \$150 000) although there are still, as one would expect, declining marginal returns. This latter measure, it should be noted, encourages respondents to compare themselves with those who are better off than them – and there are always people better off than you.

Evidence of the kind just presented, which shows a positive, albeit declining, relationship between income and well-being, is often contrasted with time series data which suggest that, in the UK, the US and some other developed countries, well-being (measured in terms of life satisfaction or self-assessment of overall happiness) has not risen over the last 30–50 years despite substantial increases in national income and despite the fact that most incomes in these countries are below the point (as identified for example in the cross-sectional study just described) at which further increases have no or little impact. This 'Easterlin paradox' is named after the academic who identified it.[3]

There are a number of possible explanations for the paradox, all of which probably have some merit. One is that, in developed economies, and except for those right at the bottom of the income distribution, it is largely levels of relative as opposed to absolute income that drive well-being. I am happier than you because I am richer than you, but if your income doubles and my income doubles nothing changes: I am no more or less happy.[4] This is not just because high relative income appeals to our competitiveness, or because it is used as a status marker, although both of these are true, but also because there are a number of goods whose supply cannot rise in line with economic activity and access to which will therefore always depend on relative income, on where in the income distribution one sits. Examples of these are houses with large gardens, holidays in beautiful and deserted nature reserves, homes in the catchment areas of the top 10 per cent of state schools[5] and goods used as status symbols. There are also many personal and professional services which do not benefit from productivity increases arising from technological advances and which therefore get more expensive in real terms as general prosperity rises. It may be that access to these kinds of goods and services has far more influence on well-being than access to the kinds of goods whose supply rises and price falls in line with productivity increases, such as consumer durables, computer games and books (abstracting from any status or exclusivity they confer).

A similar point is made by Amartya Sen, who argues that 'relative deprivation in the space of commodities' may lead to 'absolute deprivation in our ability to lead the life we choose to lead'.[6] In other words the ability to lead the life we choose – plausibly a prime driver of life satisfaction – is in part a function of relative income. What we need depends on our income, but also on income levels in society as a whole (or some combination of society as a whole and our neighbourhood). There are a large number of statistical studies supporting different variations on this hypothesis.[7]

This explanation of the paradox is in some ways counter-intuitive. It seems to run against the common-sense feeling that having a bit more money, in absolute as well as relative terms, may increase opportunities for the kinds of activities that encourage fulfilment and happiness (pursuing a hobby, having friends to stay, going on holiday, etc.) or remove some of the obstacles (poor child care facilities, poor medical care, poor transport, the daily struggle for survival). In fact when analysed it turns out that many of these increased opportunities result from increased *relative* income, because the kinds of goods and services they depend on don't get more plentiful or cheaper as a result of productivity increases; nonetheless it seems unlikely that the relative income explanation is the whole story – and fortunately there are other hypotheses.

A second, related, explanation is that what drives well-being is not so much income (or even relative income) but increase in income. We get satisfaction from getting richer and from improved products and services, but quickly adjust to our new level of wealth and if we do not continue to get richer revert to our old level of satisfaction. There is evidence for this so-called 'hedonic treadmill': a number of studies show a relationship between growth *rates* and absolute levels of well-being, implying that steady levels of growth will lead to steady levels of well-being.[8] On the other hand the US study referred to above does show well-being rising with income, suggesting that the hedonic treadmill is only an explanation of the paradox to the extent that well-off people tend to enjoy rising incomes.

A third explanation is the possibility of negative influences on life satisfaction that have counterbalanced the positive impact of higher incomes in the countries where time series data suggest well-being has been flat. As Stefano Bartolini argues in this volume (Chapter 6), there is evidence that some of the most likely candidates for these influences, such as the sharply increased social isolation in the US[9] or increased workplace stress, are probably linked in some way to the increased pressures associated with rising incomes. Timo Hämäläinen (this volume, Chapter 2) argues that increased prosperity can bring too much choice and a loss of sense of coherence. Both these points are extremely plausible, and they show, not that rising incomes are valueless (which simply relying on the relative income explanation would do), but that the value of rising incomes *delivered in the way they have been* may be reduced or cancelled out by side effects. This is a strong candidate, because the time series data vary between developed countries – the paradox is not universal.

Fourthly, the time series data sets on which the paradox rests mainly use life satisfaction as the measure of well-being, and this may lead to measurement issues. The surveys ask respondents to make a judgement as to how satisfied they are with their lives. In making this judgement, respondents will apply a frame of reference, and that frame of reference may be the current world, that is, one that moves with the times and rises with general income levels (this is sometimes expressed as 'rising expectations'). In this case the rising frame of reference may cancel out the effect of rising well-being. This explanation may seem similar to the relative income and hedonic treadmill explanations, but it is different in an important way: the two earlier explanations imply that well-being really does stagnate; the frame of reference explanation suggests that well-being may well rise, but the standard against which it is judged also rises. Thus, even if rising incomes had led to increased well-being, it would not be picked up in the survey data.

In addition the response may be influenced by norms about how to answer such questions – for example, it may be that, while not everyone will answer 7 out of 10, many people think that 7 out of 10 is an appropriate response for a normal person. This, and the fact that well-being is measured on a bounded scale (0–10), may reduce the sensitivity of the measurement tool and thus the extent to which it records changes over time.

On balance most academics in the field do not think these (and other) measurement problems are enough to explain the paradox entirely, but clearly they exist (see also measurement problems discussed by O'Hara and Lyon, this volume, Chapter 4) and may be part of the overall story.[10]

The following, then, can be concluded:

- In any society, at any given time, income increases will have a significant impact on well-being up to a certain level, although what this level is and how easy it is to define this level tightly will vary from society to society.
- It is quite likely – but not proven – that increasing a society's overall income reduces the well-being associated with any given level of income; this means that the gains brought about by an across-the-board increase in income without any redistribution are reduced.
- There may be little point in increasing national income if this results in reduced social capital or increased workplace stress – or has other damaging effects on well-being.

2.   Equality Is Positively Associated with Well-being, although the Relationship Is Complex

The standard textbook case for equality is that marginal utility falls with rising income – an extra £1 brings more utility to a poor person than to a rich person. Therefore other things being equal the more equality the more utility. However, other things are not equal: too much equality and redistribution blunts work incentives (or so goes the standard argument) and therefore reduces output and utility. The optimum level of equality (leaving aside any social justice considerations) is therefore at the point where 'the gains from further redistribution are just outweighed by the losses from the shrinking of the cake'.[11] The same case applies substituting well-being for utility.[12]

The discussion in the previous subsection suggests that the optimum level of equality as determined by this calculus is high. In the US, happiness stops rising at household income levels above $75000 – the marginal well-being of an extra £1 for people above this level is not just low but zero (if well-being is defined in terms of affect – that is, feelings and emotions) – and the curve flattens quite significantly at $50000.[13] In other words, the loss of well-being amongst the less well off that results from inequality is not compensated for by much gain amongst the better off, so the cake has to get a lot bigger to justify it – even when the less well off get their share of the cake. In fact in recent years in many Western countries median incomes have stagnated and lower-quartile incomes have often fallen despite rising GDPs – the less well off have *not* been getting their share of the cake.[14] What this means is that most people would be better off with more equality and less growth, and even the well off wouldn't be that much worse off in well-being terms.

Of course, affect isn't the only measure of well-being, and, as we have seen, returns to income continue above $75000 when well-being is defined as how well a life scores in comparison with the best possible life. So perhaps the gains in well-being of the better off resulting from inequality do count for something and do help to balance the losses of the less well off. At this point our earlier discussion of the Easterlin paradox becomes relevant. We established that, to the extent that the 'relative income' explanation of the Easterlin paradox was true, growth would not increase the well-being of either the better off *or* the less well off (excepting those right at the bottom of the income distribution), since growth does not increase relative income. This reduces the extent to which inequality can be justified by the growth it results in. Again, redistribution looks like the better option.

As I have already made clear I am *not* suggesting that relative income is the complete explanation of the paradox or that absolute levels of income have no role. Rather I am saying that relative income almost certainly is important to well-being, and, to the extent that it is, the case for inequality is reduced. Nor am I denying that, in the short to medium term, growth is needed to avoid *reductions* in living standards, economic instability and unemployment,[15] all of which, as we will see, are damaging to well-being. A degree of inequality may be the price we have to pay to deliver this necessary growth – although, as the success of the Nordic countries shows, some societies do not seem to need very much of this magic ingredient.

There is some evidence that inequality may be damaging to well-being in ways that go beyond these effects. In some unequal societies, material aspirations are particularly strong and cannot all be met. The result is not just a zero-sum game but a negative-sum game: the dissatisfaction of those with unmet high aspirations outweighs the satisfaction of those with met high aspirations.[16]

This evidence is largely qualitative. There is however quantitative evidence that, controlling for income levels, inequality has a negative impact on both mental and physical health,[17] which in turn are strongly correlated with well-being. Inequality is also linked to other social ills (such as crime) which plausibly affect everyone's well-being. Another potential consequence of inequality is insecurity: intuitively, we would expect more equal societies to produce a greater sense of security amongst their members, which we know contributes to well-being. So for example a higher ratio between unemployment benefit rates and an estimate of the expected wage increases life satisfaction for both the unemployed *and* the employed.[18]

There are also statistical studies suggesting a more general positive relationship between well-being and equality,[19] but the evidence is not straightforward because of the number of other factors that are difficult to control for. Latin American countries, for example, boast relatively high levels of life satisfaction[20] *and* high levels of inequality,[21] while there is evidence that some low-income but potentially mobile groups actually like inequality.[22]

3. Unemployment Is Very Damaging to Well-being

The evidence on this is particularly clear cut:

- The unemployed have sharply lower life satisfaction scores than the employed (5–15 per cent lower), are 19 per cent less likely to have a high life satisfaction score and are 15 per cent less likely to have a high overall happiness score;[23] these results are stronger than those associated with the equivalent income loss.[24]

- The unemployed do not adapt to their circumstances in the way that those who gain or suffer income changes generally do – the impacts just described are long lasting (or, if they do adapt, the long-term unemployed suffer additional harms over time).[25]
- High levels of unemployment are associated with loss of well-being amongst the employed, presumably because they create fear of unemployment.[26]
- There is a positive association between doing at least some work and well-being amongst the otherwise retired.[27]

4. Economic Instability Is Damaging to Well-being

Again the evidence is clear cut:

- Loss of income damages well-being significantly more than a comparable gain enhances it.[28]
- Well-being is negatively associated with very high growth rates, presumably because of the disruption almost always accompanying very high growth.[29]
- Job security is the job feature most commonly cited by employees as desirable.[30] Casual workers enjoy lower levels of well-being than full-time workers.[31]
- Inflation is also negatively associated with well-being, although the overall impact of inflation is significantly less than the impact of unemployment; volatile inflation rates are worse than steady inflation rates.[32]
- Levels of wealth are more strongly related to levels of life satisfaction than are levels of income; this may partly be because wealth allows consumption above income, but may also be because of the value of economic security which wealth provides.[33]
- Major structural changes in the economy will have a negative impact on the individual's sense of coherence, which is an important determinant of health and well-being (Hämäläinen, this volume, Chapter 2).

5. The Various Components of a 'Good Job' (in Addition to Income) Are Strongly Associated with Well-being; This Includes the Right Amount of Work – Not Too Much but Not Too Little Either

The evidence on this consists partly of correlations of certain features of jobs and subjective measures of well-being and partly of survey data on the features of jobs that people value. The following are key findings:

- Most people in Europe say they would like to work fewer hours – a survey a few years ago revealed that over 50 per cent of European Union workers said they wanted to reduce their working week to an average of 34 hours and that they would 'even accept a corresponding drop in income to achieve this'.[34] However, there are also data showing that part-time workers enjoy lower levels of well-being than full-time workers[35] (although those who choose to work part time enjoy higher levels of life satisfaction[36]). Consistent with these findings, the limited amount of evidence suggests there is an inverse U-shaped curve relating life satisfaction and hours worked, that is, that well-being rises as hours worked rise but only up to a certain point before it starts to drop as hours become excessive.[37]
- Long commutes significantly reduce well-being.[38]
- As already noted, the job feature most widely valued by employees is security; casual work is damaging to men's mental health and women's life satisfaction.[39]
- Also highly valued are good social relations at work[40] and the opportunity to do work that is interesting and stretches the employee but which he or she is good at.[41] These are linked to overall job satisfaction.[42]

However, rises in national income do not necessarily translate into better jobs in this sense. Overall job satisfaction in the UK fell between 1989 and 1997 and then rose back to 1989 levels by 2005 – in other words, it has not risen in line with national income. Similarly job satisfaction fell or was flat between 1997 and 2005 in 9 of 15 OECD countries while rising in 6.[43]

For more on well-being at work, see Flint-Taylor and Cooper (this volume, Chapter 9).

6. The Way We Consume Does Not Optimize Our Well-being, and Advertising May Contribute to This

There are three points here. The first is that many of our decisions about how to consume and spend our time do not maximize our well-being. This is because people are often not very good judges of what will make them happy.[44] (See also Hämäläinen, this volume, Chapter 2; and Bartolini, this volume, Chapter 6.) As a result we spend a relatively large amount of our time on passive pursuits such as watching television, even though the evidence is that active pursuits contribute disproportionately to well-being;[45] there have also been suggestions that passive pursuits actively induce low levels of well-being.[46] It has also been shown that societies such as the

UK that are relatively more materialistic have higher levels of mental ill health[47] and lower levels of child well-being[48] than societies (such as some in continental Europe) that are less materialistic.

The second point is that advertising may make our consumption decisions (even more) suboptimal. It is well known that advertisers aim to create emotional associations with products to drive sales and that it only works because it can exploit and exacerbate imperfections in our information processing.[49]

The third and most controversial point is an attempt to combine the first two points. Advertising induces suboptimal decisions because it encourages materialism and passive pursuits at the expense of active pursuits.[50] It is thus potentially damaging to well-being. However this is disputed, we at least do not have clear-cut evidence, and more work is needed to confirm or reject this hypothesis.

7.   Some Types of Personal Debt Are Associated with Low Levels of Personal Well-being

Short-term debt, such as credit card debt or payday debt, has a negative effect on well-being. This kind of debt is often associated with poverty, of course, but the debt itself adds to the anxiety. However, longer-term debt, such as mortgages or debts taken out to invest in assets, has not been found to have a negative impact on life satisfaction.[51]

8.   There Are Other Features of Society, such as the Strength of Personal Relationships and Social Capital, Which Are Strongly Associated with Well-being and Which, while Themselves 'Non-economic', Are Influenced by the Design of the Economy

Social capital and social relations are central to well-being, as argued by John Helliwell (this volume, Chapter 5):

- There is a positive correlation between well-being and participation in the community and volunteering, although in *some* studies when the personality variable of extraversion was added to the model the effect disappeared; in other words, while it is likely (and intuitively plausible) that there is a causal relation, it is possible there is not.[52]
- Seeing family and friends is positively associated with well-being.[53]

Given this, well-being will be influenced by the extent to which the economy allows individuals the time to volunteer and participate in the community, and to invest in their relationships with friends and family. More generally, social trust and stability enhance well-being:

- Social trust (i.e. trust in most other people) is positively associated with well-being;[54] positive responses in the UK to the question 'Do you think most other people can be trusted?' fell from about 60 per cent in the 1950s to about 30 per cent in 2002.[55]
- Children's well-being, both as children and later in life, is negatively associated with frequent moves of home.

In other words, an economy that allows people to stay living in the same place and earn a living – that encourages social stability – is likely to enhance well-being. Participation in the community is also likely to depend on a degree of social stability – and thus on the extent to which individuals can find stable work without uprooting themselves.

Finally, the environment influences well-being (as pointed out by Basu et al., this volume, Chapter 7):

- Living close to open green space has been shown to enhance people's well-being.[56]
- Negative externalities such as pollution and aircraft noise are (unsurprisingly) negatively associated with well-being.[57]

The economy needs to be managed to ensure these externalities are effectively internalized.

THE IMPLICATIONS OF THIS EVIDENCE

In this section we argue that the evidence in the previous section points towards five main priorities for economic policy:

1. a target band of income for everyone;
2. economic and social stability and full employment across all regions of a country;
3. satisfying work for all;
4. work for all in the right quantities;
5. ensuring active forms of consumption and correcting the biases created by advertising.

1.   A Target Band of Income for Everyone

The discussion of income and well-being concluded:

- In any society at any given time, individual income increases will have a significant impact on well-being up to a certain level.
- It is quite likely – but not proven – that increasing a society's overall income will reduce the well-being associated with any given level of income.

This, together with the evidence on the importance of equality that followed, makes clear that simply targeting growth is not the most efficient way of maximizing well-being. Targeting an income band is a potential alternative. In other words, our target should be *maximizing the proportion of households with an income between a lower and upper boundary* (adjusted for household type). This both is compatible with the evidence as just described and, I suggest, has a good chance of being politically viable. The values of the boundaries would be based on income/well-being curves. The headline indicator would be the proportion of households living within the boundaries.

Achieving the lower boundary of the band would mean that you could participate actively in society and could pursue a fulfilling life without the distractions of insecurity and poverty; at the upper boundary of the band the relationship with well-being would be very small.

This account of the lower boundary is essentially the idea set out by Amartya Sen, who argued nearly 30 years ago that an adequate 'living standard' for individuals is one which allows positive answers to questions such as: 'Can they take part in the life of the community? Can they appear in public without shame and without feeling disgraced? Can they find worthwhile jobs? Can they keep themselves warm? Can they use their school education? Can they visit friends and relations if they choose?'[58]

The lower boundary is considerably above subsistence, but exactly where it is will always be a matter for political and social judgement. However, decision makers can look to the kind of results cited above to guide them. For example, we saw that there is an inflection point in the curve describing the relationship between income and affect in the United States at around $50 000 – in other words, it is at about this level that the marginal impact of an extra dollar falls sharply. To use this figure is to hypothesize that, if your income is below the 'living standard', a rise in income leads to significant increases in the balance of positive over negative affect, but that, once you have achieved the 'living standard' and can answer yes to Sen's questions, then further increases in income have relatively little impact on this balance. In other words, income is a hygiene factor: its presence does not lead to happiness, but its absence makes happiness hard to achieve.

This hypothesis cannot be proved (as yet), but it is plausible and it looks like the best available guide to where the lower boundary should be. It also leads to a result not so far from median income. It's a pragmatic policy recommendation. Having said this, there is room for discussion as to which of affect or life satisfaction measures are more appropriate for this kind of decision. In general, life satisfaction measures are more responsive to changes in external circumstances;[59] on the other hand, affect measures are more immediate, that is, they are not mediated by a judgement and are therefore less susceptible to frame-of-reference effects. They may therefore be better evidence of whether someone is leading a good life in Sen's sense. More research is needed on this.

What should the top boundary be? If the inflection point in the affect curve is used for the bottom boundary, perhaps we could identify a similar point in the curve measuring comparisons with the best possible life for the top boundary. If there comes a point after which people are satisfied even by this demanding criterion, then surely the associated consumption is not a priority.

If we use this scheme for setting the boundaries, then the values of the boundaries will vary from society to society and, as the Easterlin paradox shows, over time within societies. In the US the lower boundary currently appears to be around $50000 household income (for the average household) and the upper end appears to be over $150000.[60]

2. Economic and Social Stability and Full Employment across All Regions of a Country

This falls directly out of the evidence. High well-being is associated with low levels of unemployment and high levels of job and financial security.

In some circumstances there is a trade-off between these two desirable outcomes. France, for example, is said to have chosen relatively high levels of both unemployment and job security, the UK relatively low levels of unemployment and job security. The challenge is thus to improve the levels of security and unemployment at which this trade-off takes place, to shift the curve as it were, or perhaps even to eliminate the reasons the trade-off exists. This should be an explicit objective of economic policy and could be captured in some compound measure of these two desirable components of economic security.

Several other desirable features of society contributing to high levels of well-being – stronger relationships, social trust, community involvement, children who are able to 'put down roots' – are associated with stable communities. A good economy is one which strengthens existing communities rather than requiring people to uproot themselves. The impact of economic development on communities and the extent to which it encourages dysfunctional geographic mobility should also be a priority for economic policy makers. This means that economic policy has to have a strong regional and local element.

3. Satisfying Work for All

Economic policy at the moment is almost entirely concerned with increasing output, although creating employment is seen as a desirable consequence of that. In fact the evidence suggests that economic policy should be concerned with the quality of the jobs created as well as the quantity (in fact of course job satisfaction often enhances productivity as well). The level of job satisfaction should be a specific target – a criterion used by policy makers when deciding which industries and firms to support, and an objective of programmes developed in collaboration with employers and trade unions.

4. Work for All in the Right Quantities

Long working hours are damaging to well-being. They may also make constructive use of leisure time difficult, reducing the time and energy available for the kinds of active pursuits and community engagement which are associated with high levels of well-being. Reducing the average number of hours worked (and in particular the number of hours worked by those working the most) should therefore be an explicit target for economic policy.

5. Ensuring Active Forms of Consumption and Correcting the Biases Created by Advertising

The evidence shows that the quality as well as quantity of consumption matters to well-being, and, as we have seen, it is at least likely that individuals are exposed to pressures which result in suboptimal consumption decisions. Just as a well-being-driven economic policy will target the quality of jobs, so it will target the quality of consumption, with a view to steadily increasing the proportion of consumption devoted to those activities strongly linked to well-being. This does not of course imply state direction of leisure activities, Soviet-style young pioneer camps and the banning of television. It does imply identifying the biases and barriers which result in suboptimal decisions and, where possible within the constraints of a liberal society, attempting to remove these.

AN EXAMPLE: INCREASING INCOMES CURRENTLY BELOW THE LOWER END OF THE BAND

In this section I start exploring what taking these objectives seriously might mean for policy. I do not end up with definitive proposals – the recommendations are strictly illustrative of an *approach*. I am using a UK example, but the principles apply more widely.

There is at the time of writing no clear evidence as to the lower boundary of the target income band for the UK. For the purposes of this exercise, I am assuming the lower boundary is equal to the current median wage of £26 000 ($41 600) – that is, somewhat lower than the US's $50 000.

In the UK, median wages stagnated between 2002 and 2008, have fallen since[61] and are not projected to get back to 2002 levels for several years. As in the US, even when the economy was growing, most people's incomes did not go up. If the objective is getting people above the current median wage of £26 000, that is, above the lower boundary of the target income band, then obviously conventional economic policy was not working even in the good times.

A standard explanation has been the trend towards an 'hour-glass-shaped' labour market: good and rising incomes for a growing professional and managerial elite, at the same time as a rising number of people forced into unskilled work with stagnant or declining real incomes. Two kinds of remedy are then possible. The first involves accepting that in the modern world hour-glass-shaped labour markets are inevitable. The task is to make the best of this fact: increase the proportion of the workforce in the top part of the glass and increase cash and in-kind transfers to those in the bottom part. Policies aiming to achieve this include investing in higher education, support for industries which employ graduates, increased expenditure on public and state-subsidized goods, from health care to parks and art galleries, tax credits and a generous system of social insurance. This was the Labour government's approach in the UK under Tony Blair and Gordon Brown.

There are a number of problems with this. First of all, it is not at all clear that the transfers required are politically sustainable – that they will be supported by a majority; and, even if they are, they will always remain precarious, always vulnerable to a government that wants to cut spending. In addition, this approach does not in itself address the need for satisfying work amongst non-graduates as well as graduates – the third objective set out above. It is not a well-being approach to economic policy. These problems are all the more acute given that only a minority (45 per cent) of young people in the UK do go to university, and the proportion is unlikely to rise any time soon. The top of the hour glass is not going to get that much bigger.

The alternative is to manage the economy to deliver more 'good jobs', for non-graduates as well as graduates: increasing the number of what are now good jobs and improving what are now bad jobs.

This means increasing the number of non-graduate skilled jobs and doing so in all regions of the country where there is a shortage of such jobs. Moving home is not good for building social capital and relationships, which are important to well-being, and, as we have seen, frequent moves of home are particularly bad for children's well-being, both at the time and later in life. Long commutes are also bad for well-being. Internal migration and jobs concentrated in a few major hubs cannot be part of a well-being-based economic policy.

An analysis of the sectors where such jobs are concentrated suggests that in the UK this part of the strategy requires more jobs in construction and in manufacturing.[62] Influencing the construction sector is relatively simple. Demand is heavily influenced by government policy (planning regulations, social housing subsidies and regulations, building regulations, taxation), and there is both a need for retrofit to reduce carbon emissions and an acute shortage of affordable housing – itself damaging to well-being. The question, given fiscal constraints, is whether there are levers that can mobilize resources without major increases in public subsidy; nef policy analysis shows that there are, given changes (quite radical changes) to the planning and capital gains tax regimes.[63] The resulting building programme would expand demand for skilled labour and thus the number of 'good jobs' and increase the well-being of both workers and tenants.

Strengthening the manufacturing sector is more difficult, but contrary to popular imagination it is not dying in the UK. While overall forecasts tend to be gloomy, there are pockets of expansion, suggesting that there is a basis for a growing internationally competitive sector.[64] However, this is unlikely to happen without some form of intervention: it is a classic case of widely shared benefits and concentrated costs, requiring collective action if things are to happen. The state is best placed to ensure this: hence the need for an active 'industrial strategy' focused on good jobs and thus well-being. This does not mean the state does this on its own: the approach involves close long-term cooperation between the private and public sectors.[65]

But a well-being-based economic policy must also improve what are

Table 8.1   Estimated typical pay range (per annum) for non-graduates in sample sectors

Hospitality	£9667–£24 452
Social care	£10 529–£27 000
Retail	£11 695–£27 174
Manufacturing – transport	£18 676–£34 678
Manufacturing – other	£15 222–£34 852
Construction	£15 918–£41 453*

Notes:
* nef estimates based on analysis of Sector Skill Council and ONS data. See Shaheen et al. (2012) for methodology.
£1 = approx. €1.15 and $1.60.

now bad jobs. An important part of this is addressing low pay levels in some sectors, where even relatively skilled jobs are badly paid. Table 8.1 sets out nef estimates of typical pay ranges for non-graduates in six sectors.

As can be seen, there are very significant variations between sectors, with even the best-paid non-graduates in hospitality not reaching our target. Increasing skill levels amongst non-graduates is not going to be enough in the three low-paying sectors identified here: hospitality, social care and retail.

Fortunately, government is the key employer and purchaser in the social care sector. It can itself set the wage levels, either as an employer or through the contracts it lets to providers, and ensure higher than current 'market' rates. Of course, the extra costs have to be paid for, through either higher taxes or cuts elsewhere, and any pay rises would have to be introduced over a reasonably long period to make this politically accepta-ble. Given a well-being-based economic policy, the question is not whether to do this, though, but how quickly is feasible.

In the hospitality and retail sectors the state is not the purchaser, of course. Here there is a strong case both for continuing to uprate the statu-tory minimum wage and for state action to encourage unionization. The clear (and unsurprising) evidence is that, in those countries (and regions and sectors) with strong unions, the ratio of median income growth to GDP growth has been much higher than elsewhere.[66]

Higher wages may create pressures for increased productivity, possibly shifting an industry out of a low-wage equilibrium and paying for at least some of the increase. If demand is relatively inelastic, higher wages could also lead to lower rents in two industries where rents represent a high proportion of total costs, and are ultimately a function of potential profit. Nevertheless, they are also likely to mean higher prices, particularly in the short to medium term. This is not bad in itself – changing relative prices is what redistribution means. However, it could impose unacceptably high cost increases on consumers who are already struggling, and it could force businesses to lay off staff. Unemployment, as we know, is particularly damaging to well-being. Higher prices could also provoke destabilizing inflation, which is also bad for well-being (although modest bursts of inflation may be an acceptable price to pay).[67]

Further research is needed on these impacts and the extent to which fiscal or other measures can deal with them. Again the question for a well-being-based economic policy is not whether wages should rise but the speed at which they can rise towards target levels. It is worth noting that, in the UK, the Low Pay Commission, which sets the minimum wage, has conducted this kind of analysis. It has proceeded with considerable caution, partly because the option of fiscal or other mechanisms to reduce negative impacts has not been open to it. A well-being-based economic policy would place more importance on wage increases for the low paid and would therefore explore all possible means of making this possible.

CONCLUSION: THE APPROACH TO POLICY MAKING IMPLIED BY THIS EVIDENCE

The example just given makes clear that the kind of measures needed for a well-being-based economic policy will be interventionist. Perhaps more interestingly, these measures do not fit comfortably into the schema sometimes proposed by conventional policy makers, which distinguishes between 'economic' and 'political' objectives. The former are normally stipulated to be maximizing GDP and allocative efficiency, with unemployment, for example, being a case of allocative inefficiency. Allocative efficiency is sometimes defined as 'Pareto optimality' – the situation where no one can be made better off without making someone else worse off. A quite elaborate theoretical apparatus is then presented to show that these objectives are delivered when markets work 'well'. Purely economic policy is thus a matter of identifying and then correcting market 'failures'. Of course, the resulting policies can be modified to take into account 'political' objectives, which might include reducing inequality, or protecting jobs in a marginal constituency, and this may involve a departure from Pareto optimality. A side effect of this schema is a neat division of labour between official economists and the politicians.

The objectives set out and the approach just illustrated do not involve the same kind of distinction between the economic and the political. The task is no longer to make the economy 'work' according to traditional standards, to achieve Pareto optimality and then modify outcomes; it is to change the way the economy works. Having said this, we can still make a clear distinction between those objectives grounded in evidence and those which can be characterized, fairly or unfairly, as reflecting the preferences or interests of politicians and their clients. It is just that we now draw the line in a different place. And this matters: the subtle suggestion that GDP maximization and allocative efficiency are in some way more legitimate or neutral as objectives than, say, equality has certainly had a pervasive influence (at least in the UK).

Given this, neoclassical economics is not such a useful overall frame-work for action as in the past. Of course, standard microeconomic tools still have an important role to play: when working out how to reduce unemployment in a particular region, for example, it is likely that eco-nomic analysis of potential comparative advantage will play an important part. But conventional theory does not provide an overall justification for, and guide to, the kind of government action now needed. In the past, effec-tive government leaders such as Margaret Thatcher have typically used a handful of simple principles (such as 'Find a market solution' or 'Increase choice' or 'Cut spending') to guide the work of more junior policy makers and to explain policy to the public. We need a similar set of principles.

Unfortunately we do not as yet have a well-being economic theory with the same internal consistency and elegance as neoclassical economics and perhaps we never will. We are forced back on to the kind of pragmatism illustrated in the previous section. The trouble is that theory often trumps pragmatism, and of course theory has a strong hold in finance ministries. It could constitute a block to the adoption of well-being objectives in so far as bureaucracies tend to stick with those objectives they know how to deliver.

The idea that government should pay care workers more than current market rates is an excellent illustration of this problem. It runs directly counter to 'value for money' principles often adopted in governments, and a belief system in which market-set prices are 'correct' and provide the benchmark for 'value for money' (unless you can demonstrate a market failure).

Because of this, politicians who are attracted to this agenda will need to spend a good deal of effort making government more 'joined up' – creating a coherent programme across departments. If the battle is between theory and ill-defined pragmatism, theory will have more legitimacy and is likely to win. If the battle is between theory and a coherent, evidence-based set of objectives, implemented and monitored by a leadership team all working towards the same goal, using a well-designed metric set, then the objectives have a chance of winning. This is easier said than done, of course, and joined-up government has been an unachieved objective in England or the UK since Edward I of England's Wardrobe (his private finance department) engaged in disputes with the Exchequer. But there are cases where things have been improved: in Colombia, for example, the government has set itself the target of reducing poverty defined in multidimensional terms. This requires cooperation across departments, and progress is monitored by the Presidential Council – which the President *has* to attend. The metric set and the process have by all accounts facilitated more joined-up working. It is possible to imagine a similar process for well-being, in which, to take an example from the previous section, policies on land planning, tax, skills development and regional industrial policy were coordinated to boost the buildings sector.

A final point: there will be trade-offs between the objectives derived from the well-being evidence. Although these will remain largely matters of political judgement, in the future data from large-scale national well-being surveys will be able to inform these judgements, as they will, at least sometimes, help to assess the relative impact of achieving different economic policy objectives.[68] So, as our measurements become more comprehensive, we may be able to use a well-being 'currency' to manage trade-offs – we may be able to assess the relative merits of alternative policies by measuring the impacts on well-being of their otherwise incommensurable outcomes.

NOTES

1. For a review of the evidence see L. Stoll (2012), *Well-being for Policy: A Review of the Evidence*, London: nef, section 1.1. For example, R. Layard, G. Mayraz and S. Nickell (2008), 'The marginal utility of income', *Journal of Public Economics*, **92**, 1846–57.
2. D. Kahneman and A. Deaton (2010), 'High income improves evaluation of life but not emotional well-being', *Proceedings of the National Academy of Sciences of the United States of America*, **107** (38), 16489–93.
3. R. Easterlin (1995), 'Will raising the incomes of all increase the happiness of all?', *Journal of Economic Behavior and Organization*, **27** (1), 35–47.
4. A. Clark, P. Frijters and M. Shields (2008), 'Relative income, happiness and utility: an explanation for the Easterlin paradox and other puzzles', *Journal of Economic Literature*, **46** (1), 95–144; R. Layard, G. Mayraz and S. Nickell (2010), 'Does relative income matter?', in E. Diener, J. Helliwell and D. Kahneman (eds), *International Differences in Well-being*, New York: Oxford University Press.
5. On schools see R. Frank (2005), 'Does money buy happiness?', in F. Huppert, N. Baylis and B. Keverne (eds), *The Science of Well-being*, Oxford: Oxford University Press.
6. A. Sen (1984), 'The living standard', *Oxford Economic Papers*, **36**, 74–90.
7. See for example E. Luttmer (2005), 'Neighbors as negatives: relative earnings and well-being', *Quarterly Journal of Economics*, **120**, 963–1002; B.S. Frey and A. Stutzer (2005), 'Happiness research: state and prospects', *Review of Social Economy*, **62** (2), 207–28.
8. D.W. Sacks, B. Stevenson and J. Wolfers (2010), *Subjective Well-being, Income, Economic Development and Growth*, NBER Working Paper No. 16441, Cambridge,

MA: National Bureau of Economic Research; B. Stevenson and J. Wolfers (2008), 'Economic growth and subjective well-being: reassessing the Easterlin paradox', *Brookings Papers on Economic Activity*, Spring, pp. 1–102; M.R. Hagerty and R. Veenhoven (2006), 'Rising happiness in nations: 1946–2004 – a reply to Easterlin', *Social Indicators Research*, **79**, 421–36.

9. Between 1984 and 2004 the number of Americans with 'no one to talk to' rose from 8 per cent to 24 per cent. For the link with economic growth see S. Bartolini and E. Bilancini (2010), 'If not only GDP, what else? Using relational goods to predict the trends of subjective well-being', *International Review of Economics*, **57**, 199–213.

10. For a fuller discussion of this see 'Appendix 1: Measuring well-being – the limits of life satisfaction', in J. Michaelson, S. Abdallah, N. Steuer, S. Thompson and N. Marks (2009), *National Accounts of Well-being: Bringing Real Wealth onto the Balance Sheet*, London: nef.

11. R. Layard (2005), *Happiness*, London: Allen Lane, referring to work by James Meade, James Mirrlees and Amartya Sen.

12. Note that well-being is not a synonym for the economists' concept of utility, since the latter is in practice identified with consumption preferences. It is closer to John Stuart Mill's concept of utility.

13. Kahneman and Deaton (2010).

14. F. Shaheen, C. Seaford and J. Chapman (2012), *Good Jobs for Non-graduates*, London: nef.

15. P. Victor (2008), *Managing without Growth: Slower by Design, Not Disaster*, Cheltenham, UK and Northampton, MA, USA: Edward Elgar Publishing.

16. O. James (2007), *Affluenza: How to Be Successful and Stay Sane*, London: Vermilion; T. Kasser and R.M. Ryan (1996), 'Further examining the American dream: differential correlates of intrinsic and extrinsic goals', *Personality and Social Psychology Bulletin*, **22**, 280–87.

17. R. Wilkinson and K. Pickett (2009), *The Spirit Level*, London: Allen Lane, which includes references to extensive sources on inequality and health.

18. P. Dolan, T. Peasgood and M. White (2006), 'Review of research on the influences on personal well-being and application to policy making', final report for Defra, p. 60. I have drawn extensively from this literature review and have referred to the relevant pages rather than the articles cited, which can of course be identified in the review.

19. S. Oishi, S. Kesebir and E. Diener (2011), 'Income inequality and happiness', *Psychological Science*, **22** (9), 1095–1100; L. Winkelmann and R. Winkelmann (2010), 'Does inequality harm the middle class?', *Kyklos*, **63**, 301–16; M. Berg and R. Veenhoven (2010), 'Income inequality and happiness in 119 nations', in Bent Greve (ed.), *Happiness and Social Policy in Europe*, Cheltenham, UK and Northampton, MA, USA: Edgar Elgar Publishing, pp. 174–94.

20. nef Happy Planet Index (2009).

21. Although there are reasons why life satisfaction scores may be inflated in unequal societies. Survey respondents tend to enhance their capability self-assessments relative to the mean in unequal societies as compared with respondents in equal societies. S. Loughnan, P. Kuppens, J. Allik, K. Balazs, S. de Lemus, K. Dumont, R. Gargurevich, I. Hidegkuti, B. Leidner, L. Matos, J. Park, A. Realo, J. Shi, V.E. Sojo, Y.-y. Tong, J. Vaes, P. Verduyn, V. Yeung and N. Haslam (2011), 'Economic inequality is linked to biased self-perception', *Psychological Science*, **22**, 1254–8. To the extent that life satisfaction scores reflect self-esteem, the same bias could exist in life satisfaction scores.

22. Layard (2005).

23. Dolan et al. (2006), p. 49.

24. Ibid., p. 50; A. Clark (2010), 'Work, jobs and well-being across the millennium', in E. Diener, J. Helliwell and D. Kahneman (eds), *International Differences in Well-being*, Oxford: Oxford University Press.

25. Dolan et al. (2006), p. 50; Clark (2010).

26. Clark (2010).
27. Dolan et al. (2006), p. 51.
28. For example see D. Kahneman and A. Tversky (eds) (2000), *Choices, Values and Frames*, Cambridge: Cambridge University Press, cited in Layard (2005).
29. E. Lora and J. Chaparro (2009), *Understanding Quality of Life in Latin America and the Caribbean*, Washington, DC: IADB.
30. Clark (2010).
31. Dolan et al. (2006), p. 50.
32. Ibid., p. 60.
33. Ibid., p. 42.
34. European Foundation for Improvement of Living and Working Conditions (2003), *A New Organisation of Time over Working Life*, available at: www.eurofound.europa.eu/publications, cited in N. Marks and H. Shah (2004), *A Well-being Manifesto for a Flourishing Society*, London: nef, p. 10.
35. Dolan et al. (2006), p. 50.
36. S. Abdallah and S. Shah (2012), *Well-being Patterns Uncovered: An Analysis of UK data*, London: nef.
37. Dolan et al. (2006), p. 51.
38. Ibid., p. 51.
39. Ibid., p. 49; Clark (2010).
40. Clark (2010).
41. M. Csikszentmihalyi (1997), *Finding Flow: The Psychology of Engagement in Everyday Life*, New York: Perseus Books, cited in Marks and Shah (2004), p. 9; Clark (2010).
42. Clark (2010).
43. International Social Survey Programme 1989–2005, analysed in Clark (2010).
44. D. Gilbert (2006), *Stumbling on Happiness*, New York: Alfred A. Knopf.
45. Foresight (2008), *Mental Capital and Wellbeing: Making the Most of Ourselves in the 21st Century*, London: Government Office for Science.
46. Marks and Shah (2004).
47. O. James ([1998] 2010), *Britain on the Couch*, London: Vermilion.
48. UNICEF UK (2011), *Child Well-being in the UK, Spain and Sweden*, London: UNICEF UK.
49. See for example research described in *Strategy and Business* (Booz & Co.), **60** (Autumn 2010).
50. J. Alexander, T. Crompton and G. Shrubsole (2011), *Think of Me as Evil*, Woking: WWF-UK, PIRC.
51. Dolan et al. (2006), p. 42; Foresight (2008).
52. Dolan et al. (2006), p. 52; see also nef (2008), *Five Ways to Well-being: The Evidence*, London: nef.
53. Dolan et al. (2006), p. 59.
54. Ibid., p. 55.
55. Performance and Innovation Unit (2002), *Social Capital: A Discussion Paper*, London: Cabinet Office, cited in Marks and Shah (2004), p. 6.
56. C. Maller, M. Townsend, L. St Leger, C. Henderson-Wilson, A. Pryor, L. Prosser and M. Moore (2002), *Healthy Parks, Healthy People*, Melbourne: Deakin University and Parks Victoria, cited in Marks and Shah (2004), p. 7.
57. Dolan et al. (2006), p. 61.
58. Sen (1984).
59. J. Helliwell and S. Wang (2012), 'The state of world happiness', in J. Helliwell, R. Layard and J. Sachs (eds), *World Happiness Report*, New York: Earth Institute, CIFAR, Centre for Economic Performance.
60. Obviously these figures need to be adjusted to take into account the number of adults and children in the household.
61. For more on this and the UK labour market see Shaheen et al. (2012). The problem described here has been much more long lasting in the US.

62. Ibid.
63. C. Seaford (2010), *One Million Homes*, London: nef.
64. Based on current nef analysis, unpublished.
65. Not simple, of course: UK regional and industrial policy has had a patchy record, and there has been a consistent failure to match supply and demand of skills. The new economics foundation is currently researching this topic.
66. Research presented by L. Kenworthy at Resolution Foundation seminar, London, 21 November 2011.
67. However, there is unlikely to be much impact on the UK's international competitiveness: retail is an untraded sector with a very small part in the supply chains of traded sectors; hospitality does cater for overseas visitors, and the impact of higher wages on overseas demand could be modelled. In general, though, the UK does not and cannot compete on price in international markets; the best-paid jobs tend to be in internationally traded sectors (see Shaheen et al. 2012).
68. For an official paper on the kind of cost benefit analysis tools that might support this, see D. Fujiwara and R. Campbell (2011), *Valuation Techniques for Social Cost–Benefit Analysis: Stated Preference, Revealed Preference and Subjective Well-being Approaches – A Discussion of the Current Issues*, London: HM Treasury, available at: http://www.hm-treasury.gov.uk/d/green_book_valuationtechniques_250711.pdf.

9. Well-being in organizations

Jill Flint-Taylor and Cary L. Cooper

For those in employment, the number of hours spent at work averages out at nearly 20 per cent of the total number of hours in the year (OECD 2013). The workplace is clearly one of the most important contexts to consider in any review of well-being research and practice. It is also a context in which many of the influences on individuals' well-being are in the hands of the organization they work for – with far-reaching implications for the broader lives of employees as well as their family and friends. So it is encouraging to see signs of recent progress in the way organizations approach the well-being of their employees.

In this chapter, we explore these developments and the benefits of spreading them more widely, as well as the issues that remain to be addressed. We outline a research-based model to help guide the assessment and active management of well-being in organizations, and set this in the context of the need for a more holistic approach to well-being. As discussed elsewhere in the book, for example by John Helliwell (Chapter 5) and Timo Hämäläinen (Chapter 2), an integrated, coherent life experience is very much the ideal rather than the reality for most working people. For example, Helliwell and Huang (2010) found significant differences and tensions between measures of life satisfaction and job satisfaction within the same respondent group. Specifically, they found that factors such as responsibility for decision making at work may have a positive effect on job satisfaction but a negative effect on life satisfaction. The study of how conditions in the workplace affect well-being is central to resolving such tensions.

In the workplace there are many different factors that influence well-being, ranging from specific health and safety risks to the strategic business decisions made by the leadership team. Well-being considerations are self-evident in the former, but often overlooked in the latter. Putting well-being at the heart of plans and decisions would have huge benefits for society as a whole, so our focus in this chapter is on equipping and encouraging organizations to do their best in this regard. We adopt this focus precisely because we view a person's work as a central element of what should ideally be an integrated and coherent life experience, because we recognize the power of employing organizations to influence well-being outcomes for all, and because the well-being of employees has not traditionally had a prominent place in organizational priorities.

Several interconnected trends are responsible for the current movement of well-being up the corporate agenda. These include the strengthening of the business case for investing in the well-being of employees (PricewaterhouseCoopers/DWP 2008), a growing interest in improving employee engagement,[1] and a recognition of the close relationships between mental health, employee engagement and the performance of individuals and organizations (Macleod and Brady 2008; Macleod and Clarke 2009). Underpinning all this, there are signs of improved integration between research and practice in this field, although there are still many barriers to overcome in this regard. It is essential for well-being policy to pay specific attention to nurturing the progress that organizations have made, as well as pushing the boundaries of what can and must be achieved by challenging outdated assumptions and presenting alternatives for the sustainable success and well-being of individuals, organizations and society as a whole.

CHANGING TIMES: IMPLICATIONS FOR WORK AND WELL-BEING

As we have heard said by many politicians in many countries, we are now living in turbulent times (Weinberg and Cooper 2012). Following the crisis in the global banking sector, the implications for ordinary businesses and individuals have been beyond enormous. For most working people, there have been major consequences for their health and general well-being and for those of their family. Most working people in the developed and developing world have experienced increased job insecurity, longer working hours, more bottom-line management styles, more presenteeism[2] and a poorer work–life balance. As people feel more insecure, they work longer to show their employers that they are committed, in an effort to prevent their names appearing on the next tranche of redundancy announcements. This has direct consequences for the families of these workers, who are spending less time with their partners or spouses and their children, which creates the vicious circle that problems at home begin to interfere with effective performance at work. The evidence is clear – consistently working long hours damages people's health, their performance and their family relationships (Burke and Cooper 2008).

Another generic issue is debt – as the economies in many countries slip further into low or negative growth, the level of personal and household debt tends to rise. Research shows that there is a strong link between debt and depression (Cooper et al. 2009). Depression is now the leading cause of morbidity in the world. Between one in four and one in six people in the world (including both developed and developing countries) have suffered from depression in the past, are currently suffering from it or will suffer it in the future. As Charles Seaford observes (this volume, Chapter 8), economic activity is important to well-being, but the link is not a simple one. So we need to understand more about how these relationships work. Stefano Bartolini's discussion of well-being, money and human relationships (this volume, Chapter 6) is of particular relevance here.

What happens to people in the workplace contributes in certain very specific ways to the extent and prevalence of these common mental health problems. Clearly there is a direct if complex relationship between employment, or lack of it, and levels of debt and depression. Even those who manage to stay in regular employment are likely to experience the uncertainties and effects of cost-cutting and restructuring programmes. Other important influences include how employees are managed, how they are dealt with when they experience ill health and other personal or family problems, how many hours they work, how intense these hours are, and so on. All these factors have been thoroughly researched and operationalized in the form of a workplace well-being model described below.

There are also demographic issues to be incorporated into the picture. People are living longer, and this has a number of implications in the context of working lives – given the economic imperatives, many will have to work longer before retiring. Then there is also the question of increased elder care responsibility for those who are already burdened by the pressures of the workplace. Another important demographic pressure is that more women are working than ever before, which creates additional problems for two-earner families and, indeed, for single working parents.

These changing societal demographics are overlaid on to a more intense and pressured working environment. Unsurprisingly, managers are not immune and are likely to be suffering as much as their subordinates. Yet there are many managers who, when under stress, behave in maladaptive ways that further damage the people around them. This source of workplace stress is an added burden on ordinary working people, which has been highlighted by many researchers over the years (Langan-Fox and Cooper 2011).

So we can see how negative pressures are building up in today's world, and how pressures such as the pace of change and the unsustainable drive for ever-increasing consumption create complex and interwoven effects across all aspects of our lives. Nevertheless, it would be mistaken to assume that well-being policy should focus simply on reducing pressure. Pressure can be positive (e.g. realistic, motivating goals) as well as negative (e.g. stressful work overload), and a lack of pressure can be as damaging to both well-being and performance as too much pressure (Podsakoff et al. 2007).

There are many opportunities for exploiting new developments and challenges to enhance well-being in today's workplace and in society as a whole, but so far much of this is potential rather than actuality. The online blogging and publishing community provides vivid illustrations of how open-mindedness and innovative thinking can help people and business to thrive by taking advantage of social change and new technology. For example, in a *Fast Company* feature titled 'This is Generation Flux', Robert Safian (2012) gives detailed illustrations of important social, economic and technological contributions being made by people who thrive on complexity and rapid change. A different angle is provided by an article in the *Economist*'s online *Technology Quarterly*, which describes the 'maker' movement – a trend for individuals and small groups to create and share a range of innovative products using affordable technology (*Economist* 2011). It will be important for more rigorous academic research and well-being policy to follow suit, or we risk relying too heavily on the sporadic success of creative individuals and small groups.

THE ASSESSMENT OF WELL-BEING IN ORGANIZATIONS

The Importance of Psychological Well-being

The above discussion shows how important it is to give particular attention to those aspects of well-being that relate to our mental health, and that this is not just a matter of removing stressors from the environment but also of realizing potential opportunities for growth and flourishing (Keyes 2002). To reflect the importance of positive as well as negative experiences for mental well-being, we use the term 'psychological well-being'. Psychological well-being is interdependent with, but distinct from, social well-being and physical well-being (see Robertson and Cooper 2011 for a detailed discussion).

The concept is not a new one – psychological well-being can be defined as a combination of eudaimonic and hedonic elements (Ryff and Keyes 1995). Eudaimonic well-being is represented by terms such as 'self-acceptance', 'environmental mastery', 'positive relationships', 'personal growth', 'purpose in life' and 'autonomy'. Hedonic well-being is represented by terms such as 'happiness', 'subjective well-being' and 'positive emotions'.

Psychological well-being has always been at the centre of workplace risk assessments of stress levels among employees in organizations. Until recently it has not, however, played a large part in the various programmes that organizations put in place to support employees and reduce sickness-related costs. Often going under the title of 'wellness', these initiatives have typically included health promotions (e.g. smoking cessation and healthy eating campaigns) and a range of facilities to support and encourage physical exercise. Now, however, we are seeing a more holistic approach emerging, as a result of a growing body of evidence demonstrating the strong relationships between psychological well-being and organizational performance (see the section 'Strengthening of the business case' below for a discussion of the 'business case' for well-being).

The rest of this chapter addresses the questions of how to measure well-being in the organizational context (with particular but not exclusive emphasis on psychological well-being), the actions organizations should take to play their part in creating the right conditions for individuals and the organization to thrive, and why this is important for organizational performance as well as employee well-being. We refer to well-being in this context as 'employee well-being', to emphasize organizations' responsibilities for actively managing the impact of workplace pressures on the well-being of their employees. This term is not intended to imply that an individual's well-being is one thing at work and another at home.

Sources of Workplace Pressure and Support

We have already noted that pressure can be positive as well as negative, with the implication that getting the balance right is essential for well-being. Support, such as collaborative relationships with team members, is clearly instrumental in helping to achieve this balance. One of the first things that organizations need to do, therefore, is to measure current sources of pressure and support, alongside measures of psychological well-being and physical health. The findings can then be explored in more depth through discussion and consultation, with the aim of designing and implementing interventions to address well-being risks and build on existing positive practices.

To ensure that organizations' well-being assessments and interventions are robust, coherent and informed by research findings and best practice experience, it is essential to apply a tried-and-tested model of the sources of workplace pressure and support. This is something that most annual employee surveys do not attempt to do – their purpose is much broader than the assessment of well-being, and their design rationale is to reflect current organizational issues and priorities in as concise a survey measure as possible. When it comes to interventions, in the field of well-being these are typically fragmented across a range of specialist departments and institutional stakeholders, such as occupational health, health and safety, and training – with each using its own specific professional models and techniques.

Auditing Employee Well-being

Fortunately, research and practice in stress auditing (assessing the risks of stress across an organization) have provided a coherent picture of the main sources of workplace pressure (HSE 2001; Faragher et al. 2004; Schaufeli et al. 2006). The resulting frameworks have been widely applied in stress auditing over the past two decades. It is true that private sector organizations have generally been much less likely than their public sector counterparts to engage in this form of assessment. Nevertheless, there is now a large body of data and research findings to support the evaluation of existing models of sources of workplace pressure, and to facilitate the updating of these models to include positive psychology measures as discussed above.

The UK Health and Safety Executive (HSE) Stress Management Standards are one such framework (Yarker et al. 2008). Another, which has been updated recently to incorporate measures of positive psychology and engagement, is the ASSET model (Johnson 2010). The ASSET model summarizes the sources of workplace pressure and support into six main categories: resources and communication; control;[3] balanced workload; job security and change; work relationships; and job conditions (aspects of the job directly related to physical conditions and job satisfaction) (Figure 9.1).

Currently even those audits that incorporate indicators of engagement and positive psychological well-being still typically approach the sources of pressure in the format of a stress risk assessment. It is likely, however, that in future this approach will be adapted to accommodate the recognition that the sources of workplace pressure can be (a) sources of positive pressure, (b) sources of negative pressure and (c) sources of support. So, for example, work relationships may create positive pressure if one feels motivated to do one's best for a supportive and collaborative team of colleagues. Conversely, poor relationships with team colleagues may create negative pressure by making it difficult to rely on their input to the achievement of your objectives. When it comes to work relationships as a source of support, an example would be willingness among colleagues to fill in for each other during times of absence or high workload.

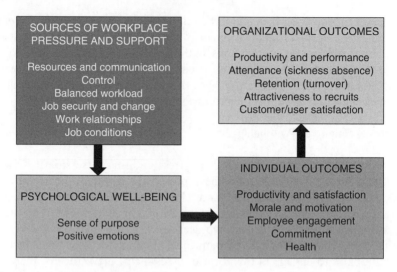

Figure 9.1   The ASSET model of employee well-being

The detailed design of a well-being audit and the practicalities of implementation are illustrated and discussed in a number of case study chapters in Robertson and Cooper's book on well-being in organizations (Robertson and Cooper 2011). The main points to emphasize here are the importance of involving stakeholders in the set-up phase, communicating the purpose of the exercise to all involved, and sharing the findings in an appropriate way once these are available.

THE ACTIVE MANAGEMENT OF WELL-BEING IN ORGANIZATIONS

Strengthening of the Business Case

Over the past decade or so, evidence has been steadily mounting for the business benefits of improving employee well-being. For example, Cropanzano and Wright found a strong correlation between psychological well-being and work performance in their five-year longitudinal study (Cropanzano and Wright 1999). In the UK's National Health Service (NHS), an independent study by Steve Boorman found that health and well-being indicators were positively related to lower MRSA ('superbug') infection rates, increased patient satisfaction and lower levels of spending on agency staff (owing to better retention and lower levels of sickness absence among permanent staff) (Boorman 2009).

In common with the research by Cropanzano and Wright, many of the studies that assess desirable business outcomes have focused on psychological well-being as a predictor variable. Other examples are an influential study of nearly 8000 separate business units in 36 companies, which found employee engagement and psychological well-being to be positively correlated with a range of desirable outcomes including customer satisfaction, productivity, reduced sickness absence and reduced turnover (Harter et al. 2003).

The relationship between employee well-being and customer satisfaction has been replicated by several studies and is particularly well established (Bernhardt et al. 2000). The relationship between well-being and productivity has been studied at the business unit level, as in the studies by Harter et al. (2002), and at the individual employee level, as in a study by Donald et al. (2005).

The latter study found that 23 per cent of variance in (self-reported) employee productivity was explained by scales measuring psychological well-being, perceived commitment of the organization to the employee, and concerns about resources and communication (in a sample of 16 000 UK employees). Specifically, three factors, when combined, showed a positive relationship with higher employee productivity ($R = 0.48$, $R^2 = 0.23$, $p < 0.001$). The three factors and their relationship to productivity are:

1. better psychological well-being (lower score on risks to mental health (standardized $\beta = -0.33$);
2. greater perceived commitment from the organization (standardized $\beta = 0.17$);
3. greater access to resources and information (lower score on concerns about these issues, standardized $\beta = -.10$; sample item measuring concerns, 'I am troubled that I do not feel I am informed about what is going on in this organization').

Another angle on the business case comes from research by the Sainsbury Centre for Mental Health (2007), which found evidence to suggest that presenteeism due to employee mental ill health accounts for approximately 1.5 as many working days lost as absenteeism (see Table 9.1). The Sainsbury Centre (2007) paper explains the ways in which information was drawn together from a range of different sources to estimate the levels and costs of presenteeism in the UK. Central to the approach is work that has been done estimating typical ratios of presenteeism to levels of sickness absence. The level of presenteeism due to mental ill health in the UK was estimated by drawing on international evidence,

Well-being and beyond

*Table 9.1   Estimated annual number of working days lost through
            presenteeism attributable to mental ill health in an organization
            with 1000 employees (United Kingdom)*

Workforce size	1000
Estimated annual number of sick days attributable to mental ill health	3240
Estimated ratio of presenteeism to absenteeism	1.5
Annual working days lost through presenteeism	4860

Table 9.2   The prevalence of presenteeism

	Health 'good'	Health 'not good'
No absences	35% (healthy and present)	28% (presentees)
Some absences	13% (healthy but not always present)	24% (unhealthy and not always present)

Source: Robertson and Cooper (2011, p. 19).

including studies from the US, Canada and Australia. Some of the estimates are summarized in Table 9.1.

The severity of this issue becomes clear when we see how prevalent the problem of presenteeism is. Table 9.2 shows the picture for a sample of nearly 40 000 employees in the UK, who responded to a detailed, standardized survey that included specific questions about health (mental and physical) and about number of days' absence from work. As work is known to have positive benefits for well-being (Robertson and Cooper 2011), the goal is not to ensure that all those suffering from any kind of illness are absent from work for the duration. However, the detailed, item-level analysis underlying the 'health not good' figures in Table 9.2 showed a clear picture of a majority who would have benefited from at least some time off work for recuperation.

Although these studies are persuasive, it has often been the case that similarly robust research findings in the field of human resource management have failed to influence those who hold the purse strings within employer organizations. Yet, even in the difficult economic climate of recent years, it appears that organizational practice is keeping up better this time (Robertson and Flint-Taylor 2010). Evidence for this includes willingness to invest in regular, large-scale employee surveys, senior management support for measuring and improving issues related to engagement[4] and well-being, and overall increased spend on well-being provision in the UK (CIPD 2011).

The reasons for this positive trend are undoubtedly complex and varied, but one of the main catalysts is likely to be the close collaboration between academic researchers and the providers of the commercial tools and services that support measurement and intervention in this field, as in the case of the Gallup studies reported by Harter et al. (2003) and studies on the sources of workplace pressure reported by Donald et al. (2005). Such collaboration ensures that academic rigour and expertise are directed towards those problems that practitioners in organizations are most concerned about. It also provides a clear channel for the implementation of useful findings by consultants and their clients in human resources and organizational development.

There is, however, a need to ensure that organizations are encouraged to move beyond broad, high-level surveys and 'quick-fix' interventions, to a more detailed analysis of specific risks (to engagement, well-being and organizational performance), followed by interventions designed to achieve sustainable improvements in employee engagement and well-being over the longer term. A short survey covering a broad range of issues – the typical annual employee survey – is a useful starting point. However, it can be tempting for organizations to focus on scores at the expense of drilling down further into the real issues, and to measure improvement against the results of the next survey without attempting any further validation. In other words, following the results of a short survey, further work should be carried out to drill down into the underlying issues (for example, by convening groups of employees to discuss the survey results and make suggestions regarding possible solutions), to identify actions to be taken to address these issues, and to agree a set of outcome measures against which improvements can be evaluated.

Observation of current practice in organizations suggests that such follow-up is not sufficiently widespread, and that it is common to evaluate improvements almost exclusively through re-surveying. This approach risks creating a false sense of achievement when actual improvements have been slight, or when the survey results or follow-up interventions have been manipulated by leaders and teams whose performance-related financial bonus is directly tied into improving their survey scores.

Clearly, the business benefits of employee well-being and engagement are appreciated more now than ever before, with leaders and managers being held accountable for delivering improvements within their teams and organizations – typically on an annual basis but sometimes even more frequently. This is a positive development, but as well-being rises up the corporate agenda it becomes both more challenging and more essential to exercise common sense, discipline, integrity and critical evaluation to ensure real, sustainable improvements in well-being.

Progress in Paying Attention to Psychological Well-being

We have already mentioned the close connection between employee engagement and well-being, and the role that this currently plays in raising well-being up the corporate agenda. It appears that educating leaders and managers in what it takes to keep employees engaged has opened the door to a dialogue about psychological well-being at work. This is very welcome, given our observation above that employee 'wellness' programmes have tended to emphasize physical health initiatives, with psychological well-being interventions largely confined to stress awareness training and remedial support provided by occupational health employee assistance programmes, rather than a broad emphasis on promoting good psychological well-being.

Even now this is still the dominant approach to well-being (CIPD 2011). Yet the research evidence is clear: outcomes of improved psychological well-being include fewer illnesses, even serious illnesses such as coronary heart disease (Kuper and Marmot 2003), and fewer stress-related absences (Cooper and Quick 1999). There is clearly a long way to go yet in terms of raising the general profile of mental health and well-being at work (Foresight Mental Capital and Well-being Project 2008). Nevertheless, an increasing number of organizations are now building on their interest in employee engagement to explore the additional benefit of measuring specific indicators of psychological well-being. This new trend is driven at least in part by the recognition that even the best employee engagement initiatives cannot deliver sustainable results, over the long term and in a challenging economic environment, without a detailed assessment of psychological well-being to guide the design and delivery of robust interventions (Robertson 2007; Robertson and Cooper 2010).

It appears that human resource practitioners' quest for sustainable solutions has begun to make organizations more receptive to the concept of the detailed well-being audit, an employee survey that goes beyond asking for attitudes and opinions to gather data about respondents' situations and experience, using detailed research-based indicators of stress, positive psychological well-being and associated factors. The benefits of these detailed, organization-wide assessments are well established. For example, based on a comprehensive review of scientific findings, the UK government's Foresight project recommended 'The collection of wellbeing data against Key Performance Indicators and the undertaking and implementation of annual wellbeing audits' (Foresight Mental Capital and Well-being Project 2008, p. 29).

However, even when the benefits of this approach are acknowledged, there are still many practical barriers to overcome before it becomes widely adopted. One problem is that of 'survey fatigue', where the frequent use of surveys makes it difficult to gain employees' commitment and cooperation with a detailed exercise to measure psychological well-being. Another is the interference effect from the design of the annual employee survey – where employees and their managers become used to a certain format of questions and reporting, and find it difficult to adapt to the different style and structure of the in-depth well-being audit. Thirdly, organizations are often nervous about asking what they perceive to be negative questions about potential stressors in the work situation – yet such questions are an essential part of assessing psychological well-being.

Clearly there is a need to continue both research and policy development to persuade organizations of the importance of auditing psychological well-being on a regular basis, and to help the advocates of this approach to overcome the practical barriers to its implementation.

From Risk Management to Resilience and Positive Psychological Well-being

In this regard, recent developments in research and theory have much to offer. In particular, current academic interest in positive psychological well-being provides a robust foundation and impetus for reshaping the organizational stress risk assessment model to include positive as well as negative well-being indicators. In this way, once again, there is a potential alignment between organizational interests and good science – organizations prefer to emphasize the positive where they can, while researchers have established that positive emotions, sense of purpose and other psychological well-being constructs have value in their own right, over and above the avoidance of stress (Fredrickson and Joiner 2002).

Developments in the field of positive psychology have been discussed elsewhere in this volume, so in this chapter we will touch on some of the specific implications for well-being in organizations. Apart from stimulating a shift from stress auditing to a more comprehensive assessment of psychological well-being, positive psychology has much to offer in the design of effective interventions for improving employee morale and organizational performance.

In particular, Barbara Fredrickson's 'broaden-and-build' conceptualization of positive emotions (Fredrickson 1998, 2001) has wide-ranging implications for practitioners seeking to raise levels of morale, confidence and creativity among individual employees, as well as for leaders and managers striving to maintain positive challenge pressure on their teams and promote innovation while avoiding burnout stress. The core message for organizations is that simply minimizing stress is not sufficient to ensure well-being or performance.

The work of Seligman, Csikszentmihalyi and colleagues has also been influential in shifting the focus from stress management to the promotion of positive psychological well-being (Seligman and Csikszentmihalyi 2000; Seligman et al. 2005). As long ago as the early 1990s, Seligman and colleagues were at the forefront of adapting therapeutic techniques from clinical psychology for use in workplace training programmes in the US and the UK (Seligman 1990; Proudfoot et al. 2009). The aim was to improve participants' ability to succeed and thrive in the face of tough challenges, such as selling insurance or getting a new job after having been unemployed for six months or more.

In spite of robust findings demonstrating the benefits of this training approach for individuals and organizations, longer-term take-up was poor, even among the sponsoring organizations that had benefited financially and in other ways from their participation in the research programme. The programmes were branded as 'resilience training' – designed to help individuals cope better with work-related pressures. Resilience was typically defined in this context as the ability for an individual to bounce back from setbacks, and to keep going in the face of tough demands and difficult circumstances. Although the training approach was seen as different to a compliance-driven approach to managing workplace stress, it appears that most corporate cultures were not ready to embrace anything so closely associated with psychological therapy and the problems of anxiety and depression – however impressive the financial benefits were.

In the past few years the situation has taken a more positive turn, with organizations becoming more open to this kind of intervention. There are various possible explanations for this. One is likely to be the widespread recognition that we live in times of ongoing change, uncertainty and resource constraints – and that this situation is likely to endure. Another factor is the influence of positive psychology, as mentioned above. Even resilience is now seen as being about more than recovery from stressful or potentially stressful events – it is also about the sustainability of that recovery and the lasting benefit of coping well with the situation (Reich et al. 2010).

These are promising developments. However, organizations have a natural bias towards short, inexpensive interventions that emphasize the positive. This can all too easily result in going for 'quick-fix' training interventions that draw a few simple messages from positive psychology at the expense of more holistic, in-depth approaches. So, for example, there is a risk of focusing on 'strengths-based' approaches derived rather simplistically from Seligman's more recent work on character strengths and virtues, at the expense of applying the more challenging but possibly more powerful techniques and insights from his work on resilience development.

Seligman himself has adhered to a comprehensive approach, incorporating both the earlier work on resilience and more recent insights from positive psychology into the US Army Master Resilience Trainer (MRT) course (Reivich et al. 2011). This course is a ten-day programme that teaches resilience skills to non-commissioned officers (NCOs), who are also equipped to roll the resilience training out to the soldiers under their command. The course includes modules on resilience, building mental toughness, identifying character strengths and strengthening relationships. Although the military work context is different in many ways to the typical context in a corporation or non-military public sector organization, the model incorporates some of the best proven concepts and techniques for developing resilience and should, therefore, be of interest to organizations in all sectors. It is worth noting, however, that the Army Master Resilience programme is not without controversy. At the very least, as Mihaly Csikszentmihalyi observes (this volume, Chapter 10), 'extreme caution is in order' in such circumstances where psychologists and the military work in a close alliance.

More broadly, the work of Dennis Charney (Charney and Nemeroff 2004) pulls together a number of research findings and practical techniques in the form of a prescription for resilience. Based on the study of the attributes and coping strategies of individuals confronting dangerous and challenging situations, Charney's work provides a good foundation for the design of resilience training programmes and other personal development interventions.

In all this, it is important to recognize the need for individuals to take responsibility for their own well-being, in relation to developing resilience, managing the risk of stress and making the most of character strengths and opportunities to flourish. It is, however, the organization that holds the balance of power when it comes to managing the sources of positive, motivating challenge (challenge pressure) and negative causes of stress (hindrance pressure) in the work environment. In the next subsection, we outline a research-based framework to help guide organizations in this important but difficult endeavour.

Candidate Selection and Talent Management – The Well-being Angle

As well-being rises up the organizational agenda, questions are being asked about how best to promote individual and organizational health by adapting the way we assess candidates for recruitment and promotion. For some time, specific well-being criteria such as resilience have been incorporated into assessments for particularly challenging roles. More broadly, most well-designed competency frameworks include one or more well-being criterion statements, usually related to the ability to sustain effort and quality of output under pressure. Beyond this, well-being tends to be implicit or a by-product of performance-related criteria – for example, in the work on person–job and person–organization fit.

A detailed review of relevant research and an attempt to answer the question of what organizations should be doing to promote well-being through selection and assessment is provided by Flint-Taylor and Robertson (2013). Their discussion addresses three broad issues:

- how to ensure that an individual is in the best possible shape for current and future roles;
- how to ensure that employees have a positive impact on general organizational well-being;
- how to ensure that managers and leaders in particular have a positive impact on the well-being and performance of the individuals and teams who report to them.

The authors conclude that, although there is a large body of research and practice to draw on, this is not an area where academics and practitioners work closely together and there is much that still needs to be done to make the best use of the available findings and to investigate the issue of well-being from the angle of selection and assessment. One of the most promising recent strands of research in this area is the study of employee proactivity in organizations (Thomas et al. 2010).

Future research and practice should also pay sufficient attention to the question of values and person–organization fit, from an employee well-being perspective. This is consistent with the call by Timo Hämäläinen (this volume, Chapter 2) to move beyond emphasis on capability towards a holistic approach that includes both objective and subjective measures and facilitates more coherent and sustainable decisions for individuals, organizations and society as a whole.

When it comes to managing the pipeline of talented employees in an organization, there is a complex interaction between the issues of equality (ensuring equal opportunity) and diversity (celebrating differences and valuing everyone) on the one hand, and the issue of well-being on the other. Bullying, harassment and discrimination policies are now well established in most large organizations, and in most developed countries the law offers good protection for those at risk of such behaviour, although it can often be hard for individuals to get the full benefit of these safeguards.

Even when these policies are working well, there are other considerations linking equality, diversity and well-being. For example, responsibilities outside the workplace make it difficult for many people to progress in an organizational environment where long hours are the norm. This problem affects more women than men, and well-intentioned attempts to address it by promoting work–life balance can backfire in terms of the progression of women (Caproni 2004). Such problems in turn affect the overall performance and well-being of the organization, according to research demonstrating the benefits of gender diversity on corporate boards (e.g. Terjesen et al. 2009).

Well-being Interventions

Post-audit interventions

Well-being interventions in organizations may be classified as primary, secondary or tertiary (Quick and Tetrick 2003):

- *Primary interventions* seek to manage stress risks and improve well-being by addressing the underlying causes of current barriers to well-being – they are termed 'primary' because they tackle the 'root cause' of the problem in the form of systems, processes or other organization-level factors. Increasingly, as the benefits of positive emotions are given greater attention, there is interest in how to increase opportunities for flourishing, even where there are no major barriers or problems. Primary interventions are often broad, organizational development initiatives, but they may also be more specific, involving for example the redesign of a particular job or the resolution of a technology problem.
- *Secondary interventions*, such as stress awareness courses or resilience training, focus on helping employees to cope with pressure and to take responsibility for managing their own well-being. They are termed 'secondary' because they are seen as the second line of defence – they help individual employees to manage the risks that organizational systems, processes and so on pose for their well-being, but they do not seek to remove the problem from the workplace environment.
- *Tertiary interventions* include employee assistance programmes and other counselling provision, and are targeted at employees whose health has already been negatively affected by the problem. They are termed 'tertiary' because they are regarded as the last (third) line of defence – it is important to have them in place, but they should not be relied on at the expense of taking action to prevent damage to employees' well-being (through primary and secondary interventions).

All three levels of intervention have an important part to play in the enhancement of well-being in organizations. It is, however, particularly important to ensure that sufficient investment is made in primary interventions, as these are likely to prove most effective in the long term, although they are also likely to be the most demanding in terms of effort, stakeholder buy-in and resource.

Leadership and management

Leaders and managers have a particular responsibility when it comes to managing the sources of pressure in the workplace. It is in this context that employee well-being emerges most clearly from the specialist preserve of occupational health and other professions and into the mainstream of organizational life.

The impact of leaders and managers – positive and negative – on employee well-being is now well documented (Barling and Carson 2008; Robertson and Flint-Taylor 2009). Data from exit interviews reveal that dissatisfaction with their manager is one of the most frequently cited reasons for people leaving their employer, while meta-analyses have shown that the quality of relationship between employee and manager predicts turnover (Griffeth et al. 2000).

Recent studies of leadership style and workgroup well-being have provided more information on the ways in which leaders influence productivity, well-being and performance (Flint-Taylor and Robertson 2007). Development programmes based on the findings from this research have shown how leaders can be supported to improve their active management of the sources of workplace pressure and support (Flint-Taylor et al. 2011). Central to this approach is the recognition that leaders can be 'lopsided' in the way they provide challenge and support for those who report to them, and the related finding that leader personality traits or other attributes 'taken to extreme' can result in a negative impact on employees even though in moderation the same attribute acts as a leadership strength (Flint-Taylor 2008).

This effect has been discussed by some authors in terms of the 'dark side' of personality (Burke 2006), or in terms of 'derailers' – negative characteristics that lurk in the background threatening to undermine an otherwise promising leadership career and can eventually throw it off track altogether. Our own research, and that of authors such as Kaplan and Kaiser (2006), suggests a much finer line between leadership strengths such as assertiveness and leadership 'risks' such as aggressiveness. One of the implications of this perspective is that all leaders need to develop skill in the active management of the risks inherent in their leadership strengths, especially when it comes to optimizing their personal impact on levels of positive (challenge) pressure and negative (hindrance) pressure in their teams' work environment.

Some of the latest research in this area makes use of the ASSET six sources of workplace pressure and support framework to investigate how leaders exert their influence on the workplace factors that drive employee well-being (Robertson et al. 2011). This research is ongoing, with early findings suggesting that leader personality influences workgroup well-being significantly but indirectly. The impact on well-being seems to take place through the way the leader's personality predisposes him or her to manage situational factors such as workload or relationships. The implication is that leaders can learn to improve their impact through more skilful management of these situational factors.

This finding has important and encouraging implications for the design of leadership development interventions, suggesting that there is a real-istic opportunity to improve leaders' impact on well-being by educating them in how to manage the six sources of workplace pressure and support more effectively – even though their personality can be expected to remain stable over time. Leaders need to understand the potential impact of their personality, but their development efforts should be on learning how to flex their style and behaviour to make the most of their natural character strengths and to manage the risks that these bring with them.

Personal resilience development
Earlier in this chapter we referred to workplace training programmes for improving personal resilience. In practical terms these involve a range of exercises to help participants acquire or strengthen some of the main strat-egies used by people who cope well with difficult and stressful situations. For example, participants are shown how to pick up negative biases in their thought patterns, and how to challenge these incorrect assumptions so that they come to view events and challenges from a more realistic and helpful perspective (a technique known as 'reframing'). Other exercises include techniques for identifying and observing a resilient role model, reflecting on what really matters to you, working out how to overcome your own personal barriers to exercise, and addressing the need to maintain a strong social support network even when you are under pressure at work.

An additional angle to the development of personal resilience emerges once we apply the sources of workplace pressure and support framework. This involves helping individual employees to understand how they are likely to react to changes in each of the six sources of pressure, and using these insights to anticipate and manage both the sources of pressure and support (to the extent that these are within their control) and their own reactions. So, for example, depending on our personality, some of us may be more susceptible to problems with our work relationships but resilient in the face of high workloads, while others may quickly become stressed by poor communication with their managers, and so on.

As with leadership development, this approach offers benefits for personal resilience development by introducing the framework of sources of workplace pressure to the design of the training. This approach is described in detail in Cooper et al. (2013).

Well-being interventions in practice – case studies
A number of successful case studies are documented in Robertson and Cooper (2011). These studies include:

- *in the UK*: a programme of assessment (an ASSET stress and well-being audit) and interventions to improve well-being at London Fire Brigade, resulting in a reduction in sickness absence rates due to stress anxiety/depression (SAD) from 20 per cent of all absence to 11 per cent of all absence – calculated as a direct saving to the organization of over £1.8 million (Finn and Tinline 2011);
- *in the USA (and globally)*: a global initiative to build an organizational culture of health in the largest health care company in the world (Johnson & Johnson), contributing to a healthier-than-average workforce and a reduction in health risk measures, as shown in Table 9.3 (Isaac and Ratzen 2011, p. 136);
- *in Germany*: development of a comprehensive corporate health management system for well-being (Kuhn and Pelster 2011), which achieved success on a number of indicators, including sick-leave rates below the industry average;
- *in the Netherlands*: use of internet-delivered interventions in worksite health promotion, the evaluation of which concluded that 'the responsiveness to user needs, in terms of both the content of the intervention and its functionality, makes the Internet highly appropriate to deliver worksite health promotion interventions' (Crutzen 2011, p. 182).

Table 9.3   Health risk indicator improvement at Johnson & Johnson over time

	1995–99	2002	2007	2009
Tobacco use	12%	8.5%	4.0%	3.9%
High blood pressure	14%	12.2%	6.6%	6.3%
High cholesterol	19%	10.4%	7.0%	5.3%
Inactivity	39%	40.5%	33.5%	20.4%

NATIONAL GUIDANCE AND POLICY INITIATIVES

Well-being at work has been the subject of a number of reviews, reports and policy guidance initiatives in the UK. In addition to the Foresight review (Foresight Mental Capital and Well-being Project 2008) mentioned above and the HSE (2001, 2009) guidance on stress management, important examples include Dame Carol Black's (2008) review and recommendations and the National Institute for Health and Clinical Excellence (NICE) (2009) guidance on promoting well-being at work.

CONCLUSION

Working in organizations has a profound effect on people's well-being, and this effect extends well beyond the boundaries of the work context. The conditions people experience at work have an impact on their overall physical health and psychological well-being, and this impact extends to families, friends and society as a whole.

While it is important for people to take responsibility for managing their own well-being, employing organizations have a central role to play in creating the right conditions in the workplace. In the assessment and improving of well-being in the workplace, psychological well-being has been shown to be particularly important for organizational performance as well as for individual health and happiness.

The best place for an organization to start is with a robust, research-based framework to guide the measurement of employee well-being and the workplace factors that affect it, such as work relationships, physical working conditions, workload, availability of resources and clear communication. These factors need to be assessed in depth – a short survey can be a positive first step, but even a more detailed survey needs to be followed up by consultation and further investigation in order to identify the best course of action for improving levels of well-being among employees. The subsequent interventions should be evaluated on the basis of previously agreed outcome measures, taking care not to place too much reliance on improvements in survey scores without substantiating evidence.

Whereas in the past much of the work in this area focused on stress management, a broader approach is now gaining ground. This approach draws in recent insights from the field of positive psychology, and makes use of an expanding range of developmental interventions at both organizational and individual levels. It is particularly important to understand and manage the impact that leaders and managers have on the well-being of teams and on the organization as a whole.

There are now a number of policy guidelines recommending best-practice approaches for organizations to follow. These guidelines provide a wealth of practical advice, and increasingly they also address what we have called the 'business case' for acting to improve employee well-being. However, the experience of people working in the field suggests that, in spite of recent progress and the strong evidence for financial and other benefits, organizational practice is rather patchy and there is a worrying tendency to go for the 'quick-fix' approach at the expense of effective, enduring improvements in well-being.

This suggests to us that a priority for well-being policy is the question of how best to influence the leaders and stakeholders of organizations, large and small. Building on the business case is important but not sufficient in itself, at least in the narrow sense of proving financial and performance outcomes. An important consideration is the pressure that various stakeholder groups can bring to bear. Institutional investors such as the large banking corporations can be a negative force for well-being in organizations, for example by pushing short-term solutions driven by narrow interests. They can, however, also be a positive force, as we are seeing in the pressure some asset management institutions are applying for companies to increase the representation of women on their corporate boards. There are many other categories of stakeholder groups, some with a stake in promoting social change as a whole rather than focusing specifically on organizations.

All these groups should be taken into account in developing well-being policy. We already know a lot about what organizations should do. The priority now is to equip and mobilize those groups who can persuade organizations to put well-being at the centre of their strategic plans and operational processes.

Finally, both within and beyond the context of formal organizational structures, we believe it is important for well-being policy to encourage the exploitation of opportunities presented by the current pace of change, as well as the management of risks. For example, new technologies are opening up the possibility of radically different ways of working, some of which (*Economist* 2011) promote well-being by allowing individuals much greater freedom and autonomy within healthy, collaborative work relationships. Such opportunities should be sought out, supported and actively promoted rather than being left to blossom or fail through chance.

NOTES

1. See Robertson and Cooper (2011, pp. 27–31) for a detailed discussion of the many different definitions of employee engagement. Here we use the term to mean 'the individual's

involvement and satisfaction with as well as enthusiasm for work' (Harter et al. 2002), together with 'a positive attitude held by the employee toward the organization and its values' (Robinson et al. 2004).
2. Presenteeism 'is defined in terms of lost productivity that occurs when employees come to work ill and perform below par because of that illness' (Cooper and Dewe 2008).
3. Employees' sense of feeling in control of events, as when their suggestions about the work are listened to.
4. See Robertson and Cooper (2011, p. 31) for definitions and more on different approaches to engagement.

REFERENCES

Barling, J. and J. Carson (2008), *The Impact of Management Style on Mental Well-being at Work: State-of-science Review: SR-C3*, Foresight Mental Capital and Well-being Project, London: Government Office for Science.

Bernhardt, K.L., N. Donthu and P.A. Kennett (2000), 'A longitudinal analysis of satisfaction and profitability', *Journal of Business Research*, **47** (2), 161–71.

Black, C. (2008), *Working for a Healthier Tomorrow*, London: Stationery Office.

Boorman, S. (2009), *NHS Health and Wellbeing*, Boorman Review, London: Department of Health.

Burke, R.J. (2006), 'Why leaders fail: exploring the dark side', in R.J. Burke and C.L. Cooper (eds), *Inspiring Leaders*, Oxford: Routledge, pp. 237–46.

Burke, R.J. and C.L. Cooper (2008), *The Long Work Hours Culture: Causes, Consequences, and Choices*, Bingley, UK: Emerald Publishers.

Caproni, P.J. (2004), 'You can't get there from here', *Journal of Applied Behavioral Science*, **40** (2), 208–18.

Charney, D.S. and C.B. Nemeroff (2004), *The Peace of Mind Prescription*, Boston, MA: Houghton Mifflin Harcourt.

CIPD (2011), *A Barometer of HR Trends and Prospects 2011*, London: CIPD.

Cooper, C.L. and P. Dewe (2008), 'Well-being – absenteeism, presenteeism, costs and challenges', *Occupational Medicine*, **58** (8), 522–4.

Cooper, C.L. and J. Quick (1999), *Stress and Strain*, Oxford: Health Press.

Cooper, C.L., J. Field, U. Goswami, R. Jenkins and B. Sahakian (2009), *Mental Capital and Wellbeing*, Oxford: Wiley-Blackwell.

Cooper, C.L., J. Flint-Taylor and M. Pearn (2013), *Building Resilience for Success: A Resource for Managers and Organizations*, Basingstoke: Palgrave Macmillan.

Cropanzano, R. and T.A. Wright (1999), 'A five-year study of the relationship between well-being and performance', *Journal of Consulting Psychology*, **51**, 252–65.

Crutzen, R. (2011), 'On the use of Internet-delivered interventions in worksite health promotion', in I.T. Robertson and C.L. Cooper (eds), *Well-being: Productivity and Happiness at Work*, Basingstoke: Palgrave Macmillan.

Donald, I., P. Taylor, S. Johnson, C.L. Cooper, S. Cartwright and S. Robertson (2005), 'Work environments, stress and productivity: an examination using ASSET', *International Journal of Stress Management*, **12** (4), 409–23.

Economist (2011), 'More than just digital quilting', *Economist, Technology Quarterly*, Q4, 3 December, available at: http://www.economist.com/node/21540392.

Faragher, E.B., C.L. Cooper and S. Cartwright (2004), 'A shortened stress evaluation tool (ASSET)', *Stress and Health*, **20**, 189–201.

Finn, M. and G. Tinline (2011), 'Improving well-being at London Fire Brigade', in
I.T. Robertson and C.L. Cooper (eds), *Well-being: Productivity and Happiness
at Work*, Basingstoke: Palgrave Macmillan.

Flint-Taylor, J. (2008), 'Too much of a good thing? Leadership strengths as
risks to well-being and performance in the team', paper presented at the
British Psychological Society Division of Occupational Psychology Annual
Conference, Stratford.

Flint-Taylor, J. and I.T. Robertson (2007), 'Leaders' impact on well-being and
performance: an empirical test of a model', paper presented at the British Psychological Society Division of Occupational Psychology Annual Conference, Bristol.

Flint-Taylor, J. and I.T. Robertson (2013), 'Enhancing well-being in organizations
through selection and development', in R.J. Burke and C.L. Cooper (eds), *The
Fulfilling Workplace*, Farnham: Gower, pp. 165–86.

Flint-Taylor, J., J. Durose and C. Wigley (2011), 'Keeping pressure positive:
improving well-being and performance in the NHS through innovative leadership development', in I.T. Robertson and C.L. Cooper (eds), *Well-being:
Productivity and Happiness at Work*, Basingstoke: Palgrave Macmillan.

Foresight Mental Capital and Well-being Project (2008), *Final Project Report*,
London: Government Office for Science.

Fredrickson, B.L. (1998), 'What good are positive emotions?', *Review of General
Psychology*, **2**, 300–319.

Fredrickson, B.L. (2001), 'The role of positive emotions in positive psychology:
the broaden-and-build theory of positive emotions', *American Psychologist*, **56**
(3), 218–26.

Fredrickson, B.L. and T. Joiner (2002), 'Positive emotions trigger upward spirals
toward emotional well-being', *Psychological Science*, **13**, 172–5.

Griffeth, R.W., P.W. Hom and S. Gaertner (2000), 'A meta-analysis of antecedents and correlates of employee turnover: update, moderator tests, and research
implications for the next millennium', *Journal of Management*, **26** (3), 463–88.

Harter, J.K., F.L. Schmidt and T.L. Hayes (2002), 'Business unit level outcomes
between employee satisfaction, employee engagement and business outcomes: a
meta-analysis', *Journal of Applied Psychology*, **87**, 268–79.

Harter, J.K., F.L. Schmidt and C.L.M. Keyes (2003), 'Well-being in the workplace
and its relationship to business outcomes: a review of the Gallup studies', in
C.L.M. Keyes and J. Haidt (eds), *Flourishing: Positive Psychology and the Life
Well-lived*, Washington, DC: American Psychological Association, pp. 205–24.

Helliwell, J.F. and H. Huang (2010), 'How's the job? Well-being and social capital
in the workplace', *Industrial and Labor Relations Review*, **63**, 205–28.

HSE (2001), *Tackling Work-related Stress: A Managers' Guide to Improving and
Maintaining Employee Health and Well-being*, Sudbury: HSE Books.

HSE (2009), *How to Tackle Work-related Stress: A Guide for Employers on Making
the Management Standards Work*, Sudbury: HSE Books.

Isaac, F. and S. Ratzen (2011), 'Building an organizational culture of health', in
I.T. Robertson and C.L. Cooper (eds), *Well-being: Productivity and Happiness
at Work*, Basingstoke: Palgrave Macmillan.

Johnson, S. (2010), 'Organizational screening: the ASSET model', in S. Cartwright
and C.L. Cooper (eds), *Oxford Handbook on Organizational Well-being*, Oxford:
Oxford University Press.

Kaplan, B. and R. Kaiser (2006), *The Versatile Leader: Make the Most of Your
Strengths – Without Overdoing It*, San Francisco, CA: Pfeiffer.

Keyes, C.L.M. (2002), 'The mental health continuum: from languishing to flourishing in life', *Journal of Health and Social Behavior*, **43**, 207–22.

Kuhn, K. and K. Pelster (2011), 'The development of a comprehensive corporate health management system for well-being', in I.T. Robertson and C.L. Cooper (eds), *Well-being: Productivity and Happiness at Work*, Basingstoke: Palgrave Macmillan.

Kuper, H. and M. Marmot (2003), 'Job strain, job demands, decision latitude, and risk of coronary heart disease within the Whitehall II study', *Journal of Epidemiology and Community Health*, **57**, 147–53.

Langan-Fox, J. and C.L. Cooper (2011), *Handbook of Stress in the Occupations*, Cheltenham, UK and Northampton, MA, USA: Edward Elgar Publishing.

Macleod, D. and C. Brady (2008), *The Extra Mile: How to Engage Your People to Win*, London: Prentice Hall Financial Times.

Macleod, D. and N. Clarke (2009), *Engaging for Success: Enhancing Performance through Employee Engagement*, London: Department for Business, Innovation and Skills.

National Institute for Health and Clinical Excellence (2009), *Promoting Mental Wellbeing through Productive and Healthy Working Conditions: Guidance for Employers*, London: NICE.

OECD (2013), *OECD Factbook 2013: Economic, Environmental and Social Statistics*, Paris: OECD Publishing.

Podsakoff, N.P., J.P. LePine and M.A. LePine (2007), 'Differential challenge stressor–hindrance stressor relationships with job attitudes, turnover intentions, turnover, and withdrawal behavior: a meta-analysis', *Journal of Applied Psychology*, **92**, 438–54.

PricewaterhouseCoopers/DWP (2008), *Building the Case for Wellness*, London: PricewaterhouseCoopers.

Proudfoot, J.G., P.J. Corr, D.E. Guest and G. Dunn (2009), 'Cognitive-behavioural training to change attributional style improves employee well-being, job satisfaction, productivity, and turnover', *Personality and Individual Differences*, **47**, 147–53.

Quick, J.C. and L.E. Tetrick (2003), *Handbook of Occupational Health Psychology*, Washington, DC: American Psychological Association.

Reich, J.W., A.J. Zautra and J.S. Hall (eds) (2010), *Handbook of Adult Resilience*, New York: Guilford Press.

Reivich, K.J., M.E.P. Seligman and S. McBride (2011), 'Master Resilience Training in the U.S. Army', *American Psychologist*, **66** (1), 25–34.

Robertson, I.T. (2007), 'Using business psychology to close the well-being gap', *Selection and Development Review*, **23**, 13–19.

Robertson, I.T. and C.L. Cooper (2010), 'Full engagement: the integration of employee engagement and psychological well-being', *Leadership and Organization Development Journal*, **31** (4), 324–36.

Robertson, I.T. and C.L. Cooper (2011), *Well-being: Productivity and Happiness at Work*, Basingstoke: Palgrave Macmillan.

Robertson, I.T. and J. Flint-Taylor (2009), 'Leadership, psychological well-being and organizational outcomes', in S. Cartwright and C.L. Cooper (eds), *Oxford Handbook of Organizational Well-being*, Oxford: Oxford University Press.

Robertson, I.T. and J. Flint-Taylor (2010), 'Well-being in healthcare organisations: key issues', *British Journal of Healthcare Management*, **16** (1), 18–25.

Robertson, I., J. Flint-Taylor, G. Hodgkinson and M. Healey (2011), 'Leader personality and workgroup well-being', British Academy of Management Conference.

Robinson, D., S. Perryman and S. Hayday (2004), *The Drivers of Employee Engagement*, Brighton: Institute for Employment Studies.

Ryff, C.D. and C.L.M. Keyes (1995), 'The structure of psychological well-being revisited', *Journal of Personality and Social Psychology*, **69**, 719–27.

Safian, R. (2012), 'This is Generation Flux: meet the pioneers of the new (and chaotic) frontier of business', *Fast Company*, 9 January, available at: http://www.fastcompany.com/magazine/162/generation-flux-future-of-business.

Sainsbury Centre for Mental Health (2007), 'Mental health at work: developing the business case', Policy Paper No. 8, London: Sainsbury Centre for Mental Health.

Schaufeli, W.B., A.B. Bakker and M. Salanova (2006), 'The measurement of work engagement with a short questionnaire: a cross-national study', *Educational and Psychological Measurement*, **66**, 701–16.

Seligman, M. (1990), *Learned Optimism: How to Change Your Mind and Your Life*, New York: Knopf.

Seligman, M.E.P. and M. Csikszentmihalyi (2000), 'Positive psychology: an introduction', *American Psychologist*, **55** (1), 5–14.

Seligman, M.E.P., T.A. Steen, N. Park and C. Petersen (2005), 'Positive psychology progress: empirical validation of interventions', *American Psychologist*, **60**, 410–21.

Terjesen, S., R. Sealy and V. Singh (2009), 'Women directors on corporate boards: a review and research agenda', *Corporate Governance: An International Review*, **17** (3), 320–37.

Thomas, J.P., D.S. Whitman and C. Viswesvaran (2010), 'Employee proactivity in organizations: a comparative meta-analysis of emergent proactive constructs', *Journal of Occupational and Organizational Psychology*, **83**, 275–300.

Weinberg, A. and C.L. Cooper (2012), *Stress in Turbulent Times*, Basingstoke: Palgrave Macmillan.

Yarker, J., E. Donaldson-Feilder, R. Lewis and P.E. Flaxman (2008), *Management Competencies for Preventing and Reducing Stress at Work: Identifying and Developing the Management Behaviours Necessary to Implement the HSE Management Standard: Phase 2*, London: HSE Books.

PART IV

Policy responses

10. The politics of consciousness

Mihaly Csikszentmihalyi*

One of the outcomes of the Enlightenment in the West has been questioning the accountability of rulers and governments. Although most civilizations recognized that good rulers contributed to the welfare of their people while bad ones brought about misery and strife, until quite recently bad government was seen as a failure of rulers to live up to their responsibilities to a divine power, rather than to the people.[1] Basically, the idea was that a good government should provide safety and prosperity; but, if it failed to do so, the duty of the people was to suffer through it and hope for the best. As common people began to acquire power in Europe, however, the questions began to be debated: 'What exactly should be expected of government? What justifies its existence?'

One perspective was advanced by the German philosopher Gottfried Wilhelm Leibniz, who answered the question in his *Codex Juris Gentium* of 1693 by claiming that 'the careful and constant pursuit of happiness' was a 'natural right' of human beings, which governments had to protect. A little over 80 years later, Thomas Jefferson (who was influenced by many other sources, especially John Locke) wrote the fateful lines in the Declaration of Independence of the United States which claim that governments are instituted to secure certain inalienable rights, among which are 'Life, Liberty, and the Pursuit of Happiness'.

In the past 200 years, this phrase has become a commonplace, and most people would agree that one reason governments have legitimacy and are granted power by the people is because they try to secure everyone's right to 'pursue happiness'. The issue, however, is agreeing what this pursuit of happiness entails.[2] Does it simply mean that government should protect the property of citizens, as George Mason and other colleagues of Jefferson argued, following Locke's lead, equating *happiness* with *property*? Did it mean that government must protect free trade and business entrepreneurship? Was the pursuit intended to apply to individual happiness or only to public order and prosperity?

These are questions one would think psychology might help in finding answers for. After all, Aristotle had a point in defining humans as *zoon politikon*, that is, beings whose life is contingent on a *polis*, or communal social arrangement. For better or for worse, the achievements that distinguish humans from other life forms, even from the great apes with whom we share at least 95 per cent of our genetic material,[3] are all dependent on interactions embedded in a rule-bound matrix that we loosely refer to as 'culture'. From language to technology, from religion to science, what is most 'human' is also the most 'cultural'.

Yet psychology, in the hope of discovering universal laws of behaviour that – like the laws of physics – are independent of time and place, has mainly focused on studying human behaviour abstracted from its cultural context. From Wundt's laboratories in Leipzig to Skinner's mazes at Harvard, experimenters were willing to sacrifice what was most interesting about humans in the hope that objective and precise measurements of molecular bits of behaviour would eventually build into a meaningful explanation of what men and women actually are, and why. But, in so doing, psychology has mainly become irrelevant to issues involving actual social and political decisions.

Of course, there have always been exceptions. Freud wrote *Civilizations and Its Discontents*; after the Second World War Adorno and his followers tried to explain the roots of authoritarian personalities; and Israeli psychologists helped establish the kibbutzim, where a scientific educational system was supposed to produce individuals free from the neuroses that bourgeois families tended to produce. Even B.F. Skinner tried his hand at extrapolating the findings of behaviourist psychology to the public arena. His book *Walden Two* was a stimulating, if somewhat unrealistic, attempt to imagine a community run by the mechanistic laws of utilitarian exchange.

But these and other such forays, until recently, remained marginal to the advance of psychology as a science, with the result that its impact outside the confines of academia is relatively insubstantial. The advent of positive psychology seems to be ushering in a change in this state of affairs.[4]

One of the first signs has been the effort to include measures of psychological well-being into the area of social indicators. By the 1990s several psychologists who have become recognized pioneers in positive psychology in the United States had begun to campaign to include measures of life satisfaction (Ed Diener) and happiness (Daniel Kahneman in the USA, Ruut Veenhoven in Europe) in the large-scale surveys that policy makers have been using more and more to assess the economic and social conditions of the population. Large-scale polling organizations, such as the Gallup Institute founded by the psychologist Don Clifton, also started to add measures of psychological well-being to their surveys.

It is too early to determine to what extent these early developments indicate a greater use of psychological knowledge in the public arena. Some signs, such as the interest shown by politicians in Scotland and in the UK as a whole for taking seriously psychological well-being in their plans, seem to bode well for the future. At the same time, working hand in hand with established power structures is a delicate matter. It becomes easy for psychologists to be co-opted to fulfil government policies and, in the process, to forget their responsibilities to the scientific role of critical objectivity.

For instance, when Daniel Kahneman gave a keynote address at one of the early positive psychology conferences in Washington, DC, he warned the audience that if psychologists wanted to have influence in the political arena they would have to adopt some of the theoretical models and language of economists, because politicians respected economists while they didn't think psychologists had much to bring to the table. The problem is that, at least in the USA, economists have long lost a critical stance towards the system in which they operate. They pick and choose from economic theory those assumptions that fit the interests of the dominant capitalist institutions, and turn a blind eye to the realities that do not support those interests: for instance, that the so-called 'free market' is often rigged in favour of special interests, or that universal suffrage means that all citizens have an equal say in how the country is run. It would be a pity if, in order to gain acceptance from the current ruling 1 per cent, psychologists had to give up the freedom to see and think outside the limits of convenient conventions.

Another large-scale application of positive psychology to social issues has been Marty Seligman's contract with the US Armed Services to train military personnel to become more self-reliant, or, as the hype for the project says, 'indestructible'. This is, of course, not the first time that a symbiotic relationship between psychology and the military has been forged. The vogue for intelligence testing received its major boost early in the twentieth century when the Army adopted the Stanford–Binet test to screen recruits for the First World War; then, in the Second World War, the US Air Force commissioned J.P. Guilford, a psychologist teaching at the University of Southern California who was to become president of the American Psychological Association after the war, to develop tests for measuring the creativity of fighter pilots. The intent of Seligman's project is very laudable. At the same time, it is another instance where extreme caution is in order. It does not take much imagination to conceive that such an alliance might lead to a slippery slope where all sorts of less desirable military aims might be abetted by psychologists. So we seem to be stuck in a predicament where we are damned if we do and also if we don't. Is there a way out of this uncomfortable situation?

I would start approaching the question of how positive psychology can relate to the issue of governance with an obvious axiom: if people are given a choice to delegate some of the power over their lives to another human agency (e.g. a government), they will do so only to the extent that they perceive that agency will help them achieve what they expect to make them happy. The Mongol hordes followed their khans freely, expecting to be led to loot by their leaders. The Chinese followed their emperor's will in large part because they believed that he was the representative of the heavenly powers that through him would provide rain, good crops and a prosperous life. This perspective differs from that of Jefferson and the Enlightenment philosophers in that it does not assume that humans have a right to pursue happiness (or any other *natural* right). It simply says that, if a government fails to allow its people to pursue happiness, it is likely to fall.

THE GREATEST EXPERIMENT OF ALL TIMES

There could have been no clearer confirmation of this axiom than the recent collapse of communist governments all across the globe, notably that of the Soviet Union and all the satellite countries under its rule. What made this sudden turn of events so unexpected was that these governments, influenced by the Leninist–Stalinist model, had achieved almost total control over the behaviour of their populations. And, according to the laws that psychologists as well as laypersons trusted to explain human behaviour, when people have been taught a set of beliefs from birth onward in the schools, the media, the workplace and public meetings, they were supposed to accept those beliefs. When they knew that resistance to the regime entailed torture and often death, while collaboration could lead to power and a comfortable life, they would conform to the orders from above. The science of psychology would have predicted that the hundreds of millions of people born under Soviet rule, who had no knowledge of any other way of life, who had no power and no realistic ways to change the status quo, would be turned into subservient robots destined to remain slaves of their masters unless freed by some outside agency.

Yet, as we now know, this is not what happened. The masses took it upon themselves to throw off their chains, without help from outside and against all reason. And, as a minor side effect, the events of the last decade of the last millennium also served to lay for ever to rest the behaviourist hegemony in American psychology, nourished by laboratory observations of rodent behaviour. Clearly, there seemed to be something more to human behaviour that had eluded the experimenters. One global process involving hundreds of millions of 'subjects' disproved the conclusions built on thousands of carefully arranged experiments: men and women did not simply enact 'learned' behaviours shaped by schedules of reinforcement, even when these lasted for many decades, and the punishments involved pain and the loss of life. Clearly, there seems to be something more to human behaviour than what experimenters have focused on in highly restricted and controlled laboratory settings.

But what, exactly?

Modern psychology had no grounds for answering such a question. There was no theoretical basis to explain what has happened in global politics during the last few decades. Even the most humanistic theories of the last century were interpreted as saying that human beings were entirely determined by their genetic programmes and by environmental conditions to follow a set of basic instructions. Maslow's need hierarchy, for instance, was interpreted to mean that only after the needs for survival, safety, belonging and so forth were secured were men and women motivated to act according to 'higher-order' needs. Yet it was known that, for instance, gang members in urban slums killed each other more because of slights to their self-esteem than because of needs lower on the pyramid, or workers left their jobs for lack of challenges even when their safety and security needs were not entirely fulfilled. In other words, psychological theory had not been able to free itself from the paradigms of the older natural sciences, which deal with laws governing inanimate matter. It had not yet been able to come to terms with the existence of *consciousness* – the evolutionary development that allows men and women to organize their own previous experiences and then imagine alternatives to existing reality, thereby making it possible to initiate changes relying on the agency of consciousness itself, independent of external conditions.

THE REQUIREMENTS OF HUMAN CONSCIOUSNESS

The evidence from recent historical events suggests that we cannot explain human behaviour adequately without taking into account the increasing role of consciousness in human affairs. For instance, the visionary French palaeontologist and Jesuit priest Pierre Teilhard de Chardin predicted at the midpoint of the twentieth century that future wars would be fought no longer just to gain territory, or resources, or in defence of one's faith or ideology, but to liberate, or to expand the consciousness of people.

Consciousness in this context is defined as the information that an organism has of its own experience, ordered in terms of: temporal categories – past, present and future; spatial categories such as me versus us versus them; affective groupings such a good and bad; cognitive categories like true and false – and so on. On the basis of such information, then, individuals have the possibility of making decisions that might contradict the behavioural programmes set down by genetic and cultural instructions, thereby introducing a certain amount of freedom of choice, or autonomy, into the repertoire of human behaviour.[5]

It could be argued that any system – and certainly every living organism – has some form of consciousness, in that the organism must be 'aware', at some level, of its internal states as well as the conditions in its immediate environment. In humans, however, this awareness has developed into an autonomous system that not only registers information, but also is able to initiate action. With the development of the forebrain, we became able to *reflect* on what was happening in consciousness, and act as if the content of consciousness was part of a reality to which we had to respond, adapt or change. And increasingly with time the reality of consciousness has become the paramount reality of our species.

Now we have developed this new way of conscious life, it has become increasingly difficult to live a good life if consciousness is prevented from operating by conditions imposed from outside agencies. So, if we want to know how psychology can help us understand historical events and political changes, we need to ask: What is it that consciousness requires from the social covenant? What are the social and political conditions that allow consciousness to flourish? Of course, many of these conditions have been well known for a long time. But most of them pertain to what corresponds to the 'lower-order' needs of Maslow. The Roman emperors knew that bread and circuses were a good way to keep the loyalty of citizens. King Henry IV of France knew that a 'chicken in every pot' went a long way to keep his subjects happy. It took many centuries and several bloody revolutions to realize that people also needed freedom and hope if they were to follow willingly the rules and laws of a political system. But for consciousness to flourish even more is needed.

There are three basic conditions, I shall argue, that human consciousness needs in order to be able to flourish. First is *freedom* – at the simplest level, the freedom to decide what consciousness should contain, and then the freedom to decide what it should consider true, good and beautiful. The second is *hope*, or the expectation that the future will be at least as good as the present. The third one is the opportunity to find *enjoyable experiences*, or flow, in everyday life. Of course, one could list many other desirable conditions, but I think those either are included in these three or are less essential. For instance, it could be argued that consciousness also needs to experience meaning, or a sense of belonging. But meaning is a component of hope, and belonging is not so much a condition for the good functioning of consciousness per se, but of existence in general.

The Freedom of Consciousness

Let me describe an experience that illustrates quite clearly the issues involved in the first of these conditions, that of freedom. During a visit to Budapest in the 1980s – the first time I had been back to the city in almost half a century – I was invited by some young relatives to go out with them on a Saturday evening. It was to be a teenage party in the basement of the house of some of their friends in Pest. I laughed at their request, explaining that I was too old to dance – or even sit – at a loud musical evening. 'Oh no,' they reassured me, 'it's not that kind of party. We just meet to read poetry.' I assumed they were kidding, but, sure enough, when the party started 20 or so adolescents were sitting around the walls in the basement and took turn reading their favourite poems, some old, some not yet published. And here and there, now and then, some of the young men and women dried a tear running down their cheeks as a hundred-year-old verse was recited.

It was hard to believe this was happening in the mid-1980s, in a metropolis behind the Iron Curtain. So I asked one of my young cousins how come they spent a couple of weekends together every month, reading poetry. He shrugged as if the question was naive:

> Well, we need to hear some truth once in a while. We don't get it in school, or in the papers, or on the TV. Our parents are afraid of discussing with us the things that matter for fear of getting us in trouble with the secret police. Poets are the only ones we trust, because they say the truth even if they have to disguise it to get it printed . . . but we know how to read their code.

This was just one case, but it is a good example of how the need for truth is one thing human consciousness needs, and will fight for if the powers that be are not willing to provide it. Just imagine how it feels when you cannot trust any of the information that is being aimed at you. It feels as if the content of your consciousness is unreliable, that it contains mostly lies. In other words, you cannot trust the contents of your own mind. Under such conditions, consciousness is no longer free to operate as an autonomous agent influencing behaviour.

It follows that a political system cannot exist for long unless it allows people to feel in control of their own consciousness. This means that government has to be transparent and trusted. Citizens need to feel that they are not being manipulated, that the information they receive is not distorted, and that they have a choice about what to believe and what to feel. When too many people conclude that politics is simply a mechanism for allowing the few to exploit the many, the system of governance loses its credibility, and the loyalty of the masses.

Consciousness and Hope

For consciousness to operate smoothly, it must have access to hope. When a person believes that the future is going to be worse than the present, the incentive to work – or even to live – diminishes until it disappears. Organisms with less well-developed forebrains can apparently hold only a short time span in their consciousness, extending less than an hour into the future.[6] But humans, who can imagine their entire life span, and its eventual end, need to have reasonably positive expectations for the future in order to be able to go on. Why try if we are convinced that our efforts will make no difference? Deprived of hope, consciousness becomes idle and atrophied, eventually falling into what the ancients called the deadly sin of *sloth* – or, as the social critic Woody Allen so well illustrated this condition: 'Whosoever shall not fall by the sword or by famine, shall fall by pestilence; so why bother shaving?'

Positive psychology has recognized the importance of hope for individual happiness. But again, the broader socio-political implications of hope have rarely been dealt with. Yet already, over 2000 years ago, when the Roman Republic was facing one of its frequent crises, the great politician Cicero was warning his countrymen: 'Our capital is invested in hope rather than in money; if that hope is abandoned, all else will be amassed only to be lost later on.'[7] In other words, faith in a better future is what keeps people motivated to work for the common welfare, to support the *res publica*. A nation or an organization – no matter how rich and powerful it has become – will start decaying as soon as its people can no longer imagine a better future for themselves.

What are the political implications of this need to feel that better days are possible? Certainly it does not imply that the government should decide what its citizens should hope for. But it does suggest that one of the essential tasks of government is to keep working hard to identify targets for growth – material ones, of course, but also social, cultural and even 'spiritual' ones – that will open up goals for the aspiration of its citizens. In this respect one should not underestimate the power of symbolic actions on the part of government: the race to the moon; the holding of Olympic Games; the building of great public spaces, parks and imposing buildings – these all show a commitment to a future that promises more than just survival and material comfort, but that indicates concern for promoting goals that are more permanent and fulfilling. Obviously, however, symbolic gestures only work if they are aligned with true purpose and are backed by action; otherwise they become another tool for diminishing consciousness, rather than enriching it.

Building more directly on positive psychology approaches to hope, we should consider how governments can foster the two components of hope that have been identified at the individual level, namely *agency* and *pathways*.[8] In other words, citizens must believe that they can attain their goals in life, and they should have access to the tools for getting there. If the majority of people feel that many of the desirable goals – such as health care, education, a home and a decent job – are unattainable, and even if attainable they can never find the means for reaching the goals, resentment will build in the population, until it turns into either resigned apathy or the sparks that will start a revolution – with unpredictable, although usually tragic, consequences.

Consciousness and Enjoyment

Not long ago I had the opportunity to have an interesting conversation with the president of an ancient European nation, one that not many centuries ago was a powerful player on the international stage, and at the forefront of excellence in the arts and the sciences. 'Tell me', he said. 'What can we do to keep our best young people from leaving to have a better life in some other country?' I was not sure what he meant, but then he explained that in the past few decades the brain drain in his country had become a real problem; too many well-trained, smart and ambitious young people were leaving because, 'Let's face it', he said, 'we have become too complacent and boring. There is so little that is new and interesting for them to do here.'

The problem this statement was complaining about knows no boundaries, and affects the wealthy countries as well as the poor ones. In Saudi Arabia it is manifest when young sheikhs, who a few generations ago showed their mettle racing camels, now race Mercedes in the desert, while in some Arctic communities without roads they are building drag-racing strips so the young people can use the cars purchased with oil money. In the USA some of the Native American reservations have the highest mortality rates in the world for young people, because the ancient art of leading sheep on horseback from pasture to pasture is no longer practised; young men try to recapture the enjoyable experiences their ancestors had by driving at night, intoxicated – and all too often dying in the process. In the poorest countries of Africa young boys are recruited and armed by commercial and political interests to bring terror into the countryside. Just as in the last century with the Hitler Jugend in Germany or Mussolini's Balilla in Italy, bored, hopeless young men with nothing better to do are seduced by the promise of adventure to support governments that cannot find anything better for them to do.

But it is not enough just to provide the illusion of action. Otherwise one falls back on the *panem et circenses* that failed the Romans when they could no longer motivate their citizens with meaningful tasks or the compulsory State activities of the North Korean party exercises. Conscious beings need to feel that they choose what to do, and that this is a challenging endeavour that brings them to increasingly higher levels of mastery. As Fausto Massimini[9] and Paolo Inghilleri[10] have eloquently argued, cultural evolution is a product of the enjoyment we derive from acting as autonomous agents, creating new things, thinking new thoughts and improving on old practices.[11] As Dante Alighieri wrote back around 1312 in his political treatise *De Monarchia*: 'In every action . . . the main intention of the agent is to express his own image; that is why every agent, whenever he acts, enjoys the action. Because everything that exists desires to be, and by acting the agent unfolds his being, action is naturally enjoyable.' This is true even of dogs bred for hunting, who are visibly transformed when stalking a prey; it is even more true of humans, who feel truly alive only when they are doing something they are good at doing – free of government impositions blind to the necessity of such free agency.

The few studies published about the relationship between political participation and subjective well-being, however, show how difficult it is to prove Dante's claim. The major problems are in disentangling cause and effect. Although several studies show correlations between well-being and civic action such as voting in elections or political protest, it is rarely clear whether individuals with high psychosocial well-being are more likely to engage in political action or whether it is the political involvement that results in greater well-being.[12] Furthermore, when a positive correlation is found, it is difficult to determine whether it is the political action per se that is correlated with the higher well-being, or the social context in which the action is embedded. Finally it is important to differentiate kinds of political participation that might enhance consciousness from those that do not. For instance, voting in the cantons of Switzerland is related to positive psychosocial well-being,[13] but the relation tends to be negative or non-existent in countries where voting in presidential elections is obligatory, such as Argentina, Bolivia, Brazil or Chile.[14]

Despite the current lack of strong evidence that political engagement benefits individual well-being – for which longitudinal studies will be needed – it is highly probable that, when people cannot express themselves in meaningful action, the body politick will be in trouble. It is likely that under such conditions people will feel increasingly frustrated, or engage in disruptive activities to prove that they exist and that they matter.

Up to now in this chapter I have been writing as if all political systems were interested in governing with the full support of the citizenry and for the benefit of all. Of course, that is an ideal that is rarely approached in history. In our times, the happiest countries are also the ones with the most democratic, orderly and peaceful governments.[15] According to work using international survey data completed by the new economics foundation,[16] the five happiest countries are Denmark, Switzerland, Austria, Iceland and the Bahamas: all relatively wealthy and peaceful countries with populations ranging from 320000 to about 8.5 million inhabitants. The largest countries on the list of 178 nations are all faring rather badly: the US is down in 23rd position, China 82nd and Russia 167th. Unfortunately, some of these large masses, and mid-size countries bent on asserting themselves, such as Iran or North Korea, could easily erupt and cause a conflagration that would put an end to life on earth. At this point positive psychology can offer little practical advice to political entities that are not interested in improving the well-being of their citizens. But of course that is not a reason for not trying, and whatever contribution we can make to alleviate the tyranny of government should be one of the most worthwhile challenges that our profession could confront.

CONCLUSIONS

The 'politics of consciousness' is simply an extension of existing views of how governmental responsibility intersects with the well-being of citizens by taking into account the human need that has been the last to evolve in time: the need to preserve and enrich consciousness. We have seen that for consciousness to flourish three separate but overlapping conditions are necessary: to be able to use attention freely, and to decide what is true and desirable; to have grounds for hope in a better future; and to be able to express one's own strength and purpose in meaningful activities.

Providing for the survival, safety and comfort of citizens is of course also essential, and has been long held to be the responsibility of good government. But no matter how wealthy, free and peaceful a population might be, if the consciousness of its members atrophies, the community will suffer and decline.

NOTES

*   With many thanks for the assistance of Kyle D. Bond, Jeanne Nakamura, and the editors of this volume for their helpful suggestions.
1. J. Israel (2006), *Enlightenment Contested: Philosophy, Technology, and the Emancipation of Man*, Oxford: Oxford University Press.
2. See G. Wills (1979), *Inventing America: Jefferson's Declaration of Independence*, New York: Random House.

3. J. Cohen (2007), 'The myth of the 1%', *Science*, **29** (316), 1836.
4. A summary of studies in positive psychology that deal with the relationships between individuals and institutions, including political ones, can be found in Peter H. Huang and Jeremy A. Blumenthal (2009), 'Positive institutions, law, and policy', in Shane J. Lopez and C.R. Snyder (eds), *Oxford Handbook of Positive Psychology*, New York: Oxford University Press, pp. 589–98.
5. Mihaly Csikszentmihalyi (1993), *The Evolving Self*, New York: HarperCollins.
6. M. Seligman, P. Railton, C. Sripada and R. Baumeister (2012 in press), 'Navigating into the future or driven by the past', *Perspectives*.
7. Marcus Tullius Cicero (2002), *Letters*, trans. D.R. Shackleton Bailey, Cambridge, MA: Harvard University Press, p. 189.
8. See C.R. Snyder (1994), *The Psychology of Hope*, New York: Free Press.
9. Fausto Massimini, Paolo Inghilleri and Antonella delle Fave (1996), *La Selezione Psicologica Umana*, Milano: Cooperativa Libraria IULM.
10. Paolo Inghilleri (1999), *From Subjective Experience to Cultural Change*, New York: Cambridge University Press.
11. Csikszentmihalyi (1993).
12. For a summary, see Constance Flanagan and Matthew Bundnick (2011), 'Civic engagement and psychosocial well-being of college students', *Liberal Education*, **97** (2), 1–9.
13. A. Stutzer and B.S. Frey (2006), 'Political participation and procedural utility: an empirical study', *European Journal of Political Research*, **45** (3), 391–418.
14. Rebecca Weitz-Shapiro and Matthew S. Winters (2008), *Political Participation and Quality of Life*, Inter-American Development Bank Working Paper No. 636, Washington, DC: Inter-American Development Bank.
15. Robert Inglehart and H.D. Klingmann (2000), 'Genes, culture, democracy, and happiness', in E. Diener and E.M. Suh (eds), *Culture and Subjective Well-being*, Cambridge, MA: MIT Press, pp. 165–83.
16. See N. Marks, S. Abdallah, A. Simms and S. Thompson (2006), *The (Un)Happy Planet Index: An Index of Human Wellbeing and Ecological Impact*, London: nef.

11. Well-being, capitalism and public policy: from generalization to granularity

Geoff Mulgan

In this chapter I look at some of the ways we should consider two questions: first, how governments can influence well-being; and, second, how capitalism influences well-being. I argue that in both cases the aggregate pictures tell us less than we might hope. However, the more detailed pictures both of public programmes and of the influences of different aspects of capitalism can be very instructive. The implication is that we need to choose our levels of granularity with care.

PUBLIC POLICY – WHAT HAVE WE LEARNED?

Governments today can measure happiness. To a lesser extent they can influence it and grow it. The goal of increasing public happiness has become a more overt aim for public policy in many countries, sitting, sometimes uneasily, alongside more familiar goals such as economic growth, national security and social justice. The pressures for change include the growing body of research on the causes (and correlations) of happiness and the long-run rise of public concern for quality-of-life issues, sometimes attributed to the rise of 'post-materialist' values.[1] But there are also ancient antecedents, and the overt aspiration for governments to increase happiness can be found in the Western, Islamic, Hindu, Chinese and Buddhist traditions.[2]

Some of the recent writing about well-being has exemplified 'policy-based evidence' or 'ideology-based evidence' – selective use of facts and analysis to bolster conservative, utilitarian, liberal, libertarian, socialist or green beliefs. The left seize on data that suggest that inequality and unemployment correlate with unhappiness, while the right seize with equal conviction on the data showing the importance of marriage and faith. Yet the data do not fit neatly into any ideological patterns. In time, the large data sets becoming available – such as the 200000-person sample being surveyed by the UK's Office of National Statistics – look set to change the terms of debate, just as GDP measures became a focal point for national political argument 70 years ago, but also ended up transforming how economic dynamics were understood.

The UK data are a good illustration. These data confirm the U pattern of life satisfaction over the life span, the negative impact of unemployment, and the importance of relationships. But they challenge the assumption that leisure is preferable to work – those working over 46 hours a week had almost identical levels of life satisfaction to those working 31–45 hours, scoring a fraction higher on both satisfaction and anxiety. Professionals score higher in general, but so do the self-employed.

The broader implications of data such as these are still uncertain, and there are as many reasons to question them as there still are to question GDP measures – particularly their comparability over time and place. Where GDP has been primarily a measure of aggregates it's likely that the greatest use of well-being data will come from disaggregation – understanding in more detail the differences between parts of society, whether categorized by socio-economic class, age, race or culture. Knowing that one country scores 7.2 and another 7.3 by contrast will tell us very little.

There is even less clarity on the policy implications. Some specific policies are being tested in fields ranging from schools and family policy to health care and the environment. Behavioural interventions are, for example, being tested more rigorously.[3] But no one can confidently predict that any specific policy will lead to measurable improvements in well-being. In this respect the field shares the weaknesses of much psychology, which lacks either strong evidence of underlying causation (although longitudinal studies are steadily improving its understanding) or reliable evidence for many of its remedies. This is true not just of acute conditions but also of more everyday ones. As Parks et al. put it a few years ago, 'we know very little about how to improve the lives of people whose days are free of overt mental dysfunction but are bereft of pleasure, engagement and meaning'.[4]

Policy makers also face the challenge of definition – what exactly are they trying to grow or maximize? There has been an extensive literature on the definition of happiness, but different policies may result if the goal is to maximize pleasure or present happiness, life satisfaction or some other measures such as fulfilment. As the UK survey evidence shows, the implications will also be different if the aim is to reduce unhappiness or to maximize happiness. Actions to reduce unhappiness may focus on issues such as stress and severe mental illness. If aggregate happiness is the primary goal, however, the main focus may be on such issues as interpersonal trust.

Such choices about ends will influence, for example, how much weight to give to unemployment versus income; one answer[5] suggests that the relative priority of both should be determined by the effect of each on well-being. But well-being will never be the only criterion by which policy choices of this kind are judged. Moreover, even if it was, we should be just as interested in the dynamic effects of any policy intervention (i.e. what impact it might have on well-being in five or ten years) as we are interested in its immediate effects. For public policy, as in daily life, there are bound to be trade-offs between happiness now and happiness in the future. Other examples of the difficulties involved in making happiness a policy goal include the trade-off of feelings of safety relative to opportunities for fun (which often involves very different preferences amongst different age groups), whether to promote tranquillity or vitality, how much to empha- size overall satisfaction in life, or whether to stretch people (i.e. seeing some dissatisfaction now as necessary for greater fulfilment later).[6]

Well-being has to be situated alongside, and sometimes in tension with, other goals such as national security, the interests of future generations or moral virtue. It would be very surprising if it became a dominant or even unique goal. The implication of some writings is that government could become a purely technical exercise of adjusting policies to optimize well- being. From the perspective of the 2010s this looks neither very likely (the gaps in knowledge are vast) nor very desirable (since it would remove any need for moral or political argument).

The same is true of the commonly held, opposite, view that govern- ments should only seek to maximize freedom. This monist view is equally incoherent when pushed too far, and equally crude. This is why all real communities and societies negotiate limits to freedom, whether children's freedom to avoid school or adults' freedom to use drugs.

So what should governments do? Recent experience suggests that we need to distinguish three very different levels of government action to influence well-being. At each level there are legitimate arguments about whether the state has any business being involved in promoting happiness – or whether it should solely concern itself with promoting either freedoms or capabilities. But at least the options which then follow are becoming clearer.

LEVELS OF CAUSATION

The first level concerns the overall design of systems of government and their functioning. Such fundamental things as the maintenance of peace, the rule of law, and democracy matter greatly. We have fairly strong evidence that these tend to correlate with well-being, and probably cause it, and there are obvious reasons why this should be the case. Being in a nation at peace does not of itself cause happiness, but it removes many obvious causes of unhappiness. Overall levels of public spending by contrast do not have a reliable impact on happiness – many attempts to find patterns have failed, perhaps not surprisingly given the many different compositions of public spending across the world.

At a second level there are policies. At this level the evidence is weakest. We simply don't know how different policies on marriage will affect well-being, even though we know that marriage correlates with it; we don't know whether more or less compulsory schooling or curriculum content has a positive or negative effect; overall education has surprisingly little clear impact on happiness (perhaps because expectations often rise faster than the possibility of meeting them). We might expect more rights to parental leave and flexible time to have an effect, but we can't prove it. And we can't say for certain whether, for example, later retirement ages or laws promoting work sharing have the impacts we might expect them to.

Here the problem is partly a matter of insufficient evidence, but there is also the problem of causation. It's not hard to hypothesize possible causal links between a particular policy and an outcome in terms of well-being, but the reasoning soon becomes very thin. Take taxes, for example: do lower taxes make people happy? In principle, more disposable income should have some effects on well-being. But the effects will depend on whether people see the tax cut as fair, whether they approve of any linked changes to spending, or whether the tax cut leads to changes in spending or investment. Then, even if there is a one-off effect, expectations may quickly adjust, leaving well-being levels where they were before.

At a third level however the picture is more positive. The more detailed level of programme or service design turns out to be rich in experiment, and some accumulating evidence. This more granular level may also be the better one for making sense of happiness in all its forms and for finding plausible accounts of causation. There are now dozens of different approaches being taken in schools to promote resilience or empathy, some with evidence about effects. There is a very fertile field of practice around public health and preventing mental illness. For example, detailed manuals now set out the effects of different kinds of exercise on both physical and psychological health. The same is true in relation to active ageing – from exercise and volunteering to paid employment (in Canada paid employment came top in a recent survey as the most satisfying activity for the over-65s). We also have some suggestive evidence on the impact of urban planning on well-being, via such things as commuting time (which correlates inversely with happiness) or fear of crime (some more detailed analysis and references can be found in my chapter for the Oxford University Press *Handbook on Wellbeing*[7]). Many examples are collected on the website Action for Happiness, which includes evidence on options for action at the level of individual schools or neighbourhoods.[8]

There are some clear possible research agendas for advancing knowledge at the programme level. One is more use of rigorous randomization to assess which interventions work, and for which groups. We might expect these to highlight the importance of careful segmentation – interventions may work well for particular groups and for people with particular cultural characteristics, but not for others. Over-aggregated randomized control trials will be of little use – the best approaches will use genuine randomization but with highly targeted groups, distinguishing for example what works for the housebound over-80s and working-class young men, middle-class working mothers and middle-aged men with long-term conditions. One size will certainly not fit all.

We might also expect progress in understanding the effects of environments on population well-being.[9] The salutogenic approach was foreshadowed in projects such as the Peckham experiment in the 1930s in London, which emphasized the environmental actions that could improve population health. It seems likely that whole-town or neighbourhood approaches which, for example, increase walking and cycling, or expand mutual interactions, may have an effect both on the distribution and the mean of well-being.

Judging even these more granular policies is bound to be hard, simply because of the challenge of keeping some variables constant while others change. But it would be interesting to make the most of natural experiments, comparing, for example, how happiness evolves in societies where the costs associated with economic crises are widely shared (e.g. through work sharing or pay cuts) against those where they fall disproportionately on a minority who lose their jobs.

The next few years should be interesting – the combination of more policy and programme experiment, more data, and more sophistication in using methods to evaluate policy should combine to take the field far beyond the relatively flimsy state of current knowledge.

CAPITALISM – WHAT HAVE WE LEARNED?

If the state faces challenges as we learn more about well-being, what about the economy and, in particular, the capitalist system? Capitalism promises happiness, and its legitimacy derives from the extraordinary speed with which it has achieved material improvement. But the critics of capitalism have for two centuries warned that capitalism imprisons the worker on a treadmill of work, as the salaryman sacrifices his life to the corporation in the hope of promotions that may never come. The consumer becomes trapped on a treadmill of ever greater consumption, jumping from anticipation to anticipation but never being truly satisfied, while small investors are imprisoned by the hopeful dream that their stocks will suddenly make them wealthy without the inconvenience of work. All are vulnerable to that ill-defined but ubiquitous epidemic of the modern world – depression.[10] It's not just those at the bottom who suffer. Max Weber viewed the investment mindset as unnatural: 'a person does not "by nature" want to make more and more money';[11] and Karl Marx wrote of the trap the capitalist himself falls into, as he 'relentlessly drives human beings to production for production's sake ... [A]s such he shares with the miser the passion for wealth as wealth ... [C]ompetition forces him continually to extend his capital for the sake of maintaining it, and he can only extend it by means of continual accumulation.'[12]

Nineteenth-century Britain led the world in industrialization, but it was also believed to suffer from high suicide rates, and this encouraged many critics in continental Europe to ascribe them to too much freedom and overly high expectations: as Avner Offer put it, 'affluence breeds impatience and impatience undermines well-being',[13] or, in the more extreme words of Franco Berardi, capitalism has become an 'unhappiness machine'[14] widening the gulf between the capacity of the brain and the expanding volume of information and pressures that are bombarding it.

But these generalizations are not easy to substantiate. Richard Easterlin recently updated his famous research showing the lack of correlation between growth and satisfaction with the conclusion that, in:

> sixteen developed countries with time series at least 21 years in length, there is no significant relation between the rate of economic growth and the improvement in life satisfaction. In seven countries transitioning to free market economies with time series that are at least 14 years in length and include a measurement before or close to the beginning of transition, there is no significant relation between the rate of economic growth and the improvement in life satisfaction. In thirteen developing nations spanning Asia, Africa, and Latin America with time series at least 10 years in length (the average being 15 years), there is no significant relation between the rate of economic growth and the improvement in subjective well-being. Pooling the data for all thirty-six countries above, there is no significant relation between the rate of economic growth and the change in life satisfaction.[15]

Other research seems to confirm the picture with a levelling off as income rises.[16]

Korea, the miracle economy of east Asia, is a good example of how capitalism can apparently corrode well-being. In the 1950s it had a GDP lower than much of Africa, but over the next few decades vaulted ahead to the ranks of the most prosperous nations. Per capita GDP in Korea increased from $800 in 1970 to $19 000 in 2008. Yet, according to the OECD, the level of life satisfaction among Koreans decreased from 61.1 per cent to 47.3 per cent between 1990 and 2002.[17] Egypt is another example: in late 2010, just before the regime fell, only 9 per cent of Egyptians were described as thriving, less than for Palestine and Yemen, despite 5 per cent growth that year. The figures had fallen in previous years for all but the richest, again despite strong economic growth.[18] Progress should mean a longer life, lived more richly, with more fulfilment. Although money and consumption can serve time they can also degrade it.

Yet the evidence isn't straightforward.[19] One reason for the levelling off of the correlation between happiness and economic wealth is simply that each marginal increment of income produces a smaller absolute increase in happiness. When mapped on a log scale, there is a fairly close fit between income and happiness.[20] More money doesn't increase the experience of happiness, but it does improve stated satisfaction with life, presumably because it improves people's sense of relative success.

More detailed analysis also suggests why the data come out as they do. The Gallup World Poll asks people what emotions they experienced the previous day. People in relatively rich nations report themselves as more likely to have felt love and enjoyment and less likely to have experienced anger, depression or boredom. Patterns over time are similar, with trends towards greater happiness (the US is a particular exception).

So growth has some impact on happiness. But what is surprising is how little. A good case study was the crisis of the late 2000s. In the UK in 2007 average life satisfaction levels were 7.3; in 2008 the figure rose to 7.5; it fell marginally to 7.4 in 2009 and was back up to 7.5 in 2010, after the severest recession in several generations, and a sharp rise in unemployment. In the US the Gallup daily poll found a drop of only 2 per cent reporting being happy the previous day (from 89 to 87) during the course of 2008. Why was this? Why should a downturn make people happier, even if only marginally? It's possible that people had to spend more time with friends or family and quite enjoyed doing so, that low interest rates kept the majority feeling prosperous, that expectations had become more realistic, or that they felt more fellow-feeling than at the height of the boom. A better answer is simply that all measures of happiness tend to be fairly slow to move; measures of unhappiness, perhaps surprisingly, don't move in tandem with measures of happiness and may be more sensitive. Unemployed people in the US are 20 per cent more likely to report worry on any given day than people with jobs, but they are only 5 percentage points less likely to report happiness.[21] Recessions, it turns out, increase stress and anxiety a lot – particularly where debt is involved.

Another answer is that we quickly revert to a set point of happiness, even after serious shocks like illness, disability or the death of a spouse, a challenge both to political action and to the promise of the market.[22] Another is simply that so many of the factors shaping happiness, like genetic make-up or childhood experiences, sit well beyond the reach of any conceivable market.[23] Some influences can be bought: physical attractiveness for women and height for men correlate with reported happiness, and can be influenced by consumption of the right makeover. Even blood pressure roughly correlates (inversely) with happiness at the level of whole nations, and in principle is amenable to influence by what we buy and consume. Yet much of what matters most for happiness is beyond the reach of money.

Another factor may be social norms. One interesting study a decade ago suggested that the effects of inequality on happiness are refracted through prevailing social and ideological norms. The US population were less troubled by inequality because of their acceptance of the idea that, even if incomes were unequal, everyone has the chance to succeed: the data showing that social mobility in the US is lower than in many other developed countries, and may be declining, either didn't matter or weren't known.[24] The unnerving implication could be that policy makers should do what they can to sustain hope – even where it's unjustified.

The claims that capitalism causes misery are at best unproven. But so is the claim that capitalism reliably grows well-being. These claims are as doubtful as the mirror claims that either public spending or the absence of public spending has a causal effect on happiness. What may follow is the need to pose the question in more detail, at the level of daily life rather than aggregates. This conclusion clearly echoes what I have already said about public policy and government action.

Recent detailed evidence on the relationship between market economies and happiness may be more illuminating. In the workplace, the detailed mix of pay, autonomy and recognition is likely to influence well-being. For some, long hours are associated with great job satisfaction; for others, long hours are a direct source of misery. Generalizations are bound to mislead.

The same is true of consumption. One of the leading investigators of the relationship between consumption and happiness concludes that 'people who strongly orient towards values such as money, possessions, image and status report lower subjective well-being'.[25] Symptom and cause are interwoven: blocked relationships and dissatisfactions lead people to focus on material goods, which then renders them less able to make and keep good relationships. A 'materialist value orientation' develops through 'experiences that induce feelings of insecurity and exposure to social models that encourage materialistic values'.[26] Show young men extremely attractive women and they will judge others more negatively. In one study 81 male dormitory residents watching a popular TV show, whose main characters were three strikingly attractive females, were asked to rate a photo of an average female (described as a potential blind date for another dorm resident). These rated the target female as significantly less attractive than did a comparable control group, and another study found that men who were exposed to photographs of physically attractive women subsequently became less satisfied with their current heterosexual relationships and rated their partners as less attractive.

The initial impressions of romantic partners – women who were actually available to them and likely to be interested in them – were so adversely affected that the men didn't even want to bother. Self-assessments of attractiveness also change. Women who are surrounded by other attractive women, whether in the flesh, in films or in photographs, rate themselves as less satisfied with their attractiveness – and less desirable as marriage partners. As Nairn et al. have shown, these pressures may be reaching ever younger, as advertisers target girls under 13, urging them to buy make-up and fashion as the easiest route to popularity and happiness.[27] But consumer research shows that too much attention to materialistic values and possessions has a negative impact on psychological well-being.[28] The effects on self-esteem are fairly obvious. But there is also a more general effect on attitudes.[29] The more that people attach importance to material objects the more they risk feeling let down, since the new fashion, make-up or perfume is unlikely to achieve all that it promises. Too much attention to material things may also get in the way of other relationships. This was the finding of a study to examine the empirical links between watching, wanting and well-being in UK children.[30] It discovered that children who spend more time in front of the television or computer screen are more materialistic. Children who are more materialistic tend to have lower self-esteem and a lower opinion of their parents, and children who have a poor opinion of their parents also argue with them more and have a lower opinion of themselves.[31]

There are also clearly reinforcing links between materialism and anti-social behaviour. Children who communicate less with their parents, or receive negative messages from them, tend to focus more on money.[32] They then become more vulnerable to the messages from business. Much advertising depends on creating insecurity from upward social comparisons that leave slim women feeling fat, beautiful people feeling ugly and successful people feeling inadequate.[33]

Here the different types of capitalism have different effects. Spend per capita on advertising has been four times greater in America than in mainland Europe, and twice as great in the UK. What effect does this have on the mood of a society? Does it lead to a more materialistic orientation – to choosing harder work so as to earn more cash rather than more time with the family or friends? It appears so. Does it then disappoint in terms of happiness? Again, it appears so, with a tendency to make up for disappointment with addictive behaviours. Robert Frank explored some of these patterns in the US.[34] He asked people to consider a choice between two worlds. One, world A, is a world where you earn $110000 per year, and others earn $200000. The other, world B, is a world where you earn $100000 per year, and others earn $85000. A majority of Americans, it turns out, choose world B. Why? It could be envy, but it's also a recognition that the visibility of those richer than us makes us dissatisfied. The very dissatisfaction which can act as a spur for hard work and risk taking can also just end up as a trap, particularly in an environment where it's hard to avoid media that offer Porsches and Patek Philippe watches, luxury holidays and sports cars. H.L. Mencken once defined a wealthy man as one who earns $100 a year more than his wife's sister's husband.[35] The same pressures that drive some to work harder drive others to debt. We know that happiness isn't achieved just by owning things or earning more. Learning to be happy often means learning to sustain emotional connections, and learning how to teach others about our needs, and ourselves about how to meet the needs of others. Yet capitalism often encourages a narcissistic preoccupation with self that is one of the least likely routes to happiness.

But the heart of the matter may be simpler than this. Lord Acton once wrote that all progress depends on dissatisfaction. Certainly a dynamic capitalist economy depends on dissatisfaction – to drive workers to work, and consumers to consume. Perhaps a dynamic society does too, and constantly navigates the balance between too little satisfaction and too much.

But the main message of this research is surely that we need to look at the right level of focus. In our own lives it will be a subtle mix of pressure and support, cooperation and competition, that best promotes well-being. The same is true of societies or organizations.

SOME CONCLUSIONS

A recent book suggested, in relation to both economic goals and the goal of increasing well-being, that, 'if the complete planning of society is not possible because planners cannot have all the information that would be necessary to achieve their objective, then partial planning is also impossible'.[36] This is surely a non sequitur. Every wealthy country has used more than 'partial planning' to maximize wealth, from Germany or Japan to the USA's highly activist industrial and technology policy. Complete planning in relation to the economy is neither feasible nor desirable. But this leaves a substantial space for partial planning, and conscious policy action to influence economic growth as one of a number of important goals for any society.

Similar considerations apply to well-being as a policy goal. No government has ever taken GDP maximization as the only goal of public policy (the closest has possibly been communist China, which did incorporate it into performance measures). Citizens and stakeholders of all kinds have much more complex and varied needs and would soon evict a government that was solely obsessed with GDP. They would probably do the same to a government that became too obsessed with well-being.

For now this is not a serious risk. Governments are only just beginning to understand well-being, let alone to adopt policies to improve it. In 50 years we might have reason to worry about too much attention to well-being. For now the much bigger concern is how little serious attention is paid.

Hopefully the flood of data will open up new ideas and new ways of thinking, both on public policy and on the role of economic systems. But as this happens we should beware of generalizations: the greatest value of the data will come from disaggregation not aggregation, and the most effective actions are likely to be fine-grained too.

NOTES

1. Ronald Inglehart (1990), *Culture Shift in Advanced Industrial Society*, Princeton, NJ: Princeton University Press; Ronald Inglehart, Miguel Basáñez, Jaime Díez-Medrano, Loek Halman and Ruud Luijkx (eds) (2004), *Human Beliefs and Values: A Cross-cultural Sourcebook Based on the 1999–2002 Values Surveys*, Mexico City: Siglo XXI.
2. I set out some of these in my 2006 book *Good and Bad Power*, London: Penguin.
3. The Behavioural Insight Unit in the UK government's Cabinet Office is testing a range of policy interventions, some of which will be relevant to happiness.
4. M. Seligman, A. Parks and T. Steen (2004), 'A balanced psychology and a full life', *Philosophical Transactions of the Royal Society: Biological Sciences*, **359**, 1379–81.
5. Seaford (this volume, Chapter 8), for example.
6. E. Diener, C. Nickerson, R.E. Lucas and E. Sandvik (2002), 'Dispositional affect and job outcomes', *Social Indicators Research*, **59**, 229–59.
7. (forthcoming), *Handbook on Well-being*, Oxford: Oxford University Press.
8. www.actionforhappiness.org.
9. Discussed by Bartolini (this volume, Chapter 6) and Basu et al. (this volume, Chapter 7).
10. Alain Ehrenberg (2008), *The Weariness of the Self: Diagnosing the History of Depression in the Contemporary Age*, Montreal: McGill-Queen's University Press.

11. Max Weber ([1930] 2005), *The Protestant Ethic and the Spirit of Capitalism*, London: Routledge, p. 16.
12. Robert Heilbroner (1985), *The Nature and Logic of Capitalism*, New York: Norton, writes particularly well about the anxieties endemic to capitalism.
13. Avner Offer (2006), *The Challenge of Affluence: Self-control and Well-being in the United States and Britain since 1950*, Oxford: Oxford University Press, p. 82.
14. Franco Berardi, *La fabbrica dell'infelicità: New economy e movimento del cognitariato*, Rome: DeriveApprodi.
15. http://www.nationalaccountsofwellbeing.org/learn/need/easterlin-still-challenge.html.
16. A. Kohut (2007), *Global Views on Life Satisfaction, National Conditions and the Global Economy*, Pew Global Attitudes Project, 2007, Washington, DC: Pew Research Center, available at: http://pewglobal.org/files/pdf/1025.pdf.
17. See the speech by the Korean statistics commissioner Insill Yi, drawing on an OECD 2009 report, 'Quality of life index in Korea: why we need it and how to apply', available at: http://www.oecd.org/dataoecd/56/29/44118771.pdf, pp. 1–2.
18. Abu Dhabi Gallup (2011), 'Egypt: the arithmetic of revolution', March.
19. Stevenson and Wolfers challenged the view that there is no link, and their paper set off a wave of intensive argument over what the data actually show. B. Stevenson and J. Wolfers (2008), 'Economic growth and subjective well-being: reassessing the Easterlin paradox', *Brookings Papers on Economic Activity*, Spring, pp. 1–87.
20. D. Kahneman and A. Deaton (2010), 'High income improves evaluation of life but not emotional well-being', *Proceedings of the National Academy of Sciences of the United States of America*, **107** (38), 16489–93.
21. See www.gallup.com/poll/139604/worry-sadness-stress-increase-length-unemployment.aspx. This research also finds that the incidence of worrying is higher for those who have been unemployed longer, while the incidence of happiness is only slightly less for the long-term unemployed.
22. E. Diener, R.E. Lucas and C.N. Scollon (2006), 'Beyond the hedonic treadmill: revisions to the adaptation theory of well-being', *American Psychologist*, **61**, 305–14.
23. N. Donovan and D. Halpern (2002), *Life Satisfaction: The State of Knowledge and Implications for Government*, London: Cabinet Office.
24. A. Alesina and R. MacCulloch (2004), 'Happiness and inequality: are Europeans and Americans different?', *Journal of Public Economics*, **88**, 2009–42.
25. Tim Kasser (2003), *The High Price of Materialism*, Cambridge, MA: MIT Press, p. 13.
26. Richard Ryan and Edward Deci (2000), 'Self-determination theory and the facilitation of intrinsic motivation, social development, and well-being', *American Psychologist*, **55**, 68–78.
27. Agnes Nairn, Jo Ormond and Paul Bottomley (2007), *Watching, Wanting and Wellbeing: Exploring the Links – A Study of 9 to 13-Year-Olds*, London: National Consumer Council.
28. D. Kanner and R.G. Soule (2003), 'Globalization, corporate culture, and freedom', in Tim Kasser and A. Kasser (eds), *Psychology and Consumer Culture: The Struggle for a Good Life in a Materialistic World*, Washington, DC: American Psychological Association, pp. 49–67.
29. Juliet B. Schor (2004), *Born to Buy: The Commercialized Child and the New Consumer Culture*, New York: Scribner.
30. Research on adolescents also shows the corrosive effects of media culture. See Nairn et al. (2007).
31. Schor (2004). Moniek Buijzen and Patti M. Valkenburg (2003), 'The effects of television advertising on materialism, parent–child conflict and unhappiness: a review of research', *Applied Developmental Psychology*, **24**, 437–56; Moniek Buijzen and Patti M. Valkenburg (2003), 'The unintended effects of television advertising: a parent–child survey', *Communication Research*, **30**, 483–503.
32. G. Moore and R. Moschis (1984), 'The impact of family communication on adolescent consumer socialization', *Advances in Consumer Research*, **11**, 314–19.

33. Women exposed to perfume advertisements with attractive slim models become less satisfied with their own appearance; M. Richins (1991), 'Social comparison and the idealized images of advertising', *Journal of Consumer Research*, **18** (1), 71–83.
34. Robert Frank (2000), 'Why living in a rich society makes us feel poor', *New York Times Magazine*, 15 October, available at: http://partners.nytimes.com/library/magazine/home/20001015mag-frank.html.
35. A study confirmed Mencken's definition. David Neumark and Andrew Postlewaite examined the behaviour of a large sample of pairs of American sisters, one of whom did not have a job. Analysing all the factors that might influence the sister to find a paid job, they found that relative income was the most powerful: a woman in their sample was 16 to 25 per cent more likely to seek paid employment if her sister's husband earned more than her own. D. Neumark and A. Postlewaite (1998), 'Relative income concerns and the rise in married women's employment', *Journal of Public Economics*, **70** (1) (October), 157–83.
36. P. Booth (ed.) (2011), . . . *And the Pursuit of Happiness*, London: Institute of Economic Affairs, p. 34.

12. Well-being for growth and democracy in the EU

Agnès Hubert*

Is leisure an asset or a liability for the economy? Why should activities such as cleaning, cooking and caring be considered productive only when they are performed outside of the household? Should air pollution be taxed? Are health policies designed for adding life to years? Is the *way* that services are delivered sufficiently taken into account in schools, care institutions, hospitals, prisons and workplaces? Should the well-being cost of unemployment be deducted from the cost of active labour market policies? How should macroeconomic policies be designed, decided and implemented in order to integrate the findings of well-being research? What are the life management skills that should be made compulsory in school curricula? Are civic activities adequately supported and recognized as being meaningful to the general improvement of well-being? Is 'sense of coherence' a measurable indicator of well-being?

These questions, which sample some of the issues discussed in this book, are particularly topical in policy-making circles. Some of the required information and policy measures relating to these issues already exist at regional, national and EU levels. For example, time-use surveys provide gender-disaggregated information on the time spent doing household chores, as well as on caring for relatives. A global greenhouse gas reduction strategy is implemented by the EU to fight climate change and improve the quality of the environment. A European pact for mental health and well-being was launched in 2008, and a pilot European Innovation Partnership on Active and Healthy Ageing (EC 2012) is committed to delivering an increase of two healthy life years by 2020. Lastly, the questionnaire of the third wave of the European Quality of Life Survey[1] investigates the sense of coherence across the populations of European nations.

The practical value of these examples is to provide evidence that decision makers at all levels can challenge their established mental models and policy practices. Indeed, these examples demonstrate that market activities are no longer seen as the exclusive gauge of a successful society. Indicators and improvements in data collection create new knowledge to identify and analyse the impact of a change in perspective. They provide evidence to design more efficient policies. This knowledge is particularly necessary in times of credit restrictions, as it reveals the potential of non-monetary resources which can be mobilized for the achievement of well-being (Eriksson and Lindström, this volume, Chapter 3).

The scope of reflection encompassed by this book is wide. Far from the piecemeal approach just described, the ambition to develop a holistic frame-work of what counts for the well-being of citizens is very timely and should serve to enrich the current debate on 'GDP and beyond'. The European Commission has, with the OECD and the statistical offices of Member States, taken a leading role in the development of new data and indica-tors to correct the inadequacy of GDP as the sole measure of wealth. This work has received an impetus with the widely discussed publication of the Stiglitz–Sen–Fitoussi report (Stiglitz et al. 2009) on the one hand and from the EU's Europe 2020 strategy[2] on the other. Furthermore, this initiative reached an important stage in August 2013, as a report on the implementa-tion and outcomes of the actions put forward in the communication 'GDP and beyond: measuring progress in a changing world' (EC 2009) was issued by the European Commission (SWD (2013) 303 final). This shows that much has been done to improve the availability, timeliness and accuracy of data, as well as instigating ongoing progress on social and environmental indicators. It also underpins that this has not been matched by sufficient theoretical research on the determinants of well-being in affluent societies.

It is therefore timely to take stock of progress made in the development of new indicators, but also to debate and decide on the direction of future work, for its relevance to policy making and integration in decision-making processes, in the light of the wide understanding of well-being contained in this book. The European Parliament has suggested the devel-opment of 'a tiered strategy for the beyond GDP approach that would show how to pragmatically implement the new approach in day-to-day political work' (EP 2011); think tanks are arguing for the necessity of a more integrated approach of social justice and climate change (Degryse and Pochet 2009), and civil society organizations call for democratic debates on 'What is wealth today?'[3] Issues concerning *how* policy makers can move more visibly beyond GDP are coming to the centre stage. While much progress has been made by experts and statisticians, and new com-mitments were made at the UN's Rio+20 conference to advance the international debate on a system of environmental economic accounts, it is clear that the discussions of well-being should move out of specialized circles and enter the public arena. As argued in several of the contributions to this book, participation generates trust, which is a prerequisite for the enhancement of well-being.

In this chapter, I will argue that the EU has substantial and long-term interests in these developments. This is not only because of its commitment to the 'GDP and beyond' discussions, but also because 'promoting well-being' is an objective of the Union.[4] It is also the key to its largest current interlinked challenges of growth and democracy. Indeed, the questions regarding how to relaunch economic growth in Europe after the crisis and how to overcome the lack of democratic support for the EU are linked and are both crucial for the smooth continuation of European integration. The perspective opened by Antonovsky's (1987) research on the sense of coherence upheld by the needs for comprehensibility, manageability and meaningfulness of life, as theorized by Timo Hämäläinen (this volume, Chapter 2) and a number of the multidisciplinary inputs in this volume, opens new avenues to direct European policies to invest in well-being as a productive factor, either in a utilitarian perspective, to more efficiently fulfil the superior needs of an educated and ambitious society, or in an Aristotelian perspective, to pursue a meaningful existence. This nevertheless requires a slight change of focus (to effectively make social and ecological sustainability the ultimate goal of all relevant policies) and of process (to develop participative governance to foster social relationships, trust and sense of coherence). The European Union is a challenging place to test and promote this approach.

THE ROLE OF THE EUROPEAN UNION

'Well-being' has been an explicit objective of the Union since the Treaty of Lisbon signed in Portugal in December 2007. Under various denominations, one of the objectives of the EU has, from treaty to treaty, increasingly been focused on balancing economic development with social and environmental sustainability: 'improving the quality of life of its citizens' was added as an objective to the Treaty of Maastricht (1992) and 'sustainable development, high levels of employment and economic and social cohesion' to the Treaty of Amsterdam (1997). The concern for well-being has therefore existed for a while and, as demonstrated by the range of initiatives mentioned in the second paragraph of this chapter, EU policy makers have already integrated determinants of well-being into individual policies. At a meta level, strategies for environmental sustainability including climate change as well as health, consumers, education and social framework initiatives have been creating a process of change towards innovative policies and participative processes for over a decade. However, formally, the means to promote the well-being of people at the EU level, both in secondary legislation and in policy practice, are limited.

Most of the policies concerned (social, education, health, environment) are 'shared competences', which means that Member States retain the main responsibility and EU action is conditional upon proven added value, in line with subsidiarity and proportionality[5] requirements. In brief, the EU can be a catalyst for change in these fields and can steer, support and accompany reform processes, but it does not have much of a say in policy instruments like binding legislation or fiscal policy measures which can effectively create change.

Despite the strong interest shown by a number of Member States and regions of Europe in adapting their policies to changing needs, the economic crisis has unfortunately put the concern for well-being lower on the priority list of decision makers who have recently had to focus on macroeconomic emergencies. Also, whilst a limited interpretation of the role of the EU in the relevant fields may have been sufficient in the past, it is no longer so. Indeed, in the aftermath of the economic crisis, contested cooperation between the EU and its Member States on welfare and growth could be the Achilles heel of Europe's capacity to recreate the conditions for its future prosperity.

GROWTH FOR WELL-BEING IN EU POLICY

Economic growth matters for well-being, 'but only up to a certain level, which varies from society to society' (Seaford, this volume, Chapter 8). The 'Easterlin paradox' (Easterlin 1974), complemented by the message of the former dean of Harvard University (Bok 2010) that 'Prosperity does not necessarily bring happiness as economic growth has gone hand in hand with mental and behavioural disorders, family breakdown, social exclusion, diminished social trust', is evidenced by the contributions in this volume. This message is starting to be understood by policy makers.

Economic growth is no doubt necessary, as we are experiencing the effects of a major economic downturn, but equally happiness is a factor of prosperity. Indeed, as the chapters of this book suggest, happiness makes people more productive (Flint-Taylor and Cooper, this volume, Chapter 9), less costly to public services (Eriksson and Lindström, this volume, Chapter 3) and more reasonable (Basu et al., this volume, Chapter 7). Although a healthy economy is by no means the only shared determinant of well-being, the economic crisis has highlighted the interdependence of national economies, which, in turn, has put pressure on the EU to find ways to restore growth. The questions are: What type of growth? How can we enter the virtuous circle of happiness that produces growth? And can environmental and social sustainability be a competitive factor for European economies?

In his September 2009 political guidelines, the president of the European Commission (Barroso 2009) announced a change in the growth strategy which had been pursued in the last decade: 'This is not the time for business as usual or for routine – what we need is a transformational agenda.' This position was based on his analysis of the long-term changing social realities that were taking place in European societies, on the disappointing results of the Lisbon Strategy for growth and jobs (2000–2010) and on the need to overcome the financial mess which had generated the crisis in the first place.

What do people need to be happy? Convinced that the incremental adaptations of the existing welfare systems were neither adequately responding to new social risks, nor sustainable, the European Commission commissioned an assessment of the new social trends and realities in Europe (Liddle and Lerais 2007). The outcomes revealed a range of often paradoxical findings, summarized in the following paragraphs.[6]

There has been a remarkable increase in life expectancy in the last century (from 43.5 years in 1900 to 75.5 in 2000 and an expected 82 in 2050); we have experienced 60 years of relative peace, medical science has made significant progress and we have better living and working conditions than ever before. But we tend to concentrate on the downside in terms of retirement expenditure, sustainability of welfare systems and the risk of a generation divide in terms of sharing the financial implications of ageing.

There have been dramatic improvements in educational levels, but one-fifth of schoolchildren do not reach basic standards of literacy and numeracy. Six million young people leave school without any qualifications, and most young people including those with secondary and tertiary schooling find it difficult to access the labour market. Similarly, the proportion of women finishing tertiary education has significantly increased in the last two decades, but this is not fully reflected in the labour market or in women's position in economic and political decision making. The gender pay gap is still 17 per cent on average, gender stereotypes persist and women are too often compelled to choose between family and work.

Declining birth rates could reflect choice in an affluent society to have fewer and better-educated children, but surveys reveal that this choice is constrained by a complex combination of factors (uneven sharing of parenting responsibilities, suboptimal child care facilities, the housing situation and family-unfriendly work practices) which do not reflect the expressed desire for maternity or paternity.

Changing family patterns bring more freedom to individuals, but marital break-ups, single parenthood and the weakening bonds of the extended family create tension in terms of work–life balance and caring responsibilities.

In terms of the labour market, in particular where the knowledge economy has started to replace hard working conditions in industry and services, the workforce has had to cope with an increase in the pace of change, be it for acquiring new skills, adjusting to new business models or adapting to shifting consumer preferences. Working patterns and working conditions have become more diverse and irregular, with more flexible forms of contracts, the spread of part-time working, greater mobility and more changes throughout a lifetime between different jobs and between periods of employment and non-employment. This resonates with the analysis of Flint-Taylor and Cooper (this volume, Chapter 9) on addressing new needs in organizations.

Differences in income and opportunities are widespread across regions, and between rural and urban areas, as well as within and between Member States. Almost one in four people in Europe are threatened with poverty or social deprivation. The incidence of child poverty remains high, and is rising in several Member States, with higher risks of exclusion and poverty later in life.

There is a trend towards the individualization of values and an atomization of culture – a focus on the individual and the consumer rather than on society as a whole (see Hämäläinen, this volume, Chapter 2, on selfishness, 'short-termism' and path-dependence, and Bartolini, this volume, Chapter 6, on consumerism), and new issues of tolerance and respect for others ('the Reasonable Person Model', in Basu et al., this volume, Chapter 7). Yet new forms of solidarity are emerging, including through new leisure and cultural activities.

Globalization has increased people's exposure to diversity, stimulating curiosity and enriching societies. But it has prompted anxieties about cultural diversity and intercultural dialogue, as well as about Europe's capacity to assert its common values. In this context, migration is testing the effectiveness of Member States' integration strategies and creates new forms of exclusion, though it can be beneficial for both migrants and the receiving countries.

The importance attached to traditional forms of political participation is decreasing, and trust in public institutions is often low. Yet there is a quest for new, more flexible forms of civic participation and a desire to shape the future. The IT revolution and new communication tools have spawned new forms of dialogue and civic participation. But there is evidence of a 'digital gap', with low-educated, older and economically inactive citizens having difficulty in making use of these new technologies.

The production and consumption patterns that underlie the affluence enjoyed in many parts of Europe have implications, including on climate change and increased pressures on natural resources. Reversing these negative impacts of current lifestyles will mean adjusting behaviour and will have significant social impacts.

The raft of changes linked to globalization, ageing and the shift to a knowledge-based society is generating a feeling of insecurity and anxiety among citizens. Poll results suggest that present generations believe their children will experience a significant reduction in quality of life compared to what they have experienced. The economic and financial crisis compounds this upheaval. In this context, new social problems are emerging, such as stress and depression, obesity, environment-related diseases and lack of exercise. These add to traditional problems of social isolation, mental illness, drug and alcohol abuse, criminality and insecurity.

The policy answer to these challenges suggested by the Commission has been to encourage Member States to engage in a new 'life chances social vision' for Europe based on creating opportunities for people but also guaranteeing access to essential services and providing solidarity with the most deprived. This was supported by a social investment strategy to 'tap Europe's full human potential, broaden life chances for all' and 'advance well-being and quality of life in Europe' (EC 2008). The 'renewed social agenda' adopted by the Commission in July 2008 translated this new vision into a commitment to use EU social instruments (directives, social dialogue, funding, partnership and screening of policies) to develop the 'opportunities, access and solidarity' approach. The seven priority areas identified (children and youth; more and better jobs, and new skills; mobility; longer and healthier lives; combating poverty and social exclusion; fighting discrimination and promoting gender equality; opportunities, access and solidarity on the global scene) resonate positively with the holistic framework suggested in this volume, which links well-being to social and mental needs, the workplace and social and physical environments. The renewed social agenda has influenced policy making by strengthening the coordination between different policy areas (health, employment, education and culture, research) and pushing some new issues for the empowerment of citizens (early childhood education and care (EC 2011a), social innovation (EC 2011b), corporate social responsibility, a 'holistic' approach to health, consumers and food policy for 'healthier, safer and more confident citizens'). The approach of the renewed social agenda which has now been reformulated in the Social Investment package (EC 2013a) has also contributed to changing the mindset of policy makers: more attention has been given to answering new needs, to investing in people's capabilities and to promoting social inclusion. From September

2008 the financial crisis turned political attention away from the renewed social agenda, but a year later a new EU growth strategy, Europe 2020, revived the 'opportunities access and solidarity' agenda within the new framework of 'smart, sustainable and inclusive growth'.

THE EUROPE 2020 STRATEGY FOR SMART, SUSTAINABLE AND INCLUSIVE GROWTH

The financial crisis has brought proof of the interdependence of European economies, but it has also created a lasting burden of debt likely to put new pressures on social cohesion and environmental progress. It was widely recognized that 'business as usual would lead to a gradual decline of Europe'.[7] After dealing with bad banks, correcting the financial markets and trying to re-establish financial stability with increased policy coordination, the priority has been to develop longer-term policy instruments to create jobs, better lives and new sources of growth to restore the competitiveness of European economies.

Implicitly, the 'smart' (developing an economy based on knowledge and innovation), 'inclusive' (fostering a high-employment economy delivering social and territorial cohesion) and 'sustainable' (promoting a more resource-efficient, environment-friendly and competitive economy) agenda, which was agreed by the European Council for 2010–20, is betting on the specific strength of European economies: their welfare and environment policies. This has set the scene for a 'socially and environmentally sustainable' economic strategy based on knowledge and innovation as the way to re-establish a competitive economy.

Both the relative affluence of European societies and the consequences of the financial and economic crisis have thus boosted the need to transform our definition of growth. In this context, the Europe 2020 strategy is a political recognition that major policy re-engineering of growth and well-being has started with increased attention to social, innovation and environment-friendly policies. The fact that it is a major policy framing document which will guide the policies of 27 states for several years gives a political direction. By fixing precise targets to be reached by 2020,[8] policy makers have announced where we are heading and have made themselves accountable for results expressed in measurable targets.

Employment, the reduction of CO_2 emissions, energy efficiency, the use of alternative energy, education (school dropouts and university graduates) and distributional issues (poverty assessed by material deprivation, by joblessness and on a percentage of median income) are now firmly on the dominant policy framework of the EU and Member States. Although this new strategy is a step forward in highlighting the distribution of material wealth and other social goods (health and education) as well as economic and environmental sustainability as prerequisites for creating growth in well-being, it does not cover all the dimensions of well-being, including some of the more subjective dimensions advocated in this book. The 'GDP and beyond' initiative has been furthering discussions amongst experts on relevant indicators.

BEYOND GDP: REFRAMING WELL-BEING IN THE EU AGENDA AND DEBATES

The EU is now one of the major international actors in the search for measures of progress beyond GDP. The inadequacy of GDP as a measure of human progress was initially brought on the EU agenda by environmental concerns. The Kyoto conference in 1997 set European leadership the task of establishing standards to mitigate climate change, and within the first decade of the new millennium EU political activity on environmental issues increased exponentially, creating a demand for more comprehensive information to support policy decisions in the field. In 2006, the success of the UK's government's Stern Report (Stern 2006) in reviving the public debate on the cost of what is not accounted for in GDP[9] gave a further impetus to bring these issue into the open. This conjunction of events encouraged the European Commission together with the European Parliament, the Club of Rome, the WWF and the OECD to host a major conference to debate 'GDP and beyond' at the end of 2007. The objective was to discuss which indicators were most appropriate to measure well-being and how they could best be integrated into political decision making. There were 650 participants, including government officials, elected politicians, civil society members, think tank members, and people from industry and key institutions such as the World Bank and UNDP, who attended this event, which was furthered by a communication on 'GDP and beyond: measuring progress in a changing world' (EC 2009) in which the European Commission proposed to implement five key actions[10] to improve indicators that better reflect policy and societal concerns.

As mentioned earlier, the Commission announced in the communication its intention to report on the implementation and outcomes of these actions near the end of 2012. In the light of this report which was adopted in August 2013 (EC 2013b), further action will be decided. A lot of progress has been made by the European Statistical System (ESS)[11] to improve data collection, analysis and the production of indicators. A clear sense of purpose and impetus was given to the implementation of the 2009 communication by policy developments: the renewed EU Sustainable Development Strategy (European Council 2006) and the Europe 2020 growth strategy. For the former, Eurostat has published every two years a report making use of 100 sustainable development indicators to monitor progress towards the objectives and targets of the strategy. For the latter, the surveillance mechanism, which is based on the headline targets on employment, education, inequalities and climate change, has very clearly relied on improved information produced by the Statistical Office of the European Union (Eurostat).

The European Statistical System committee adopted a report (of the so-called 'sponsorship group') on 'Measuring progress, well-being and sustainable development' in November 2011. It was produced as a result of a cooperative project co-chaired by Eurostat and the French national statistical office (INSEE) and led by Member States' high-level representatives working together, with the aim to adapt the official statistical systems to be better equipped to meet changing needs. It establishes a plan for improving European statistics to implement the 12 recommendations of the Stiglitz–Sen–Fitoussi Commission report and those of the 'GDP and beyond' communication. These actions cover three priority areas:

1. strengthening the household perspective and distributional aspects of income, consumption and wealth within the household (including broadening income measurement to non-market domestic activities and leisure time);
2. multidimensional measures of quality of life (including the development of synthetic indicators which combine different variables that are strongly correlated);
3. environmental sustainability (including landscape and biodiversity indicators and developing environmental accounts in the area of water and waste).

Furthermore, such European research projects as 'BRAINPOoL' (Bringing alternative indicators into policy) and 'E-Frame' (European framework for measuring progress) are running research in parallel to developments on measurement and policy.

The debate on sustainable development and well-being has also been kept alive by international events such as the Rio+20 UN conference in June 2012 on the environment, and the fourth OECD World Forum on 'Statistics, Knowledge and Policy' in New Delhi in October 2012.

The reporting exercise of 2013 came at the right time to bring the discussion from the measurement to the political level. A major conference in Amsterdam in February 2014 will help in shaping future directions and engaging in a 'learning process' with citizens. This should involve the presentation of new EU data, survey and analytical developments as national statistical offices improve their convergence, and discussions on indicators for social and environmental sustainability as well as future developments including the theories which uphold well-being approaches and policies. This could (and actually does already) happen at local and national levels. There are also major reasons for bringing the issue of well-being to the front of the European Union agenda.

The first is that, in the course of the last few years, measuring progress-related issues has become a movement, involving statistical offices but also local, regional and national actors in the EU. Sets of indicators aimed at representing and monitoring well-being have been developed and/or are being discussed at national level: in the Netherlands (the Netherlands sustainability monitor), in Germany (the German system of social indicators and the German system of sustainable development indicators) and in the UK (the Measuring National Well-being Measurement Programme, which has been very high-profile and includes the addition of direct measures of experienced well-being – i.e. subjective well-being indicators – to the UK's largest national survey). Similar efforts are in progress in Hungary (as set out in the Hungarian Statistics Office report 'Establishing indicators for measuring social progress'). In addition, regional and local initiatives are burgeoning everywhere in Europe. They involve local authorities, NGOs, and grassroots groups which have created community-led responses to climate change, shrinking energy supplies, and social solidarity as well as new ways of building resilience and happiness.[12] This wealth of experiences should be made visible, discussed and exchanged. Its contribution to the design policies that create well-being would be enhanced by political recognition and discussions at the highest level. Moreover, such a debate would be greatly beneficial to EU structural policies, which are being revisited to help overcome the crisis and within the next EU budgetary exercise have started building on mutual exchange and use of indicators.

The second reason is about growth and competitiveness. The crisis imposes large constraints on public budgets and on people; hence there is a need to make the most efficient use of scarce financial resources while maintaining what have been shown to be the strengths of Europe in time of financial crises: its internal market, its social resilience,[13] its multicultural education and research, its migration and its so-called 'green and white economy', that is, its health and care services and eco-friendly industry. Opening up the dialogue on indicators and on the holistic understanding of well-being argued in this book could provide better guidance to policy makers and European citizens. The policy frameworks emphasizing outdated well-being challenges tend to give the wrong signals and lead to the wrong decisions and to waste. The 'salutogenic approach' (Eriksson and Lindström, this volume, Chapter 3), for instance, upholds that a society where people can be in control of their life and develop a sense of coherence is more likely to be sustainably healthy and reduce the costs of welfare policies. The same goes for human resources management in corporations, as illustrated by Flint-Taylor and Cooper (this volume, Chapter 9). Further along this road, the challenging paradox underlined by Bartolini (this volume, Chapter 6) directly points to some of the destructive effects on well-being of certain forms of consumption that are measured positively in GDP.

The third reason concerns democracy. The term 'democracy' refers here to the empowerment of people to take part in decisions which affect them, which is, as illustrated by O'Hara and Lyon (this volume, Chapter 4), Helliwell (this volume, Chapter 5) and Flint-Taylor and Cooper (this volume, Chapter 9), a major determinant of well-being. It refers also to the specific challenge which the European Union is facing to establish a positive connection with its citizens. Citizens are increasingly disillusioned with the EU's capacity to make a difference in addressing their concerns about social conditions, the economic situation and the environment. The low voter turnout at the European elections, the rejection of EU treaties, and the rise of populist movements which advocate political and economic protectionism are seen by many as evidence of this disenchantment with policy responses to current conditions. The financial crisis and the concentration on macroeconomic issues have also increased the perception that European policies are not primarily concerned with improving citizens' lives. Building a narrative that resonates with citizens' ideas concerning the quality of their and their children's lives is therefore an important consideration if European integration is to be taken further.

CONCLUSION: WHAT THE EU CAN CONTRIBUTE

While it has only limited normative competences in the policy fields most directly concerned (health, education, social and environment policies), the EU contribution to influencing well-being has to be exerted at multiple levels (see Mulgan, this volume, Chapter 11): at the meta level (maintenance of peace, the rule of law, security, the deepening of democracy and, in the case of the EU setting up macroeconomic parameters, regulating the single market and agreeing rules in major policy fields) and at the granular level (e.g. by mobilizing European instruments, including the structural funds to promote social innovation, youth initiatives and policies aimed at the empowerment of actors). As to the second level (policies), the most effective interventions take place at national or local or even workplace level, but, in some important policy fields, political recognition and legal and/or financial support by the EU can stimulate and complement actions at other levels. Gender equality is an example of an issue for which, in many Member States, EU leverage has been decisive despite initially limited competences (Hubert 1998). Environmental policy is another telling example. Also let's remember that pursuing well-being involves trade-offs and a major change of perspective, which can be shifted by spreading evidence that a more efficient, just and sustainable type of prosperity is within our reach.

Where EU action is most needed is to develop the political take-up that will allow well-being to 'count' in policy making. The conference of 2007 and the 'GDP and beyond' communication of 2009 have mobilized the European statistical community on the creation of new data and new indicators. Much progress has been made by statisticians to improve the timeliness and accuracy of data and analytical instruments for measuring the distributional and environmental aspects of growth. The aim is to provide access to knowledge about the quality of the air we breathe, the water we drink, the costs of energy and how to save it, the distribution of income within households, how people spend their time, their expectations and the degrees of satisfaction with their lives. These efforts are still ongoing. A more favourable frame of reference for economic, social and environmental growth has been created with the Europe 2020 strategy. The governance process to monitor macroeconomic (and some social and environmental) dynamics is proactively aiming at reaching targets beyond the market value of goods and services produced. The stocktaking exercise of 2013 will at some stage result in a new road map for actions to adapt to a fast-changing context. The financial and economic crisis has reshuffled the cards, accelerated change and increased complexity. 'Business as usual would lead to a gradual decline of Europe', said the president of the European Commission.[14] The new holistic approach proposed in this book suggests the aim of creating an environment where 'coherent' citizens can participate in the long-term (as opposed to 'short-termist'), innovative (as opposed to path-dependent) and empathic (as opposed to selfish) choices that shape their lives and the societies we live in (see Hämäläinen, this volume, Chapter 2). This requires, as a first step, agreement on clear and widely shared indicators to steer policy and to provide tools for citizens to be in control and develop fulfilling lives.

NOTES

*   The author writes here in her personal capacity. Views expressed do not necessary reflect the position of the European Commission.

1.   The European Quality of Life Survey, which has been conducted by the European Foundation for Working and Living Conditions (EUROFOUND) since 2003, started its third wave in 2012.

2.   Europe 2020 is the EU's strategy to promote smart, sustainable and inclusive growth for the period 2010–20. Concretely, the Union has set five objectives – on employment, innovation, education, social inclusion and climate/energy – to be reached by 2020. Each member state has adopted its own national targets in each of these areas. An annual monitoring process underpins the strategy.

3.   This debate was organized by the Forum pour d'Autres Indicateurs de Richesse (FAIR), a network of civil society organizations working on wealth indicators.

4.   The objectives of the European Union are 'to promote peace, its values and the well-being of its people' (TEU art. 3.1) and to work towards 'sustainable development, full employment, social progress and the quality of the environment' (TEU art. 3.3).

5.   The principles of subsidiarity and proportionality are set out in article 5 of the Treaty of the European Union to regulate the exercise of powers by the EU. Subsidiarity is the idea that a central authority should only perform those tasks which cannot be performed effectively at a more immediate or local level, and according to the principle of proportionality the content and form of the action must be in keeping with the aim pursued.

6.   These changes are further documented in an analysis of the results of the EU Surveys on Income and Living Conditions by Professors Atkinson and Marlier (2010).

7.   J.M. Barroso, presenting the Europe 2020 strategy to the European Parliament.

8.   http://ec.europa.eu/europe2020/europe-2020-in-a-nutshell/targets/index_en.htm.

9.   The report predicted that the overall costs of climate change would be equivalent to losing at least 5 per cent of global GDP each year, now and for ever. Including a wider range of risks and impacts could increase the loss to 20 per cent of GDP or more.

10.   The five key actions are: to complement GDP with highly aggregated environmental and social indicators; to provide near-real-time information for decision making; to report more accurately on distribution and inequalities; to develop a European Sustainable Development Scoreboard; and to extend national accounts to environmental and social issues.

11.   The ESS is the partnership between the Community statistical authority, which is the Commission (Eurostat), and the national statistical institutes (NSIs) and other national authorities responsible in each member state for the development, production and dissemination of European statistics. This partnership also includes the EEA and EFTA countries.

12.   For example, 'Action for Happiness', founded by well-being expert Richard Layard, with Geoff Mulgan and Anthony Seldon, is a UK-based group with an international membership, which is focused on local, community-led ways of creating happiness. See also http://www.transitionnetwork.org/.

13.   To illustrate: social investment strategies have produced a return on investment; old age poverty is 8 per cent in the EU as opposed to 22.4 per cent in the US; between 2000 and 2011 the employment rate among 15- to 64-year-olds increased in Europe by 2 per cent while declining in the US by 7 per cent and in China by 3 per cent; health care expenditure represents less than 10 per cent of GDP in the EU as an average and 17.5 per cent of US GDP, while life expectancy is superior in the EU (79.4 against 78.3).

14.   J.M. Barroso, presenting the Europe 2020 strategy to the European Parliament.

REFERENCES

Antonovsky, A. (1987), *Unraveling the Mystery of Health: How People Manage Stress and Stay Well*, San Francisco, CA: Jossey-Bass.

Atkinson, A. and E. Marlier (2010), *Income and Living Conditions in Europe*, Luxembourg: Eurostat Statistical Books.

Barroso, José Manuel (2009), 'My vision: political guidelines for the next Commission', European Commission.

Bok, Derek (2010), *The Politics of Happiness: What Government Can Learn from the New Research on Well-being*, Princeton, NJ: Princeton University Press.

Degryse, C. and P. Pochet (2009), 'Changer de paradigme: la justice sociale comme prérequis au développement durable', Working Paper No. 2009:02, ETUI, Brussels.

Easterlin, Richard (1974), 'Does economic growth improve the human lot?', in Paul A. David and Melvin W. Reder, *Nations and Households in Economic Growth: Essays in Honor of Moses Abramovitz*, New York: Academic Press.

EC (European Commission) (2008), 'Renewed social agenda: opportunities, access and solidarity in 21st century Europe', COM(2008) 412.

EC (European Commission) (2009), 'GDP and beyond: measuring progress in a changing world', COM(2009) 433.

EC (European Commission) (2011a), 'Early childhood education and care: providing all our children with the best start for the world of tomorrow', COM(2011) 66.

EC (European Commission) (2011b), 'Empowering people, driving change: social innovation in the European Union', Bureau of European Policy Advisers (BEPA).

EC (European Commission) (2012), 'Taking forward the Strategic Implementation Plan of the European Innovation Partnership on Active and Healthy Ageing', COM(2012) 083.

EC (European Commission) (2013a), 'Towards Social Investment for Growth and Cohesion – including implementing the European Social Fund 2014–2020', COM(2013) 083.

EC (European Commission) (2013b), 'Commission Staff working document: progress on GDP and Beyond actions', SWD(2013) 303 final.

EP (European Parliament) (2011), Report on 'GDP and beyond: measuring progress in a changing world', 2010/2088(INI), rapporteur Anna Rosbach.

European Council (2006), 'Renewed EU Sustainable Development Strategy as adopted by the European Council on 15/16 June 2006'.

Hubert, A. (1998), *L'Europe et les femmes*, Rennes: Editions Apogée.

Liddle, R. and F. Lerais (2007), 'Europe's social reality', European Commission background document, consultation paper from the Bureau of European Policy Advisers.

Stern, Nicholas (2006), 'Stern review on the economics of climate change', commissioned by the UK government.

Stiglitz, J.E., A. Sen and J.-P. Fitoussi (2009), *Report by the Commission on the Measurement of Economic Performance and Social Progress*, available at: www.stiglitz-sen-fitoussi.fr.

13. Policies for well-being and health

Pekka Puska

The general aim of political decision making in any country is or should be to do good to people, i.e. to protect and to promote their well-being. In the process, there are obvious basic needs and services that relate to them: to protect peace (the army), to protect order (the police) and to provide other basic needs of food, accommodation and so on. An important task is also to protect the health of the people from epidemics and diseases.

But with the modern development of societies these basic needs are not enough. People are increasingly interested in decision making related to more immaterial values, especially concerning human well-being and the well-being of the environment. This brings up the question not only about the limits of societal responsibility for citizens' well-being, but also of what well-being is, and how it should be measured – and ultimately promoted. These questions are extensively discussed in several chapters of this book.

Numerous surveys on the question of what people value show that health is usually very high on the list (e.g. Diener and Scollon 2003). But what do we mean by health? Is it lack of diseases or good 'subjective health', well-being or high happiness? This relates to the question: what should be the target of public health work and health policy, and more broadly of societal policies for well-being?

LEVELS OF HEALTH AND WELL-BEING

Traditionally health work has dealt with major diseases: their treatment and prevention. Gradually less severe health problems have received attention, as well as the need to promote 'functional capacity', 'positive health' and good well-being. Happiness has also come into the picture, although in this continuum happiness seems to be farthest from the possibilities of political decision making. Happiness is said to have very strong genetic and intrinsic determinants (Lyubomirsky 2007).

These changing societal needs seem to relate to the changing pattern of public health. In earlier times poor public health outcomes were driven by infectious diseases, high child mortality and low life expectancy. Public health work and public policies have led to a greatly reduced public health burden of infectious diseases, to reduced early mortality and to much improved life expectancy.

Instead, contemporary public health outcomes are much more strongly influenced by some chronic non-communicable diseases (NCDs) – notably cardiovascular diseases, cancer, diabetes and chronic lung diseases. This now is the case not only in the industrialized countries, but also in the developing world. In fact, some 80 per cent of NCD deaths currently occur in the developing world, where much of that mortality is in the working-age population. About half of this NCD mortality is cardiovascular – heart disease and cerebrovascular stroke. In the developing world, the NCD burden has become not only a public health problem, but also a great hindrance for social and economic development (WHO 2011).

Based on scientific understanding of the aetiologies, there has been substantial success in prevention and control of major NCDs in the developed world, for example in my own country, Finland. This has also led to global actions by the World Health Organization (WHO). One culmination of this was the special UN High-level Meeting of the General Assembly on the Prevention and Control of Non-communicable Diseases in New York in September 2011. The political outcome declaration of this high-level meeting urged member states and international organizations to strengthen their work fighting NCDs to produce improved global public health, and in this way to contribute to sustainable social developments in the developing world (United Nations 2011).

In addition to the physical NCDs, increasing attention is also being put on poor mental health as a growing public health problem. Depression especially seems to be growing and making a big contribution to ill health worldwide. This development has led to searches not only for treatment but also for means of mental health promotion.

ENTRY POINTS FOR HEALTH AND WELL-BEING POLICY WORK

When discussing policies for well-being, we should naturally understand what we mean by well-being. It is clearly more than health, even subjective health, as often assessed in health surveys (personal assessment of one's health, in contrast to diseases and their symptoms). And it is clearly not the same as happiness. Since happiness is a mental or emotional state of well-being, well-being as a whole has broader connotation; for example, Gouch et al. (2007) define well-being as 'what people are notionally able to do and to be, and what they have actually been able to do and to be', indicating that well-being is a more appropriate prime topic for policy.

On the other hand, since health in a broad sense is an important component of well-being, policies for health are important. This relates to the question of the entry points for interventions and policy. There are different levels – from diseases to comprehensive well-being.

Diseases as an entry point for policy are naturally always important, since they are the targets for prevention and treatment. In modern societies, health services are expected to treat diseases – in an evidence-based and cost-effective way. Also, since many, if not most, major diseases are largely preventable, health services should contribute to prevention, with its human and economic merits.

However, from a public health point of view diseases are not the most appropriate entry points for policy, although good policies are needed for effective health care.

From a public health point of view, population-based prevention clearly has the greatest potential. It is based on the reduction of major *risk factors* at the level of populations. The risk factors of major NCDs are closely associated with certain behaviours or lifestyles, especially related to tobacco, alcohol, diet and physical activity. Since these risk factors and risk-related behaviours are usually not specific to only one disease, but relate to many diseases, WHO speaks of 'integrated prevention'. It means that, instead of vertical-disease-specific preventive programmes, the interventions and policies target as entry points the common risk-related behaviours in the population, through health promotion programmes and policies. This is much the approach advocated in the UN Political Declaration of the High-level Meeting of the General Assembly on the Prevention and Control of Non-communicable Diseases.

There is little doubt that if policies can influence risk-related lifestyles there will be broad public health benefits, in terms of reduction in several diseases – and not only reduction in diseases, but also improvement of functional capacity and subjective health. This has been shown, for example, by the development in Finland of effective risk reduction policies (Puska et al. 2009).

Much attention has recently been given to *social determinants* as another entry point. This approach was emphasized by the WHO Commission on Social Determinants of Health (WHO 2008). There the emphasis is on 'the causes of the causes', as the chair of the Commission, Sir Michael Marmot, has put it. This approach notes the importance of the conditions in which people grow, play, work, live, and spend their leisure time.

The social determinants approach also puts a lot of emphasis on the role of socio-economic factors and on the major health inequities related to socio-economic differences. It emphasizes the importance of education and poverty reduction, and of attention to disadvantaged groups. A WHO Conference on Social Determinants of Health summarized this approach in its political declaration (CSDH 2008).

Attention to social determinants extends political decision making far beyond traditional health policies. There the drivers of policies are often other than narrowly defined health factors. From the health point of view this calls for 'health in all policies' (Puska 2007) or 'whole-of-government' policies.

The social determinants approach has at least two problems from the health point of view. First, the relationship between the determinants and health outcomes is complicated and may depend on the cultural situation. For example, improving a person's financial situation may not automatically lead to better health. In addition, at the population level there is a general experience that up to a certain level increases in the national economy are related to increased rates of chronic NCDs.

Second, attention to social determinants may divert the attention from evidence-based and effective but unpopular restrictive or regulatory policies on risk factors. Restrictive policies are often unpopular with large segments of the population, not to speak of the opposition of the private sector to many regulation policies. Let's take the example of tobacco. Globally some 6 million people in the world die annually from tobacco (approximately 10 per cent of all deaths). There are evidence-based policies (taxation, smoke-free regulations, and complete prohibition of advertising) that are quite effective even without complementary policies on social determinants of smoking. Obviously, different approaches – both supportive and restrictive, direct public health policies and broad social-determinants-based health promotion – are needed and complement each other.

The next level and possible entry point for policy is the *salutogenic approach* (Eriksson and Lindström, this volume, Chapter 3). This approach does not start from diseases or even their risk factors or determinants of risk factors. This approach addresses the questions of what creates health, rather than looking for the causes of disease. It emphasizes 'generalized resistance resources' that allow people to resist diseases (Antonovsky 1987). This is said to mean the 'process of enabling individuals, groups, organizations and societies to emphasize abilities, resources, capacities, competences, strength and forces in order to create a sense of coherence and thus perceive life as comprehensive, manageable and meaningful' (Eriksson and Lindström, this volume, Chapter 3). While this sounds good, there is long way to go to define precise practical policies resulting from it.

Especially in the Nordic countries, policies for well-being are often linked with '*welfare* policies'. The Nordic welfare state model is usually understood to encompass policies in which the society takes care of its citizens in numerous vulnerable situations, such as ill health, poverty, disability and old age. While this approach clearly also has to do with well-being, it mainly deals with financial issues and service delivery, and not with broader aspects of well-being.

The alternatives presented above on different categories of policies for well-being clearly do not cover the broad spectrum of well-being policies. However, they are all useful and needed and not mutually exclusive. While broad policies for well-being should be searched for and implemented, at the same time obvious risks of diseases and unfavourable life situations should be removed, and inequities in health and well-being should be reduced.

FROM ECONOMIC GROWTH TO SUSTAINABLE WELL-BEING

Let us discuss some further aspects of contemporary policies for well-being.

Financial and economic issues often dominate both public discussions and policies when well-being is the issue. Several chapters in this book discuss the relationship between well-being and economics, which is a complex issue. Certain economic resources are definitely needed, and relative poverty clearly reduces well-being. However, after a certain level, both for individuals and for nations, increases in economic wealth do not lead to substantial improvements in well-being (Seaford, this volume, Chapter 8).

As to public health, we notice that, above certain rather low levels of GNP, public health correlates very little with GNP, that is, the wealth of the nation. Thus, for example, life expectancy, and in broader terms health and well-being, in Costa Rica is as good as in the USA, even if GNP per capita in the US is four times greater than in Costa Rica.

This notion has led to a search for other development indices than GNP to measure and follow the well-being of nations. At the end of the day the objective of public policies should not be economic growth but the good and well-being of people (Bartolini, this volume, Chapter 6). Kofi Annan has said that, 'when planning the future, we must remember that people don't live only for economics; instead, economic development and production must serve people'. Many indices for monitoring the well-being of people have been developed, and it would be a very important step to be able internationally to develop and agree on an index that effectively describes the well-being of nations.

Economic growth is often justified as the means to serve well-being. Strengthened commercial activity, intensive marketing, and the use of energy and natural resources are often seen as important vehicles for economic growth, which is said to be needed to finance services for well-being. But the opposite argument is that this kind of economic growth often leads to problems for health and well-being that call for expensive corrective services that would not be needed with less intensive economic growth. Obviously the challenge for a well-being approach to policy is to combine sustainable economic activity with the improved well-being of people.

This discussion relates also to the issues of globalization, that is, the increasing interaction between nations and increasing global influences on any nation. Globalization is inevitable and leads to many positive consequences. But, as the ILO World Commission on the Social Dimension of Globalization noted, it also leads to negative consequences for humans and environments (ILO 2004). The contemporary epidemic of NCDs in the developing world is clearly very much a consequence of globalization. The Western tobacco industry, food and beverage industry, alcohol industry and others have through extensive marketing, trade agreements and so on helped push Western unhealthy lifestyles to the low- and middle-income countries. 'McDonaldization' or 'Coca-cola-ization' is fattening people all over the world. The Western tobacco industry has moved its marketing machinery to the developing world, where its products are responsible for most of the tobacco-related mortality in the world.

The challenge, as the ILO Commission put it, is that the international community needs to take action to counteract the negative social consequences of globalization. Some similar measures have already been undertaken with regard to climate change. And for public health the Framework Convention on Tobacco Control (WHO 2003) has been a landmark. But much more needs to follow.

WHOSE RESPONSIBILITY?

In the field of health promotion there has been much conceptual development from early health education to modern comprehensive health promotion. Since the Ottawa Charter, much emphasis has been put on the 'ecological approach', that is, on efforts to influence the physical and social environment. The First International Conference on Health Promotion in 1986 in Ottawa shifted attention from 'educating people' to influencing physical and social environments to be conducive for health (WHO 1986). The origins of health problems and the potential for salutogenic support are in the environment. Thus the famous slogan since Ottawa has been:

'Make the healthy choice the easy one.' The role of environment is well emphasized by Basu et al. (this volume, Chapter 7).

This discussion often leads to the debate on the limits and needs for regulation: the 'nanny state' debate. Discussions on regulation usually involve whose responsibility the health-related aspects of people's lifestyles are. The private sector emphasizes people's own responsibility and refers to regulation as the 'nanny state'. Health activists point out that people's lifestyles are to a large extent dependent on social and physical environments – hence amenable to policies. This is especially the situation with children; nobody can realistically say that the responsibility for children's choices should be with the children.

Regulation is often unpopular – not only within industry but also often among parts of the population. These groups usually recommend use of educational or other preventive activities instead of restrictive regulation measures. But the paradox is that the most popular measures are often the most ineffective, while the most effective measures are often the most unpopular. Thus, for example, increases in tobacco or alcohol tax are often unpopular, although they are clearly effective, and furthermore do not cost money – on the contrary up to a certain level they will bring money into the government coffers.

Studies also show that people generally value health and well-being, and would like to behave accordingly. Thus most smokers, including those among the lower socio-economic groups, say that they would like to stop smoking. Most obese people would like to lose weight (Helakorpi et al. 2012). Thus the problem of health promotion – and more broadly of well-being policies – is to help people to do and achieve what they want but often find difficult.

EVIDENCE AND POLICY

An important issue in discussing policies for health and well-being is the question of evidence. It is fashionable to emphasize and ask for evidence-based policies. Obviously policies should be based on hard evidence, for example, on causes of diseases or on obstacles to the well-being of the population. But issues of evidence become very complex when we talk of broad programmes or policies for health and well-being. Narrow evidence from limited perspectives may not be able to address comprehensive needs. Furthermore, societal policies are not justified or decided only by evidence, but by the values and democratic wishes of the people.

This also leads to discussion of the origins of social innovations for well-being and of the leadership of social change processes: top down or bottom up. Many innovations clearly come from scientific discoveries; experts can be the change agents. At the same time it is often the grassroots levels and those who shape popular opinion who lead social innovations for improved well-being.

Deepened democracy, grassroots movements and people's health movements can often be the vehicles for policy changes for improved well-being. At the same time legislation can be very important in stabilizing and helping to maintain the new developments. There are often great expectations that 'technical implementation' of good policies will lead to major changes. However, we can question whether policies pull people or people pull policy. At the end of the day it is a social change process where each continuously influences the other.

A good example is the dramatic change that has taken place with regard to smoking in Western societies, with huge beneficial public health consequences and societal implications. The change from the situation where tobacco and smoking were part of the economy and culture everywhere to the current situation where smoke-free is the norm and smoking is pushed to a marginalized role has been a dramatic societal change over the last few decades.

This change in smoking has clearly been a social change process where the initial change agents were the scientists informing the general public about the dramatic harm of tobacco use, but where tobacco-control legislation has gradually been implemented and strengthened hand in hand with reductions in smoking, people's growing intentions to stop and their changing attitudes.

FINAL COMMENTS

So what are my final comments on policies for well-being? Without doubt, most of the above-mentioned policy approaches are relevant – and not mutually exclusive. At the same time, future policies for well-being in societies should go beyond these. It is most likely that some more profound changes in national policies are needed.

Such changes would mean a greater emphasis on policies that increase social interaction, and social support between people, for giving and receiving (Helliwell, this volume, Chapter 5). This would have implications for planning the physical environments of communities. It would mean more walking outdoors and indoors, which at the same time would increase physical activity – that itself has a strong beneficial impact on both physical and mental health. It is well known that physical activity is a strong means to reduce depression (Kirkwood et al. 2008).

New policies for well-being would also likely mean policies to restrict intensive commercialism, marketing and consumerism (Bartolini, this volume, Chapter 6). This would mean certain restrictive and regulatory policies both nationally and globally, to reduce the harmful social consequences of globalization. Such measures would certainly support sustainable health development in terms of NCD health and have beneficial environmental effects.

But, in addition to regulatory policies to protect people, positive policies are needed to enable people and communities to develop positive initiatives and practices for well-being. New policies for well-being would also mean new arrangements in work life and at worksites (Flint-Taylor and Cooper, this volume, Chapter 9). Such policies would increase flexibility and people's ability to control their own work more.

And finally new policies would mean a deepening of the democratic process (Csikszentmihalyi, this volume, Chapter 10). With this development people themselves, with increased education and informed about scientific evidence, would better be able to influence their life circumstances for better health, well-being and environments.

REFERENCES

Antonovsky, A. (1987), *Unraveling the Mystery of Health: How People Manage Stress and Stay Well*, San Francisco, CA: Jossey-Bass.

Diener, E. and C. Scollon (2003), 'Subjective well-being is desirable, but not the summum bonum', paper presented at the University of Minnesota Interdisciplinary Workshop on Well-being.

Helakorpi, S., A.-L. Holstila, S. Virtanen and A. Uuutela (2012), *Health Behaviour and Health among the Finnish Adult Population, Spring 2011*, THL Report No. 45/2012, Helsinki: National Institute for Health and Welfare (THL).

ILO (2004), *A Fair Globalization: Creating Opportunities for All*, World Commission on the Social Dimension of Globalization, Geneva: ILO.

Kirkwood, T., J. Bond, C. May, I. McKeith and M. Teh (2008), *Mental Capital through Life: Future Challenges*, Foresight Mental Capital and Well-being Project, London: Government Office for Science.

Lyubomirsky, S. (2007), *The How of Happiness: A Practical Guide to Getting the Life You Want*, London: Sphere.

Puska, P. (2007), 'Health in all policies', *European Journal of Public Health*, **17** (4), 328.

Puska, P., E. Vartiainen, T. Laatikainen, P. Jousilahti and M. Paavola (eds) (2009), *The North Karelia Project: From North Karelia to National Action*, Helsinki: Terveyden ja hyvinvoinnin laitos.

United Nations (2011), Political Declaration of the High-level Meeting of the General Assembly on the Prevention and Control of Non-communicable Diseases, United Nations General Assembly, available at: http://www.un.org/ga/search/view_doc.asp?symbol=A/66/L.1.

WHO (World Health Organization) (1986), *Ottawa Charter for Health Promotion*, Geneva: WHO.
WHO (World Health Organization) (2003), *WHO Framework Convention on Tobacco Control*, Geneva: WHO.
WHO (World Health Organization) (2008), *Closing the Gap in a Generation: Health Equity through Action on the Social Determinants of Health*, final report, Geneva: World Health Organization, available at: http://whqlibdoc.who.int/publications/2008/9789241563703_eng.pdf (accessed 22 March 2009).
WHO (World Health Organization) (2011), *Global Status Report on Noncommunicable Diseases 2010*, Geneva: WHO.

14. Practical models for well-being-oriented policy

Juliet Michaelson*

INTRODUCTION

The 'how' of policy delivery is as important as – or even trumps – the 'what' of policy initiatives. This is what John Helliwell contends in his contribution to this volume (Helliwell, this volume, Chapter 5). While 'trumping' is a bold claim, many of this book's chapters have emphasized the importance of *the way things are done* in promoting, for example, coherence, relatedness, meaning, reasonableness, positive challenge and therefore, ultimately, well-being (see Hämäläinen, this volume, Chapter 2; Eriksson and Lindström, this volume, Chapter 3; Basu et al., this volume, Chapter 7; Flint-Taylor and Cooper, this volume, Chapter 9).

This does not mean downplaying the importance of the 'what'. This volume's contributions also highlight evidence that decisions made within areas such as macroeconomic policy, urban planning and advertising regulations are likely to have impacts on population well-being (see Helliwell, this volume, Chapter 5; Bartolini, this volume, Chapter 6; Basu et al., this volume, Chapter 7; Seaford, this volume, Chapter 8). Policy makers should pay serious attention to this and to similar evidence from the field of well-being research. Increasingly, summaries of this evidence are being produced specifically for a policy audience (for example, Dolan et al. 2006; Diener et al. 2009; Stoll et al. 2012). As Geoff Mulgan argues, such evidence does not guarantee positive impacts of any particular policy initiative that it inspires (Mulgan, this volume, Chapter 11). But considered policy making informed by this evidence is more likely to succeed in improving human well-being – that is, enabling people to experience their lives as going well – than policy making carried out in ignorance of it.

Much of this 'what' evidence is produced by researchers working within 'well-being economics', and is therefore of a form familiar to policy making within a classical economic paradigm: for example, comparing the relative impacts of inflation and unemployment on well-being (Blanchflower 2007). Moving outside these familiar forms by being asked to think about the 'how' of policy may seem more daunting to decision makers used only to thinking about 'hard outcomes'. In particular, problem solving about the 'how' makes explicit the need to rely less on formal decision criteria (precise sets of rules, such as those used in conducting cost–benefit analyses) and more on heuristics – 'experienced-based techniques' which allow us to 'dynamically adjust and learn rules of thumb' (Marks 2010).

In this chapter I introduce the dynamic model of well-being, which I argue can help both the 'what' and the 'how' of policy making oriented towards promoting well-being. The model draws together a large number of theoretical approaches to, and empirical evidence about, well-being. It was developed by colleagues at the new economics foundation (nef), a politically independent think tank based in London which works on new forms of economics and public policy that can deliver social justice, environmental sustainability and human well-being. Our position as an intermediary between academic researchers and policy makers creates an impetus for us to create models which, while rigorously based on the evidence, can be turned to practical use in the deeply pragmatic business of policy making. This chapter aims to illustrate how we set out to achieve this, by exploring our dynamic model of well-being and its links, first, to our work on co-production and, second, to our well-being communication tool, the Five Ways to Well-being.

THE ORIGIN OF THE DYNAMIC MODEL OF WELL-BEING

We first developed the dynamic model of well-being in a piece of work for the UK Foresight Programme. Foresight sits within the UK Government Office for Science with the aim of helping the government 'think systematically about the future', using scientific evidence and futures analysis. Its major projects are in-depth, two-year studies which compile a 'comprehensive evidence base on major issues looking 20–80 years into the future'.[1] The project review that was published in 2008 had as its topic 'mental capital and well-being', collecting evidence in five broad areas from over 400 leading experts and stakeholders (with a Science Co-ordination Team led by Cary Cooper, a contributor to this volume).

The second phase of the project involved analysis of policy options in response to the evidence gathered in the first phase, for which nef was asked to consider approaches to measuring well-being and their utility for policy making (Thompson and Marks 2008). In the course of this task we had to deal with the fact that, in order to measure something, it is necessary first to define the concept which you aim to measure (this, of course, is one of the key principles which motivated the production of this volume, as explained in Chapter 1). Creating the dynamic model was an attempt to do this by presenting a way of conceptualizing well-being. But the model does more than just define a concept, because it also provides a way of grouping the wealth of empirical evidence from different sources about well-being into four clear, memorable domains. The approach it encapsulates builds on our conviction that subjective measures of well-being present a robust and meaningful way of understanding humans' experiences of their lives (Centre for Well-being 2011; Michaelson et al., forthcoming). Our intention, therefore, is that the model is simple enough to be accessed by policy makers at a moment's recall, to call up an overview of the well-being evidence at a far more intuitive level than referencing dense literature reviews.

Our starting point for creating the model was the high-profile *Review of Research on the Influences on Personal Well-being and Application to Policy Making* for the UK Department for Environment, Food and Rural Affairs, carried out in 2006 by Paul Dolan, Tessa Peasgood and Matthew White. It outlined five different conceptual approaches to defining well-being, each of them linked to different measurement approaches (Dolan et al. 2006; Centre for Well-being 2011). These are:

- *Preference satisfaction*: the approach taken by classical economics which identifies well-being with individuals getting what they want, typically measured in terms of their income, as a proxy for what will enable them to best satisfy their preferences.
- *Objective lists*: approaches which specify sets of objective conditions which must be met in order to produce well-being. These often focus on basic material needs but may also include concepts such as freedom.
- *Functioning accounts* (these are called 'flourishing accounts' by Dolan et al., but we reserve 'flourishing' for a different use, explained below): these draw on the *eudaimonic* approach to well-being, traced back to an Aristotelian focus on what is part of 'living well', which in contemporary accounts is operationalized with reference to psychological concepts such as experiencing meaning, engagement and strong social relationships.
- *Hedonic accounts*: these focus on emotions and feelings – with well-being defined as the right balance of positive to negative feelings, usually measured in terms of feelings during a recent period.
- *Evaluative accounts*: this approach is closely identified with the measurement approach which uses individuals' assessments of how their life is going overall, or of particular aspects of their life, the most well-known example being a question about satisfaction with life overall.

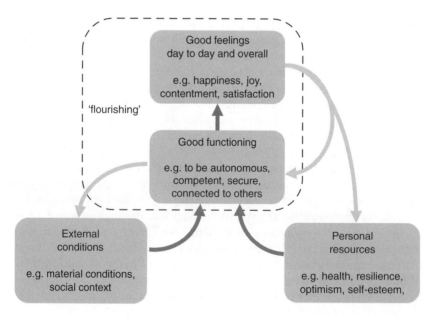

Source: Adapted from Thompson and Mark (2008); Centre for Well-being (2011).

Figure 14.1   The dynamic model of well-being

These different accounts have tended to be viewed as conflicting, and
certainly many of the proponents of specific accounts see themselves as
rectifying perceived deficiencies of others. Our approach, however, was
deliberately integrative. We found that asking a question about how the
different accounts describe elements which each contribute to an individual's well-being produced a model of a whole system with distinct elements
influencing each other. This model was used by the final Foresight Project
report to describe well-being as a 'dynamic process'.

The model is shown in Figure 14.1. It describes various different aspects
of well-being acting together, in a system influenced by key feedback
loops. The model describes a well-being process starting from two key
sets of factors: 'external conditions' (bottom left box of Figure 14.1) and
'personal resources' (bottom right). These together influence the degree of
'good functioning' (middle) – that is, positive interactions with the world –
which an individual experiences, which in turn influences the feelings the
person experiences and his or her evaluations of life overall (top). The
feedback loops between these elements work together to create a dynamic
system.

While the model as a whole describes a holistic dynamic process through which well-being arises, we identify the domains of positive feelings and evaluations, and of good functioning, as together constituting well-being. When these domains are positive, a person can be considered to be *flourishing*. We argue that policy makers, by measuring flourishing alongside measures of external conditions and personal resources, will be able to understand the relationships between them and therefore identify the scope for policy action to enhance well-being (Michaelson et al., forthcoming).

As I describe further the different elements of the model, I will link them to the various accounts of well-being given by contributors to this volume, to illustrate how the model can be used as an integrative tool to bring together different conceptual approaches to well-being.

THE ELEMENTS OF THE DYNAMIC MODEL

External Conditions

A large proportion of the 'well-being economics' research that is carried out by economists and social scientists (using subjective measures of well-being within large-scale survey data) contributes evidence to the importance of external conditions for well-being. Recent summaries of this evidence include MacKerron (2011) and Stoll et al. (2012). External conditions include those factors in an individual's life that are external, but proximal to the individual, as well as more distal conditions.

The proximal conditions are material and social factors including: the factors highlighted by Seaford (this volume, Chapter 8) such as income and employment status; other material factors such as housing conditions; and proximal social factors such as marital or long-term relationship status. Examples of more distal external conditions in the evidence base are the local deprivation and unemployment rates, air pollution and, as highlighted in contributions by Bartolini (this volume, Chapter 6) and Basu et al. (this volume, Chapter 7), the walkability of urban environments. Social factors are also a crucial element of distal external conditions, with aspects of the social context such as average levels of membership in organizations and social trust having effects distinguishable from an individual's own membership and trust levels, as argued in contributions in this volume by Helliwell (this volume, Chapter 5) and Bartolini (this volume, Chapter 6) (see also Helliwell and Putnam 2004).[2]

External conditions, understood in this way, are therefore closely related to the objective list accounts identified by Dolan et al. (2006).

Personal Resources

The set of personal resources which the model highlights relates to assets which are the more inherent aspects within individuals themselves. These cover both the physical, particularly physical health, and a number of personality factors – character traits, thinking styles and so on. Physical health is well documented within well-being economics as associated with well-being, with evidence that the direction of causation runs both ways (physical health is both a contributor to and an outcome of well-being – see Diener and Chan 2011 and Stoll et al. 2012). Personality factors and cognitive traits are not always mentioned in discussions of 'well-being economics', because they are less readily measured at population level, and because they are perceived to be relatively fixed and therefore less amenable to policy intervention. But, while these characteristics are more stable than the somewhat context-depending functioning behaviours (see below), and have a strong genetic component, they can be amenable to change. Thus they have been of particular interest to positive psychologists, who aim to understand what leads to good mental health and well-being, in contrast with the focus, in the majority of the profession, on understanding mental illness: hence their focus, in thinking about the contributors to well-being, on concepts such as learned optimism as a cognitive explanatory style – 'a way of understanding how we construct our understanding of the world',[3] as well on people's individual ('character') strengths (Seligman 2002). Diener et al. (1999) call these 'traits and cognitive dispositions associated with subjective well-being', and note that they also include self-esteem, at least in individualist cultures which do not take the approach of valuing 'the group above the individual'. In fact, a large range of personality factors are well established as being associated with subjective well-being (DeNeve and Cooper 1998; Diener et al. 1999).

It is worth pausing here to examine why I have mentioned physical health but not mental health in the discussion of personal resources. Psychological health has been shown to be strongly related to well-being, with a high likelihood that those experiencing mental disorders will also experience low well-being (Diener and Seligman 2004). On the one hand, this is unsurprising, with a high degree of overlap between the concepts of high well-being and good psychological health, although there is disagreement on the extent of this overlap. Keyes (2002) argues that the concepts should be treated separately, presenting empirical evidence that suggests the presence of two distinct dimensions: one running from low to high mental *health* (that is, positive mental functioning), which he calls languishing to flourishing; and the other going between the presence and absence of mental *illness* (see also Eriksson and Lindström, this volume, Chapter 3). Others present good psychological health and high well-being as broadly synonymous, for example Huppert (2009), who adapts a general epidemiological model (Rose 1992) to propose a model which conceptualizes the population on a single spectrum going from mental disorders at one end, through languishing, to moderate mental health and finally to flourishing (i.e. high well-being, good mental health) at the other. This is closer to the approach taken by our dynamic model, which by not explicitly mentioning psychological health suggests that it largely overlaps with the overall well-being concept which the model describes. However, if it was useful to make a distinction between these concepts in a particular policy context, for example in relation to people experiencing chronic mental illness, psychological health could be explicitly highlighted within the personal resources element.

Good Functioning

The element in the central box of the dynamic model (Figure 14.1) is good functioning. This concept emerges from the eudaimonic approach to well-being, focusing on how people interact with the world around them (introduced earlier as a category in the Dolan et al. 2006 review). It is often described as a concern with 'a life well lived'. Some psychologists have focused on a single aspect of eudaimonia, perhaps most famously Csikszentmihalyi in his work on the concept of 'flow' – the sense of complete absorption that comes from pursuing an activity which is rewarding in itself (see e.g. Nakamura and Csikszentmihalyi 2002). But those psychologists who have offered explicit frameworks to understand good functioning tend to agree that it is multidimensional, although they specify the dimensions in different ways. Deci and Ryan (2000) provide one account in their self-determination theory. This emerged from their investigations of the types of goals associated with high well-being, through which they identified autonomy, competence and relatedness as three basic psychological needs necessary for self-motivated, meaningful behaviour. Others have gone on to suggest security as a potential fourth basic psychological need (Kasser 2006). Ryff (1989) and Keyes (2002) identify six dimensions of psychological well-being – self-acceptance, positive relations with others, personal growth, purpose in life, environmental mastery, and autonomy. As in these frameworks, functioning in our model focuses on the basic behaviour types which are part of well-being, although there is deliberately no specification of the life domains (e.g. work, family life) or particular activities through which these behaviours should be accessed.

It is interesting to reflect on how many of the contributions to this volume present frameworks that provide alternative ways of conceptualizing good functioning. Eriksson and Lindström (this volume, Chapter 3) comment on the similarity of the elements of sense of coherence theory – seeing the world as comprehensible, manageable and meaningful – to Deci and Ryan's (2000) self-determination theory. (One distinction between the two may be that sense of coherence theory focuses on qualities and perceptions of the external world, whereas self-determination theory focuses on individuals' (perceptions of their) own behaviours.) Basu et al. (this volume, Chapter 7) note the further similarity of their Reasonable Person Model triad – of building mental models, functioning effectively and taking meaningful action – to these other frameworks. While not suggesting specific models, other contributors to this volume can also be seen as taking broadly functioning approaches to well-being in the emphasis they place on social relationships (Helliwell, this volume, Chapter 5; Bartolini, this volume, Chapter 6). Rather than enter into debates about which of these is 'the right' model of functioning, I prefer to take seriously the idea that they are models – abstractions of a complex reality. This is particularly relevant in the realm of psychological constructs with notoriously fuzzy boundaries. Such models prove their worth through their correspondence with empirical evidence and particularly in their *usefulness* in specific contexts. Policy makers should therefore view the dynamic model of well-being as a portal to these different models of good functioning, from which they can select the most appropriate to the particular issue at hand.

Good Feelings and Evaluations

The element in the top box of the dynamic model of well-being (Figure 14.1) encompasses good feelings and evaluations about life – the hedonic and evaluative accounts of the Dolan et al. (2006) categorization. The life satisfaction measures used as the basis of empirical evidence in contributions by Helliwell (this volume, Chapter 5), Bartolini (this volume, Chapter 6) and Seaford (this volume, Chapter 8) draw directly on this element of the model.

While this element is perhaps the most readily associated with the well-being agenda in popular discourse, the aim of the model is to place feelings and evaluations in a wider context. The model describes good feelings and judgements about life as arising from an interaction of external conditions, personal resources and good functioning. Hence a concern with citizens' feelings need not be seen as a distraction, or a soft option, for policy makers, but instead a meaningful way of tracking the results of policy action in other domains.

Feedback Loops

The 'dynamism' of the model's title arises from the flows between its different elements, not just those which go from the bottom upwards, but also in feedback relationships in the other direction. While many different feedback relationships could be identified, we choose to highlight three we regard as especially important.

Two feedback loops start from good feelings. The first, well established in the psychology literature, is the role of emotions in creating changes in the body, as well as 'readiness to act' in specific ways, in response to certain types of stimuli. Thus, for example, fear engages the flight mechanism, while positive emotions signal the benefits of continuing with a current activity (Marks 2011). The second feedback loops posits further benefits of positive emotions. It is the loop between good feelings and personal resources, based on the evidence established by Barbara Fredrickson's broaden-and-build theory, which shows that experiencing positive feelings broadens people's scope of possible action and, over time, builds up personal resources such as psychological resiliency and coping skills (Fredrickson 2001). The model also describes a feedback loop between good functioning and external conditions, based on evidence that functioning well in the world enables people to better shape the conditions around them. For example, autonomy has been identified as a determinant of health behaviours and educational achievement (Thompson and Marks 2008); and the degree to which individuals relate successfully to each other is likely to be related causally to the quality of the social context around them (as Helliwell and Putnam 2004 suggest when they highlight a possible direction of causation from personal disposition and subjective well-being to social circumstance[4]).

SIMILARITIES TO OTHER CONCEPTIONS OF WELL-BEING

It should not be surprising that the dynamic model, as an integrative model, has much in common with other conceptions of well-being. I have already noted that its broad conception of functioning creates synergies with a range of eudaimonic theories of well-being, including sense of coherence (Hämäläinen, this volume, Chapter 2; Eriksson and Lindström, this volume, Chapter 3) and the Reasonable Person Model (Basu et al., this volume, Chapter 7). It also clearly has much in common with models which emphasize both feeling and functioning, such as Seligman's PERMA, which identifies the five elements of well-being as positive emotion, engagement, (positive) relationships, meaning and accomplishment (Seligman 2011). Huppert and So's operational definition of flourishing identifies ten 'mirror opposites of the symptoms of common mental disorders' to arrive at a set of features across the feeling, functioning and personal resources elements of the dynamic model (Huppert and So 2011).[5] The influence of earlier models can also be detected. A similarity with Maslow's (1943) hierarchy of needs can be seen in the dynamic model's efforts to acknowledge both the material and psychological realms, although the hierarchy itself is deliberately excluded, replaced with a system of dynamic flows. Sen's capabilities theory (Sen 1984; discussed by Hämäläinen, this volume, Chapter 2) is echoed in the dynamic model's inclusion of a focus on the interaction between external conditions and good functioning – Sen's 'capabilities' could be described in terms of the dynamic model as those external conditions which enable (society-specific) elements of good functioning.

Aked (n.d.) argues that the dynamic model draws on four key concepts from systems thinking and work on complex adaptive systems: interrelatedness, emergence, feedback and non-linearity. Thus the model seems to have things in common with the conception of well-being as a 'function of whole systems', outlined by O'Hara and Lyon (this volume, Chapter 4). And there are obvious parallels with the model of the key determinants of well-being suggested by Hämäläinen (this volume, Chapter 2), which is also at least partly drawn from complexity thinking. The dynamic model of well-being and Hämäläinen's model share a very similar structure. Both start from two key building blocks around environment and resources and progress through elements of activity and functioning to an ultimate concern with feeling and experience. There are of course differences in the two models in the precise way in which their elements are delineated, and, as discussed further below, Hämäläinen's model includes a layer of daily activities between environment or resources and more generalized functioning which is elliptically omitted from the dynamic model. But the similarity of the two models is striking, particularly given that they were developed separately and each draws on a somewhat different selection of the social scientific literature.

USING THE MODEL IN POLICY MAKING

The foregoing description of the elements of the dynamic model shows how it provides a framework for policy makers to make sense of the wealth of evidence about the factors that constitute, and that are associated with, well-being. This is of particular utility when they are considering the 'what' issue of where to invest public funds. Policy making which attended to the evidence on how strong the associations between different external conditions and well-being were, and used this evidence to guide decisions about where to target public spending, would very likely be more effective in improving well-being outcomes overall. The 'personal resources' element also has 'what' implications, particularly for investment in parenting, early years and education provision, which can affect the development pathways of character traits (Foresight Mental Capital and Well-being Project 2008; Aked et al. 2009) – with growing evidence on how provision such as resilience training can also affect such traits in adults (Reivich et al. 2011).

The advantage of using the model for these sorts of decisions is that, while it draws on a huge wealth of well-being evidence, it does not require policy makers to have an in-depth familiarity with this evidence to begin applying a well-being approach to their work. At one level, it simply provides an understanding for those working on a particular policy issue, for example housing or early years education, of how their efforts contribute to the overarching goal of promoting population well-being. At another level, it could prompt questions across the whole of a government department, such as 'Are we attending to all the domains of the dynamic model of well-being across our activities?'

But crucial to the challenge with which this chapter began – guiding thinking about the 'how' of policy – is the central, functioning element of the model. It suggests a need for serious attention on how the *way* in which policy is implemented enables people to function well in terms of experiencing things like autonomy and control, competence and a sense of manageability, relatedness, and a sense of meaning. One of the ways the model can do this is by giving rise to the sort of heuristic rules of thumb mentioned earlier. For example: 'Implementing policy through a delivery method that promotes autonomy is to be preferred to one which does not.' Another way is through the use of specific approaches to policy that are designed to promote the elements of good functioning. One such approach which has aimed to systematically achieve this through the way that public services are delivered is co-production, although its links to eudaimonic well-being have rarely been made explicit.

In what follows, I focus on the co-production approach in some detail, to examine how it relates to the elements of good functioning that I have outlined. I then go on to examine various tensions involved in implementing good functioning in policy.

AN APPLICATION TO THE 'HOW' OF POLICY: CO-PRODUCTION

The new economics foundation has been among those leading the development of co-production as a way of delivering services. But co-production
did not emerge as a direct response to well-being evidence. Rather, it grew
out of the work of a number of thinkers including Elinor Ostrom, Edgar
Cahn and Neva Goodwin who recognized the value of family and community relationships and the activity that takes place within this non-market,
'core economy' sphere (Stephens et al. 2008). This led to the insight that
the design of public services should acknowledge the importance of social
relationships and trust, and the skills and abilities which people have to
offer – hence nef's working definition of co-production: 'Co-production
means delivering public services in an equal and reciprocal relationship
between professionals, people using services, their families and their
neighbours. Where activities are co-produced in this way, both services
and neighbourhoods become far more effective agents of change' (Boyle
and Harris 2009).

   The work of nef in developing the theory and practice of co-production
(much of it in partnership with the UK's innovation foundation,
NESTA) has led to the identification of six interlinked key features of
public services which take this approach, first described in a publication
with the neatly descriptive title *Public Services Inside Out* (Boyle et al.
2010). These are:

1. *Recognizing people as assets.* The recognition of people as assets aims
   to provide an alternative perspective to that of seeing people who use
   public services as simply having 'problems to be fixed', instead taking
   the view that they are people who, 'whatever . . . problems they might
   have, also have huge experience, skills, often time – certainly the
   human ability to connect with other people'. Such recognition aims to
   produce a 'critical underpinning shift in values that makes the other
   elements [of co-production] possible' (Boyle et al. 2010).
2. *Building on people's existing capabilities.* This means moving away
   from the 'deficit model' of public services, which assumes that their
   role is to step in where people are not able to do things for themselves,
   towards an understanding of their role as helping to *develop further*
   what people are already able to do.
3. *Mutuality and reciprocity.* Co-produced public services should recognize the benefits of reciprocal relationships, and encourage them to
   develop between service users and professionals, and among service
   users themselves. Service users should be seen as 'equal partners in

designing and delivering services', and not 'passive recipients' (Boyle et al. 2010).

4. *Peer support networks.* Such networks create means for people to share knowledge and skills to support each other in a structured way, with explicit links to appropriate professional support.

5. *Blurring distinctions.* This draws on the insight that, in order to draw fully on people's capabilities and develop reciprocal relationships through fundamental changes in people's involvement in the design and delivery of services, the distinctions between professional 'producers' of services and those who 'consume' them will become blurred.

6. *Facilitating rather than delivering.* A co-production approach encourages public service agencies to view themselves and their purpose differently, not as actors who must *provide* services, but as *facilitators of change* for individuals, families and communities.

These are not a set of dry theoretical principles, but a set of features that grew out of observations of copious examples of policy practice in the UK and beyond, many of which are described in detail in *Public Services Inside Out* (Boyle et al. 2010). Examples include:

- schools which enable pupils to identify issues that they are passionate about and help them acquire the skills to take action on those issues;
- a social housing provider which encourages tenants to earn credits for volunteering to help run the services of the housing association, which can then be used to access local services; and
- support services for disabled people which help the people develop their personal and community networks rather than just 'delivering care'.

Many more examples are provided by members of the UK's co-production practitioners' network;[6] still more are referred to by contributions in this volume, for example Helliwell's examples about how institutions are managed (this volume, Chapter 5).

So with an origin outside well-being research, and development deeply rooted in practice, is it coherent to describe co-production as a practical application of the functioning element of the dynamic model of well-being? An examination of the conceptual underpinnings of the key features of co-production suggests that this description is highly appropriate.

Figure 14.2 presents a schema summarizing the close conceptual links

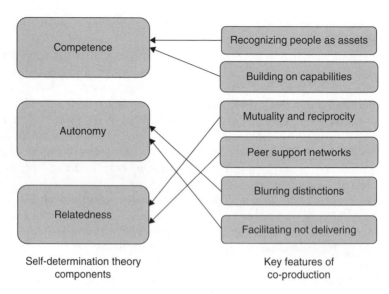

*Figure 14.2   The links between good functioning, represented by the
components of self-determination theory, and the key features
of co-production*

between co-production and well-being, using the three basic psychological
needs of self-determination theory to represent good functioning.[7] The
fact that each co-production feature is shown as linked to only one
component of self-determination theory should be regarded as a simplifi-
cation for clarity of presentation – in reality, the six co-production features
are highly mutually reinforcing, with porous boundaries between them;
hence the true picture is likely to be one of complex multiple relationships.
Despite this complexity, the six key features of co-production do seem to
cluster in three groups which correspond very plausibly to the three components of self-determination theory.

The first and second key features, *recognizing people as assets* and
building on people's existing capabilities, clearly share an approach
towards users of public services as capable, with abilities to offer. This
recognizes what Deci and Ryan (2000) call the 'fundamental' need of
competence 'to engage optimal challenges and experience mastery' – that
is, to be challenged at an appropriate level and learn to master situations. Only by regarding their users as people with something to offer
can public services provide opportunities for meeting this fundamental
need for competence. The alternative – regarding them simply as people
with problems that professionals must solve – prioritizes the competence

of the professionals but dismisses the competence of the people they are aiming to help.

The third and fourth key co-production features, *mutuality and reciprocity* and *peer support networks*, both focus on fostering relationships between people. This clearly builds on the fundamental need for relatedness, described by Deci and Ryan (2000) as the need 'to seek attachments and experience feelings of security, belongingness, and intimacy with others'. It also encompasses Helliwell's claim that 'humans are pro-social beings' (Helliwell, this volume, Chapter 5).

The fifth and sixth co-production features, *blurring distinctions* and *facilitating rather than delivering*, aim to overturn conceptions of public services as providers 'doing to' users. By blurring distinctions between producers and consumers, and moving from delivering to facilitating, the focus is on incentivizing people's active engagement with services, involving them in making decisions and using their own experience on behalf of themselves and others. This addresses the need for a sense of autonomy, which Ryan and Deci (2000) describe as people's need to 'experience their behaviour as self-determined', free from external control.

Understood according to these key features, co-production can therefore be regarded as an approach to public services that clearly represents an implementation of the dynamic model of well-being to the 'how' of policy. While I have focused on the links between co-production and good functioning, situating good functioning in the context of the dynamic model as a whole helps to describe the likely wider benefits of a co-production approach. Stephens et al. (2008) describe the risk that a non-co-production model of public services, where professionals 'deliver narrow units of help to passive clients', will lead to 'their costs ... spiralling out of control and their targets [failing] to reduce the needs they are trying to address'. Thus co-production is not simply about good functioning for good functioning's sake, but, as the dynamic model suggests, is fundamentally about improving people's external conditions and personal resources, as well, of course, as their feelings and experiences.

Viewing the co-production approach through the lens of the dynamic model of well-being suggests a way to understand these wider benefits. Services that support people's good functioning are likely to be more effective, because they will be better designed to meet people's basic psychological needs. If improved functioning helps people's external conditions and personal resources to improve in the long term, this is likely to reduce demands on, and costs to, public services in the future. For example, an individual whose involvement with co-produced services has strengthened his or her social networks and boosted his or her self-esteem will be less

likely in the future to fall into difficulties which require the further intervention of publicly funded services.

TENSIONS IN IMPLEMENTING THE DYNAMIC MODEL

While the dynamic model of well-being describes a holistic system with
dynamic flows between its elements, when it is used to guide policy decisions there will inevitably be tensions between its different components,
requiring choices and trade-offs. Some of these will arise at the level of
the 'what'. For example, a context of restricted government revenues is
likely to necessitate choices about the level of public funds which should
be spent on developing people's personal resources in the first years
of life (which Aked et al. 2009 describe as a form of long-term public
investment) versus the funds that should be spent on improving current
external conditions. When choices of this nature are to be made, policy
makers will need to move beyond broad frameworks and use detailed
empirical evidence about likely impacts of different factors on well-being.
The UK Treasury has begun one means of doing this, exploring how
subjective well-being data can be used to establish values for a range of
social costs and benefits via the empirical relationships between income
and well-being, and well-being and other factors (Fujiwara and Campbell
2011).

Other tensions will emerge within the 'how'. Some will arise from the
different ways in which key concepts are translated during policy implementation. For example, expanding choice for users of public services has
gained much policy attention in the UK in the last few years – and this
might be interpreted as a way of operationalizing the autonomy element of
functioning. But here, too, a move beyond the model overview is required,
towards a careful reading of the well-being evidence, which in fact suggests
a disjunction between autonomy and choice. Research on autonomy has
established that, of the factors which contribute to intrinsically motivated
behaviour (our 'inherent tendency to seek out novelty and challenges, to
extend and exercise one's capacities, to explore, and to learn'), it is the
one which depends on an 'internal perceived locus of causality' (Ryan
and Deci 2000). That is, behaviour that makes me feel autonomous needs
to feel as though it originated within me. This is clearly a distinct type of
behaviour from choosing between options, although the two may sometimes overlap. Even if some choice can be good for autonomy, it has been
established that increasing choice too far has negative effects on well-
being (Schwarz 2004; Hämäläinen, this volume, Chapter 2). For example,

research has shown that adding additional options in a choice situation creates conflict which 'induces people to avoid decisions' (Schwarz 2004). Thus adding too many options may even reduce people's ability to engage in autonomous behaviour. Policy implementation needs to pay attention to the detail of these differences.

Further tensions are likely to arise between other dimensions of functioning. For example, a recent evaluation of services for vulnerable people carried out by nef identified a tension between promoting people's autonomy on the one hand and security on the other. Professionals involved in the service prioritized the safety and security of service users to an extent which often prevented them exercising their autonomy, even in the context of an intervention designed to improve users' choice and control (Stephens and Michaelson 2013). The fact that this was a situation of trade-off, with a resulting need for balance between autonomy and security, was not recognized by those involved in the details of implementation. This suggests that a better understanding of the dynamic model by professionals might help improve their ability to promote the *multiple* dimensions of good functioning, by acknowledging the need to balance them against each other.

A TOOL FOR COMMUNICATING: THE FIVE WAYS TO WELL-BEING

I have described the dynamic model as deliberately not specifying particular activities which give rise to flourishing. This conceptual generality provides flexibility which allows the model to be applied to a range of different questions and issues, as this chapter has attempted to demonstrate. But, if the aim is to communicate widely about how well-being can be promoted, it becomes advantageous to move away from conceptual generality towards concrete examples. This is the approach taken by nef's Five Ways to Well-being, explicitly developed as a set of communications messages. I describe the Five Ways to Well-being briefly in this section, and show how they relate to the dynamic model.

Like the dynamic model, the Five Ways emerged from the review of the UK's Foresight Project on Mental Capital and Well-being. Their development was motivated by the idea of using the wealth of evidence gathered by the review to create a popular public health message, modelled on the successful physical health dictum to eat 'five fruit and vegetables a day'.

The Foresight evidence was examined to identify particular activities which individuals could reasonably be expected to undertake in everyday life, and which were empirically supported as being associated with improved well-being. A process of long-listing and then short-listing used four criteria to select activities, to ensure the activities would:

- be evidence-based, with an empirical basis for claiming a link to improved well-being;
- have 'universal' appeal – across age groups, for example;
- be targeted at the individual – so that people would have the capacity to make the recommended changes in their own lives; and
- take account of the need for variety across the set of activities.

This led to the selection of five headline activities: connect; be active; take notice; keep learning; and give (Aked et al. 2008). Each of these was associated with messages outlining example activities, designed to be 'facilitative' rather than 'prescriptive' (Marks 2010). The messages are shown in Figure 14.3.

With very little direct promotion activity by nef or Foresight, other than the production of a set of colourful postcards designed to disseminate the messages, the Five Ways to Well-being have become very widely used by groups and organizations in the UK and beyond. A review of their uses

Connect . . .
With the people around you. With family, friends, colleagues and neighbours. At home, work, school or in your local community. Think of these as the cornerstones of your life and invest time in developing them. Building these connections will support and enrich you every day.

Be active . . .
Go for a walk or run. Step outside. Cycle. Play a game. Garden. Dance. Exercising makes you feel good. Most importantly, discover a physical activity you enjoy and that suits your level of mobility and fitness.

Take notice . . .
Be curious. Catch sight of the beautiful. Remark on the unusual. Notice the changing seasons. Savour the moment, whether you are walking to work, eating lunch or talking to friends. Be aware of the world around you and what you are feeling. Reflecting on your experiences will help you appreciate what matters to you.

Keep learning . . .
Try something new. Rediscover an old interest. Sign up for that course. Take on a different responsibility at work. Fix a bike. Learn to play an instrument or how to cook your favourite food. Set a challenge you will enjoy achieving. Learning new things will make you more confident as well as being fun.

Give . . .
Do something nice for a friend, or a stranger. Thank someone. Smile. Volunteer your time. Join a community group. Look out, as well as in. Seeing yourself, and your happiness, linked to the wider community can be incredibly rewarding and creates connections with the people around you.

Figure 14.3   The Five Ways to Well-being messaging

carried out in 2010 found they had been used in communication campaigns to encourage individual action, to shift the context within organizations, and to shape strategy and policy (Aked and Thompson 2011).
Prominent examples include:

- the UK city of Liverpool's 2020 Decade of Health and Wellbeing,
  which uses the Five Ways to Well-being as an overarching framework for policy action and city-wide communication;[8]
- the high-profile use of the Five Ways by the Mental Health
  Foundation of New Zealand;[9] and
- the 'Everyday Happiness' project involving 1600 Norwegian
  kindergartens.

Like the dynamic model of well-being, the Five Ways to Well-being
bring together a wealth of well-being evidence in an easy-to-remember
framework. As I have already noted, it eschews the conceptual generality of the dynamic model for a set of more specific activities. In this way
it has things in common with the 'everyday activities and roles' domain
of Hämäläinen's model of well-being (Hämäläinen, this volume, Chapter
2), highlighting daily activities through which good functioning can be
achieved. However, elements of the 'basic behaviours' of good functioning
are discernible within the Five Ways. They start and end with the social
and pro-social 'connect' and 'give' of relatedness. 'Keep learning' suggests an activity key to promoting meaning, engagement and competence.
While the call to 'be active' is focused on physical activity, it also has a
connotation of taking an autonomous, active rather than passive attitude
towards the world. 'Take notice', based on evidence on the effectiveness
of mindfulness techniques in promoting well-being, perhaps suggests the
first stage of seeing the world as coherent, given the properties of mindful
activity of focusing the mind on present activities and thoughts rather than
the past or future, as noted by Hämäläinen (this volume, Chapter 2).

The Five Ways to Well-being's grounding in evidence and links to
theory should give policy makers confidence in using them, as a tool,
particularly where policy makers aim to communicate about well-being.
Examples of practice to date suggest the Five Ways can also be useful as
a policy framework, going beyond their original intended purpose when
they were aimed at individual-level action. For instance, the public health
provider in and around Wigan, a town in the north-west of England,
used the Five Ways to Well-being as the theme around which its 2011
Public Health Annual Report was organized. The report took an approach
of mapping the assets which exist locally, within each of the Five Ways
themes, and asked how existing assets could be built on to further improve

well-being (Arden 2011). This deliberately inverted the standard public health approach of assessing needs (a deficit model) to instead produce a focus on the positive – mirroring the approach of positive psychology that underlies much current well-being thinking (Michaelson and Hämäläinen, this volume, Chapter 1). This illustrates how using the Five Ways to Well-being as a framework is a useful way in to ensure that policy addresses a range of aspects of good functioning.

CONCLUSION

In this chapter I have described how the dynamic model of well-being emerged from an attempt to integrate different accounts of well-being, using a systems approach to think about the links between them. The resulting model sees well-being as a dynamic process, emerging from the interactions between external conditions and personal resources, which influence the extent of good functioning and in turn positive feelings and evaluations, with feedback loops in the reverse direction of influence.

Because of its integrative nature, the model provides an understanding of how various accounts of well-being, such as those in contributions within this volume, fit together. It also provides a guide to the elements which previous models of well-being have chosen to emphasize.

I have suggested that the model is best used as an overall guide to comprehending well-being – an easy way to understand and remember the wealth of evidence on which it is based, which can guide broad thinking about both 'what' and 'how' questions in policy implementation. I have highlighted co-production as a practical approach to policy implementation which captures much of the dynamic model's insights for the 'how', with the six key features of co-production clustering into key elements of good functioning.

However, it is clear that policy implementation will uncover tensions between different parts of the model, which are best made explicit and given proper consideration by policy makers and practitioners. Here, and wherever specific decisions are required over and above the broad direction of policy implementation, it will be necessary to go beyond the overview provided in the model and engage with the fine detail of the substantial empirical evidence.

Finally, I introduced the Five Ways to Well-being as a tool designed for communicating about well-being, but which has also been demonstrated to be a useful high-level policy framework. Unlike the dynamic model of well-being, the Five Ways specify particular well-being-enhancing activities, but also manage to capture a number of the key elements of good functioning at the core of the dynamic model.

NOTES

*   This chapter represents my presentation of work developed over a number of years by colleagues past and present at the Centre for Well-being at nef. In particular I acknowledge the contributions of the following people as key to developing the work presented here (and my ongoing thinking): Nic Marks, Sam Thompson, Saamah Abdallah, Nicola Steuer, Jody Aked, Charles Seaford, Laura Stoll, Sorcha Mahony and Sagar Shah. In addition, I acknowledge the work of my colleagues who have led nef's development of co-production, which is presented here (briefly – but I hope not too much to the detriment of the depth of work undertaken). This has been led by my colleagues David Boyle, Lucie Stephens, Anna Coote, Julia Slay and Joe Penny. I also thank the authors of the other contributions in this volume, which have provided another important input to my thinking in writing this chapter.
1.   See http://www.bis.gov.uk/foresight/about-us.
2.   My thanks to John Helliwell for highlighting to me that previous published versions of the model did not place enough emphasis on social context within the external conditions element.
3.   I am grateful to Nic Marks for suggesting this description of learned optimism.
4.   I am grateful to my colleague Sarah Lyall for pointing out that the evidence which suggests how elements of good functioning and personal disposition are able to *enhance* an individual's external conditions should not be regarded as providing evidence that an individual's *poor* circumstances can be attributed to either the individual's poor functioning or his or her disposition.
5.   The similarity between Huppert and So's operational definition of flourishing and the dynamic model of well-being is not unexpected, given the work of Felicia Huppert and nef's Nic Marks, together with other collaborators, to design the well-being module on Round 3 of the European Social Survey, using an explicit schema of 'feeling and functioning'. This influenced the development of both subsequent models. For an account of the development of this module, see Huppert et al. (2008).
6.   The network, a legacy of nef and NESTA's joint work on co-production, can be accessed online at http://coproductionnetwork.com.
7.   Although, as noted above, self-determination theory can be seen as one of a number of theoretical frameworks which can also be used to explain good functioning, I have used self-determination theory here for its conceptual clarity and empirical underpinning.
8.   Information available at http://www.2010healthandwellbeing.org.uk/index.php.
9.   See http://www.mentalhealth.org.nz/page/1180-5-ways-to-wellbeing.

REFERENCES

Aked, J. (n.d.), 'A systems approach to understanding well-being', working paper.

Aked, J. and S. Thompson (2011), *Five Ways to Well-being: New Applications, New Ways of Thinking*, London: new economics foundation.

Aked, J., N. Marks, C. Cordon and S. Thompson (2008), *Five Ways to Well-being: The Evidence*, London: new economics foundation.

Aked, J., N. Steuer, E. Lawlor and S. Spratt (2009), *Backing the Future: Why Investing in Children Is Good for Us All*, London: new economics foundation.

Arden, K. (2011), *5 Ways to Well-being: Public Health Annual Report 2011 – Prescription for Well-being: Making the Most of Ourselves*, Wigan: Public Health Directorate.

Blanchflower, D.G. (2007), *Is Unemployment More Costly than Inflation?*, NBER

Working Paper No. 13505, Cambridge, MA: National Bureau of Economic Research.

Boyle, D. and M. Harris (2009), *The Challenge of Co-production: How Equal Partnerships between Professionals and the Public Are Crucial to Improving Public Services*, London: NESTA.

Boyle, D., J. Slay and L. Stephens (2010), *Public Services Inside Out: Putting Co-production into Practice*, London: NESTA.

Centre for Well-being (2011), *Measuring our Progress: The Power of Well-being*, London: new economics foundation.

Deci, E.L. and R.M. Ryan (2000), 'The "what" and "why" of goal pursuits: human needs and the self-determination of behaviour', *Psychological Inquiry*, **11**, 227–68.

DeNeve, K.M. and H. Cooper (1998), 'The happy personality: a meta-analysis of 137 personality traits and subjective well-being', *Psychological Bulletin*, **124**, 197–229.

Diener, E. and M. Chan (2011), 'Happy people live longer: subjective well-being contributes to health and longevity', *Applied Psychology: Health and Well-being*, **3**, 1–43.

Diener, E. and M.E.P. Seligman (2004), 'Beyond money: toward an economy of well-being', *Psychological Science in the Public Interest*, **5**, 1–31.

Diener, E., E.M. Suh, R.E. Lucas and H.L. Smith (1999), 'Subjective well-being: three decades of progress', *Psychological Bulletin*, **2**, 276–302.

Diener, E., R. Lucas, U. Schimmack and J. Helliwell (2009), *Well-being for Public Policy*, New York: Oxford University Press.

Dolan, P., T. Peasgood and M. White (2006), *Review of Research on the Influences on Personal Well-being and Application to Policy Making*, London: Defra.

Foresight Mental Capital and Well-being Project (2008), *Final Project Report*, London: Government Office for Science.

Fredrickson, B. (2001), 'The role of positive emotions in positive psychology: the broaden-and-build theory of positive emotions', *American Psychologist*, **56**, 218–26.

Fujiwara, D. and R. Campbell (2011), *Valuation Techniques for Cost Benefit Analysis: Stated Preference, Revealed Preference and Subjective Well-being Approaches – a Discussion of the Current Issues*, London: HM Treasury.

Helliwell, J.F. and R.D. Putnam (2004), 'The social context of well-being', *Philosophical Transactions of the Royal Society B*, **359**, 1435–46, reprinted in F.A. Huppert, B. Keverne and N. Baylis (eds) (2005), *The Science of Well-being*, London: Oxford University Press, pp. 435–59.

Huppert, F.A. (2009), 'Psychological well-being: evidence regarding its causes and consequences', *Applied Psychology: Health and Well-being*, **1**, 137–64.

Huppert, F.A. and T.T.C. So (2011), 'Flourishing across Europe: application of a new conceptual framework for defining wellbeing', *Social Indicators Research*, doi: 10.1007/s11205-011-9966-7.

Huppert, F.A., N. Marks, A. Clark, J. Siegrist, A. Stutzer, J. Vitterso and M. Wahrendorf (2008), 'Measuring well-being across Europe: description of the ESS well-being module and preliminary findings', *Social Indicators Research*, **91**, 301–15.

Kasser, T. (2006), 'Psychological need satisfaction, personal well-being, and ecological sustainability', report for the new economics foundation.

Keyes, C. (2002), 'The mental health continuum: from languishing to flourishing in life', *Journal of Health and Behaviour Research*, **43**, 207–22.

MacKerron, G. (2011), 'Happiness economics from 35000 feet', *Journal of Economic Surveys*, doi: 10.1111/j.1467-6419.2010.00672.x.

Marks, N. (2010), 'Think before you think', in R. Biswas-Diener (ed.), *Positive Psychology as Social Change*, Dordrecht: Springer.

Marks, N. (2011), *The Happiness Manifesto*, New York: TED Books.

Maslow, A.H. (1943), 'A theory of human motivation', *Psychological Review*, **50**, 370–96.

Michaelson, J., C. Seaford, S. Abdallah and N. Marks (forthcoming), 'Measuring what matters', in F.A. Huppert and C. Cooper (eds), *Interventions and Policies to Enhance Well-being*, Chichester: Wiley-Blackwell.

Nakamura, J. and M. Csikszentmihalyi (2002), 'The concept of flow', in C.R. Snyder and S.J. Lopez (eds), *Handbook of Positive Psychology*, New York: Oxford University Press.

Reivich, K.J., M.E. Seligman and S. McBride (2011), 'Master Resilience Training in the US Army', *American Psychologist*, **66**, 25–34.

Rose, G. (1992), *The Strategy of Preventive Medicine*, Oxford: Oxford University Press.

Ryan, R.M. and E.L. Deci (2000), 'Self-determination theory and the facilitation of intrinsic motivation, social development, and well-being', *American Psychologist*, **55**, 68–78.

Ryff, C.D. (1989), 'Happiness is everything, or is it? Explorations on the meaning of psychological well-being', *Journal of Personality and Social Psychology*, **57**, 1069–81.

Schwarz, B. (2004), *The Paradox of Choice: Why More Is Less*, New York: HarperCollins.

Seligman, M.E.P. (2002), *Authentic Happiness: Using the New Positive Psychology to Realize Your Potential for Lasting Fulfillment*, London: Nicholas Brealey.

Seligman, M.E.P. (2011), *Flourish: A New Understanding of Happiness and Well-being – and How to Achieve Them*, London: Nicholas Brealey.

Sen, A. (1984), 'The living standard', *Oxford Economic Papers*, **36**, 74–90.

Stephens, L. and J. Michaelson (2013), *Buying Things Together*, London: HACT.

Stephens, L., J. Ryan-Collins and D. Boyle (2008), *Co-production: A Manifesto for Growing the Core Economy*, London: new economics foundation.

Stoll, L., J. Michaelson and C. Seaford (2012), *Well-being Evidence for Policy: A Review*, London: new economics foundation.

Thompson, S. and N. Marks (2008), *Measuring Well-being in Policy: Issues and Applications*, report commissioned by the Foresight Project on Mental Capital and Well-being, Government Office for Science, London: new economics foundation.

Index

adolescents *see* young people
advertising 145, 153, 161–2, 176, 178,
    229–30, 234–5, 291–2
aesthetics, environmental 200
affluence 21, 155, 288, 302, 303
    see also prosperity; wealth
ageing 83–4, 286, 300, 302
agency 20, 114, 279
Aked, J. 330, 331, 336, 338, 339
allocative efficiency 238–9
altruism 8, 32, 35–6, 127
American consumerism 145–8, 175, 177
    and debt 149–52
    financing of 172–4
    see also NEG capitalism
anti-social behaviour 291
Antonovsky, A. 24, 27, 28–9, 42, 54,
    58, 60, 68, 69–74, 79–80, 81, 85,
    87, 107, 197, 202, 314
Antonovsky, H. 48–9, 71, 72
anxiety 107–8, 131–2
Ashby's Law of Requisite Variety 41,
    42, 45, 51
ASSET model of employee well-being
    149–50
attractiveness, physical 290, 291
Aung San Suu Kyi 196
autonomy 76, 247, 327, 329, 331, 334,
    335, 336–7

banks 174–5, 205–6
Barrington-Leigh, C.P. 129, 133, 196
Bartolini, S. 152, 153, 155, 156, 162,
    163, 164, 165, 170, 177, 178, 241
Baumeister, R.F. 21, 30, 31, 34–5, 47,
    59, 188, 282
Beer, S. 40, 41, 42, 44, 47, 57–8, 60, 61,
    106
belonging 27, 81, 133, 276
Berman, M.G. 188, 192
Beveridgian goals 17

'Beyond GDP' agenda 3–4, 297, 304–7
Bilancini, E. 165, 241
birth rates 300
Black Swans 41, 144
Bonatti, L. 152, 167
bounded rationality 42, 48
Boyle, D. 332–3
brain 30–31, 44, 47, 59–60, 125–6, 139,
    276, 288
brain drain 279
breakdown 42, 59, 70, 108
broken windows theory 36, 59, 200
Burke, R.J. 245, 260

candidate selection 257–9
capability approach (CA) 58
    advantages 20
    influence 19–20
    use in developing more holistic
        framework 24
    vague definition 22–3
    weaknesses 21–3
capacity
    cultural 113
    growth in, and transformation
        108–10
    improving control 45–8
    mental
        limited 44–5
        and nature 192–3
capitalism 42, 144, 287–92
    see also NEG capitalism
Casti, J.L. 26, 41
Chan, M. 131, 326
change, organizational 82
children
    child-centred approach 55–6
    educational levels 300
    effects of noise 190
    frequency of house moves 231, 234,
        236

and materialism 159, 291
and nature 194
parental involvement 30–31
responsibility for choices 317
school fatigue 60
urban environments 156
see also young people
Chinese language 103
choice
disjunction with autonomy 336–7
and micro-externalities 25
problem of 21, 27–8, 29–30, 35,
42–3, 50–51, 58, 191
reducing 48–52
selfish 36
value of 20
Cimprich, B. 192, 193
cities
low-density 171–2
modern 155–8, 176
climate change
costs of 309
creating change towards policies 298
implications of affluence 302
mitigation measures 304, 316
as source of stress 107
co-production approach 12, 332–6
coherence
and health 39–40
need for 6–7
as primary need 107
and sustainability 38–40
see also sense of coherence (SOC)
collapse theme 106–10
combinative capabilities 46, 60
communication tool 337–40
communities
collaborative 41, 46, 129, 132
and complexity gap 51–2
income maintenance programmes
135–6
walkable 156–7, 199
see also environments
community gardens 135, 202–4
commuting 37, 49, 286–7
compensating differentials 135–6
competitiveness 146, 243, 306–7
complexity
gap 40–41, 43, 44, 51–2
reducing 48–52, 107–8, 114–15

comprehensibility 28, 29, 32, 42, 46,
48, 72, 91, 210
conscious thought 44–5
consciousness
future 46, 60
human 10, 102
orders of 101–2
politics of 271–4, 281
psychological behavioural
experiment 274–5
requirements 275–6
enjoyment 279–81
freedom 277
hope 278–9
and transformation 109–10
construction sector 236–7
consumerism *see* American
consumerism
consumption
and advertising 161–2, 229–30,
234–5
collaborative 52
current culture 36
financing of 172–4
and happiness 290–291
linking of personal traits to 161–2
patterns 302
potential 145, 175
see also American consumerism
control capacity 45–8
Cooper, C.L. 4, 245, 246, 250, 252, 254,
262, 264–5
cooperation 12, 127, 139, 183
coordination mechanisms 52
credit crunch 174–5
Csikszentmihalyi, M. 5, 32, 47, 51, 73,
109, 115, 242, 256, 282, 327
cultural norms 50
cultural paradigm, development of new
42, 56–7
cultural transition and well-being
98–100, 114–15
methodology, epistemology and
reality
cultural bias 103
diverse viewpoints 104
measuring or creating reality 102
orders of consciousness 101–2
scientific neutrality and moral
inversion 103–4

standard science in well-being
studies 100–101
policy implications 111–12
cultural learning 113–14
towards a learning culture 112–13
in uncertain and incoherent times
104–7
breakdown 108
coherence as primary need 107
reducing complexity 107–8
transformation and growth in
capacity 108–10
cybernetic governance crisis 40–3

de-Shalit, A. 20, 22, 23
debt
of American consumer 149–52,
172–4, 177
link with depression 246
and well-being 222, 230
Deci, E.L. 5, 9, 158, 160, 184, 197, 202,
294, 327–8, 334–5, 336
decision-making
political 311, 314
problems 29–30, 33–4, 43–5, 58
path-dependence 36–8
selfishness 35–6
short-termism 34–5
relation to capability approach 22
defensive strategies 107–8
democracy 196, 298, 307, 318, 319
depression 33, 246, 288, 312, 318
Diener, E. 2, 4, 68, 73, 84–5, 131, 164,
169, 240, 241, 282, 293, 294, 311,
321, 326
diseases 28, 69, 76–7, 84–6, 311–13,
314–16
disposition 53, 341
dissatisfaction
link to progress 292
of those with unmet aspirations 227
downshifting 37–8, 48
dynamic model of well-being
application to the 'how' of policy
332–6
elements of
external conditions 325
feedback loops 329
good feelings and evaluations 328
good functioning 327–8

personal resources 326–7
and the five ways to well-being
337–40
origin of 322–5
similarities to other conceptions of
well-being 329–30
tensions in implementing 336–7
use in policy making 330–331

Easterlin paradox 21, 223, 226, 233,
288, 299
ecological approach 101, 316–17
economic crisis
American consumers and debt
145–52
causes of relationship decline
low density cities 171–2
materialism 158–62, 169–70
prosperity vs poverty 155–8
implications 245, 289, 302, 303,
306
NEG capitalism 152–5
in America 162–5, 168–72
in Europe 165–8
implosion of 172–5
reasons for 59, 144–5, 175–7
South Korea's response to 138
economic growth
2020 strategy for 303–4, 308
move towards well-being 315–16
relation to environmental decay
154
relation to happiness 288–90
and US expenditures 162–3
for well-being in EU policy 299–303
see also NEG capitalism
economic instability 228
economic policy and well-being 221
evidence and policy 221–2
consumption and advertising
229–30
economic instability 228
equality, positive associations
226–7
'good job' components 228–9
income, importance of 222–5
'non-economic' features of society
230–231
personal debt 230
unemployment 227–8

implications of evidence
  consumption and advertising
    234–5
  number of hours worked 234
  satisfying work 234
  stability and full employment
    233–4
  target band of income 232–3
  increasing incomes example 235–8
  policy making approach 238–40
economic prosperity 155–8, 161
economic stability 177, 233–4
educational levels 286, 300
effectiveness 75, 90, 188
Eklund, L. 77, 78, 80
elder care 83, 137–8, 139
emotional closeness 48, 71
emotions, negative 131–2
employee well-being 9–10
  ASSET model of 149–50
  job security 228, 229
  organizational arrangements and
    information overload 49–50
  and SOC 81–3
  see also organizations and well-
    being; psychological well-being;
    workplace well-being
empowerment 12, 77–8, 79–80, 307–8
enjoyment 279–81
Enlightenment 99, 100, 104, 105, 115,
  271, 274
environmental constraints 25, 37
environmental damage in cities 171–2
environments 157–8
  community gardens 135, 202–4
  effects on population well-being
    287
  enabling participation 207–8
  microcredit 205–7
  mixed use, front porches and
    pedestrianism 198–9
  to promote meaningful action 202
  to promote social interaction and
    model building 197–8
  and reasonableness 196–7
  restorative 192–5
  to restore directed attention 191–2
  safety and aesthetics 200
  shared green spaces 199–200
  as small experiments 209–10

supportive, to foster reasonableness
    in policy 185–6
  to sustain directed attention 190–191
  third places 200–201
  wayfinding and exploration 201–2
  youth involvement 204–5
  see also living environments
equality
  associations with well-being 226–7
  gender 308
  in the workplace 258–9
Eriksson, M. 26, 59, 68, 69, 70, 71, 72,
    73, 75, 78, 79, 80, 81, 84, 86, 89,
    90, 91, 92
eudaimonic dimension 5, 76, 247, 323,
    327
Europe, NEG capitalism in 165–8, 170,
    176
European Commission (EC) 296, 297,
    300, 302, 304, 308
European Statistical System (ESS)
    304–5, 309
European Union (EU) 296–8
  2020 strategy for growth 303–4, 308,
    309
  contribution to influencing well-
    being 307–8
  growth for well-being in policy
    299–303
  reframing well-being 304–7
  role of 298–9
Eurostat 305
evaluations about life 323, 328
everyday activities 24–5, 52, 339
  see also functionings
evolutionary breakdowns and
    breakthroughs 41–2
expenditures, American trends in 162–4
exploration and wayfinding 201–2
external conditions, in well-being
    model 324–5, 330, 331, 335–6

familiarity 196–7, 201–2
families 53–4, 167, 230–231, 245,
    300–301
feedback loops 131–2, 324, 329
feelings, good 328
Feldt, T. 71, 72, 82
Fitoussi, J.-P. 99, 297
five ways to well-being 337–40

Flint-Taylor, J. 252, 258, 260
flourishing 24–5, 76–7, 323–5, 330, 341
flow activities 51, 327
Foresight Mental Capital and Well-being Project 254, 263, 322, 324, 331, 337–8
Fredrickson, B.L. 255, 329
freedom of consciousness 277
freedoms 20–21, 29, 41, 285
Freud, S. 108, 272
Frey, B.S. 137, 159, 160, 240, 282
front porches 198–9
functioning
  accounts 323
  effective 193
  good 78, 324–7, 339–40
functionings
  fertile 22
  relation to capability approach 22–3, 58
future consciousness 46, 60

Gallup World Poll 101–2, 272, 289
Gandhi 113
GDP
  and American consumption 146, 148, 163–5, 178
  Beyond 3–4, 297, 304–7
  increase in 155
  as indicator of well-being 18, 284, 297
  maximizing 238, 239, 293
  in South Korea 289
gender equality 308
generalized resistance resources (GRRs) 68, 71
Gintis, H. 35, 127
givers and receivers 129–30
global health 88–9
globalization 301–2, 316
GNP 315
'good job' components 228–9
governance 40–3, 57–8, 274
governments
  attention paid to well-being 293
  and construction and public service sectors 236, 237
  and economic policy 239–40
  influence on well-being 283–7
  politics of consciousness 271–81
  Scottish 55, 61

Grameen Bank 205–6, 207
green spaces, shared 199–200
Grinde, B. 188, 189

Hämäläinen, T.J. 21, 26, 29, 37, 38, 39, 40, 41, 45–6, 57, 60, 61, 105, 111, 112
happiness
  determinants 311
  difficulties in defining 284–5
  European trend 167–8
  factors affecting 139, 286–92, 299
  and governments 274, 283
  and health outcomes 131
  link with social activity 127–9, 130, 133
  pursuit of 271
  relation to income 232–3
  studies 98–9, 309, 339
  US trend 164–5, 178
Happy Planet Index (HPI) 99
Harter, J.K. 251, 253, 265
health
  and economic growth 315–16
  entry points for policy work 312–15
  evidence and policy for 317–18
  feedbacks 131
  health care systems 17
  health ease–dis-ease continuum 69–70, 86
  initiatives 339–40
  and internal coherence 39–40
  levels of 311–12
  and personal resources 326–7
  and proximity to nature 193–4, 195
  responsibility for 316–17
  salutogenic approach to 28–9, 68–92, 287
  and social context 136, 137–8
  and the workplace 245, 246, 252, 262
  see also diseases; mental health
Health For All policy 88–9
hedonic dimension 76, 224, 247–8, 323
Helliwell, J.F. 3, 128, 129, 133, 134, 136, 137, 138, 185, 195, 196, 197, 209, 244
heuristics and biases approach 44–5, 48
holistic framework 17, 23–6, 297
homo economicus 1, 44, 57

hope 278–9
household size 30, 51
'how' of policy delivery 137–8, 321–2,
    331, 332–7
HSE 249, 263
Huang, H. 134, 137–8, 244
Hubert, A. 308
human beings
    distinguished from other life forms
        271–2
    evolutionary success of 59
    holistic model 57
    myopic nature of 151
    principal needs 24–5, 27
    as pro-social beings 129–30, 335
    requirements of consciousness
        275–81
    as social beings 125–9
human-centric perspective 20, 50
humanization 112
Huppert, F.A. 4, 5, 24, 131, 240, 327,
    330, 341
hyperbolic discounting 34

I-Space model 113, 116
income
    and choice 58
    equality 226–7
    example of increasing 235–8
    inequality 54, 146, 175, 178, 290, 301
    relation to well-being 2, 20, 129, 134,
        135–6, 139, 222–5, 286, 288–9
    target band for all 232–3
indicators of well-being
    creating new, more relevant 304–7,
        308
    GDP as inadequate 18, 284
    health risk 262
    linking economic and social 99–100
    psychological well-being 254–5, 272
    and SOC 90
    subjective happiness as insufficient
        20
individualization of values 301
Indonesian tsunami 132, 134
industrialized societies
    complexity of everyday life 21
    contradictions and incoherence in
        23, 38
    deprivation problems in 20

in nineteenth century Britain 288
    transformation of 22, 29
    urbanization of 35
information and reasonableness 184–5
information overload 49–50
interdependence 37–8, 52, 58, 184, 303
Irvine, K.N. 206, 209

Kahneman, D. 31, 34, 42, 44, 60, 115,
    127, 132, 139, 240, 241, 242, 273,
    294
Kaplan, R. 186, 187, 192, 194, 197,
    199, 202, 208, 209
Kaplan, S. 186, 187, 188, 192, 197, 202,
    205, 206, 209
Kasser, T. 137, 158, 159, 160, 240, 282
Kegan, R. 102, 106, 109, 116
Keyes, C.L.M. 5, 17, 24–5, 26, 58, 73,
    76–7, 115, 247, 326, 327
Kiva 206–7
knowledge base, individual 45–6
Koelen, M.A. 43, 77–8
Kuo, F.E. 188, 193, 200
Kyoto conference 304

labour market 170, 235, 300–301
Laszlo, E. 23, 38–40, 41–2, 46, 57
Law of Requisite Variety 41, 42, 45, 51
leadership 260–261
learning
    cultural 113–14
    orders of 111
    second-order 111–13
    towards a learning culture 112–13
Levin, D.M. 100–108, 116
life expectancy 300, 312
life management
    new types of 21
    problems 29–30, 53–5, 60
    skills 46, 47–8, 51
life satisfaction
    as appropriate measure 233, 241
    debt 230
    economic growth and 288–9
    and government institutions quality
        138
    and job satisfaction 244
    levels of wealth 228
    measurement issues 225
    negative influences on 224–5

and number of hours worked 229,
284
role of SOC on 82
and social networks 129, 133
trends in Europe 168
and trust 134
and unemployment 227
Lindström, B. 26, 43, 59, 68, 69, 70, 71,
72, 73, 75, 77, 78, 81, 84, 86, 87,
89, 90, 91, 92
liquid modernity 105, 109
living environments 25, 28–9
challenging 53–4, 55
coherent 49–50
and decision-making 48
impact on well-being 42
relation to capability approach 21–2
see also environments
Lombardo, T. 46, 60
Lyon, A. 210

Machiavellian intelligence 126
manageability 28–32, 42, 46, 48, 72, 79,
82, 91, 210
managers 82, 246, 260–261
manufacturing sector 236–7
market economy 159–61
Marks, N. 99, 100, 241, 242, 282, 322,
324, 329, 338
Maslow, A.H. 24, 27, 101, 102, 107
Maslowian needs 24–5, 27, 107, 275,
276, 330
materialism
and advertising 145, 161–2, 176
and anti-social behaviour 291
generating poor relationships 158–9
growth of, in America 169–70
market economy spreading 159–61
materialist value orientation 176, 291
media promoting 161–2
poor relationships generating 159
Maturana, H.R. 23, 38, 61
Mayer, C.-H. 72, 81, 82
meaningful action
environments to promote 202–8
link to meaningfulness 210
reasonable person model 187,
188–90
meaningfulness 28, 32, 42, 48, 72, 79,
82, 210

Measuring National Well-being
Programme 3, 306
media 47, 145, 161–2, 170, 176
meditation 47
mental capacity
and complexity of everyday life 106
effect of media 47
effect of meditation 47
effect of social relationships 47–8
effect of traffic and commuting 49
and information 185
limited 27, 44–5
reasonableness and effective
functioning 190–195
mental health
distinctions 326–7
as flourishing 76–7, 326–7
pressures on 32–3
problems
extent of 17, 106–7
increasing attention to 312
relation to capability approach 21
in the workplace 246, 251, 254
and SOC 59, 78, 82
understanding of 86–7
see also health
Michael, D.N. 29, 40, 42, 57, 105, 111
Michaelson, J. 3, 323, 325, 337
microcredit 205–7
migration 301
military personnel 103, 115, 257, 273
mixed use (buildings) 198–9
model building
environments to promote 197–8
link with comprehensibility 210
reasonable person model 186–7
monetary incentives 160
moral inversion 103–4
motivations 57, 158, 160–161, 207
Mulgan, G. 59
mutual benefit 127
mutuality, in public services 332–3, 335

nanny state 317
nature
and coherence 49
policy opportunities
to preserve 194–5
to revitalize and integrate 195
restorative benefits of 192–4

needs *see* Maslowian needs;
    satisfaction of needs
NEETs (not in employment, education
    or training) 53–4
nef (new economics foundation)
    71, 100, 236–7, 322, 332, 337,
    338
NEG (negative endogenous growth)
    capitalism
  in America 162–5
    expansion of low-density city
        171–2, 176
    growth of materialism 169–70
    thriving 168–9
  antidote to 177
  buying alone 152–5
  in Europe 165–8
  reasons for implosion of
    credit crunch 174–5
    financing of American
        consumption 172–4, 177
  and social relationship decline
        155–62, 175–6
non-communicable diseases (NCDs)
    312, 313, 314, 316
Nudge strategy 48
Nussbaum, M.C. 20, 21, 23, 37

objectification 158
objective lists 323
O'Hara, M. 21, 29, 43, 45, 98, 110,
    113, 115
open citizen deliberation 48
orders of consciousness 101–2
orders of learning 111
organizations and well-being 244–5,
    263–4
  active management of
    attention to psychological well-
        being 254–5
    candidate selection and talent
        management 257–9
    case studies 262
    leadership and management
        260–261
    personal resilience development
        261–2
    post audit interventions 259–60
    strengthening business case
        250–253

    towards resilience and positive
        psychological well-being
        255–7
    well-being interventions 259–62
  assessment of
    auditing employee well-being
        249–50
    importance of psychological well-
        being 247–8
    sources of workplace pressure and
        support 248–9
  defence strategies 108
  implications of turbulent times
        245–7
  national guidance and policy
        initiatives 263, 264
  salutogenic approach 82–3
  see also workplace well-being
Ottawa Charter 88, 92, 316–17
outsourcing 51

Pareto optimality 238–9
participation
  in communities 189, 207–8, 230–231
  opportunities 48
  political 280, 297, 301
  significance of 12
  youth 204–5
path-dependence 36–8
pathways 279
pedestrianism 198–9
peer support 48, 139, 333, 334, 335
personal resources 81, 324–5, 326–7,
    331, 335, 336
personality factors 326
Peterson, C. 184, 196
physical exercise 248, 286, 318
physical stimuli 49
planning blight 22
policies for well-being and health
  from economic growth to sustainable
        well-being 315–16
  entry points for 312–15
  evidence and policy 317–18
  as level of causation 286
  levels of health and well-being
        311–12
  new 1–12, 90–91
  responsibility for 316–17
  summary of 318–19

policy
applications 137–8
building evidence base for better
136–7
delivery, 'what' and 'how' of 137–8,
321–2, 331, 332–7
European Union 298–303, 306–8
implications
of cultural transition 111–14
little clarity on 284
salutogenic framework 88–92
initiatives for organizational well-
being 263
making
approach to 238–40
use of dynamic model in 330–331
opportunities, for nature 194–5
public 91–2, 283–7, 292–3
responses 10–12
supportive environments to foster
reasonableness in 185–6
theory-driven 89–90
see also economic policy and well-
being
politics of consciousness 271–81
population-based prevention 313
poverty 53, 155–8, 207, 240, 301
precariousness 82, 170
preference satisfaction 323
prefrontal cortex 59–60, 126, 127
presenteeism 245, 251–2, 265
pro-social behaviour 129–32, 189
problem of choice *see* choice: problem
of
product choice 35, 50
production patterns 302
prosperity 155–8, 299
see also affluence; wealth
psychological well-being
attention to 254–5
dimensions of 327
importance of 247–8
measures as social indicators 272–3
towards positive 255–7
transformation and problem of
choice 26–33
psychology 5, 85, 98–9, 103, 115, 159,
256–7, 271–5, 284, 329
psychosphere 100, 102, 105, 110, 115
public services features 332–6

Puska, P. 313, 314
Putnam, R.D. 73, 133, 136, 162, 163,
171, 185, 196, 197, 198, 325, 329

quality of life (QoL) 27, 59, 87
Quick, J. 254, 259

reality
of consciousness 10, 276
measuring or creating 102
reasonableness 8–9, 182–3
and community 196–208
environments as experiments
209–10
and information 184–5
mental capacity and effective
functioning 190–195
in policy, supportive environments
for 185–6
reasonable person model (RPM) 210
being effective 188
meaningful action 188–90
model building 186–7
and subjective well-being 183–4
reciprocity 332–3, 334, 335
regulation 50, 115, 314, 317
resilience 73–5, 85, 255–7, 261–2
river of life 86
Robertson, I.T. 247, 250, 252, 254, 258,
260, 261, 262, 264–5
Ryan, R.M. 5, 9, 197, 202, 294, 327–8,
334–5, 336

Saarinen, E. 39, 41, 45, 46, 60
Sabel, C. 41, 50, 55
safety, environmental 200
Sagy, S. 48–9, 71, 72
salt 113
salutogenic framework 68–70
concepts explaining well-being 72–3
empowerment 77–8, 79–80
flourishing 76–7
resilience 73–5
defining well-being 84–7
as entry point for policy 314
generalized resistance resources 71
policy implications 88–92
research evidence base 78, 81–4
sense of coherence (SOC) 70–71
measuring 71–2

Sarracino, F. 167, 170
satisfaction of needs 25–6
Schor, J. 161, 169–70
Schwartz, B. 3, 21, 27, 191
science
science, technology, engineering and
mathematics (STEM) 111
scientific neutrality and moral
inversion 103–4
in well-being studies 100–101
Scottish strategy 55–6, 61
Seaford, C. 241, 243
self-determination theory 327–8, 334,
341
self-related cognitions 53
selfishness 35–6
Seligman, M.E.P. 2, 5, 73, 115, 164,
189, 256, 257, 282, 293, 326, 330
Sen, A. 20, 21, 23, 58, 99, 223–4, 232,
240, 297, 330
sense of coherence (SOC)
concept of 28–9, 68, 70–71, 74, 79
correlation with mental health and
quality of life 59
definition 70
as determinant of health and well-
being 19, 24–6
individual 39–40, 42, 228
as measure of well-being 90
measuring 71–2
people with strong 88, 89
and policy 89
policy experiments 55
similarities to RPM 184, 210, 328
similarity to self-determination 328
strengthening 81–2
theory 328
two-way effect of 71
weakened 32–3
service provision 55–6
short-termism 34–5
sickness absence 83, 250–251
smoking 314, 317, 318
SOC *see* sense of coherence (SOC)
social activity 126–9
social agenda, renewed 302–3
social capital
as antidote to NEG capitalism 177
decline of 164, 168, 176
effect on long-term well-being 37

influenced by design of economy
230–231
and interpersonal relationships 153
trends in America 144, 162–3, 167
in walkable communities 156–7
social context of well-being 125, 138–9
broadening scope of policy
applications 137–8
building evidence base for better
policies 136–7
health feedbacks and pro-social
brain 131
humans as pro-social beings 129–30
humans as social beings 125–9
measuring 133
negative emotions 131–2
trust 133–5, 139
use of subjective data to value
135–6
social determinants approach 313–14
social exclusion 53–6
social interaction
environments to promote 197–8
link with pedestrianism 199
social networks
life satisfaction and 129, 133
watchfulness and response 132
social norms 290
social problems
emergence of new 302
link with income inequality 54
social regulations 50
social relationships
causes of decline
long working hours 58
low density cities 171–2
materialism 158–62, 169–70
modern cities 155–8
modern society lifestyles 31–2, 43
influenced by design of economy
230–231
and mental capacity 47–8
restoring centrality of 7–9
rocking the boat 37
South Korea 138, 289
Soviet Union 41, 274
Stephens, L. 332, 335, 337
Stern Report 304
Stiglitz Commission 3, 20
Stiglitz, J.E. 2, 20, 99, 166–7, 297

stress 51, 59, 69–70, 71, 78–9, 81–2, 246–9, 254–7, 259, 262
sub-prime mortgages 150, 172, 174
subjective well-being (SWB) 85, 115
    benefits for givers and receivers 129–30
    determinants of 138–9
    and political participation 280
    and reasonableness 183–4
    use of data to value social context 135–6, 336
Sullivan, W.C. 188, 193, 200
support economy 51
sustainability
    and coherence 38–40
    environmental 36, 202, 298–9, 305
    towards more sustainable lifestyles 43
        improving control capacity 45–8
        limited mental capacity 44–5
        preventing social exclusion 53–6
        reducing variety and choice 48–52
sustainable well-being
    and coherent decision-making 38, 43
    need for new theory of 23, 56
    and policy 315–16
    requirements 38
    as ultimate goal 57
synergy 70–71, 86, 91
System 1 and System 2 thinking 132, 139
systems intelligence 41, 46, 60
systems theory 42

talent management 257–9
technology
    development 57
    digital gap 301
    effects of 47, 50
terror management 159
'Think' 48
third places (other places besides home and work) 200–201
Thompson, S. 241, 282, 322, 324, 329, 339
Tierney, J. 21, 30, 31, 34–5, 47, 59
toxic assets 173–4, 177
traffic 36, 49, 156, 199

transformation
    and growth in capacity 108–10
    societal 23, 26–33
trust
    in governments 138, 277
    social 167, 178, 231, 332
    as social glue 125
    as special 133–5, 139
    in the workplace 134, 139, 168

uncertainty 22, 29, 43–4, 105–6, 114
unconscious thought 44–5
unemployment 138, 227–8, 233, 238, 289
United Nations 3, 19, 312
United States (US) *see* American consumerism; NEG capitalism
urban renewal schemes 103–4

variety *see* choice
virtuous cycle 210
vulnerabilities 53

walkability 156–7, 199
Wall Street 172, 174, 177
Wang, S. 3, 128, 129, 134, 196, 242
wayfinding and exploration 201–2
wealth 2, 228, 289, 292
    see also affluence; prosperity
welfare state 37, 50, 53, 315
well-being
    defining 84–7, 114, 323–4
    determinants of 22, 23–4, 26–7, 37
    five ways to 337–40
    levels of 311–12
Western lifestyles 316
'what' of policy delivery 137, 321–2, 331, 336
WHO (World Health Organization) 84, 87, 88, 106, 312, 313–14, 316
willpower 34–5, 42, 48, 59
Wolff, J. 20, 22, 23
Wood, J.K. 110, 113
Wood, L. 198, 200
workplace well-being
    components of a 'good job' 228–9
    increase in pace of change 301
    long working hours 59, 165–6, 229, 234, 245, 290

organizational arrangements and
    information overload 49–50
satisfying work 234
self control 59
and SOC 81–2
trust 134, 139, 168
work presence 83
see also employee well-being;
    organizations and well-being;
    psychological well-being
worldviews, differing 105–6

x-events 41, 144

young people
    and consciousness 277
    involvement in community
        environment 204–5
    and life-management problems
        53–6
    SOC study 78, 81, 83
    see also children